255|21.12.09
AF743794
20 070 390 28
UNIVERSITY OF NORTHUMBRIA AT NEWCASTLE LIBRARY
WITHDRAWN

PROFITS AND LOSSES

UNIVERSITY OF NORTHUMBRIA AT NEWCASTLE LIBRARY
WITHDRAWN

PROFITS

AND

LOSSES

BUSINESS JOURNALISM AND ITS ROLE IN SOCIETY

CHRIS ROUSH

UNIVERSITY OF NORTH CAROLINA, CHAPEL HILL

Marion Street Press, Inc.
Oak Park, Illinois

NORTHUMBRIA UNIVERSITY
LIBRARY
ITEM No. 20 070 390 28
CLASS No. 070.44965 Rou

Cover design by Gloria Chantell

Copyright © 2006 Chris Roush

All Rights Reserved

ISBN 1-933338-05-9
Printed in U.S.A.
Printing 10 9 8 7 6 5 4 3 2 1

Marion Street Press, Inc.
PO Box 2249
Oak Park, IL 60303
866-443-7987
www.marionstreetpress.com

To my wife, Mindy, for her patience.

Contents

Introduction

As used today, the term *business journalism* refers to all reporting and writing that is written not only about businesses but also about the economy. In addition, it commonly includes other beats such as labor, workplace, technology, personal finance, investment, and consumer reporting, in addition to investigative reporting focusing on these topics. Some consider business reporting to be all reporting about business, even though the story may not have a strict business angle.

How did these various forms of reporting come together in today's media? It's the common theme of money and how it is earned and spent, not only by businesses but also by consumers. Yet most journalism histories downplay or even ignore the important role many business journalists or business reporting has played in society. That's despite the fact that in a ranking of the best journalism of the 20th century compiled by New York University's journalism department, three of the top six works selected had a specific business angle.[1]

Think about how your life would be different if it weren't for business journalists from the past century. Would cars, vans, SUVs, and trucks be as safe as they are? Maybe, but reporting about unsafe vehicles spurred the automakers to make changes to their construction sooner rather than later. Would we all feel secure in the food that we're buying from grocery stores and restaurants without the Food and Drug Administration's role in ensuring sanitary conditions? Probably not — the FDA's creation was spurred by writing about food such as spoiled meat being sold to unsuspecting consumers.

Writing about business has caused these and other changes. Even today, as society struggles with issues such as pollution, drugs that were once deemed safe but have killed, and SUVs that cause a higher than normal death rate in accidents, we are relying on journalism that is focused on business to help solve our problems.

This book provides the first history of business journalism as the term is used today and argues that no journalism has had a bigger impact on past lives or will have as big an impact on future society as business reporting. The book revisits past journalism achievements with the viewpoint of today's definition of "business journalism." It is an attempt to provide some perspective to this increasingly important field and some analysis of where it has come from and where it is headed.

Media have had a profound effect on business and the economy. This was recognized as far back as 1942, when Harold Innis wrote in the *Journal of Economic History* that, "Widening of markets, the effectiveness of competition, lowering the costs of production, the spread of the price system, the evolution of a sensitive monetary structure and the development of equilibrium economics have followed the development of the newspaper."[2]

However, business journalism's importance to society resulted despite paltry coverage of business-related issues for many decades. Look at the mass communication outlets that you use in your everyday life. What percentage of these media are devoted to business-related stories, or stories that affect people's spending? If it's the nightly broadcast news, it's likely to be two to three minutes of a 30-minute broadcast, or 10 percent at the most. In most cases, it's a simple 15-second time slot that regurgitates how the stock market performed during that day. A morning show on a major network station recently aired a 20-second spot on the possibility that the Federal Reserve might raise interest rates later that day. But there was no explanation or context as to what the move might mean for the average consumer. The show simply moved onto the next story. Other mainstream media aren't much better. The average newspaper devotes only about 15 percent of its space for stories to the business section, although that percentage has increased in recent years.[3]

The media tend to focus on the biggest stories that theoretically have the largest impact. But it could be argued that the media – and society – need a better understanding of the important role that business journalism has played in shaping society and making it a better place to live because of the personal effect that business and the economy has on so many people. Yet in 2005, many media outlets devote two and three times the attention and space to their coverage of sporting events and athletes than they do business.

Without a better understanding of the role business journalism has played in the past and could play in the future, journalists today may fail to grasp its important role and lose their focus on why business journalism is so important to people.

Without a better understanding of the role business journalism has played in the past and could play in the future, journalists today may fail to grasp its important role and lose their focus on why business journalism is so important to people. The role is becoming even more important as media increasingly become controlled by larger and larger corporations that may be unwilling to hurt their bottom line for the sake of reporting on issues that may negatively affect large advertisers. Media conglomerates produce an enormous amount of business-related stories, but the temptation is increasingly focusing solely on the bottom line and not on the good of society. "Especially in times of financial pressure, there is a temptation to create coverage whose primary objective is to attract advertisers rather than serve readers," said former *Wall Street Journal* deputy managing editor Barney Calame, a former president of the Society of American Business Editors and Writers. "Good journalism can and should do both."[4]

Some in the media understand this role clearly. In being named the new editor of *The Tennessean*, the daily newspaper in Nashville, Everett J. Mitchell said in late 2004 that the newspaper needed, among its other goals, to be the "watchdog of business."[5] *Newsweek* business columnist Allan Sloan, a giant in the field, recently called business stories "a story about life that will have a few numbers in it" and added "business is actually fun if you look at it the right way."[6]

Business journalism isn't just for the executive or the investor. Business journalism affects everybody. We all have jobs, or we rely on someone who has a job to help maintain our way of living. Should that job be lost, our living standard might change. Indirectly, we all care about business and the economy. And in the media, business journalism still has a vast, untapped audience. Studies at the Readership Institute at the Media Management Center of Northwestern University show that business coverage ranks in the middle when compared to other reporting. "Newspapers, generally, have not maxed out their opportunity to grow readership through this coverage," said Mary Nesbitt, managing director of the institute.[7]

Why do some readers shy away from business or economics stories? For the person who knows little about the world of commerce, business journalism can appear stodgy and boring – perhaps even threatening – at first glance. The perception of business and consumer writing is that the stories are full of numbers and can be tedious to read. That is the fault of the media that have not emphasized business coverage in the past and have not understood its significance. Media that realized the importance of business journalism and placed an emphasis on writing and reporting on the corporate world in a way even the novice can understand are the ones that improved society and its understanding of the importance of business and the economy.

Despite the problems of business journalism in the past, its record of impact on society overcame the handicap. And today, increasingly, some of the best and brightest reporters are looking at the business desk as a place to make their mark in journalism and on society. Thirty years ago, after *Washington Post* reporters Robert Woodward and Carl Bernstein broke the Watergate scandal, budding journalists wanted to cover politics. Although the media often downplay business news, with the scandals of Enron, WorldCom, Adelphia, and others, reporters today are seeing that business stories are the ones increasingly leading the news broadcast or being placed on the front page because these stories are the ones with the biggest impact. An evolution in media coverage occurred as more individuals have become investors in the stock market. Today, more than 50 percent of U.S. households own stock.

Despite this evolution in thought among journalists, business reporting has still fallen on its face more than a few times in recent years. Even basic business stories often lack "depth, understanding and context," said Glenn Lewin, author of *Covering Business* (Marion Street Press, Inc.). Many media outlets lauded Enron's management as being forward-thinking and creating a wonderful place to work before the energy company's disastrous downfall.

If society is to keep improving, it must rely on the media to keep pushing its watchdog role, particularly as it relates to ever-growing and influential businesses. Said former *Wall Street Journal* reporter Kent MacDougall, "Any fall-off in news media scrutiny of business practices and malpractices reduces the effectiveness of the early warning system that the press provides in alerting the public and the government to business abuses that require correction."[8]

Business journalism must play a large part even as some media outlets appear to be shunting business-related stories to the back page as they struggle to produce higher profits. The life of business journalism as a backwater of the media ended a long time ago, and reporters must continue their aggressive coverage of business to protect consumers of all types. "Business is obviously one of the powerful, driving forces of American society," said *Boston Globe* editor Martin Baron. "Business, as much as government, has shaped America.

News organizations were remiss in ignoring the subject for so long."[9]

Today, most of the bigger media outlets compete against each other daily with their business coverage as the corporate world has a greater and greater impact on society. "Business news is now the arena where mainstream editors say they test their mettle against the competition," stated a 1999 report on the status of the American newspaper. "Business stories appear regularly and prominently on front pages and throughout the paper, having slipped the bonds of their own sections the same way business itself has infiltrated every nook of society."[10] And journalists are beginning to understand the importance of their coverage. "Business has everything – power, influence, sex, drama," said *Oregonian* editor Sandra Mims Rowe. She later added, "Business should be the backbone of the newspaper" and "now that the definition of business has expanded, you get into things that affect people's lives – everyone's life."[11]

What is more human than the desire for money? We all have it in some form or another. And business journalism, at its best, taps into the understanding of greed. For-profit companies want to make more money to please their shareholders. To do that, they sometimes have undertaken immoral or illegal steps. Even consumers have greed. Many people watch the performance of their retirement account or 401(k) plan on a daily basis. The more money they have in those accounts, the closer they are to walking away from their jobs or to a secure retirement.

Think of business journalism as the coverage that we all should read, watch, or listen to, but don't want to. Think of business reporting as the story that may make us uncomfortable because it exposes wrongdoing that may have duped us, making us feel ignorant and stupid. Think of business journalism as protecting the public from unscrupulous people in the business world.

Think of business journalism as the reporting and writing that has and will affect you in more ways than any other story. Think of business journalism as the reporting and writing that forces change in companies and industry.

We live today in a society where business news and information are increasingly vital to our livelihoods. Noted business historian Alfred Chandler argues in "A Nation Transformed by Information" that information about business has been a building block in developing society and the economy since the 1600s.

We also live today in a society where fingers are pointed at those being blamed for wrongdoing. Some of those fingers have been pointed at business journalists in recent years for failing to warn the public about the ethical lapses and illegal activities at some of the largest companies in the world – and for failing to uncover their own ethical lapses. As a result, the business journalism community is taking a long, hard look at itself in an attempt to determine where, or if, it went wrong and why. It's examining what it did right in hopes of replicating those events. It's also reflecting on where it has been and where it is headed.

Think for a minute about how media today influence our lives. We may decide to vote for a certain presidential candidate based on interviews and stories we read in newspapers or magazines. We – or our children – may pick a certain brand of cereal to eat for breakfast based on the funny commercials we see on television. A radio alert about a stock falling may cause us to sell those shares in our portfolio. An Internet consumer news site may tell us the best car to buy based on parameters we've entered. We're making these decisions based on what we might have learned through business journalism.

Mass communication in various forms and presentations affects virtually every part of our lives. The media are a tool most consumers use to learn about issues, people, and places. The media are also how we discover new products or services that we may want to try – or avoid.

And yet today, knowledge and understanding by society of the media's past effect – particularly in relation to business – are shallow at best. Many in today's society have little or no understanding that the products they buy and use, the food they eat, and other economic decisions, for the most part, can be attributed to the influence of media. The newspapers of the 18th century, for example, helped spread the word about the poor economic treatment by the British toward the colonies, leading to the American Revolution. The founding fathers of the United States, recognizing the importance of the press in their fight for independence, put the First Amendment into the Constitution, giving all newspapers the right to publish without government interference.

In the 19th century, abolitionist newspapers criticized the practice of slavery, leading to the Civil War. The columns and writing in these papers helped coalesce thought against slave ownership in the North.

In the 20th century, business media alerted the public to safety problems in vehicles and in chemicals, and led readers to examine other products. Later on, our media expanded into other forms such as magazines, radio, television, and now the Internet, and each of these has changed America and how business is perceived and viewed. Whereas it once took days for information to spread to the entire country and the rest of the world, now it takes seconds. Our lives today are often predicated on knowledge and how that information was obtained.

Throughout history, business journalism has had a profound effect on the people of the United States and other parts of the world. Its prominence in our lives grows almost daily as well.

It was business journalism, as defined by today's standards, that exposed the monopolies and trusts that ran many industries in the 19th century, forcing the federal government to break them up to increase competition and make prices more stable. This journalism uncovered unsafe conditions for workers in a number of different jobs, revealed unsanitary food and beverages being sold to consumers that would make them sick or kill them, and discovered automobiles and other manufactured items that could cause bodily harm or death.

It was business journalism that warned the public about investment schemes and poorly run businesses that take the money of unknowing investors. This type of journalism has alerted people to the dangers of chemicals and drugs that have been approved for use by humans or in the plants and livestock grown to place food on our tables. It's this type of journalism that has led to local, state, and federal regulations for dozens and dozens of industries, making everyday life safer for consumers. And it's this type of journalism that has warned when companies and businesses have attempted to circumvent those regulations or found loopholes in laws designed to regulate corporate America.

What do all these stories have in common? They all relate to some form of business journalism. To be sure, many of these writers did not set out to practice business journalism when they began researching their topics or companies. But in fact, they practiced business reporting – what legendary journalist Seymour Hersh recently called the best investigative work by reporters today, according to Northwestern University business journalism professor George Harmon. For it can be argued that business reporting – reporting in the media that discusses topics and issues related to the economy, businesses, and industries or how consumers spend their money – has had just as profound an effect on people's lives today as other types of journalism.

Footnotes

1 From "Journalism's greatest hits: Two lists of a century's top stories," F. Barringer, March 1, 1999, New York Times, p. C1. The three works of journalism in the top six with a focus on business are Rachel Carson's "Silent Spring," which discussed the effects of pesticides on the environment; Ida Tarbell's history of the Standard Oil Co., which examined one of the largest companies in the world at the beginning of the 20th century; and Lincoln Steffens's "The Shame of the Cities," which looked at how businesses were corrupting governments in major cities.

2 From "The newspaper in economic development," by H. A. Innis, December 1942, Journal of Economic History, pp. 1–33.

3 From "Follow the Money," by L. Simons, November 1999, American Journalism Review, pp. 55–68.

4 From "What worries Barney Calame about business journalism," by B. Calame, Aug. 20, 2002, American Society of Newspaper Editors. http://www.asne.org

5 From "New editor: Public service to be goal for Tennessean," by R. Lawson, Dec. 7, 2004, The Tennessean, p. 1A.

6 From "Business journalism: More than mere numbers," by A. Cashin, The muckraker, an online publication of the Boston University Department of Journalism, March 2003, available at http://www.bu.edu/com/muckraker/mar03/business.htm.

7 From "Increasing the Value of Business News," by A. Colon, The Poynter Institute, Dec. 17, 2002. http://www.poynter.org

8 From Ninety seconds to tell it all: Big business and the news media, by A. K. MacDougall, 1981, Homewood, Ill.: Dow Jones-Irwin, p. 9.

9 From "Business journalism: Is the boom over?" by M. Baron, a speech at the Society of American Business Editors and Writers business reporting and writing conference, Oct. 15, 2001, available at http://www.sabew.org/sabewweb.nsf/0/85903a45786e20bc86256b0200699c46?OpenDocument.

10 From "Follow the Money," p. 61.

11 From "Follow the Money," p. 62.

References

A. D. Chandler Jr. and J. W. Cortada. (2003). A nation transformed by information: How information has shaped the United States from colonial times to present. Oxford, England: Oxford University Press.

G. Harmon. (2004, November 29). Grading business journalism. http://www.businessjournalism.org/content/5764.cfm

G. Lewin. (2002, Summer). The watchdog role business reporters need to play. Nieman Reports, pp. 19–21.

Chapter 1

Business journalism's beginning

No family was more powerful in late 15th century and 16th century Europe than the Fuggers, who loaned money to emperors and dukes. Their first loan was to a Hapsburg archduke in 1497, and they also financed the election of Charles V as Holy Roman emperor in 1519. Eventually, their financing throughout Europe resulted in the Fugger family being given the revenues from the Spanish order of knighthood and the profits from mercury and silver mines.

To help the Fugger family keep abreast of events that might affect the interest rates they charged their clients, they hired correspondents throughout the continent to write them letters explaining local business conditions. From 1568 to 1604, hundreds of letters were sent to the Fuggers, and the information in them was used to determine whether or not to loan money and at what rate. The letters also included prices for products and services in the cities from which the letters originated. The Fuggers, most business historians agree, began what has evolved today into the complex system of providing information about business and the economy in an almost instantaneous way through the Internet, television, newspapers, and other media forms.

Business journalism's history is intertwined with the rise of commerce and business across the globe. In fact, the rise of different forms of media in itself is a business enterprise. Looking back at journalism history shows that newspapers were primarily created to help businessmen receive information about goods and services. Without newspapers – and later other media – businesses would have had a difficult time communicating with each other and likely would not have grown as fast. Even after the invention of the telegraph and the telephone, businesses used the media to promote their goods and services.

Examining early developments in business journalism helps us understand how valuable a role it played in the past. Reviewing the major developments of history shows an underlying business reason for virtually every major war, political coup, or other event that changed society. Both the Revolutionary War and the Civil War resulted in profound changes to the economy of not only the United States but of its trading partners. And during these wars, the military focused on cutting off supplies and shipments to rival forces, understanding that business was the lifeblood of any battle.

David Forsyth, who wrote *The Business Press in America: 1750–1865*, argues that in the beginnings of civilization in the Paleolithic or Old Stone Age, man communicated about his economic issues with cave drawings. The genesis of writing and the establishment of a numerical system in the Bronze Age also stemmed from economic activity, he added. Even the Hammurabi Code established forerunners of today's interest rate and minimum wage laws.

In the beginning of the printed word and publications, business news was vital to society, although the information was rarely critical of commerce, which was a developing concept in the 17th and 18th centuries. In addition, the first newspapers rarely worried about offending their advertisers with critical business coverage, though few wrote anything critical of business. Few papers had ads, and those that did were often for the paper's publisher.

Newsletters were used in the Middle Ages to help well-known trading families communicate with each other. In the German city of Augsburg, the Fuggers created a newsletter of business information related to its financial business. The newsletters had the same goal as many business newspapers and media outlets of today: to transmit important information about the markets and to analyze that information. Historian George Matthews called them "reports of those who have heard the echo of events as they reverberated through the markets of the world" and said they "represent the news as it might appear on the unedited, continuously moving tape of a press agency's teletype: true reports and false rumors, trivial occurrences and important events."[1] Among the topics discussed in the Fugger newsletters were deaths of kings and queens, wars, the arrival and departure of ships, the burning of the exchange in Antwerp, executions, and the demise of the Spanish Armada at the hands of the British in 1588.[2]

Similar newsletters developed by businesses in Holland in the 17th century made Amsterdam the European business center of the period, said history professor Woodruff T. Smith. "In the sixteenth century, it had become customary for correspondents to note on their letters the rates of currency exchange," stated Smith. "In the seventeenth century it had become procedure – a matter

Business Journalism Timeline

1568 – Fugger family begins its newsletter system of informing its customers of news that might impact European economies.

J. Fugger

1588 – British navy defeats the Spanish Armada, which signals a shift in European economic power.

1700s – British newspapers begin publishing advertisements for merchants.

1700s – Newspapers in both England and the American colonies run information about ships entering and leaving ports and their cargos.

of politeness and form – to include in business letters general economic and political information and prices of major commodities."[3]

Merchants and companies bribed diplomats to obtain such information. One famous information broker, Leo van Aitzema, collected and collated business information and gossip, and businesses and governments relied heavily on him and his competitors.[4]

Englishman Thomas Gresham III also collected information from around Europe for financial gain, acting much in the manner of a business editor. A 16th-century Englishman, Gresham was a merchant who met with Fugger agents and agents from other financial houses. He became a business consultant, maintaining a cadre of reporters and spies who sent him information about other marketplaces, and he worked for Henry VIII in eliminating England's debt in the middle of the 16th century. In 1565, Gresham successfully persuaded the British government to build a stock exchange in London patterned after the Antwerp exchange. Mid-20th-century journalism professor Julian Elfenbein argues that London replaced Antwerp as the commercial center of the world in the 16th century as a result of Gresham's work.[5] In addition, Gresham used the business information he received for his own personal gain, not to provide the news and analysis for other readers. But Gresham did develop Gresham's law, which is "Bad money drives out good."

Similar publications cropped up in other European countries in the 17th century and began including political information as well. The combination of news about business and politics and how the two interact into one medium was as important then as it is today. This business coverage was vitally important, even though it looks primitive by today's standards. Understand, however, that knowledge of a business opportunity 400 years ago was not as widely disseminated then as it can be today by the media. Receiving information about purchasing a good or service at an advantageous price a day or two ahead of a rival was valuable and highly prized.

News also had other business connections. In England, for example, people who lived out in the country traveled to country fairs in places such as Bartholomew, Donnybrook, and Stourbridge to buy supplies and swap information. The creation of a newspaper, at least in England, was the gathering of these facts traded previously at country fairs into a commodity that could be sold much like the farmer's produce or other merchandise. The first press in England was set up by William Caxton, who saw his press as a way to promote law, industry, and culture.[6] Because of the government's interference in pressuring many papers critical of politicians, some newspapers focused more on business and less on the doings of Parliament.

England had been restricting content in newspapers and other published material for more than a century through licensing. But in the 18th century, the rise of a middle class in England helped advance the newspapers. Commercial traders, merchants and manufacturers longed for information and needed newspapers to give them advantageous news that could be used to make a profit. And with the emergence of the political party system, newspapers were used to promote various viewpoints as well. Daily newspapers sprang up as a result.

These newspapers were filled with business-related matters. Many were filled with primitive advertisements for products that merchants wanted to sell to the readers. In the Sept. 15–17, 1701 edition of the *London Post,* for example, an ad offering the sale of nine "comick and tragick" novels included such spell-binding titles as "Jealousy without a Cause" and

"The Cuckold turn'd Confessor." The books were being sold by the publisher of the paper.[7] The Jan. 1, 1726, issue of *The British Gazetteer* had an ad for "The Life and Actions of Moll Flanders," offered by T. Read, whose printing shop was behind the Sun Tavern on Fleet Street.[8]

Other business matters dominated the early British newspapers. An advertisement in the Jan. 28–31, 1727, *London Gazette* placed by the law firm of Buckle and Sparrow offered a reward of 200 pound for the apprehension of businessman John Rogers, who had been declared bankrupt but had disappeared. The ad noted, "He hath cheated great Numbers of Persons of very large Sums of Money."[9] A newspaper called the *Grub-street Journal* offered this business commentary in its Jan. 28, 1731, edition:

> Great numbers of the wives and children of the coal-pit men are beginning in all the neighbouring towns, by reason their husbands have not their usual work, and are forced to draw coals about for small pay, to prevent starving. We are in great dread of them, for their numbers are very large, and no body will trust them, which makes them desperate. It is said some of the coal owners have agreed not to deliver more coals till Feb. 20, which will not only make them dear, but ruin hundreds more of working men.[10]

This notice, although probably intended for the people seeing the beggars, was typical of the type of business news that pervaded most London newspapers during its time. Other typical coverage included lists of "fugitives of debt," or people who were unable to pay money that they owed others.

One of the most important functions of the early British newspapers was to act as a conduit for commerce and trade. Newspapers regularly listed information such as the cargos of ships that had arrived at port. *The London Post* from July 22–24, 1700, noted the contents inside the *Sarah Galley*, a ship that had arrived from China on July 20. The ship brought with it more than 140,000 pieces of China Ware, 2,848 Tea Tables, and 266 Lacker'd Chests, as

BUSINESS JOURNALISM TIMELINE

1735 – JOHN PETER ZENGER IS ACCUSED OF SEDITION FOR CRITICIZING THE BRITISH GOVERNMENT ON BUSINESS-RELATED ISSUES. HE IS ACQUITTED.

ZENGER'S TRIAL

1750S – FIRST "PRICE CURRENT" APPEARS. THESE NEWSPAPERS LIST THE PRICES OF GOODS AVAILABLE IN A TOWN OR CITY.

1765 – BRITISH PASS THE STAMP ACT, WHICH LEVIES A TAX ON THE PAPER USED BY PRINTERS TO PUBLISH NEWSPAPERS.

1776-1783 – REVOLUTIONARY WAR.

1791 – FIRST AMERICAN FACTORY OPENS.

1793 – THE NEW-HAMPDEN JOURNAL, ALSO KNOWN AS THE FARMERS' WEEKLY MUSEUM, BEGINS PUBLISHING. IT IS THE FIRST U.S. BUSINESS PAPER.

well as a large supply of various teas. A retailer called "Jacob's Famous Strops" offered razors and penknifes that were "very useful for surgeons and barbers" for one shilling apiece in the Nov. 17–29, 1703, edition of the *English Post.* Customers who were not satisfied with the razors by the end of the month could get their money back, the advertisement noted.[11]

Early 18th-century newspapers in Europe curried favor with businessmen and merchants. Their advertising helped the publishers stay in business, and these businessmen were also often subscribers to the papers. Many newspapers made it clear that their contents were of interest to the business community. The Sept. 6, 1722, *Stamford Mercury* noted on its front page that its contents included "historical and political observations on the transactions of Europe" as well as "remarks on trade."[12]

The colonies and business

Newspapers in the American colonies were also seeing the same developments in their pages related to business. The *Boston News-Letter* published with a date of April 17 to April 24, 1704, had one advertisement – promoting itself and its pages. It read, "The News-Letter is to be continued Weekly, and all persons who have any lands, houses, tenements, farms, ships, vessels, goods, wares or merchandise to be sold or lett; or servants runaway, or goods Stoll, or lost, may have the same inserted at a reasonable rate."[13]

Again, the development of commerce in America was a main driving force in the rise of newspapers. In the New England states, the fishing industry led to the creation of a number of different industries, and the owners of these businesses wanted to grow and expand their operations. Merchants discovered that their goods would sell faster if they published notices in the local publications. As a result, a number of early newspapers used the word *Advertiser* in their names. And the businesses learned something about their ads that the writers and editors wouldn't learn about their copy for years. As advertisements grew in number in newspapers, many took to making outlandish claims in their ads to attract attention. But many businesses discovered that the ads that were simply written drew the most interest.

Local postmasters, who used the postal service to receive information from other colonies, developed many of the newspapers. The *News-Letter* was one of these papers. Its printer was John Campbell, who had run the Boston post office since 1700. The paper had information about meetings and proclamations – and a healthy dose of business news, such as available cargo space on ships heading back to England and legal notices. The shipping news ranged geographically from as far north as Nova Scotia and as far south as Charleston.

The *News-Letter* was started by Campbell as a way to disseminate the information he collected as postmaster, and it was sent to merchants and rich colonists. In addition to the business news, the paper contained information Campbell took out of European papers, as well as information about the West Indies. Although replaced as postmaster in 1718, Campbell continued to publish the newspaper. The new postmaster started a competing paper, the *Gazette.* In 1722, Campbell sold the newspaper, but it was published until 1776.

As the colonies began growing and expanding, however, their relationship with the British government became strained, and the main source of conflict was a business issue – taxes. Newspapers on both sides of the Atlantic Ocean covered the issue with gusto. In fact, some of the major developments in journalism of the 18th century were related to the increasing tensions in the colonies.

The best known was the case of a journalist accused of spreading scurrilous information about the governor of New York. John Peter Zenger was a printer's apprentice who had opened his own shop in New York. He was approached by businessmen in the area to start a newspaper that would rival the *New York Gazette,* controlled by the administration. His *New York Weekly Journal* appeared for the first time in November 1733 and began criticizing the British-controlled government. Among the criticisms were two that were business related. One claimed that the government wanted one-third of the price of the sale of public land. Another accusation suspected illegal land purchases. A year after opening his paper, Zenger was accused of sedition and brought to trial. When he was found innocent, newspapers rejoiced and became more emboldened in covering issues that affected their readers. No other newspaper editor was tried for sedition before the Revolutionary War.[14]

With increased freedom, American newspapers reacted with incredible scorn when the British passed the Stamp Act of 1765. The law levied a tax on the paper used by printers to publish their newspapers and by lawyers to write their legal documents. Newspapers reacted angrily against the tax, noting that it had been levied without any colonial representation in Parliament. The *Pennsylvania Journal* closed rather than publish using paper with the stamp. Its last edition stated: "EXPIRING: In Hopes of a Resurrection to Life Again." The *Maryland Gazette,* which had ceased publication, suddenly reappeared, calling itself "An Apparition of the late Maryland Gazette, which is not Dead but Sleepeth."[15] Because so many newspapers defied the law, the Stamp Act could not be enforced and was repealed. With this defiance, the colonial newspapers had begun to develop the opinion that the colonies should be able to govern their own business matters.

Although a similar tax had been in force in England for some time, and some colonial governments had taxed their residents, the Stamp Act helped newspapers sway public opinion against the British government. Even some writing in English newspapers agreed. In the Jan. 21, 1775, issue of the *Edinburgh Evening Courant,* Lord Chatham wrote, "You have no right to tax America. I rejoice that America has resisted." Added Lord Camden, "My researchers have more and more convinced me, that you have no right to tax America. I will maintain it with my last breath."[16]

What this coverage indicates is that when it came to business reporting, the newspapers of the 18th century were primarily concerned with how commerce was being affected by the policies of the government. There were few critical stories about business, and when there were, it was about a businessman who had gone out of business or who owed money. The business-related information contained in many newspapers helped the merchant or manufacturer in the course of operating his business. This information included ship schedules at the closest port and details of upcoming auctions of goods.

Some of these early newspapers failed to make the distinction made by most media today between news and advertising for businesses. Instead of the seller purchasing an ad to promote the auction, it was often considered news in the early newspapers when a group of slaves were to be sold. A story, not an ad, about the auction helped the seller generate interest in the sale.

The same can be argued about some stories in current business journalism. Stories are written about new automobiles or new products that are announced by press releases sent out by large corporations solely for the purpose of generating "free" advertising for the company in the form of media coverage. And while these stories from the media today provide some perspective on the strategy behind the new product and some commentary from independent analysts, they almost always generate a positive impression in the minds of the readers.

Has business journalism changed much from its origins as a provider of information for the merchants? On the surface, the answer appears to be no. But dig deeper, as seen in the next few chapters, and the world of journalism in America will become more independent after the Revolution. That freedom will give business journalism its first motivation to aggressively cover businesses and begin to look behind the warts of industry. And what the newspaper publishers and editors of the 19th century discovered is that businesses were as scandalous and the coverage was as readable as the juicy political gossip it once gave more coverage.

What the early newspapers did, however, was recognize that business played an important role in the rapidly changing society that was adding different kinds of shops selling various goods and services in most growing metropolitan areas. To attract those businessmen as buyers of the newspaper and as advertisers, the newspapers needed to put out a lively publication that provided information people wanted. And as commerce expanded, these newspapers realized that what was happening in the business world was what they should be recording in their pages.

Footnotes

1 From News and rumor in Renaissance Europe: The Fugger newsletters, edited by G. T. Matthews, 1959, New York: G. P. Putnam's Sons, pp. 19–20.

2 See The Fugger news-letters, edited by V. von Klarwill, 1924, London: John Lane The Bodley Head Ltd.

3 From "The function of commercial centers in the modernization of European capitalism: Amsterdam as an information exchange in the seventeenth century," by W. D. Smith, December 1984, Journal of Economic History, p. 992.

4 From "The function of commercial centers in the modernization of European capitalism: Amsterdam as an information exchange in the seventeenth century," p. 996.

5 From Business Journalism (Second Edition), by J. Elfenbein, New York: Harper & Brothers, 1960.

6 From The press and America: An interpretive history of the mass media (Fifth Edition), by E. Emery and M. Emery, Englewood Cliffs, NJ: Prentice-Hall Inc., 1984.

7 From "Early eighteenth-century newspaper reports: A sourcebook," by R. Norton, Nov. 18, 2001, available at http://www.infopt.demon.co.uk/grub/grub.htm.

8 From " Early eighteenth-century newspaper reports: A sourcebook."

9 From " Early eighteenth-century newspaper reports: A sourcebook."

10 From " Early eighteenth-century newspaper reports: A sourcebook."

11 From " Early eighteenth-century newspaper reports: A sourcebook."

12 From the Stamford Mercury, Sept. 6, 1722. British Library Newspaper Library, available at http://www.bl.uk/collections/brit18th.html.

13 From " Early eighteenth-century newspaper reports: A sourcebook."

14 From "The press and America: An interpretive history of the mass media (Fifth Edition)."

15 From "History of journalism," by M. Stephens, available at http://www.nyu.edu/classes/stephens/Collier's%20page.htm.

16 From " Early eighteenth-century newspaper reports: A sourcebook."

References

E. Emery and M. Emery. (1984). The press and America: An interpretive history of the mass media (Fifth Edition). Englewood Cliffs, NJ: Prentice-Hall Inc.

D. Forsyth. (1964). The business press in America: 1750–1865. Philadelphia: Chilton Books.

Chapter 2

The first real business publications – and journalists

Long before the Internet captivated consumers and business journalists in the 1990s, other industries caught the fancy of the press. In fact, dozens of newspapers in the early part of the 19th century focused on catering to a business audience such as farmers and merchants. But no business captivated the media during the 19th century like the railroads.

Among the business publications that were started were *The Railway Express, The Railway Examiner, The Railway Globe, The Railway Standard, The American Railroad Journal,* and *The Railway Mail.* They dissected every part of the industry, from the engineering behind steam engines to the laying of track and the amount of freight shipped by each individual railroad.

Although newspapers in the early 19th century were primarily political organs, or publications that promoted the ideas of a specific political party, the century saw important developments in business journalism. Because of the growing industrialization of the country's economy, newspapers began paying more attention to news from the business world. Specialty business news publications started, and mainstream newspapers focused more on business coverage. By the end of the century, business and economics news was a regular staple in mainstream newspapers and magazines.

The beginning of *The Wall Street Journal* in 1889 was also a major development. Today, the *Journal* is one of the country's largest circulation papers, and it is considered the preeminent medium for business news and information. It has spawned competitors in all types of media. But in the 19th century, the fact that a daily newspaper could be devoted to covering the business world was a unique business plan.

There were other major developments for business journalism. A mainstream newspaper began covering business and economic issues for the first time and hired the first financial editor. The first true business journalist – a former lawyer – argued that companies should disclose detailed financial information, a radical notion for the 19th century. Dozens of specialty business publications started, showing the demand for industry-related news and information. And overall changes in how newspapers operated as a business, such as the increase in advertising revenue, also had a profound effect on business journalism.

These developments occurred during a time of great change in the country's economy.

The Industrial Revolution occurred in the 19th century, and the building of the country's factories and the growth of the country's economy and wealth naturally meant that the media of the time would begin to pay more attention to business and industry. As the country shifted from primarily agrarian output to building machines such as railroad engines in factories and processing food in plants, the effect on the people was also tremendous. More people moved into the cities from rural areas and from Europe. The printing industry was revolutionized as well, making it easier for people to access pamphlets, books, and newspapers.

These changes are well documented in the media of the time. But what the media, with few notable exceptions, lacked was an overall understanding of the impact on society that these changes caused. The media were slow to change from focusing on government and politics to other parts of society, with business being one of those issues that would gain reader interest by the end of the century.

It is sometimes hard to understand why many 19th-century newspapers and magazines, as businesses themselves, failed to place more emphasis on writing about industry and how business was creating jobs or changing the way people lived their lives. To be sure, developments such as the railroad, the telegraph, and the telephone were hailed in daily newspapers as dramatic forces that would overhaul the world. But in comparison, the daily media virtually ignored other important business events, such as the growing labor force, or simply failed to understand what was happening and why, while smaller media not widely read understood their significance.

The first business publications

The first actual newspapers devoted to business started after the Revolutionary War. Journalism historians, particularly journalism historian David Forsyth, note that "price currents" – newspapers that offered prices of goods and services in a specific city or town – began appearing in America in the 1750s. Some of the first were a 1752 sheet printed in Nova Scotia and another in Charleston, South Carolina, in 1774, although there is no definitive answer about the first "price current" newspaper.[1] These newspapers were descendants of similar papers in the Netherlands and England published as far back as the late

Business Journalism Timeline

1795 – The New York Price Current begins publishing. This business newspaper continues for 100 years and later adds stock prices.

1827 – Journal of Commerce founded in New York.

1827 – Journeyman Mechanics' Almanac begins publishing in Philadelphia. It is considered the first labor newspaper in the United States.

1835 – The New York Herald begins publishing a money page in its newspaper. The page is considered the first business section in a daily newspaper.

1849-1862 – Henry Varnum Poor edits the American Railroad Journal. The publication reports on the stock offerings and financial conditions of railroads throughout the country.

16th century. The *New York Price Current* was established in 1795, four years after the first U.S. factory had begun operation.[2]

These price currents listed the current prices of various products offered for sale by local merchants, and they rarely, if ever, contained any editorial content. The papers were strictly information and extremely numbers intensive. Among the products listed in most price currents were cotton, flour, furs, leather, oil, skins, tobacco, and wheat. A Philadelphia price current from 1783 also listed sample wages for workers such as carpenters, sail makers, and blacksmiths. Later, 18th-century price currents in that city also included information about shipping traffic. Baltimore and Boston also had price currents published in the late 18th century in the early 19th century.[3] The *Boston Daily Advertiser* was one of these price currents. Published by Nathan Hale, the paper listed prices for foreign goods and domestic goods on the front page of its May 24, 1823, edition. Most of the rest of the four-page broadsheet contains shipping information and small advertisements from merchants.[4]

The New York paper was the most successful of these early price currents. It published its first issue in December 1795 and continued for more than 100 years under other names. And in addition to prices, it had some editorial content. It also included early stock prices and exchange rates. The *Price Current*'s success led to the first daily newspaper devoted to business, *Daily Items for Merchants,* which was published for the first time in 1815. Printed by the *Price Current* publisher, the newspaper included additional information such as insurance premium quotes, prices of freight and stock, and notices of ship arrivals at foreign ports.[5]

As the first daily business newspaper, *Daily Items* set the stage for future business newspapers. Though *Daily Items* lasted less than two years, it showed other publishers that a daily newspaper devoted solely to business and commerce could exist. Some of the price currents were taken over by mainstream newspapers and delivered to subscribers. That typically meant the end of the price current, since most subscribers to general newspapers were not interested in the information in the price currents. For a business newspaper to be successful, it would have to develop a business-related readership with news about business and the economy.

Other newspapers in the early 19th century attempted to focus on a certain industry to attract readership. The best known, according to Baird and Turnbull, were *Butchers' and Packers' Gazette,* which started in 1808; *General Shipping and Commercial List,* started in 1815; *American Journal of Pharmacy,* started in 1825; and the *American Railroad Journal,* started in 1832.[6] Journalism professor Julian Elfenbein lists the *New-Hampden Journal,* also known as the *Farmers' Weekly Museum,* which published from 1793 to 1810, as the first U.S. business paper.[7] Most of these papers contained basic statistical information.

Still other business-related papers followed the lead of the price currents and provided details of goods sold at auctions and stock sales in Boston and Philadelphia. Others focused on the sale of groceries, noted Forsyth.

All these early papers catered to the business community and provided information that merchants and other businesspeople needed to successfully operate. Without the price currents and other early business papers, the merchants, farmers, and other businessmen of the early 19th century had no way of knowing the going rate for their goods and services, and no way – other than the unreliable word of mouth – of learning information that may affect their operation.

Today, these newspapers might be considered the equivalent of a data service such as the analytical parts of the Bloomberg service, which provides prices of stocks, bonds, commodities, and other financial instruments. These newspapers contained virtually no writing during the early part of the 19th century, yet they provided a sense to the reader of general business conditions. For some of these papers, their failures signified economic slumps that affected their subscribers as well.

What today's business journalism field can take away from these early business newspapers is that even in the formative stages of the United States, there was a demand for accurate information about business and commerce, and that the media were there to provide it. What would happen for the rest of the century would be a further development of the business press, as writers and editors began to interpret the data from these early newspapers for their readers and provide more analytical content.

In retrospect, these early attempts at business journalism appear crude. But what they show is the reliance on numbers to help tell a story. Compared to business coverage later in the century that often used rumors and innuendo to entertain readers, information in the price currents and trade newspapers was factual. And for that reason, many became trusted guides to the business world. The *American Railroad Journal,* as detailed later in the chapter, would advance what today is considered business journalism more than any other 19th-century publication.

The penny press and business

The development of the penny newspapers also provided a boost to business reporting. Before the 1830s, most newspapers were sold on an annual subscription basis, but the cost was more than most people could pay. When newspapers started selling for 1 cent each day, readership dramatically rose. With an increase in readership, papers began offering more varied content that appealed to readers with different interests and varied incomes.

James Gordon Bennett's *New York Herald* was the penny newspaper that devoted a large amount of space regularly to business and economics news. Started in 1835 on Wall Street, the *Herald* developed the best financial section of any of the mainstream newspapers. Bennett was a former economics teacher, and he often wrote what he

BUSINESS JOURNALISM TIMELINE

REUTER

1849 – JULIUS REUTER FOUNDS BUSINESS NEWS SERVICE IN EUROPE.

FRANK LESLIE'S ILLUSTRATED NEWSPAPER

1858 – FRANK LESLIE'S ILLUSTRATED NEWSPAPER UNCOVERS PROBLEMS IN THE MILK BUSINESS.

1861-1865 – THE U.S. CIVIL WAR.

1861 - INTERCONTINENTAL TELEGRAPH LINE IS COMPLETED, IMPROVING SPEED OF NEWS.

called the "money page." The May 11, 1835, topic was stock speculating and the "secret conspiracy of our large capitalists."[8] Bennett often used the page to explain why stock prices rose and fell. Also on his financial reporting staff was Thomas Prentice Kettell, who began writing a financial column for the *Herald* in 1835 and is considered the first financial editor of any daily newspaper in the country. Kettell founded *United States Economist* in 1852.[9]

As Bennett explained his view of business journalism, "The spirit, pith and philosophy of commercial affairs is what men of business want. Dull records of facts, without condensation, analysis, or deduction, are utterly useless. The philosophy of commerce is what we aim at, combined with accuracy, brevity, and spirit."[10] Bennett often assigned his best reporters to the business beat, said journalism historians Michael Emery and Edwin Emery.

What is striking about Bennett's attitude toward business news is that it was one of the first times a newspaper had developed a "beat" for its coverage. Newspapers in the early 19th century did not process news stories the way they do today by having reporters responsible for specific coverage areas. In that respect, Bennett's coverage of business and economics stories was a precursor to developing a business beat at other newspapers. In comparison, other newspapers of that time provided scant analysis of the business community. Historian Willard Bleyer notes that Bennett's coverage "of financial affairs in Wall Street [was] the first attempt to cover adequately that important department of local news" and that the reporting in the *Herald* "came to be recognized as a distinctive contribution to daily journalism."[11]

In comparison, other newspapers provided business coverage in chart form. The *New York Spectator* from Nov. 9, 1835, is a typical newspaper. It contained a stock sales chart for trades from Nov. 5 on its front page, trades from Nov. 6 on page two, and trades from Nov. 7 on page three, which also included a chart of bank note prices.[12]

Bennett had competitors for business coverage in the early days of the penny press. *The Journal of Commerce* was a New York paper that actually superseded the penny newspapers. It was founded in 1827 by Arthur Tappan but edited by Gerard Hallock from 1828 to 1861. The publication remains in existence today as a weekly magazine, converting in 2000. In the 1940s and 1950s, the paper was one of the best read newspapers in the country because it published shipping schedules.

Hallock was considered an innovator in how he gathered business news. He used two small schooners to cruise the waters outside New York to find incoming ships and then come back to port with the news. When other New York papers followed, Hallock then moved to land, establishing a horse express from Philadelphia to New York that gave the *Journal of Commerce* news from Washington and the South a day ahead of other New York papers.[13]

Despite its name, the *Journal of Commerce* initially was like most other New York newspapers, focusing its pages on coverage of politics and the government. And when politics and business mixed, businessmen and politicians went to the media to address the issues. For example, when President Andrew Jackson opposed the re-chartering of the Second Bank of the United States and clashed with its president, Nicholas Biddle, both turned to the media. Biddle believed that appealing to the public through the media would restore public confidence in the bank.

Bennett also focused his attention on the Jackson–Biddle clash. He warned in 1835 that the liquidation of the Second Bank was putting pressure on New York banks and stockbrokers. Bennett constantly put pressure on Jackson and his successor, Martin Van Buren, to improve the country's economy, and he argued for a new national bank, to be based in New York. Other newspapers followed suit in criticizing the administration for problems in business. The *New York American* on April 25, 1837, blamed the outgoing Jackson administration for the failure of four of the five cotton factories in New Orleans, the failure of several New York and Philadelphia companies, and the failure of more than 150 New York merchants.[14]

In the mid-1850s, Bennett also warned about speculation in overpriced railroad stocks, a suggestion that other business journalists were also making. Before Abraham Lincoln's election in 1860, Bennett warned New York banks to sell their stocks and bonds in southern operations and collect debt from southerners.[15] Like other newspapers, the *Herald* discussed slavery, but not as it related to the operation of plantations in the South. Slavery was written about as a divisive, political issue. Still, the potential effects of a change in the slavery system on business were obvious.

Many large city newspapers like the *Herald* in the early 19th century did contain a healthy dose of business coverage, according to an analysis of five newspapers by University of Washington professor Gerald Baldasty in *The Commercialization of News in the Nineteenth Century*. Baldasty conducted a content analysis of the Charleston *Mercury*, the Charleston *Courier*, the Boston *Morning Post*, Boston *Daily Advertiser*, and the New York *Courier and Enquirer* for six-day periods in 1831 and 1832. The five newspapers gave a median of 22.9 percent of their news coverage to business and labor news. Only one category – politics – received more coverage.[16] But these newspapers contained a large amount of coverage because they were located in cities with major ports, which were a vital cog in the business community in the early part of the century.

Nonmetropolitan newspapers in the same period provided less coverage to business and labor issues, Baldasty found. He reviewed weeklies in Haverhill, Mass., Rutherfordton, N.C., and Greenville, N.C., and a daily in Albany, N.Y. in January 1832 and found that the four newspapers gave just a median of 2.3 percent of their news coverage to business and labor, with Albany ranking the highest at 6.8 percent.[17]

Interestingly, an analysis of newspaper coverage near the end of the century found a different situation. This time, Baldasty conducted a content analysis of metropolitan newspapers, large-town/small-city newspapers, and small-town newspapers. The average news coverage devoted to business and labor in the metropolitan newspapers during the week of Oct. 17–23, 1897, was 18 percent, down from nearly 70 percent years earlier. The lost space for business coverage in mainstream newspapers apparently went to leisure coverage, which saw its median percentage of content increase from 2.8 percent in 1831 and 1832 to 17.8 percent in 1897.[18] Business and labor news content in the large-town/small-city newspapers was a median 12.7 percent, while the median percentage in small-town newspapers was 20.6 percent, a dramatic rise from 1832, Baldasty found.[19]

What this content analysis shows is that by the end of the century, general circulation newspapers had become more interested in business news. Some believed that business news was an important part of their coverage – partly for economic reasons. By writing about business, more businesses were likely to advertise in the papers. Unfortunately, most of this coverage was performed in a flattering manner to the businesses and lacked any critical analysis of the companies. Baldasty provides example after example of newspapers coddling their advertisers. A St. Louis paper called a department store a "model advertiser" in an editorial after it committed to running full-page ads for a year. A Detroit paper published "practical talks" with its advertisers. The New York *World* ran an index of businesses in the city in 1885. Coincidently, the index included just businesses that were the newspaper's advertisers. One of the primary benefactors of such newspaper coverage was department stores.[20]

Ethical lapses – if the application of late 20th-century standards are employed for this discussion – were common at the end of the 19th century, but they would stain the credibility of business journalism and set a bad precedent. Business leaders would come to expect such favorable content from newspapers and other media in the next century, with many of them arguing that their companies were large advertisers. The threat was obvious: write critically about my company, and advertising will be pulled. For struggling newspapers attempting to compete against rivals, few wanted to upset large advertisers.

Still, newspapers in the latter half of the 19th century gave acceptable coverage to the major business issues of the day. When the Credit Mobilier scandal broke in 1872, most newspapers gave it front-page coverage. The scandal involved giving railroad stock to members of Congress, making it also a political story. The *New York Tribune* of Sept. 21, 1872, gave two entire columns of its six-column front page to the scandal, reprinting verbatim a letter written by Oakes Ames, one of the disgraced members of Congress.[21]

Inside that same issue of the paper was more news that showed how the mainstream newspapers had taken over the content of the price currents from earlier in the century. Page 5 of the *Tribune* included a column called "The State of Trade," which included prices for goods in various Eastern cities, prices for cattle, and prices for cotton in markets ranging from Washington to Galveston, Texas. The column next to this included "Shipping Intelligence," which listed passengers sailing for San Francisco and from Rio de Janeiro, Brazil. Below that was a list of ships that had arrived in New York and Boston, as well as ships that had arrived in English ports.[22]

Page 9 of the same newspaper included a detailed list of government and state bond sales, as well as the latest stock prices for most of the major railroads and other companies. A short description of stock trading described the markets as appearing "to have fairly settled themselves to their ordinary routine. At least the indications to-day point to a quiet closing of the week, the different departments showing much less excitement, while a more settled feeling pervades the street."[23] The rest of the page included a number of advertisements from Wall Street brokers offering stocks and bonds.

ONE OF THE MOST IMPORTANT FINANCIAL EDITORS of the latter half of the 19th century was Henry Demarest Lloyd. The financial editor of the *Chicago Tribune* from 1874 to 1880, Lloyd would later become an early forerunner of the muckrakers because of his criticism of the Robber Barons who dominated businesses after the Civil War. In addition to his writing in the *Tribune*, Lloyd wrote about monopolies and the economics of politics for *The Atlantic Monthly*, and he later wrote books that advocated the position of labor unions.

Lloyd's most famous business book was *Wealth against Commonwealth*, published in 1894. In it he criticized the size of businesses, writing: "What we call Monopoly is Business at the end of its journey. The concentration of wealth, the wiping out of the middle classes, are other names for it. To get it is, in the world of affairs, the chief end of man."[24]

Another important business journalist during the time was William Buck Dana, who was editor of the *Commercial and Financial Chronicle.* After purchasing *Hunt's Merchants' Magazine* in 1861, Dana founded the *Commercial and Financial Chronicle* in New York in 1865, and edited it until his death in 1910. The *Chronicle* was the first business weekly newspaper in the country, and Dana was a dominant force in explaining business and the economy to his readers. Trained as an attorney, Dana modeled his newspaper after *The Economist* in London, and it included unsigned editorials about current business matters as well as reports on the financial conditions of banks. By 1870, the monthly *Merchants' Magazine* was folded into the *Chronicle.* Dana's editorials included commentaries on business law and criticism of government regulation of business and labor relations.[25]

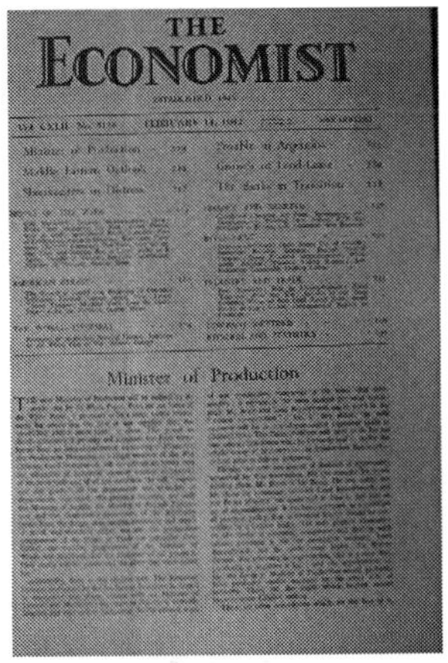
THE ECONOMIST

Minister of Production

Dana's coverage was prescient in understanding the potential of Alexander Graham Bell's telephone and how electricity would spur growth in the country. "Steam, electricity, and invention has so accelerated the pace of progress, have so re-duplicated the forces of industry and trade, that the individual has lost his place," wrote Dana in 1895. "Capital combines in corporations, not only where it is required in vast sums for railways and telegraphs, but in lumbering, mining, manufacturing, and store-keeping."[26] But he condemned the building of the Brooklyn Bridge, and he ignored the invention of the Model T Ford in 1909, one year before he died.[27]

Other newspapers and publications were not as harsh toward business during this period. A Maine newspaper, The *Portland Transcript,* billed itself as an "independent family journal of literature, science, news, markets, etc." in the latter part of the 19th century. But a review of its pages showed that the markets coverage was almost always limited to a chart listing wholesale and retail prices of goods in Portland, as well as prices of Portland stocks.[28]

The *Commercial Bulletin* in Boston gave more coverage. In its Oct. 3, 1885, issue, for example, two columns on page two were devoted to "Gossip about Trade." One of the items went into great detail about a dispute between a Boston department store, Jordan Marsh & Co., and some of its New York suppliers. Next to "Gossip about Trade," was a column titled "Failures and Suspensions," which discussed businesses that had closed. Page three was devoted entirely to the markets, with a column titled "Waifs from Wall Street," and six full columns of the ten-column page were devoted to "Reviews of Markets." The lead of the main stock story began, "The stock market has been strong during the week, uncomfortably so indeed for the bears, but it has advanced in such a listless manner and the circle of speculation has been manifestly so narrow that whether the next movement would be up or down has been extremely doubtful."[29] Even more than 100 years ago, a stock markets reporter knew how to hedge his reporting.

Still, coverage of business and the economic issues at the end of the 19th century was much broader than at the beginning. In 1882, three reporters – Charles Dow, Edward Jones, and Charles Bergstresser – started Dow Jones & Co. to sell news and gossip items to stock brokers, bankers, and speculators. Seven years later, they started *The Wall Street Journal,* a four-page newspaper devoted solely to stocks and bonds.

This was a sign of the country's growing economy as well as the increasing reliance on information about the markets and industry by people – management and consumers – making decisions about their way of life and about their companies. While much of the coverage was still overly positive, business journalism began to show signs of skepticism.

A true business journalist

One journalist in the mid-19th nineteenth century wasn't afraid to criticize the companies he was writing about. In fact, the work of Henry Varnum Poor, editor of the *American Railroad Journal* from 1849 to 1862, caused dramatic changes in the relationship between companies and journalists. In retrospect, Poor can be considered the first true modern-day business journalist for forcing companies to provide accurate information about their financial performance to investors and readers.

Poor was born on a farm in Andover, Maine, in December 1812, and his father Sylvanus Poor was the town treasurer. Although he was the first in his family to attend college, Poor received a better education for his future career as a journalist by observing his brother John Alfred Poor build a railroad system through Maine. Although he also worked as a lawyer and a lumber merchant, Henry Poor made a name for himself when he moved to New York in 1849 to become editor of *The Journal*.[30]

Poor's 13-year tenure as editor of the newspaper and his subsequent activities in publishing the *Manual of the Railroads of the United States* set the standard for journalists writing about business for rest of the century. Poor's dramatic career as a business journalist is well documented by noted business historian Alfred D. Chandler, Jr. in his 1951 master's thesis at the University of North Carolina at Chapel Hill and his 1956 book titled *Henry Varnum Poor: Business editor, analyst, and reformer.* Poor was Chandler's great-grandfather.

Before Poor arrived, the *Journal* struggled. Its owner left and went to California in early 1849 after gold was discovered. John Alfred Poor bought controlling interest in the paper and offered the job of editor to his brother. Henry Varnum Poor took his knowledge of railroad operations and changed the publication. The *Journal* previously focused on promoting the superiority of the railroad to canals and turnpikes as a way to transport goods. But unlike other business newspapers of the era, the *Journal* didn't merely recite statistics of fees and wages to transport goods across certain railroad lines. Instead, it functioned more like a traditional newspaper of the time, with articles and reports about the industry. It also provided a healthy amount of engineering and technical information for those operating railroads.

Poor advanced the newspaper as the industry's house organ, making its writing stand out from any other business paper of the 19th century – and from any mainstream newspaper. He was the first journalist writing about business to apply statistical analysis to assess a company's performance. While Poor spent a lot of time in the first few years of the publication advocating for the industry, he did so with a solid economic knowledge that explained the advantages of the railroad.

The business editor also paid particular attention to attracting investors of railroad stocks and bonds to the publication. Poor printed voluminous information – current crop production and population along the railroad's proposed route, for example – about a railroad when it was trying to sell securities, in an attempt to inform potential investors. Until 1850, Chandler noted, the media, including the *Journal*, had promoted railroad construction by wooing local governments. Talking to potential investors through the media was a new tack for any newspaper of the time.

Early on in his tenure, Poor heavily promoted new railroads in the West and South in his newspaper. To Chandler, some of the boosterism was too much:

> Poor was often unskeptical and oversanguine in making his evaluation of the prospective cost, traffic, profits and management of the new roads. Nevertheless, it should be emphasized that, in making these assertions and expressing their enthusiasm, he was voicing the opinions of many of the shrewdest businessmen and most competent railroad engineers of the day.[31]

Chandler noted that Poor would later become more selective about the railroads he supported. In the summer of 1852, for example, Poor criticized the securities offerings of the Erie and the Illinois Central railroads. He found both of them unsound.[32] The Erie offering, he noted, was not secured by a mortgage, and the railroad already had first- and second-mortgage bonds that took repayment priority. The Illinois Central, noted Poor, appeared to be managed by speculators, and the editor criticized its financial methods.[33]

Poor went a step further in his brand of business journalism. In the Feb. 7, 1852, issue of the *American Railroad Journal,* he argued that each railroad prepare a careful "exhibit" of its financial condition when trying to sell stocks or bonds to investors. This exhibit, he said, should include the company's capital stock, its debt, its estimated expenses, an estimate of construction costs, the number of miles run by its trains, and the amount received per passenger and per ton of freight per mile.[34] Poor's newspaper was the first to argue that companies disclose this information – more than 80 years before the Securities and Exchange Commission made financial statements a required public disclosure.

Later that year, Poor changed his pro-growth viewpoint about the railroad industry altogether. In the Dec. 11, 1852, issue of the *Journal,* he editorialized about the dangers of investing in highly priced railroad stocks and bonds. He grew increasingly fearful of speculators in the railroad market and told his readers that he would begin to speak out against railroad projects.[35] The next week, he criticized two railroads – the Terre Haute & Alton and the Covington & Lexington – for trying to sell securities without properly informing investors of their operations. The Kentucky railroad amended its report to include almost all the information that Poor wanted, while the Indiana railroad criticized Poor.[36]

The *Journal* increasingly turned its editorial focus away from railroad engineering and technical aspects and more toward providing information for the railroad investor. Poor initiated a list of all railroad stocks and bonds in the paper. In addition to the prices, the chart listed detailed information about each railroad, such as earnings, debt and dividends, and how many miles of track they operated. Between 1854 and 1857, Poor focused his editorial content on reforming the financial management of railroads, and then after the 1857 financial crisis, he turned his attention toward management reforms.[37] He criticized railroads for paying high dividends when they did not have the cash to continue offering investors such a payout. And he noted that railroads such as the Erie continued to borrow money even though it was highly leveraged.

Management of many railroads also needed to strengthen their understanding of how to make their roads as profitable as competitors, argued Poor. One of Poor's solutions was to have the railroad company directors publish what they had done to oversee management. He wrote:

> Were directors obliged every six months to publish what they had done, and what they proposed to do, they would have the benefit of a constant public criticism; and as men so situated are predisposed to make their statement as favorable as possible, they would be forced to act with a good degree of honesty and discretion.[38]

The suggestion was decades ahead of its time. States required the railroads to file reports on their operations, but Poor deemed those documents incomplete. His solution was to send a 600-question survey to every railroad in the country, but this proposal was dropped.[39] However, Poor continued to advocate public disclosure of operating results by the industry.

Poor stepped down as editor of the *Journal* in 1862, ending his journalism career, but his impact on business journalism was tremendous. As the chronicler of the biggest industry in the country, he was the first business reporter to demand accurate financial information from the companies on his beat. His newspaper was the first to cater to investors instead of people within the industry. And the *Journal* was the first business publication to openly criticize the industry it was covering and offer solutions to its problems.

In many ways, Poor set the standard for business journalism for decades to come. Unlike the daily newspapers, he spoke with authority about his subject because of his vast knowledge of railroads. Such expertise among journalists would not be commonly practiced among business journalists until well into the 20th century. And his detailed stock and bond listings would become a staple of newspapers.

What's surprising is that few other publications in the 19th century attempted to copy Poor's format of aggressively covering an industry. One notable exception was Albert Bolles, who was the first professor of business at the University of Pennsylvania in the 1870s. He was editor of *Bankers Magazine* in the 1880s. Like Poor, Bolles advocated for greater disclosure of bank financial information.[40] Poor showed the journalism world that individual companies could be criticized in print as long as the analysis backed up the criticism. To be sure, a number of other railroad newspapers began operation while Poor was editor of the *Journal,* but many of them took different editorial strategies and failed. Mainstream newspapers in the mid- and late 19th century could have borrowed Poor's strategy of analysis and reform when writing about industry, but only Bolles did. It would not be until *The Wall Street Journal* under Barney Kilgore in the mid-20th century that the country would see another newspaper provide such outstanding coverage and information about business.

Still, Poor's lasting impact on society was forcing companies to disclose more and better information to shareholders as a way of holding them accountable. While this concept seems standard in today's society, in the 19th century it was a unique thought. With his continued push for public scrutiny and disclosure, Poor forced companies to do something many didn't want to do. What he also did by forcing disclosure was to create greater investor confidence in Wall Street, leading to tremendous growth in the stock and bond markets for years to come. Other journalists would take on Poor's role in the early 21st century by advocating that the Securities and Exchange Commission enact Regulation Fair Disclosure, which required publicly traded companies to disclose information to the public.

Based on his influence and his impact, it is easy to call Henry Varnum Poor the first true business journalist in America. Today, however, few remember his accomplishments. But many know his last name. Standard & Poor's has been publishing financial information since 1860, when Poor began publishing the *History of Railroads and Canals of the United States*. The reference publication explained the finances and operations of hundreds of railroad and canal companies, and is considered the predecessor of all investor-related publishing in this country. In 1906, the Standard Statistics Bureau began providing company financial information. The two businesses merged in 1941 to create Standard & Poor's.

Labor papers

At about the same time that Poor began publishing his reference book on railroads, another business journalist was becoming well known across the ocean. Walter Bagehot took over as editor of *The Economist* in 1861 and remained in that position until his death in 1877. Although he was also a banker, Bagehot wrote two articles a week for the publication, focusing on a variety of issues related to business and finance.[41]

The Industrial Revolution led to an increase in laborers who increasingly wanted a voice. That voice turned out to be newspapers.

But Bagehot's writing also focused on a number of topics that had only a peripheral attachment to business. He celebrated the 100th anniversary of Adam Smith's publishing of *The Wealth of Nations* with a long examination of its meaning. He also wrote about politics and colonialism. And he wrote a long essay about the effects of the assassination of Abraham Lincoln in 1865, writing:

> The great authority attached by law to the President's office reverts to Mr. Johnson, but the far greater moral authority belonging to Mr. Lincoln disappears. There is no longer any person in the Union whom the Union dare or will trust to do exceptional acts, to remove popular generals, to override crotchety states, to grant concessions to men in arms, to act when needful, as in the Trent case, athwart the popular instinct.[42]

In addition to the newspapers focusing on economics or specific industries that started in the 19th century, another important type of business-related publication also emerged. While business and industry were growing, the plants and factories needed workers. The Industrial Revolution led to an increase in laborers who increasingly wanted a voice. That voice turned out to be newspapers.

The first labor paper was the *Journeyman Mechanic's Advocate*, which began publishing in 1827 in Philadelphia. Although the paper lasted only a year, it was a signal that workers wanted a voice in the expanding country. A year later, the *Mechanic's Free Press* newspaper also started. The *Free Press* had less propaganda and biased reporting than mainstream newspapers of the same period.[43]

Other early labor newspapers included *Working Man's Advocate* and *Free Enquirer*, both published in New York.[44] At the mainstream newspapers, only the *New York Evening Post* believed that labor issues were important enough to cover for their readers. An editorial in the Nov. 14, 1835, issue of the paper argued against the opposition of the formation of labor unions, noting that such organizations would improve society:

> Compelled to labor the extremest amount that nature can endure, and receiving for that excessive labor a compensation which makes year after year of excessive toil necessary to obtain independence, what leisure have they to devote to the acquisition of … knowledge?[45]

A year later, *Evening Post* editor William Cullen Bryant criticized a judge who had found a group of tailors guilty of conspiracy for forming a union and setting prices for their clothes. If the tailors were guilty, argued Bryant, then so were the ships that had set prices for transport to England and the newspapers that had set subscription prices. Horace Greeley of the *New York Tribune* was also an advocate for labor, arguing that women should be paid at the same rate as men and that labor should be organized for its own protection.[46]

Most other newspapers, including the *Journal of Commerce,* sided with the judge. Such an attitude toward the labor movement and unions was not uncommon in the mainstream media throughout the 19th century. Many of the mainstream papers were not fans of organized labor. After an 1891 strike at the Carnegie steel works in Homestead, Pa., *Frank Leslie's Illustrated Newspaper* chose to focus on rioting related to the strike and not on why the workers were striking:

> While the troubles in the coke region of Pennsylvania have subsided, so far as the work of production is concerned, the attempt of the operating companies to evict the striking miners from their houses has been followed by serious disorder, culminating, in one or two instances, in actual rioting, in which women, the wives of the Hungarian and Slav miners, have been prominent participants. The sheriff and his deputies were assailed with great violence in several cases, being pelted with missiles of every sort, and they appear to have been compelled to resort to the use of fire-arms in self-defense, with the result that one or two woman were killed and other persons were injured. In many instances the woman used axes and other equally dangerous implements in their assaults upon the officers. In some parts of the disaffected district it has been found necessary to re-enforce the civil authority by the presence of a company of militia.[47]

What the labor newspaper movement signified was the growing tension between the working class and industry that would contribute to the Progressive movement and would spill over in the early 20th century into a brand of journalism that aggressively attacked business. It is insightful to look at the labor papers and their content as a signal to industry that workers would like a voice and recognition. Unfortunately, too many companies and too many industries failed to notice such a movement until it was too late and workers had gone on strike.

Later in the 20th century, worker discontent would manifest itself in numerous stories followed by the mainstream press such as the call for a minimum wage, an improvement in working conditions, shorter workdays and schedules, flexible work schedules, and the demand for benefits. It was the 19th century labor papers that got the ball rolling and presented many of these issues for the first time to readers.

Advertising effect on business journalism

One of the other major changes in 19th-century media was the development of advertising. Many of the earliest newspapers contained little or no advertising and relied on selling subscriptions to stay in business. But as the economy grew and expanded, merchants and businesses wanted a way to publicize their goods and services to the general public. Naturally, they turned to the media.

Unlike many newspapers and other printed media of today, the 19th-century newspaper was open to the idea of placing advertising on its front page. This can be compared today to business news Web sites such as TheStreet.com, which has banner ads on its home page. In addition, some Gannett newspapers in the 20th and 21st centuries included ads on their front pages and section fronts, but those are a rarity.

The 19th-century ads ranged from what today would be considered classified ads to more formal display ads with various typefaces. The front page of the *Boston Daily Advertiser* from May 24, 1823, was about half full of small, classified ads of merchants selling their wares. A typical ad read: "18 cases Canton sewings, of superior quality, in cases containing 50 lbs, each, assorted – 17 lbs black, and 33 lbs of assorted colors in each case – for sale by Bryant & Sturgis, 47, Central wharf."[48] The entire back page of the four-page newspaper also included such ads.

Because these ads were small, it is unlikely that many of these advertisers had much influence on the newspapers and what was published about business and industry – not that newspapers from this era were writing critically about commerce. But the growing reliance on advertising by the media would change that relationship by the end of the century.

Larger display ads dominated the front pages of many newspapers. The front page of *The Evening News* in Detroit on Oct. 9, 1884, carried three large front-page ads for retailers that took up nearly a third of the page. All three ads conveyed the coming winter. The top ad was from department store Taylor, Woolfendon & Co. and told readers to "protect yourself from changes in the weather" by purchasing its "full lines of underwear at popular prices." Retailer William H. Elliott also offered hosiery and underwear at special prices in a separate ad, while fur maker G. Heine promoted its "fancy furs" and "seal, plush and silk cloaks" in another ad.[49]

And no product was banned from the front page. The *Wellsville Daily Reporter* in New York from Feb. 11, 1882, carried a large front-page advertisement from the Wellsville Bottling Works offering the "purest wines & liquors, whiskies, rums, brandies, gins, alcohols, which I am selling to the trade at very low rates and can offer my customers great bargains."[50]

Baldasty argues that the increase in advertising affected news content, particularly what was considered "business" journalism during the latter 19th century. Many advertisers demanded that their ads be placed in newspapers and look as if they were news stories. Some expected free publicity in the form of positive stories. Still others wanted to influence and determine what stories the newspapers would run and how certain issues would be portrayed. Department stores, for example, boycotted the New York *Evening Post* in the late 1890s because of its coverage of protective tariffs that taxed consumers returning from Europe with more than $100 in goods. The newspaper quoted women against the tariff who said that the limit was too low because clothes made abroad were better than the clothes made in New York.[51] The comment incensed the stores.

Such ad-pulling by business exists today, and certain industries seem to be particularly sensitive to negative coverage. Grocery stores and automotive dealerships, both big advertisers in newspapers, have a reputation of pulling ads after perceived negative coverage. Some business journalists receive pressure from the business side of their publications, which fear a loss of ad revenue, when it becomes known that they might be writing a critical article about a major advertiser, as discussed in Chapter 5.

But has much changed? For example, some newspapers covered the opening of Krispy Kreme doughnut stores in the late 1990s and early 21st century in their towns and cities as a cultural event that merited front-page coverage.

The bottom line for most media is that advertising provides a healthy chunk of their revenue, and without advertisers, the media outlet – and the business journalism it contains – might not exist. (There are some notable exceptions, with *Consumer Reports* being the most obvious business publication that does not accept any advertising.) What most media have attempted is to ensure the separation of the business side and the editorial side of the operation so that advertisers can't influence coverage. Most media strongly believe that the public would lose faith in their editorial content if it became known that advertisers had influenced what was written. However, as we'll later see, that hasn't always been the case with business news publications.

Business journalism as a field made great strides in newspapers in the 19th century, setting the stage for the specialty to explode in the next 100 years as industry continued to grow and society demanded more information about business and commerce. In addition, newspaper business journalism learned some painful lessons – such as the demands by advertisers and the reluctance of companies to disclose important financial information – that to a certain extent still exist today.

Footnotes

1 From The business press in America, by D. Forsyth, Philadelphia: Chilton Co., 1964, pp. 20–21.

2 From Industrial and business journalism, by R. N. Baird and A. T. Turnbull, Philadelphia: Chilton Co., 1961, pp. 233–234.

3 From The business press in America, pp. 40–41.

4 See the Boston Daily Advertiser, March 24, 1823.

5 From The business press in America, p. 38.

6 From Industrial and business journalism, p. 234.

7 From Business journalism, second revised edition, by J. Elfenbein, New York: Harper & Brothers, 1960, p. 301.

8 See the New York Herald, May 11, 1835.

9 From The business press in America, p. 300.

10 See the New York Herald, Feb. 28, 1838.

11 From Main currents in the history of American journalism, by W. G. Bleyer, New York: De Capo Press, 1973, pp. 188, 196.

12 See the New York Spectator, Nov. 9, 1835.

13 From Life of Gerard Hallock, editor of the New York Journal of Commerce, by W. H. Hallock, New York: Arno Press Inc., 1970, pp. 12–13.

14 See the New York American, April 25, 1837.

15 From Bennett's New York Herald and the rise of the popular press, by J. L. Crouthamel, Syracuse, N.Y.: Syracuse University Press, 1989, p. 91.

16 From The commercialization of news in the nineteenth century, by G. Baldasty, Madison, Wisc.: University of Wisconsin Press, 1992, p. 153.

17 From The commercialization of news in the nineteenth century, p. 154.

18 From The commercialization of news in the nineteenth century, p. 155.

19 From The commercialization of news in the nineteenth century, p. 156.

20 From The commercialization of news in the nineteenth century, pp. 118–119.

21 See the New York Tribune, Sept. 21, 1872.

22 See the New York Tribune, Sept. 21, 1872.

23 See the New York Tribune, Sept. 21, 1872.

24 See Wealth against commonwealth, by H. D. Lloyd, Englewood Cliffs, N.J.: Prentice-Hall, 1963, p. 17.

25 From Advocate for American enterprise: William Buck Dana and the Commercial and Financial Chronicle, 1865-1910, by D. Steeples, Westport, Conn.: Greenwood Press, 2002, p. 210.

26 See the Commercial and Financial Chronicle, June 1, 1895.

27 From Advocate for American enterprise: William Buck Dana and the Commercial and Financial Chronicle, 1865-1910, p. 210.

28 See the Portland Transcript, May 21, 1881, and Sept. 3, 1881.

29 See the Boston Commercial Bulletin, Oct. 3, 1885.

30 From "Henry Varnum Poor: Editor of the American Railroad Journal," a master's thesis, by A. D. Chandler Jr., at the University of North Carolina at Chapel Hill, 1951, p. 8.

31 From "Henry Varnum Poor: Editor of the American Railroad Journal," p. 131.

32 From "Henry Varnum Poor: Editor of the American Railroad Journal," p. 159.

33 From "Henry Varnum Poor: Editor of the American Railroad Journal," p. 159.

34 From "Henry Varnum Poor: Editor of the American Railroad Journal," p. 162.

35 See American Railroad Journal, Dec. 11, 1852.

36 See American Railroad Journal, Dec. 18, 1852.

37 See "Henry Varnum Poor: Business editor, analyst, and reformer," by A. D. Chandler Jr., Cambridge, Mass.: Harvard University Press, 1956, pp. 129–179.

38 From "Henry Varnum Poor: Business editor, analyst, and reformer," p. 170.

39 From "Henry Varnum Poor: Business editor, analyst, and reformer," p. 173.

40 From "Getting down to business: The development of the commercial curriculum at the Wharton School in 1910," an unpublished paper by S. A. Sass, University of Pennsylvania, pp. 72–73.

41 From Walter Bagehot, by H. R. Sullivan, London: Twayne Publishers, 1975, pp. 36–37.

42 From The best of Bagehot, by R. D. Edwards, ed., London: Hamish Hamilton Ltd., 1993, p. 19.

43 From The press and America: An interpretive history of the mass media, p. 131.

44 From The press and America: An interpretive history of the mass media, p. 131.

45 See the New York Evening Post, Nov. 14, 1835.

46 From The press and America: An interpretive history of the mass media, p. 148.

47 See Frank Leslie's Illustrated Newspaper, Vol. 72, p. 240.

48 See Boston Daily Advertiser, May 24, 1823.

49 See Detroit Evening News, Oct. 9, 1884.

50 See Wellsville (N.Y.) Daily Reporter, Feb. 11, 1882.

51 From The commercialization of news in the nineteenth century, pp. 76–78.

Chapter 3

The muckrakers and business

To today's media consumer, *Cosmopolitan* seems out of place for a discussion about business journalism. But before the magazine focused on women and fashion, it contained some of the best reporting about problems in society related to capitalism, particularly in the early 20th century. The March 1906 issue, for example, contained an expose by veteran writer David Graham Phillips about how senators in Congress were being bribed by business leaders. The September 1906 magazine included an article by Edwin Markham about child labor that led the publication to form a Child Labor Federation to push for reform.

After President Theodore Roosevelt read Phillips's article, he responded in a March 17, 1906, speech at the Gridiron Club that criticized journalists for their overly aggressive coverage. "There is filth on the floor, and it must be scraped up with the muckrake; and there are times and places where this service is the most needed of all services that can be performed," said the president. "But the man who never does anything else, who never speaks or writes save of his feats with the muckrake, speedily becomes, not a help to society, not an incitement to good, but one of the potent forces of evil."

Roosevelt's criticism did little to stem the aggressive coverage of economic problems in the country, but it did give these writers a nickname that they proceeded to wear like a badge of honor. From now on, they would be called "muckrakers."

At the end of the 19th century, a new group of journalists began emerging, taking hold of public opinion with its reporting in ways that had never been accomplished. In contrast to the reporting style at most newspapers, where reporters frequently wrote stories based on rumors and hearsay, this new breed of reporters used documents, interviews, and personal observation to tell their stories.[1] These writers were the forerunners of what is today considered the investigative reporter.

This brand of journalism grabbed the attention not only of casual readers but of politicians such as Roosevelt and regulators as well.[2] Many consider the muckrakers to be the leaders of the Progressive movement and societal change and not all that interested in business. "Their words led to a nationwide public revolt against social evils and a decade of reforms," said professor Carl Jensen, the founder of Project Censored.[3]

But a closer analysis of their writing shows that their reporting focused not just on social problems but also extensively on how the business world operated – a focus that has been virtually ignored by academia. "A half-century of scholarship has sown a near-wilderness of facts, notions, surmises, unknowns, instances and generalizations about muckrakers,"[4] said professor Harry Stein. Some of the focus on business had a huge impact. Ida Tarbell's reporting on the Standard Oil Co. was used by Roosevelt to push for increased government regulation of business. Upton Sinclair's writing about the meat packing plants led to new regulations for the food industry.

It may seem odd, initially, that these journalists focused so much on business and industry and with such fervor. The 19th century media spent much of their time writing about business from a nonbusiness perspective, viewing it in relation to other issues such as political corruption.[5] The amount and depth of coverage of business issues was on the rise, but the journalism had not yet taken a completely adversarial approach.

The so-called muckrakers of the late 19th century and early 20th century changed that, and their interest in business was driven by the changing economy. With the industrialization of the United States, more people were leaving farms and moving to cities to work in factories or plants. And with industrialization, corporations or business entities grew to a size where they became a dominant force – not only in their industry but in the towns and cities in which they operated. With their increasing influence, it became natural for journalists to pay more attention to them.

The media, which had taken on a watchdog role with the government in the 19th century, now applied the same techniques to the business world. Business and industry reacted with shock and surprise at most of the coverage it received in newspapers and magazines. Many took the position that they were providing a good for society with the jobs they offered to employees, and that their products and services were what the changing world wanted. However, underneath the good were problems, and the journalists were all too willing to expose these evils.

Society influenced and moved journalism to focus on business. The rise of the large corporations and the accumulation of great wealth led to movements to provide safeguards for the average citizen and to level the business playing field. As companies grew larger and larger, smaller competitors began complaining to the government that they were being forced out of business by unfair practices such as price cutting and even more nefarious means such as bribery and stealing. The government tried several times in the late 19th century to address these issues, but failed, primarily because the large corporations lobbied their elected officials.[6] Even legislation that was passed, such as the Sherman Anti-Trust Act in 1890, proved ineffective because it wasn't enforced.

Seeing that the government wasn't protecting the people, some reporters and editors stepped in. Virtually no major industry of the time was spared the wrath of muckraking journalists. Among those that received intense scrutiny were food companies, meat plants, oil and gas, insurance, banking, real estate, railroads, copper, and steel. Some of the reporting spread across a number of industries, such as the investigation into child labor.

The reporters and editors working on these stories did not consider themselves "business" journalists. And some, like Upton Sinclair, didn't see themselves as journalists. Their stories were written because they saw an injustice. It just so happened that the injustice was being carried out by industry. Their writing touched a nerve with society and showed people how their lives were being affected by big business. Many were unaware of the tactics used by most of these companies. And the coverage, for the first time, swayed public opinion so forcefully about business that the government was prodded into enacting laws that set forth some true regulation.

What made this brand of journalism so effective was that it showed the world for the first time how business affected virtually every part of people's lives, from the milk they drank for breakfast to the home in which they lived. Many rebelled against the notion that the head of some large conglomerate determined how much they paid for food to feed their family or for oil to heat their home and felt that the trusts were developed by industries to eliminate competition and drive up prices. The journalism coverage of these companies fed into that paranoia of big business.

Another interesting development of the muckraker movement was that the coverage of unethical, corrupt, and unseemly business operations came from a new form of media that had developed parallel to newspapers. The magazine format used more pictures as photographic technology improved. Some of the better magazines in the late 19th century used ornate drawings and photos to help tell their stories, and at least one of the muckrakers – Jacob Riis – would become as well known for his photos as for his writing.

These magazines were not for a pure business audience, however. (Such magazines would develop in the 1920s and 1930s.) Many of them were considered general interest magazines, such as *Harper's*, *America*, and *McClure's*. Although many newspapers also published investigative pieces critical of businesses during this time, it would be the magazines that would lead the media into battle against business at the turn of the century.

Ironically, many of these muckraking journalists did not write about business to expose corporations and industry. Some, such as Sinclair, wrote about business to push Socialist agendas, and the documentation of unsavory business practices to tell their stories was only a byproduct of their journalism. And while many of the

BUSINESS JOURNALISM TIMELINE

1870 – THOMAS EDISON INTRODUCES IMPROVED STOCK TICKER MACHINE.

1874-1880 – HENRY DEMAREST LLOYD IS FINANCIAL EDITOR OF THE CHICAGO TRIBUNE. HE LATER PUBLISHES A SERIES OF ARTICLES EXPOSING BUSINESS CORRUPTION AND BECOMES AN OUTSPOKEN CRITIC OF THE ROBBER BARONS.

1876 – ALEXANDER GRAHAM BELL INVENTS THE TELEPHONE, WHICH WILL EVENTUALLY IMPROVE THE SPEED AT WHICH NEWS IS DELIVERED.

CHARLES DOW

1882 – CHARLES DOW, EDWARD JONES AND CHARLES BERGSTRESSER BEGIN A WIRE SERVICE THAT DELIVERS NEWS TO INVESTMENT HOUSES ALONG WALL STREET.

investigative reporting practices used by these reporters are still used today, their ultimate goal may have been what eventually caused them to fade away and ended the muckraking movement before the beginning of World War I. If reporters from the early 20th century had written about business simply to expose wrongdoing and not to advance causes, the movement likely would have lasted longer.

Still, their effect should not be discounted. The muckrakers – through the government and public humiliation – forced companies to improve the safety of their products, to improve working conditions, and to improve worker pay. As a result, the journalists played an important role in society that should be remembered. In addition, they let corporations and businesses know that they were being watched by someone ready to expose their wrongdoing.

Ida Tarbell and Standard Oil

Ida Tarbell was born in Erie County, Pennsylvania, in 1857, near the burgeoning oil fields that would fuel the great industrial revolution. There is some dispute among scholars whether her proximity to the oil fields and her father's business in the area resulted in her fascination with John D. Rockefeller's consolidation of the industry in later years. Historian David Chalmers notes that Tarbell and editor S. S. McClure discussed writing about either the sugar or the steel trusts in *McClure's*, but decided on the oil industry after receiving a letter from fellow muckraker Ray Stannard Baker about the discovery of oil in California.[7] In her preface to *The History of the Standard Oil Company*, Tarbell wrote that the company was also selected because it was one of the few businesses that could have its history traced by trustworthy documentation through the years. Such a decision would prove valuable for the future of business journalism, for it gave other reporters a template of how to tell a story of a corrupt organization with facts and not innuendo.

Tarbell had not been brought to the magazine to write business stories. She caught McClure's attention because of her writing about Napoleon, and some of her early stories in the magazine focused on the French leader and Abraham Lincoln. The magazine had carried some business stories, such as the April 1898 article about the failure of a Wall Street firm with ties to former President Ulysses S. Grant.[8]

With assistant John Siddall, Tarbell dug into the Standard Oil Co., which was Rockefeller's company. Her writing, which began in the November 1902 issue of *McClure's* and lasted for 19 issues, was meticulous in detailing Rockefeller's early interest in oil and how the industry began. But unlike other journalists of the time, Tarbell dug into public documents across the country. Separately, these documents provided individual instances of Standard Oil's strong-arm tactics against rivals, railroad companies, and other companies that got in its way. Collected by Tarbell into a cogent history, they became a damning portrayal of big business.

Tarbell obtained testimony in court cases and before congressional committees, as well as copies of lawsuits. She talked to people inside the company and those who had competed against Standard Oil. And she was successful in gaining their trust – a step where others had failed. She noted in her writing that *The New York Sun* had sent a writer to Cleveland – where Rockefeller's company was headquartered – to write a story about Standard, but the writer was stymied in his efforts:

> You could not get an interview with him, the observer complained; even his home papers had ceased to go to the Standard offices to inquire about the truth of rumours which reached them from the outside. The hundreds of employees of the trust in the town were as silent as their master in all that concerned the business, and if one talked – well, he was not long an employee of Mr. Rockefeller. There was between the Standard Oil Company and the town and press of Cleveland none of the camaraderie, the mutual good-will and pride and confidence which usually characterize the relations between great businesses and their environment.[9]

Tarbell's writing was the first critical exposé of a large, dominant company in the United States, and it shocked readers because of the examples she provided that showed the steps a business would take to thwart competition and win business for itself. Standard Oil forced the railroads to provide it lower rates to ship its oil than what was being charged competitors. It entered markets of its competitors and sold oil at a lower price simply to force others out of business. And it used subterfuge to acquire controlling ownership in rival companies, purchasing stock silently. Her description of Rockefeller as "a business manipulator" who was "awakening a terrible popular dread"[10] was backed up by example after example where the apparent motive of Standard Oil was to make more money.

Tarbell's writing had a dramatic effect on industry and on journalism. Businesses became more wary of journalists, particularly during the early part of the 20th century. Many business leaders were on the receiving end of critical analysis of their companies and their industries for the first time. Other magazine articles copied Tarbell's reporting and writing and attacked trusts. Charles E. Russell wrote about the beef trust, while Thomas Lawson took on Amalgamated Copper, and Burton J. Hendrick attacked life insurance companies. Collectively, the reporting led to a more skeptical view of business and industry.

But Tarbell's reporting and writing of Standard Oil

BUSINESS JOURNALISM TIMELINE

1883 – DOW, JONES AND BERGSTRESSER BEGIN PUBLISHING A BUSINESS NEWSPAPER CALLED CUSTOMERS' AFTERNOON LETTER.

CHARLES BERGSTRESSER

1883 – JOHN SWINTON, MANAGING EDITOR OF THE NEW YORK SUN, STARTS JOHN SWINTON'S PAPER, WHICH ADVOCATES FOR THE RIGHTS OF WORKERS AND BECOMES ONE OF THE BIGGEST FOLLOWERS OF THE LABOR MOVEMENT.

1884 – DOW JONES PUBLISHES ITS FIRST STOCK AVERAGE. IT INCLUDES NINE RAILROAD COMPANIES AND TWO INDUSTRIAL STOCKS.

1887-89 – GENERAL ELECTRIC AND WESTINGHOUSE HIRE PUBLICITY AGENTS TO PROMOTE THEIR BUSINESSES.

stood above everything else for two reasons. It was the first portrayal of its kind, and it attacked the business operations of Rockefeller, one of the best known businessmen in the country at the time. That a prominent person in American society could lead a company that was using unsavory operating tactics was eye-opening for most people. In addition, Tarbell's detailed descriptions of Standard Oil's tactics and its development into a monopoly led the U.S. Supreme Court in 1911 to order the company be broken up into smaller companies. Although it took seven years, Tarbell's meticulous stories changed how one industry would operate for years to come and would have an effect on other industries.

Tarbell's reporting led the government to pay increased attention to monopolies and antitrust actions by companies. Indirectly, the stories led to more price competition for heating oil. And it can be argued that her reporting forced other journalists to look more critically at the large corporations beginning to dominate American industry. A review of *The Wall Street Journal* from July 1911, shortly after the Supreme Court's decision, shows that the breakup of Standard Oil was a front-page article nearly every day, while other major industries such as steel were also receiving more critical attention.[11]

The Standard Oil series set the standard for investigative business journalism. It was readable because Tarbell carefully crafted into the story the people involved in the company, primarily Rockefeller. Although the writing showed her contempt for Rockefeller, the detail and description lent credence to her animosity. And she wrote in a way that showed the conflict and effects between the large, dominant company in an industry and the smaller operators. That conflict was to become a primary story-telling method in business journalism for years to come. It would last well into the 1990s, when editors at *BusinessWeek* would ask writers to provide more of the "conflict" in their stories.

The Standard Oil series was Tarbell's first look at business and industry, and it would be her most critical. She later wrote biographies of U.S. Steel leader Elbert Gary and General Electric Co. chairman Owen Young, and her later magazine writing focused on the relationship between labor and management.[12] Her later work often sided with management and companies. For example, Baruch College journalism professor Andrea Gabor has written extensively on Tarbell's post-Standard Oil work, and she notes that Tarbell presented an uncritical view of capitalist Frederick Winslow Taylor in *American* magazine in a series that ran in 1914 and 1915 called "The Golden Rule in Business." Tarbell was also highly condescending toward immigrant labor.

But nothing could match the public's anger and distrust created by what she uncovered at Standard Oil. Today, Tarbell holds a lofty place in journalism for her reporting work of a single company. Investigative journalist Steve Weinberg calls *The History of the Standard Oil Company* "probably the greatest work of investigative journalism ever written."[13] It changed President Roosevelt's opinion of large corporations, and it changed society's opinion of big business and Rockefeller, whose philanthropy had created a positive opinion.[14]

And, ironically, Tarbell's exposé of Standard Oil would have a negative impact on business journalism's future. Rockefeller and his family would later hire publicist Ivy Lee to help restore some of the luster to his legacy. The founding of public relations and its resulting relationship with journalists arguably led to a less critical look at business and industry in future years.

Upton Sinclair and the meatpackers

Shortly after Tarbell's work on Standard Oil began appearing in *McClure's*, another publication began printing the work of another writer that detailed the problems of another industry. Upton Sinclair's exposé of the meatpacking industry in the Socialist newspaper *Appeal to Reason* had as much of an impact on society and business as did Tarbell's writing.

Sinclair was born in Baltimore in 1878 and moved to New York ten years later. His writing career had been undistinguished until *Appeal to Reason*'s owner gave him $500 and commissioned him to write about immigrant workers in Chicago's meatpacking plants.[15] Sinclair spent nearly two months observing the working and living conditions of the employees in the plants, and the newspaper serialized his account in 1905. Interestingly, the newspaper dropped the novel after only about two-thirds of it had been published.

Publisher Macmillan, which had earlier published Sinclair's *Manassas*, wanted to sell the book, however, and Sinclair sent them the manuscript of *The Jungle*. After initially agreeing to a contract, the publisher withdrew its offer. Some speculate that the publisher was pressured by the industry to avoid the book.[16] However, Sinclair found another publisher, Doubleday Page, which published a sanitized version in 1906 although it had been threatened with a libel lawsuit from meatpacker Armour & Co.[17]

The book, although a fictional tale about immigrant Jurgis Rudkos, was an immediate hit because of its realistic portrayal of life in Packingtown, as the area around Chicago where the meat plants operated was called. Workers suffered miserable conditions and worked in unbearable heat and cold. Others suffered injuries on the job that led to their death. Still others lost their jobs at the whim of their boss.

Sinclair, who was not a journalist, had set out to write a book that would advance the Socialist movement in America by criticizing how working people were being treated. Instead, as he aptly noted later in his career, his writing hit the American public in the stomach. The descriptions of the unsanitary conditions in the plants led to an uproar over healthy meat. Spoiled meat was routinely packed and sold to consumers. Rats that ran through the plants were processed along with cows. Inspectors

Business Journalism Timeline

1889 – The Wall Street Journal begins publishing.

1890 – Jacob Riis publishes "How the Other Half Lives," a book that exposes poor conditions in housing complexes in New York.

1892 – Editor of The Ladies' Home Journal announces that the publication will no longer accept advertising from patent medicine companies.

1902 – Financial World magazine starts. It will last until the 1990s.

1902 – Clarence Barron, owner of the Boston News Bureau and the Financial Journal in Philadelphia, buys The Wall Street Journal.

were bribed to turn the other way.

Roosevelt sent a scathing letter to F. N. Doubleday criticizing the book, noting that an Agriculture Department report had described meatpacking as safe. Doubleday responded that Sinclair's depictions in the book were an accurate portrayal, and Roosevelt launched an investigation.[18] In a March 10, 1906, letter written by Sinclair to Roosevelt, he told the president:

> Find a man concerning whose intelligence and integrity you are absolutely sure; send him up here, or let me meet him in Washington, and tell him all that I saw, and how I saw it, and give him the names and addresses of the people who will enable him to see it. Then let him to go Packingtown as I did, as a working-man; live with the men, get a job in the yards, and use his eyes and ears; and see if he does not come out at the end of a few weeks feeling, as did the special correspondent of the London "Lancet," whom I met in Chicago, that the conditions in the packing-houses constitute a "menace to the health of the civilized world."[19]

Later in the letter, Sinclair warned Roosevelt about the "connections" that the packers had in Washington and warned that the Department of Agriculture not be warned about an impending investigation. Instead, Roosevelt went through the Bureau of Commerce and Labor. By the end of the year, Congress had passed the Pure Food and Drugs Act and the Meat Inspection Act.

The immediate impact of Sinclair's writing, forcing new government regulations of an industry, was a first for journalism. Never before had a story caused politicians to act so swiftly to address what was perceived as a wrong in the business world. To be sure, the Progressive movement of the era aided Roosevelt. But Sinclair's writing pushed the changes.

Sinclair's book could have had a wider impact. The working conditions of the meatpackers remained abysmal for years. And bribery continued to have a place in the relationship between government and industry. But *The Jungle* raised the public's awareness of how companies were ignoring the rules and practices that society deemed acceptable. And although his writing leaned toward Socialist beliefs, the stories of long working hours, poor pay, little time off their feet, and male workers driven to alcoholism and female workers to prostitution, shocked readers who had never been inside a plant.

Sinclair had gone one step beyond Tarbell in writing from the worker's perspective. As such, his exposé of the meatpackers may have had more of an impact on society than Tarbell's writing about one of the richest men in the world for it forced people to think about working conditions and the effect on employees. And although it was not his intent, Sinclair exposed the greed of powerful businessmen for all to see. It was the businessmen who could have improved the conditions in the plants, but to do so would have lowered profits.

And Sinclair's reporting tactics of going to Packingtown and spending weeks in the plants would pave the way for a later breed of investigative business reporter, particularly at the television networks, who would go undercover and work in grocery stores and talk to salespeople with hidden cameras and microphones. What Sinclair did was simply take what he had seen in person and relay it to the rest of the world.

Sinclair's work stretches the boundaries of what is accepted business journalism, even in the early 20th century. His later books also criticized large industries, most notably *Brass Check*, a critique of the newspaper business that makes claims about the problems of corporate ownership of media that resonates today, 80 years later. Although none of Sinclair's books would garner as much attention as *The Jungle*, his contribution to business journalism was not having backed down to the large corporations that threatened his writing. By standing up for what he believed in, Sinclair set the stage for business reporters to aggressively go after critical stories that the business world didn't want told.

Lincoln Steffens and business bribery

At the same time that Tarbell was making her mark in *McClure's* with her serial about the Standard Oil Co. and Rockefeller, another of the magazine's writers was drawing attention to the behind-the-scenes bribery that many business leaders were using as part of their everyday operations.

Lincoln Steffens worked as a journalist in New York at the *Evening Post* and the *Commercial Advertiser* when McClure hired him to work for his magazine. He had been editor for four months when McClure told him to get out of the office and find out what was going on in the country.[20]

Steffens spent months in some of the country's largest cities, including St. Louis, Minneapolis, Chicago, Philadelphia, and New York. When he returned to the magazine's offices, he began writing a series of articles in *McClure's* that explained the corruption occurring in local governments. The first – on St. Louis – appeared in the October 1902 issue, one month before Tarbell's Standard Oil series began. The second, on Minneapolis, appeared in January 1903 in the same issue as one of Tarbell's Standard Oil articles and a piece by Ray Stannard Baker about miners in Pennsylvania. Combined, the three presented a powerful message about the state of America, and McClure realized the connection. The issue included an editorial stating, "We are all doing our worst and making the public pay."[21]

At first glance, the articles from Steffens, later put into a book called *The Shame of the Cities*, don't appear to have anything to do with business; uncovering wrongdoing in the corporate world was not Steffens's intent. But anyone who has read them realizes that they're a damning portrayal of how businesses operated at the turn of the 20th century. In addition, Steffens believed that businessmen of principle could right the situation.

The first article on St. Louis pointed out how business and government worked together. "Business men were not mere merchants and the politicians were not mere grafters," wrote Steffens. "The two kinds of citizens got together and wielded the power of banks, railroads, factories, the prestige of the city, and the spirit of its citizens to gain business and population."[22] In competition with Chicago, St. Louis's government leaders loaned its money at interest and placed the interest into private bank accounts, noted Steffens. He described how city vehicles were used by the families of city officials, and how public supplies were used by private businesses. Companies that refused to pay blackmail to city officials left the city. Only after a new circuit attorney was elected and began investigating the wrongdoing did things change in St. Louis.

Steffens found much of the same in Pittsburgh. The railroads that provided transportation for the steel mills had purchased their lines by out-bribing others. "This businessman, the typical American merchant, everywhere, cares no more for his city's interest than the politician does," he wrote.[23] The politicians, he added, were actually businessmen who exploited the city as if it were their private enterprise. One built a railroad for $30 million, more than the city's public debt.

Later, in his book, Steffens synthesized his thinking toward business by stating, "The typical business man is a bad citizen; he is busy. If he is a 'big business man' and very busy, he does not neglect, he is busy with politics, oh, very busy and very businesslike."[24] He said that businessmen were "self-righteous" frauds, "the chief source of corruption, and it would be a boon if he would neglect politics," and that "the commercial spirit is the spirit of profit, not patriotism."[25]

Although Steffens is espousing the anti-business sentiment that was prevalent in the early 1900s, at a time when the first large corporations had begun to dominate the marketplace, it's interesting to note that his comments about business and businessmen being the problem with government were filled with such hate. And although business had corrupted government with the Credit Mobilier scandal in the 1870s, Steffens was the first to document that business had such a widespread negative effect across the country in the operation of local governments. He demolished the belief that corruption existed only among the poor and struggling companies. His exposure of business corruption in politics led the trail for other business journalists, although little has changed. Adam Cohen, writing in *The New York Times,* noted in 2004 that "Steffens would not be surprised by the extent of the alliance between business and government today. But he would be disheartened if the American people did not start to follow his simple electoral prescription."[26]

Combined, Tarbell, Steffens, and the other muckraking journalists at *McClure's* put the business world at the forefront of American thought as to what was wrong with the country. They showed how business permeated every part of life and affected virtually everyone. And even though they did not consider themselves "business" journalists – few reporters during that time specialized – their reporting and writing set the standard for years to come.

Steffens intent in writing about political corruption was not to expose the unethical businesses. But Steffens shows that the relationship between business and government should not be ignored, and he set the tone for future business reporters to look at contracts, bids, and other relationships between business and government. Although his reporting resulted in few tangible changes, it did shed a light on a new avenue for reporters looking to protect society from corruption in the business world. Today, many media outlets pay close attention to their local government and how businesses in the community conduct their operations with the municipality.

The other muckrakers

A number of other journalists during the time also became involved in the muckraking movement, and many of their stories and books also showed how business was taking advantage of society.

One of the first was Jacob Riis, a Dane whose writing of poor housing conditions in New York in the 1890s for the New York *Tribune* led to changes in building guidelines. His 1890 book *How the Other Half Lives* drew widespread attention on the housing problems in the city. Although a police reporter, much of Riis's writing focused on unsanitary living conditions brought about by lax regulation of businesses. "He fought for city ordinances, prodded municipal officials and encouraged philanthropic assistance," noted Donald N. Bigelow. In that respect, he was covering a business issue in the same way as Steffens. Riis believed that improving the quality of housing by forcing the construction companies building the tenements to improve the standard of their work would have a positive effect on the East Side neighborhoods he frequented. The tenements "throw off a scum of forty thousand human wrecks to the island asylums and workhouses year by year," noted Riis.[27]

Other muckrakers began to pay more attention to working conditions. Edwin Markham pointed out that 50,000 children worked in the textile mills in the South, filling 12-hour days with lint dust covering their bodies. He included his findings of egregious child labor problems in a book called *Children in Bondage*. Markham was joined in the crusade to protect child workers by John Spargo, who published *The Bitter Cry of Children* in 1906, documenting the working conditions of boys in coalmines. "Accidents to the hands, such as cut, broken, or crushed fingers, are common among the boys," wrote Spargo. "Sometimes there is a worse accident: a terrified shriek is heard, and a boy is mangled and torn in the machinery, or disappears in the chute to be picked out later smothered and dead. Clouds of dust fill the breakers and are inhaled by the boys, laying the foundations for asthma and miners' consumption."[28] Ray Stannard Baker, writing in *McClure's*, also addressed the child labor issue, and then later took on the economic status of blacks, a business topic few if any dared to broach.

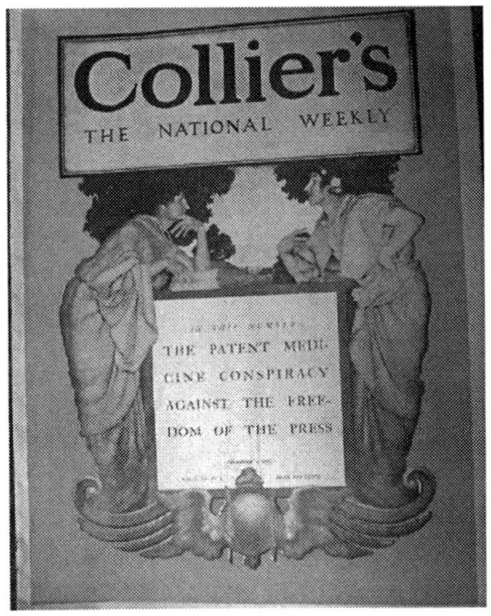

The writing of Baker, Markham, and Spargo forced the passage of child labor laws and improved working conditions. Anyone reading this work from a different generation is struck by the similarities of the working conditions a century ago in the American factories and the working conditions today in many mills and plants in Asia that employ children. Without the groundbreaking work of Baker, Markham, and Spargo, American society may not have addressed child labor as early as it did. Again, a journalist had found how greedy businesses were abusing the public.

Others tackled similar issues. John Fitch, writing in *American* magazine in 1911, attacked the 12-hour workday prominent in the steel industry at that time, noting how it was making strong men old before their time. Many other industries were using a 10-hour workday, but not steel mills, which argued that they had to operate around the clock. Fitch addressed U.S. Steel Corp. directly in his writing, noting that it could take the lead in improving working conditions for its mill employees. When his article was published, it drew the attention of Congress, which censured the company.[29] Within a decade, the steel mills had changed to an eight-hour workday.

Other muckrakers looked at dangerous products being sold to unsuspecting consumers and crusaded for regulations to protect society. In 1908, Spargo followed up his writing about the children in the coal mines with *The Common Sense of the Milk Question*, which argued for more healthy milk to improve the health of babies. His book was not the first attempt to draw attention to the issue of sanitary milk. As far back as 1858, the issue had appeared in *Frank Leslie's Illustrated Newspaper.*[30] *Ladies' Home Journal* and *Collier's* magazines, publications that had jumped on the muckraking bandwagon, were more effective in their attack on patent medicines, sold throughout the country and advertised heavily in newspapers. The editor of the *Journal* had announced back in 1892 that it would no longer accept ads from patent medicine companies.[31] But then editorials in the *Journal* in 1904 and later articles in *Collier's* pointed out that such medicines typically contained alcohol, cocaine, and morphine. In particular, the *Collier's* coverage was notable because it took to task the Massachusetts newspapers that had ignored the debate about patent medicines in the state legislature for fear of upsetting some of their largest advertisers.[32] Along with *The Jungle,* the coverage of patent medicines led to the passage of the Pure Food and Drug Law.

Another muckraker, Charles Edward Russell, exposed the corruption of some of the largest trusts in America while trying to provide reform for the worker. He wrote a scathing attack of the Beef Trust in *Everybody's* magazine in 1905, and then took on the Tobacco Trust two years later in the same publication. Both exposés were later made into books, *The Greatest Trust in the World* for the beef industry and *Lawless Wealth* for tobacco. In the latter, he commented, "We have given our praise to the money-getters. Then shall we profess astonishment that men do extreme things to get money – now that we are all discovering what that means for the rest of us?"[33]

Russell had come upon the common theme that pervaded most of the writing of the muckrakers: that the vast and growing business world was to blame for many of the problems in America. Corporations were causing their workers to get sick and die because of poor conditions, were causing some of their customers to become sick and die or become addicted to drugs, were selling products at outrageous prices, were using unscrupulous and often illegal operating tactics to drive competitors out of business, and were bribing government officials and corrupting regulations. Russell's work was rooted in the belief that public ownership of key industries was necessary to fix the problems of business, and that corporate executives had no redeeming qualities, argues journalism professor Robert Miraldi.[34]

The corner of Wall and Broad streets in lower Manhattan, wrote Russell, is where the real rulers of America worked. That corner was the headquarters of the Standard Oil Co. His conclusions may have been harsh and off the mark, but they did raise awareness of business control of many parts of society.

Although the glory days of muckraking era died out in the second decade of the 20th century, many of the muckraker's journalistic innovations – such as documenting allegations and reporting undercover – remain in use today. And while they were not what we today consider business journalists, they laid the groundwork for aggressive business coverage for years to come.

Yet today the muckrakers have a negative connotation with many people. Criticism of the muckrakers was prevalent in the 1950s, when it was argued that these writers were too often the spokespeople for the middle class.[35] Society apparently decided to ignore the good that came out of the reporting. With a small cadre of muckraking-type journalists today taking on similar industries, the results on society have not been as immediate or as widespread as those of the original muckrakers.[36]

Does this mean that society, and government acting as an agent for society, have become immune to muckraking business journalism? Hardly, as we see numerous articles and the flurry of legislation designed to protect the investor in the wake of the Enron, WorldCom, and Adelphia scandals of the 21st century. But in the early 20th century, muckraking's focus on business seemed to permeate the media, and the shock value overwhelmed readers.

What the work of the early muckrakers led to is the media's constant drive to uncover business greed, explain why it happened and what went wrong, and expose those who try to take advantage of society.

In the end, however, the muckraking movement of the early 20th century may have met its match because of its attention to business. Lewis Filler argues that pressure from business was one of the causes for the demise of muckraking.[37] Another analysis by Miraldi argues that the threat of libel lawsuits scared the muckrakers away from industry.[38]

Still, it can't be ignored that the muckrakers showed today's business journalists how to aggressively cover topics related to industry and the economy.

Footnotes

1 From Stories that changed America: Muckrakers of the 20th century, by C. Jensen, 2000, New York: Seven Stories Press, pp. 16–17.

2 From The social and political ideas of the muckrakers, by D. Chalmers, 1964, New York: Citadel Press, p. 110.

3 From Stories that changed America: Muckrakers of the 20th century, p. 16.

4 From "American muckrakers and muckraking: The 50-year scholarship," by H. H. Stein, Journalism Quarterly, Spring 1979, pp. 9–17.

5 From "The business century: How the economy became hot news in the last 100 years," by B. Saporito, March/April 1999, Columbia Journalism Review, pp. 47–52.

6 From Stories that changed America: Muckrakers of the 20th century, pp. 15–16.

7 From The history of the Standard Oil Co., briefer version, by I. Tarbell, edited by D. Chalmers, 2003, New York: Dover Publications, p. xiv.

8 From "A romance of Wall Street Street: The Grant and Ward failure," by H. Garland, April 1898, McClure's Magazine, pp. 498–505.

9 From The history of the Standard Oil Co., briefer version, p. 126.

10 From The history of the Standard Oil Co., briefer version, p. 127.

11 See the front page of The Wall Street Journal from July 1, 1911, July 6, 1911, July 7, 1911, and July 11, 1911.

12 From Muckraking! The journalism that changed America, edited by J. Serrin and W. Serrin, 2002, New York: The New Press, p. 154.

13 From "Ida Tarbell, Patron Saint," p. 29.

14 From The history of the Standard Oil Co., briefer version," pp. xv–xvi.

15 From The jungle: The uncensored original edition, p. i.

16 From The jungle: The uncensored original edition, p. ii.

17 From The jungle: The uncensored original edition, p. iii.

18 From The jungle: The uncensored original edition, p. iii.

19 From letter from U. Sinclair to President T. Roosevelt, March 10, 1906, National Archives, Records of the Office of the Secretary of Agriculture. http://www.archives.gov/exhibit_hall/american_originals/meat.html

20 From Muckraking! The journalism that changed America, p. 146.

21 From Muckraking! The journalism that changed America, p. 150.

22 From "Tweed days in St. Louis," by L. Steffens, October 1903, McClure's Magazine, pp. 577–588.

23 From "Pittsburg: A city ashamed," by L. Steffens, May 1903, McClure's Magazine, pp. 24–39.

24 From The shame of the cities, by L. Steffens, 1904, New York: McClure, Philips & Co., p 3.

25 From The shame of the cities, p. 4.

26 From "'The Shame' that Lincoln Steffens found has not left our country," by A. Cohen, April 11, 2004, The New York Times, p. 10.

27 From How the other half lives: Studies among the tenements of New York, by J. Riis, 1963, New York: Hill and Wang, p. 3.

28 From The bitter cry of children, by J. Spargo, 1968, New York: Times Books, p. 175.

29 From Muckraking! The journalism that changed America, p. 28.

30 From Muckraking! The journalism that changed America, p. 47.

31 From Muckraking! The journalism that changed America, p. 310.

32 From Muckraking! The journalism that changed America, pp. 310–314.

33 From Lawless wealth: The origins of some great American fortunes, by C. E. Russell, 1908, New York: BW Dodge & Co., pp. 278–279.

34 See The pen is mightier: The muckraking life of Charles Edward Russell, by R. Miraldi, 2003, New York: Palgrave McMillan.

35 From "American muckrakers and muckraking: The 50-year scholarship," pp. 9–10.

36 From "Financial reporting: Lessons of the Enron collapse," by J. Madick, Winter 2003, Harvard International Journal of Press/Politics, pp. 3–7.

37 From "American muckrakers and muckraking: The 50-year scholarship," p. 11.

38 From "Scaring off the muckrakers with the threat of libel," by R. Miraldi, Fall 1998, Journalism Quarterly, pp. 609–614.

References

R. Miraldi (2003). The pen is mightier: The muckraking life of Charles Edward Russell. New York: Palgrave McMillan.

J. Riis. (1963). How the other half lives: Studies among the tenements of New York. (Third edition.) With introduction by D. Bigelow. New York: Hill and Wang.

U. Sinclair (2003). The jungle: The uncensored original edition. With foreword by E. Lee. Tucson, Arizona: See Sharp Press.

I. Tarbell (2003). The history of the Standard Oil Co., briefer version, edited by D. Chalmers. New York: Dover Publication.

Chapter 4

A depression in business journalism

Howard Carswell graduated with a degree in engineering from Purdue University in 1925, but instead of going into that field, he entered journalism. He spent several years as a copyreader for the business and financial section for the *Chicago Tribune,* and was working at the paper during the 1929 stock market crash. Later, he worked at *The Wall Street Journal*'s Washington bureau for a short time before joining the financial section of the *New York World-Telegram* in 1934.

So, in 1938, when Carswell wrote a scathing critique of business journalism, he was speaking from experience. "The big city press does not supply its male readers with what they want in the way of business and financial news," he wrote in *Public Opinion Quarterly.* "Editorial direction is out of touch with the public." To be more specific, Carswell noted that most business coverage still focused on the stock market, which few readers wanted during the Great Depression. "Coverage should envisage the whole panorama of business, industry, and finance – of technology and research; promotion and advertising; retail, wholesale, and foreign trade; problems of management and competition."[1]

Carswell's viewpoints accurately reflect the decline in strong business reporting that had existed during the muckraking movement. Many leaders of the muckrakers moved onto other subjects. Ida Tarbell, a reluctant muckraker, continued to write about business subjects, but her journalism was much less adversarial. Upton Sinclair, more of a crusader, continued to advocate socialist-type reforms but never again attacked an industry other than his crusade against newspapers in the book *The Brass Check.* Even Sinclair later admitted that reforming the meatpacking industry was not the goal of *The Jungle.*

Business journalism continued to evolve with the changing country, and there were some bright moments. In 1920, John J. Leary, Jr. of the *New York World* won a Pulitzer Prize for his coverage of the coal strike a year earlier.[2] It was the first Pulitzer won by a reporter covering a business or economic issue. The first magazine aimed at mainstream readers and devoted solely to business issues started in 1917 with the introduction of *Forbes.* B. C. Forbes had been a columnist with the *New York American,* but thought that his understanding of business and the economy could be put to better use in a magazine format.[3] Two years later, *The Wall*

Street Journal started *Barron's*, a weekly financial newspaper named after its current editor. And in 1923, Washington journalist W. M. Kiplinger published his first issue of the *Kiplinger Washington Letter*.[4]

While these developments may seem small, each would have a lasting significance in business journalism. Leary's Pulitzer Prize was a milestone and likely caused other mainstream newspapers and magazines to pay more attention to labor issues, if not general business coverage. The creation of additional publications for business readers showed that there was more of a demand for coverage of industry and economic issues than many media outlets had considered. The readers of these publications ranged from executives and workers in businesses to investors and other professionals.

The early part of the 20th century also brought a new medium in radio, and radio news outlets covered business issues in many of the same ways as had other media.

But what is noticeable about business journalism in the first half of the 20th century is that the overall quality of the coverage declined. With a few exceptions, the business and economics news desk at a magazine or a newspaper became the backwater where old reporters were put out to pasture. Other reporters who couldn't successfully cover other beats were given business to write about. As author John Quirt stated in describing business journalism in the early 20th century, the business section at all but the top newspapers "attracted piddlers and diddlers more interested in gathering cash than news" and then added the following indictment:

> It also was a dumping ground for burned-out city-side reporters and others looking for a place to camp until retirement. Younger reporters sometimes started in "biz" before escaping to more prestigious beats, and those who got stuck there did not always bother to acquire deep knowledge of what they were writing about. Very little space was set aside for their stories in any event, and there was very little opportunity to display them on page one.[5]

Carswell argued that the problem with business news coverage was that it did not possess the broadest reader appeal to businesspeople during this time. "Coverage is still focused on the securities market, however unconcerned most of the readership may be," he wrote. "The New York Stock Exchange is treated as the fountainhead of all news of the business and financial world." He also called much of the coverage "routine and repetitious much of the time. It is technical to the lay reader and lacks popular interest."[6]

Exacerbating the problem was the rise of public relations, and many PR practitioners used business journalists to place favorable coverage in publications for their clients. The reporters and editors could have resisted, of course, but in many cases they were being offered money or other bribes. Other business journalists were working both sides of the fence, writing press releases that were then sent to the media.

Further hurting business journalism's reputation was its first big failure in covering a major business and economic story – the stock market crash of October 1929 and the ensuing Depression. Like a good portion of the coverage of the stock market in the 1990s before the technology bubble burst and stock prices fell, media coverage of Wall Street in the 1920s and even into the early 1930s mostly failed to recognize the significance of the fall of the market and the effects it would have around the country and the rest of the world.

Business journalism entered a dark period where the coverage, after making gains during the period of the muckrakers, regressed.

Labor reporting

However, one area where parts of the media did continue to show some aggressiveness during the first part of the 20th century was in labor issues. With the industrialization of the economy, more and more workers were joining unions. These unions were meeting resistance from corporations, and the two groups often clashed. Newspapers and magazines often covered basic labor issues such as strikes and better working conditions, but it was actually the specialized labor newspapers that performed the task more thoroughly.

An analysis of labor coverage shows a stark contrast between the mainstream media and labor-oriented newspapers. Even as far back as 1944, it was determined that union and labor movements were "treated unfavorably on the top news programs" of the four major radio networks.[7] In addition, many media outlets, which had full-time labor reporters during the 1940s and 1950s, dropped coverage so that today few regularly cover labor and union issues.[8]

Mainstream coverage was typical. In *The New York Times* on Oct. 16, 1902, the left-hand column of the front page carried a story about a coal strike in Pennsylvania ending. Its lead was basic: "The great anthracite coal strike is settled."[9] Although the story noted the importance of the event – that President Theodore Roosevelt appointed a panel to settle the dispute, a first for the government – it ignored the demands of the workers. Three years later, when the *Times* covered a Supreme Court decision declaring the state's 10-hour workday unconstitutional, the bulk of the story focused on the judges' opinions.[10]

There were some exceptions. Westbrook Pegler won a Pulitzer Prize in 1941 for the *New York World Telegram* for his coverage of scandals in organized labor that led to the conviction of a union official.[11] A year later, Louis Stark of *The New York Times* won a Pulitzer for a series of articles

BUSINESS JOURNALISM TIMELINE

LINCOLN STEFFENS

OCTOBER 1902 – MCCLURE'S BEGINS PUBLISHING LINCOLN STEFFENS' "SHAME OF THE CITIES" SERIES. IT UNCOVERS CORRUPTION BETWEEN BUSINESSES AND GOVERNMENT.

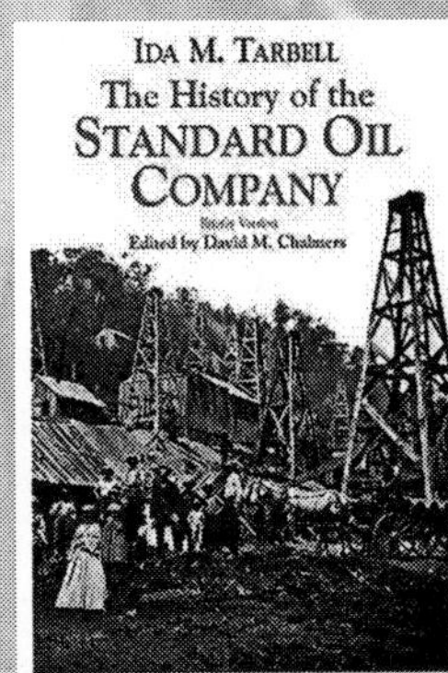

NOVEMBER 1902 – IDA TARBELL'S SERIES OF STORIES ON THE STANDARD OIL CO. BEGINS IN MCCLURE'S MAGAZINE. IT WILL RUN FOR 19 ISSUES.

covering labor.[12] For decades, the *Times* was one of the few major newspapers that devoted time and space to labor.

The labor newspapers, however, presented a much more balanced view of organized workers and flourished between 1880 and 1940, primarily because of the growing labor movement but also because of the mainstream media's lack of understanding of labor issues. One of the major labor journalists of the late 19th century was John Swinton, who had been managing editor of the *New York Sun* but left in 1883 to start his own paper, aptly named *John Swinton's Paper.*[13] In it, he advocated for the rights of workers and became one of the biggest followers of the labor movement into the 20th century. In 1887, Swinton wrote:

> There will soon be but two parties in the field, one composed of honest workingmen, lovers of justice and equality; the other...composed of kid-gloved, silk-stockinged, aristocratic capitalists and their contemptible toadies.[14]

Swinton's opinion – and expressing an opinion was common in articles in virtually every newspaper of the time – summed up the conflict that led to the need for labor coverage.

Many of the labor publications in the early 20th century were associated with Socialist or Communist movements in the United States. *Appeal to Reason,* the weekly newspaper that hired Upton Sinclair to write about the Chicago meatpacking plants, was a Socialist paper that circulated more than 700,000 copies in 1913. The *Daily Worker,* which was the Communist paper, had a circulation of 100,000 during the Depression.

Most of the labor papers simply wanted to help workers improve their condition in life. Many advocated for better working conditions or higher wages and shorter hours. Others in the early 20th century discussed issues such as integrating black and white workers or providing education to workers who didn't know how to read and write. *Progressive Women* took on issues that related to the work of women. The *Mechanic's Free Press* and the *Working Man's Advocate* attacked companies that used children as workers.[15]

What many of these papers accomplished was providing a voice for the workers in their goal of improving their lives, and they also exposed problems in the workplace. Many counteracted the mainstream press, which they considered hostile to their cause, according to Jon Bekken.[16] Some newspapers treated the labor newspapers with critiques. The *Commercial Advertiser* in New York called labor editors "poor and deluded," while the *Wayne County Advocate* in upstate New York called the labor press "rabble."[17] A series of stories on the history of organized labor in *The Wall Street Journal* in 1922 concluded by stating, "Whatever 'incalculable benefits' organized labor has conferred on its members, these benefits have been obtained at an incalculable cost to the rest of humanity."[18] Even then, the *Journal* had a pro-business attitude to its pages.

In 1935, the federal government passed the Wagner Act, which gave unions the right to collectively bargain with companies. In many respects, the new regulations were what the labor press had been lobbying for decades – an equal footing at the bargaining table.

Most of the labor reporting in the past half century has shifted and is now focusing more on what is commonly called "workplace issues." Many media believe that they're covering labor issues by running such stories. But research has shown that the media – large conglomerates in many cases – are simply using the concept of reporting and writing about the workplace to give off an appearance that they cover labor.

In addition, professor Christopher Martin argued that the media today have framed labor issues in a way in which the actual concerns of organized workers are ignored. Labor stories are written from a consumer's perspective, Martin stated, trivializing the concerns of the workers while emphasizing the effect of strikes on consumers who want to purchase the goods and services produced by the workers.[19]

As labor reporting stands today, it is a minor part of business journalism even though 12.9 percent of all working people in the United States belong to a union, according to statistics from the U.S. Department of Labor.[20] That number is down from a high in the 1950s, when approximately one-third of all workers belonged to some union. The decline in overall union membership has led to the closure of hundreds of labor publications, including the 2002 demise of the *Racine Labor,* a newspaper in Wisconsin that existed for 60 years and provided an alternative to the local newspaper.

And while the mainstream media have been criticized for ignoring good labor stories, there hasn't been any movement to add coverage. Labor writer Michael Hoyt argued that "a lot of good labor stories are simply ignored. A rich harvest goes to waste."[21] Daily newspapers, weekly news magazines, and nightly news broadcasts regularly cover strikes, but without strikes, coverage of labor issues is scant.[22] One notable exception has been the movement to unionize Wal-Mart stores. William Serrin, a former labor reporter at *The New York Times,* argued that most editors don't know or care about labor reporting. "It was just something you had to have in the paper, like obits."[23] Even when labor is covered, unions defending worker rights is called "troublemaking," while the media like to tell workers to learn to live with layoffs, and treaties such as NAFTA will help them.[24]

Perhaps no part of business journalism needs to be re-examined more than labor reporting. In the early 21st century, *BusinessWeek* and *The Wall Street Journal* are the only media outlets that cover labor extensively. Open any other printed media or watch the nightly news, and you'll rarely see a story about labor. With more than 15 million

BUSINESS JOURNALISM TIMELINE

1903 – AMERICAN TELEPHONE AND TELEGRAPH CO. HIRES ONE OF THE FIRST PUBLIC RELATIONS AGENCIES.

1905 – APPEAL TO REASON RUNS PART OF UPTON SINCLAIR'S SERIES ON WORKING CONDITIONS AT MEATPACKING PLANTS IN CHICAGO.

1905 – CHARLES EDWARD RUSSELL ATTACKS THE BEEF TRUST IN ARTICLES IN EVERBODY'S MAGAZINE.

NOVEMBER 1905 – COLLIER'S MAGAZINE RUNS A SCATHING ARTICLE SHOWING HOW PATENT MEDICINE COMPANIES HAD INFLUENCED WHAT WAS BEING WRITTEN ABOUT THE INDUSTRY IN MASSACHUSETTS NEWSPAPERS. THE ARTICLE CHANGES PUBLIC PERCEPTION ABOUT THE INDUSTRY.

1906 – DOUBLEDAY PAGE PUBLISHES TONED-DOWN VERSION OF SINCLAIR'S THE JUNGLE. BY THE END OF THE YEAR, CONGRESS PASSES THE PURE FOOD AND DRUGS ACT AND THE MEAT INSPECTION ACT.

potential readers belonging to unions, the media need to revisit their past – primarily the past of labor newspapers – and look at how labor was once covered and consider adding more stories. There are plenty of interesting and informative labor stories to cover that would give society a better picture of why unions are declining in membership and what many union leaders are doing to combat newly aggressive corporations and industries, but there are few media that want them, believes Serrin.[25]

The market crash

The coverage of the stock market leading up to and including the October 1929 stock market crash also left a lot to be desired. Many stories about the market leading up to the crash ignored the potential for losses in the market, and many advised investors to continue pumping money into stocks. In retrospect, much of the coverage was similar to the coverage that the stock market received in the 1990s during the most recent bull market. Comparing the two seems to show that business journalism didn't learn anything by reviewing history because the field didn't carefully examine the earlier coverage.

Some newspapers noted the great bull market of the 1920s and wondered when it would end. Writing in the special features section of the Nov. 15, 1925, *New York Times* financial editor Alexander D. Noyes commented:

> During the last quarter century, there have been only four of what Wall Street calls its "major bull movements" and what the general public calls a speculative mania. Frequently a movement of the kind in this period, with speculation rising to huge proportions, would be interrupted by violent downward reaction, after which the speculation would be renewed on an even more extensive scale.[26]

Noyes would constantly worry about the overheated stock market for the next four years, and his writing would run counter to most of the other coverage in New York newspapers. As in the 1990s, when some business journalists cautioned about the overpriced market, such warnings were ignored by the investing public and drowned out by the overwhelming volume of other stories promoting the market. After 1924, when the market began a five-year period of upward trajectory, the newspapers were noticeably bullish along with most of the rest of Wall Street. In 1928, when Congress examined the practice of brokerage firms lending money to clients to borrow stock, *The Wall Street Journal* criticized the meddling, noting that, "They talk of a 'pyramid' of speculations, forgetting that the pyramid is the most stable form of all building with the broadest possible base...Nothing can be so easily liquidated in this country as the speculative position in stocks."[27]

The *Journal* had yet to reach its position in American journalism as one of the most aggressive media outlets in covering and criticizing business, industry, and Wall Street. Even so, it was recognized in the 1920s as the leading publication when covering the markets, and its position on issues related to investing was closely watched. Unfortunately for its readers, its bullish position toward the rising stock market never changed before October 1929.

On July 1, 1929, the *Journal* reported that "conditions financially and commercially were never sounder than now."[28] A week later, the newspaper commented that traders had stopped trying to estimate a top to the market, and the paper predicted that the market would rise indefinitely. In August, the paper commented that the outlook for the rest of the year was "brighter than at any time in recent years."[29] Even when stocks began falling in early October, the *Journal* remained confident, noting that prices were still much higher than they were a year earlier.

Noyes, meanwhile, offered a different viewpoint about the market. He had joined the *Times* in 1920 after 30 years as the financial editor of the New York *Evening Post*, and his experience in following the market during previous bubbles such as 1901 was invaluable. Noyes was "one of only a few voices that chose not to sing in the all-bulls' choir."[30] Noyes questioned the viability of the loans that brokers gave customers to purchase stocks and stated his belief that either the market had changed so that "the old rules are wholly abrogated" or that "its reversal, when it comes, may be severe in proportion to the violence of the movement which is interrupted."[31]

Except for *The Commercial & Financial Chronicle*, the *Times* was the only media outlet that provided good judgment about the market in 1929, said J. K. Galbraith in *The Great Crash 1929*. The remaining publications, said the noted economist, "reported the upward sweep of the market in admiration and awe and without alarm."[32]

The *Journal* introduced a Pacific Coast edition on Oct. 21, 1929. A week later, the market crashed. And how it covered the precipitous drop contrasted sharply with the *Times*. Although the *Journal* would later be embarrassed by its coverage, it was not alone. Another newspaper, the *New York Daily Investment News*, ran a huge headline on Oct. 25, 1929, the Friday before the crash, when stocks rallied. It read, "Stock market crisis over."[33]

On Oct. 28 and Oct. 29, the Dow Jones Industrial Average – an index created by *The Wall Street Journal* – recorded two of its four largest drops ever. Yet on the morning of Oct. 30, the newspaper led with a headline "Stocks steady after decline" and a lead that read, "The stock market passed through its record day of business on Tuesday with the general level of prices reaching new lows. There were signs of support buying, however, as well as investor purchases having some effect on the widespread break."[34]

Compare this optimistic coverage with what appeared

BUSINESS JOURNALISM TIMELINE

1906 – JOHN SPARGO PUBLISHES "THE BITTER CRY OF CHILDREN" ABOUT WORKING CONDITIONS THAT BOYS FACE IN COALMINES.

1907 – THE U.S. CHAMBER OF COMMERCE STARTS NATION'S BUSINESS.

1911 – U.S. SUPREME COURT ORDERS BREAKUP OF STANDARD OIL CO.

1911 – JOHN FITCH, WRITING IN AMERICAN MAGAZINE, ATTACKS THE 12-HOUR WORKDAY PROMINENT IN THE STEEL INDUSTRY, NOTING HOW IT WAS MAKING STRONG MEN OLD BEFORE THEIR TIME.

1914 – PUBLICIST IVY LEE IS HIRED BY THE ROCKEFELLER FAMILY TO CHANGE PUBLIC OPINION ABOUT KILLINGS RELATED TO STRIKES AT ITS COLORADO MINING OPERATIONS.

1915 – NEW YORK FEDERAL RESERVE BANK BEGINS HOLDING WEEKLY NEWS CONFERENCES.

on the front page of the *Times* on the same day. Its lead read, "Stock prices virtually collapsed yesterday, swept downward with gigantic losses in the most disastrous trading day in the stock market's history. Billions of dollars in open market values were wiped out as prices crumbled under the pressure of liquidation of securities which had to be sold at any price." In the fourth paragraph, the story reiterated that the day was "the most disastrous in Wall Street's history."[35]

On Nov. 1, the *Times* – which had its own market index that competed with the Dow Jones Industrial Average – ran a three-column head noting that stocks had gone back up, but its coverage was still cautious. At the bottom of the front page, it also ran a story about the Ford Motor Co. cutting prices of its cars in a bid to boost the economy. The *Journal*, meanwhile, gave a sunnier picture. "The sun is shining again, and we will go on record as saying some good stocks are cheap because John D. Rockefeller said it first. Only the foolish will combat John D.'s judgment."[36]

It was the *Journal* that looked foolish, and as a result its subscriptions suffered during the Depression, falling from around 52,000 to 28,000; reporters and editors who didn't lose their jobs received pay cuts. Its readers would have been better off by perusing *Variety*, the show business newspaper. "Its headline read: Wall Street lays an egg."[37] And it took a while for other business journalists to understand the gravity of the market collapse on the rest of the country. The Jan. 15, 1930, issue of *Forbes* included a cover article on how the country could forestall entering a depression – even though the crash had already plunged the country into one.[38]

The *Times*, meanwhile, carried on in an I-told-you-so attitude. Its editorial on Oct. 26, written just before the crash, criticized the "orgy of speculation" that had driven the market and itself speculated, "We shall hear considerably less in the future of those newly invented conceptions of finance which revised the principles of political economy with a view solely to fitting the stock market's vagaries."[39] Noyes, meanwhile, had his own criticism, noting that the market decline "was the financial community's return to common sense."[40] His writing conveyed a cautionary tone about whether the country's economy could rebound.

The failure of one ofthe major publications in business journalism to accurately portray the stock market in the late 1920s and understand the importance of the October 1929 crash symbolized that Wall Street reporters were not as savvy as many believed. Like the market bubble in the 1990s, these reporters had been convinced by their sources – analysts, brokers, investment bankers, and others – that the dynamics of the market had changed and that stock price evaluations were entering a new stage where underlying fundamentals of the companies no longer mattered. It was a bitter pill for many business journalists to swallow, but it was obviously a lesson the field would have to learn once again.

Business journalism didn't learn its lesson for some important reasons. For one, few, if any, business journalists in the late 20th century bothered to review the coverage leading up to the 1929 market crash to look for parallel events that might have forecasted the 2000 market drop. And many top business journalists may have become so confident in their understanding of how the markets operate that they let arrogance blind them to what may have been obvious with clearer vision.

In the 1920s, the level of greed in society had again become a major part of business journalism coverage. Only this time, some business journalists also got caught up in that greed, giving the field a huge black eye and causing tremendous lost credibility for business journalism and the market.

Unlike the market bubble that burst in 2000, however, the run-up in stock prices in the 1920s was not generally blamed on overly positive Wall Street coverage. Still, business journalism failed society in not comprehending the overheated stock prices and the approaching depression. It was a failure that could be used as Exhibit A of the poor business journalism being practiced in the second quarter of the 20th century, a body of reporting that lacked analysis and understanding so desperately needed in the field.

The rise of consumer reporting

The stock market crash and ensuing economic malaise, however, did have one positive outcome for business journalism. During the country's Depression in the 1930s, there arose a brand of journalism that would help overhaul business journalism. This type of reporting focused on how consumers invested their money and offered advice on how people could get more for their money. Today, this type of reporting is often called "personal finance" reporting or "consumer" reporting, and the journalists who write these stories are almost always on the business desk.

Two events in journalism in the 1930s spurred this focus on money and how consumers used money. The first was the creation of *Consumer Reports,* which began publishing in 1936, and which helped define consumer reporting by analyzing products that people were purchasing. The second was the writing career of Sylvia Porter, who began writing a column on personal finance for the *New York Post* in 1936.

The origin of *Consumer Reports* began three years before the first issue when Arthur Kallet, an engineer and director of Consumers' Research, and Frederick Schlink, an engineer, published *100,000 Guinea pigs: Dangers in everyday foods, drugs, and cosmetics.* The book, according to its introduction, is "intended not only to report dangerous and largely unsuspected conditions affecting food, drugs, and cosmetics, but also, so far as possible, to give the consumer some measure of defense against such conditions."[41] In 1972, an updated version came out called *200,000 Guinea pigs.* In May 1936, *Consumers Union Reports* published its first issue. It included articles on milk, breakfast cereals, soap, and stockings, ranking each of them Grade A and Grade B. Another article argued that credit unions are better than banks, while yet another analyzed Alka-Seltzer and criticized its effectiveness, stating that its claims "vanish like the gas bubbles in the air."[42]

Consumer Reports was revolutionary. (The name of the magazine was changed in 1942 to make it accessible to all readers, not just union members.) And it was criticized by other publications. *Reader's Digest* attacked the publication in 1939, and *Good Housekeeping,* whose Seal of Approval had been called a fraud by the Consumers Union, accused *Consumer Reports* of prolonging the Depression.[43]

Never before had journalists joined with researchers to assess the quality and efficacy of products being purchased by consumers. The publication was immediately successful. By 1940, it started asking readers questions about products, and by 1946, circulation had reached 100,000. Subscriptions reached 400,000 just four years later, and in 1952, the magazine published its first frequency-of-repair table for automobiles.[44]

What *Consumer Reports* did that no other publication had ever attempted was to have products tested by scientists before they were included in an article. In addition, the results of similar products, through scientific tests, were compared to each other, allowing readers to determine which product was more suited for their needs. The magazine became known for its aggressive coverage of products and wasn't afraid to criticize companies.

For example, a 1942 article showed that the differences in tar and nicotine were insignificant when it came to the harmfulness of smoking, fully a decade before additional concerns about smoking cigarettes were published. (Cigarette maker Lorillard launched a national campaign taking advantage of the article, which showed that one of its brands was "lowest in nicotine and tars." The Federal Trade Commission ordered a cease-and-desist order for the ad campaign, noting that its ads were false and misleading because it only printed a small part of the *Consumer Reports* article.[45])

For a while, even the federal government attacked Consumers Union, placing it on the House Un-American Activities Committee's list of subversive organizations. But by 1970, the National Commission on Product Safety recommended the creation of the Consumer Product Safety Commission, primarily a result of *Consumer Reports* and its work in discovering unsafe products. By 1992, the magazine had more than 5 million subscriptions.

Part of the success of *Consumer Reports* was due to the fact that the economy was changing. After World War II, the pent-up demand for consumer products made the magazine a natural byproduct of the growing economy. And as it gained credibility with its accurate reports, more consumers came to look to it for advice before buying products. In addition, its credibility was enhanced by the fact that it took no advertising.

As a result, media began using consumer reporting as one of the mainstays of their business coverage. In particular, television found that consumer reporting that compares products by price and uses is favored by viewers, and many stations have full-time consumer reporters to help people fix their problems with faulty products or with unsatisfactory service from retailers and companies. *U.S. News & World Report* now has a section called "News you can use" that often has consumer-related stories, and even traditional publications such as *BusinessWeek* have included consumer reporting. *BusinessWeek* has a "personal finance" section in the back of the weekly magazine that often offers advice on the best products to buy in certain categories, such as stereos. And it has a columnist, Steve Wildstrom, writing reviews of computer gadgets. The *Wall Street Journal* also has similar consumer reporting on electronics for its readers.

But will consumer reporting last in the mainstream media? Journalism critic Kent MacDougall noted in 1981 that the number of full-time consumer reporters fell from a peak of 500 in 1974 to 200 by 1980, and those that remained "concentrated on snappy, inoffensive superficialities rather than significant exposes of consumer rip-offs."[46] Today, the number of full-time consumer reporters in the mainstream media is estimated at about 100, and many media feel pressured to avoid consumer issues because of advertising concerns. Some people argue that *true* consumer reporting like that in *Consumer Reports* is virtually dead at other magazines and newspapers.

SYLVIA PORTER ALSO WAS A "CONSUMER REPORTER" by some definitions in that her writing helped many consumers of financial instruments such as stocks, bonds, and insurance. But in today's terminology, Porter is considered more of a "personal finance" reporter, an important facet of business journalism.

Porter graduated from Hunter College in 1932 and worked as an assistant in a Wall Street investment bank. Later, she wrote columns about bonds for *American Banker* for $2 apiece while publishing *Reporting on Governments*, a newsletter about government bond issues. Turned down by the Associated Press when she applied to be a business reporter, Porter was hired by the *New York Post* in 1936 and began writing a column with the title "S.F. Porter says." The initials were intentional. The newspaper didn't want its readers to know that it was a woman in her 20s offering thousands and thousands of people financial advice.[47]

But Porter quickly gained a following. Her explanation of arcane financial subjects such as government bonds and term life insurance was done in a way that everyone could understand. In that respect, she was one of the first business journalists to write in layman's terms rather than Wall Street's terminology. In addition, she began her writing at a time when the Depression had caused virtually everyone to be more cautious with their hard-earned money.

The businessmen would discuss financial issues that they didn't think she'd understand, but then they would read about them the next day in the Post.

By the 1940s, Porter's column used her full name as well as her picture. Porter's column covered financial issues other than investment advice. Her Feb. 28, 1947, column in the *Post* focused on consumer opinion long before consumer confidence was measured on a monthly basis.[48] Porter's May 22, 1947, column tackled the decline in individual savings, which she blamed on higher prices.[49] On July 3, 1947, she wrote about how consumers were dipping into savings to make purchases.[50]

But her forte was investing. At the same time she was writing columns assessing the nation's economy, Porter was also dispensing investment advice. Her March 20, 1947, column discussed a new savings bond from the federal government.[51] Her May 7, 1947, column was about money that the government owed consumers who had not cashed in expired savings bonds.[52] Her May 20, 1947, column noted that stocks valued at less than $10 appeared to be outperforming higher priced issues.[53] And her July 15, 1947, column addressed the issue of what bonds to purchase for different investors.[54]

Porter also wrote about investing as it related to companies. She recalled going to financial meetings dressed in her "Kitty Foyle dresses with little white collars and little white cuffs and looking oh, so innocent."[55] The businessmen would discuss financial issues that they didn't think she'd understand, but then they would read about them the next day in the *Post.* Once she attended a convention of investment bankers and overheard a group of them discussing secret negotiations about an upcoming sale of Ford Motor Co. stock. The bankers had thought she was one of the wives and then wondered how the story made it into the *Post.*[56]

Porter's column was syndicated across the country and at one point was run in more than 400 newspapers, giving her business writing a much broader audience than New York. In 1960, her column had a readership of more than 23 million, and she became the only business journalist to appear on the cover of a mainstream news magazine when she was on the Nov. 28, 1960, cover of *Time.* It was a fitting tribute to the first mainstream business journalist widely known around the country. As *Time* put it, "More car buyers, more stock market investors and more plain everyday consumers listen to Sylvia Porter than to any other economic writer in the profession."[57]

Her advice was followed. In 1959, when she wrote about a 5 percent bond being issued by the government, investors flocked to brokerage firms to buy them. In April 1960, when she urged readers to write to their brokers or the New York Stock Exchange for pamphlets on investing, more than 16,000 followed up.[58]

The problem with business journalism, Porter believed, was that too many of the business pages in newspapers and magazines, and increasingly business coverage on television, were written or spoken in a language she called "bafflegab." Porter was the first to argue that business coverage would be more helpful to readers if they could understand it. When writing about the nation's currency hoard, she began by writing, "You wouldn't by any chance have $460 tucked away in your pocketbook or wallet or laying around the house this minute, would you? As a typical American, that's the astounding total you're now supposed to be holding in cash."[59] Her lead allowed the average consumer to understand what could have been a difficult subject.

Time noted that Porter's writing was superior: "Sylvia has no equal at reducing vital but complex subjects, such as the Federal Reserve System to manageable size. She is sometimes miles ahead of the competition in spotting trends: she was one of the first to see the business recession of 1958, made a splash by spotting the travail of Miami's resort-hotel business."[60]

There were other business writers in the 1940s and 1950s whose writing was closely followed on Wall Street. Joseph A. Livingston, who wrote for the Philadelphia *Evening Bulletin*, arguably was respected more than Porter by those in the investment community. In 1946, Livingston, then with the *Philadelphia Record*, had begun a survey summarizing economic forecasts from the government, economists, banks, and businesses. He continued the survey when he moved to the *Bulletin* in 1948 and the *Inquirer* in 1972. Because he was a journalist, Livingston knew economists who worked for Wall Street firms, companies, and forecasting firms, and he developed contacts in academia. The survey exists today as the Livingston Survey, the oldest review of economic forecasts, and is collected by the Federal Reserve Bank of Philadelphia.[61]

But Porter had broader appeal, and she was able to market her personal finance tips to a wider audience through books. She also spoke on economics and personal finance issues constantly across the country.

Amid all the problems with business journalism in the first half of the 20th century, *Consumer Reports* and Sylvia Porter expanded the field and added credibility at a time when it needed it most. They also showed that business journalism, at its best, was able to assess the economy and society and give consumers what they needed.

The dark ages

Unfortunately, *Consumer Reports* and Sylvia Porter were bright spots in what can be considered the dark ages of business journalism. From the 1920s to the 1960s, few newspapers, magazines, or other media outlets distinguished themselves with business coverage.

Part of the problem was the motives of many of the business journalists during the time. Because there were no professional business journalism organizations during the time, reporters and editors involved with producing business coverage had no set standards or ethical guidelines to follow except for their own beliefs of right and wrong. And other journalism organizations at the time that did have ethical codes or codes of conduct didn't bother to address many of the issues that were specific to business journalism.

Journalists were poorly paid and overworked in the early 20th century, and they generally welcomed what publicists had to offer, "especially the free passes to their attractions," noted journalism professors Fred Fedler and Denise DeLorme.[62] Editors also came to benefit from a visit by a publicist to the newsroom for he usually brought along handouts that could be used to fill space in the newspaper.[63] Some journalists acted as publicity men for the businesses in the area and would send releases to the newspapers where they worked.[64]

Further issues sullied the reputation of business journalism in the early 20th century. Clarence Barron, who owned *The Wall Street Journal*, ordered stories promoting companies in which he owned stock. Former *Fortune* editor Marshall Loeb described the business journalists of the time as "either hacks in eyeshades or dandy dilettantes who looked like escapees from The Great Gatsby – or crooks."[65]

Were these practices unethical? In today's business journalism world, they would likely result in the journalist being censured or fired. But in the early 20th century, journalism had no set ethical standards, and journalists didn't perceive any problems in what they did. When a publicist brought a release to a newspaper about the circus, an editor might publish it, thinking that the paper's readers wanted to know about the circus and the paper was providing the information.

In addition, business journalists were being manipulated for financial benefit. "If a railroad baron wished to manipulate his company stock, he leaked a story to a news agency where it would be circulated at once and trading in the stock affected within an hour or so, bullish or bearish," according to an early history of Dow Jones and *The Wall Street Journal*. "The baron would pocket the profit, losers be damned." [66] Journalists at the time knew of the practice, but did not condemn it.

Other problems existed. Companies began developing public relations departments to handle media inquiries about their business, beginning with General Electric Co. in 1897. Businesses began to aggressively court journalists any way they could. The publisher of the *San Francisco Bulletin* received a monthly check for $125 from the Southern Pacific railroad, and additional checks from a gas company and other companies, in return for positive coverage.[67] The implication was clear: don't write anything unfavorable about our operations, or the checks will stop.

But what these business journalists were doing was taking the first step down a slippery slope. Tickets to the fair turned into bigger offers of bribery. And once some of these activities became known to the readers, business journalism suffered a black eye.

Even *The Wall Street Journal* was not immune to such indiscretions. Author Edward Scharff notes that many of its reporters and editors played the market in the 1920s, buying stocks of many of the companies they wrote about:

> What drew most young men to the *Journal* was an open secret having nothing whatever to do with the fabled fun of the news business or the romance of the rolling presses. Newspapermen and radio newscasters were

> privy to inside information that could practically guarantee profits in the stock market. In addition, they were paid – sometimes handsomely – to work in conjunction with speculative rings and stock syndicates.[68]

Scharrf later asserted that it was common knowledge on Wall Street that reporters from all the big newspapers could be bought. Noted business historian Maury Klein's research backs him up. He notes that one publicity man spent $286,279 on articles favorable to his pool's stock before the October 1929 crash. Another published *The Stock and Bond Reporter*, a publication that touted favorite stocks in pools in return for information. The financial columnist for the New York *Daily News* wrote about stock tips given to him by a trader. In return, he received the profits from a trading account.[69]

An investigation later discovered that business journalists for at least eight papers promoted stocks in their writing in return for bribes. The most embarrassing incident occurred at *The Wall Street Journal*, where reporters who wrote "Broad Street Gossip" and "Abreast of the Market" wrote positive stories about specific companies and the stocks in return for money in the 1920s. The revelations about the *Journal* reporters came out during hearings by the Senate Banking and Currency Committee in 1932, more than three years later, when Congressman Fiorello LaGuardia produced canceled checks written to the *Journal* reporters from publicist A. Newton Plummer. The stories based on the bribes had gone as far back as 1923.[70] The *Journal* ran the story about the testimony before the committee on page 11 the next day.

The *Journal* had no specific rules against its business journalists playing the market. But it did have a written regulation that its staff should "bend over backwards to avoid any action, no matter how well intentioned, that could provide grounds for even suspicion," said author Jerry Rosenberg.[71] The regulation, however, was written in vague language and could have been interpreted in various ways. After the scandal broke, the paper instructed its staffers to avoid writing that would affect a stock's price and to avoid using inside information before it became available to the public.

But the damage had been done – both to the reputation of *Journal* and to the image of business journalism. It would take years for the field to recover, and the ethical transgressions of business reporters in the early 20th century likely precipitated the poor reputation of writing about industry and the economy among the entire journalism field that existed well into the 1970s.

Footnotes

1 From "Business news coverage," by H. J. Carswell, October 1938, Public Opinion Quarterly, pp. 613–621.

2 See BusinessJournalism.org, which has a section devoted to business journalists winning Pulitzers. The first one listed is actually more about political coverage than business, thus the designation of Leary's award as the first for a business journalist. http://www.businessjournalism.org/content/3378.cfm

3 From The press and the world of money: How the news media cover business and finance, panic and prosperity and the pursuit of the American dream, by J. Quirt, Byron, Calif.: Anton/California-Courier,

1993, pp. 85–86.

4 See http://www.newsbios.com/newslum/timeline.htm. Kiplinger's would later become a leading personal finance magazine.

5 From The press and the world of money, p. 86.

6 From "Business news coverage," pp. 613–621.

7 See "Labor in the radio news: An analysis of content," by L. Sussman, Fall 1945, Journalism Quarterly, pp. 207–215.

8 From "Downtime for labor," by M. Hoyt, March/April 1984, Columbia Journalism Review, pp. 36–40.

9 From The New York Times century of business, by F. Norris and C. Bockelman, New York: McGraw-Hill, 2000, pp. 15–16.

10 From The New York Times century of business, pp. 22–23.

11 See BusinessJournalism.org at http://www.businessjournalism.org/content/3378.cfm.

12 See BusinessJournalism.org at http://www.businessjournalism.org/content/3378.cfm.

13 See Striking for life: labor's side of the labor question: the right of the workingman to a fair living, by J. Swinton, New York: American Manufacturing and Publishing Co., 1894.

14 From Workingmen's democracy: The Knights of Labor and American politics, by L. Fink, Urbana, Ill.: University of Illinois Press, 1983, p. 27.

15 See "The labor and radical press 1820–the present: An overview and bibliography," by K. Kelling, part of the Labor Press Project at the University of Washington. http://faculty.washington.edu/gregoryj/labor-press/Kelling.htm.

16 From "A paper for those who toil: The Chicago labor press in transition," by J. Bekken, Spring 1997, Journalism History, pp. 24–32.

17 From "Origins of the American labor press," by R. Streitmatter, Autumn 1999, Journalism History, pp. 99–106.

18 See the "Incalculable benefits" in the Wall Street Journal, Sept. 20, 1922, to Dec. 7, 1922. The specific quote came from Sept. 20, 1922, p. 1.

19 From Framed! Labor and the corporate media, by C. Martin, Ithaca, N.Y.: Cornell University Press, 2004.

20 See "Union members summary," a press release issued by the U.S. Department of Labor, Jan. 21, 2004.

21 From "Downtime for labor," p. 36.

22 See "Work, workers and the workplace: Is local newspaper coverage enough?" by S. Douglas, N. Pecora, and T. Guback, Winter 1985, Journalism Quarterly, pp. 855–860.

23 From "Labor in the mainstream press: The vanishing labor beat," by W. Serrin, pp. 9–18, in The New Labor Press: Journalism for a changing union movement, edited by S. Pizzigati and F. J. Solowey, Ithaca, N.Y.: Cornell University Press, 1992.

24 From "Workplace coverage no substitute for real labor reporting," November/December 1994 and "Moribund militants: Corporate media on (re)organized labor," January/February 1996 by J. Jackson, at the Labor Media Watch, a joint project of FAIR and the Labor Resource Center at Queens College, available at http://www.fair.org/extra/9411/wsj-workplace.html and http://www/fair.org/extra/9601/aflcio.html.

25 From "Labor in the mainstream press: The vanishing labor beat," pp. 16–17.

26 From The New York Times century of business, pp. 78–79.

27 From Worldly power: The making of the Wall Street Journal, by E. E. Scharff, New York: Beaufort Books Publishers, 1986, pp. 28–29.

28 From Worldly power: The making of the Wall Street Journal, p. 29.

29 From Worldly power: The making of the Wall Street Journal, p. 29.

30 From Rainbow's end: The crash of 1929, by M. Klein, New York: Oxford University Press, 2001, p. 16.

31 From Rainbow's end: The crash of 1929, p. 18.

32 From The press and the world of money: How the news media cover business and finance, panic and prosperity and the pursuit of the American dream, p. 37.

33 From Rainbow's end: The crash of 1929, p. 218.

34 From The press and the world of money: How the news media cover business and finance, panic and prosperity and the pursuit of the American dream, p. 40.

35 From "Stocks collapse in 16,410,030-share day, but rally at close sheers brokers; bankers optimistic, to continue aid," available at http://www.nytimes.com/library/financial/103029crash-lede.html.

36 From The Wall Street Journal: The first 75 years, New York: Dow Jones & Co., 1964, p. 25.

37 From Worldly power: The making of the Wall Street Journal, p. 32.

38 See Forbes, Jan. 15, 1930.

39 From Rainbow's end: The crash of 1929, p. 216.

40 From Rainbow's end: The crash of 1929, p. 250.

41 From http://www.consumerreports.org/main/content/aboutus.jsp?FOLDER%3C%3Efolder_id=457439&bmUID=1105635357977.

42 From http://www.consumerreports.org/main/content/aboutus.jsp?FOLDER%3C%3Efolder_id=457439&bmUID=1105635357977.

43 From http://www.consumerreports.org/main/content/aboutus.jsp?FOLDER%3C%3Efolder_id=457439&bmUID=1105635357977.

44 From http://www.consumerreports.org/main/content/aboutus.jsp?FOLDER%3C%3Efolder_id=457439&bmUID=1105635357977.

45 From http://www.consumerreports.org/main/content/aboutus.jsp?FOLDER%3C%3Efolder_id=457439&bmUID=1105635357977.

46 From Ninety seconds to tell it all: Big business and the news media, by A. K. MacDougall, 1981, Homewood, Ill.: Dow Jones-Irwin, pp. 8–9.

47 From "SABEW mourns the loss of three business journalism pioneers," by M. Kandel, October 1991, The Business Journalist, p. 1.

48 From New York Post, Feb. 28, 1947. Available in the Western Historical Manuscript Collection,

University of Missouri, Columbia, Mo.

49 From New York Post, May 22, 1947. Available in the Western Historical Manuscript Collection, University of Missouri, Columbia, Mo.

50 From New York Post, July 3, 1947. Available in the Western Historical Manuscript Collection, University of Missouri, Columbia, Mo.

51 From New York Post, March 20, 1947. Available in the Western Historical Manuscript Collection, University of Missouri, Columbia, Mo.

52 From New York Post, May 7, 1947. Available in the Western Historical Manuscript Collection, University of Missouri, Columbia, Mo.

53 From New York Post, May 20, 1947. Available in the Western Historical Manuscript Collection, University of Missouri, Columbia, Mo.

54 From New York Post, July 15, 1947. Available in the Western Historical Manuscript Collection, University of Missouri, Columbia, Mo.

55 From "SABEW mourns the loss of three business journalism pioneers," p. 1.

56 From "SABEW mourns the loss of three business journalism pioneers," p. 1.

57 From "Sylvia & you," Time, Nov. 28, 1960, pp. 46–52.

58 From "Sylvia & you," pp. 46–52.

59 From "Sylvia & you," p. 47.

60 From "Sylvia & you," p. 47.

61 From "The Livingston survey: Still useful after all these years," by D. Croushore, March/April 1997, Business Review, Federal Reserve Bank of Philadelphia, pp. 1–3.

62 From "Journalists' hostility toward public relations: A historical analysis," by F. Fedler and D. DeLorme, a paper submitted to the Association for Education in Journalism and Mass Communication 2002 Convention, Public Relations division–research category.

63 From "Journalists' hostility toward public relations: A historical analysis."

64 From "Journalists' hostility toward public relations: A historical analysis."

65 From "Words to profit by: Business coverage is now expansive and honest. It wasn't always so," by M. Loeb, Dec. 7, 1998, Time, p. 213.

66 From What's News, Dow Jones: Story of the Wall Street Journal, by W. Neilsen and F. Neilsen, Radnor, Pa.: Chilton Book Co., 1973, p. 33.

67 From "Journalists' hostility toward public relations: A historical analysis."

68 From Worldly power: The making of the Wall Street Journal, p. 25.

69 From Rainbow's End: The Crash of 1929, p. 151.

70 From Worldly power: The making of the Wall Street Journal, pp. 37–38 and Rainbow's end: The Crash of 1929, p. 151.

71From Inside the Wall Street Journal: The power and the history of Dow Jones & Co. and America's most influential newspaper, by J. Rosenberg, New York: Macmillan Publishing Co., 1982, p. 58.

Chapter 5

The effects of public relations and advertising

On Jan. 14, 2005, Mike Buffington, the president of the National Newspaper Association and the owner of four community newspapers in Georgia, wrote a letter to Lee Scott, the chief executive officer of Wal-Mart Stores, Inc., the largest company in the world. In the letter, Buffington told Scott that he had been contacted by a Hill & Knowlton public relations representative letting him know that executives from the Bentonville, Ark.-based company were available for interviews to discuss criticism about its labor practices, unfair treatment of workers, and how its stores affect small-town retailers.[1]

Buffington said that he and many other newspaper publishers "are insulted by this Wal-Mart PR effort," noting that the company's core market is the small towns in which he and other National Newspaper Association members publish newspapers, yet the company refused to advertise in many of these papers. "When under fire from various critics, you turn to us to help you fight back," wrote Buffington. "Adding insult to injury, you expect us to give you free space to do that with PR solicitations such as the one I received...So why is it that community newspapers in America are good enough to help fend off critics with free PR, but we're not good enough for your paid advertising?"[2]

(Despite Buffington's letter, Wal-Mart did not expand its advertising campaign designed to improve its image to smaller newspapers. But in late November 2005, nearly a year later, the world's largest retailer did place full-page ads in 336 small newspapers in Missouri and Oklahoma as a test to determine whether they increased sales and traffic at its stores in those states.)

The day before Buffington's letter, Wal-Mart had placed large advertisements in 100 metropolitan newspapers across the country, but none in smaller cities or town newspapers. In a *USA Today* article in the Money section two days before Buffington's letter, Scott was quoted as saying that the "negative press and criticism" had hurt employee morale, but that he didn't think the public relations strategy by the company would "diminish the criticism."[3] His goal was strictly for the company – he wanted Wal-Mart workers to feel better about their jobs.

In dozens of newspapers across the country, such as *The New York Times, Chicago Tribune,*

Fort Worth Star Telegram, *Philadelphia Inquirer*, and *Arkansas Democrat Gazette*, stories about Wal-Mart's public relations and advertising blitz appeared in the business section.[4] Stories also appeared on networks such as ABC, CNN, and Fox News and on business-related Web sites such as CBSMarketWatch.com.[5]

Wal-Mart is not alone in cajoling the media – particularly the business media – to write stories in an attempt to improve its corporate image. Throughout history, the relationship between the business world and business journalism has been an ongoing tug of war in which both sides attempt to accomplish specific goals. The business journalist wants access to corporate executives and company information to report and write stories. Often, these journalists must work with the company's public relations or corporate communications staff to obtain interviews or information.

Their media outlets also want these businesses to place advertisements in their newspapers or on their airwaves or Web sites. Without such ads, many media would struggle to survive, and the lack of advertising from business in the past has forced media such as the *New York Herald-Tribune* to go out of business.

On the other side of the fence, businesses use the media to advertise their products and services. Without the media, they would struggle to find a way to let potential customers or shoppers know about what they have to offer and at what price. In addition, businesses, particularly large companies, hire workers whose job it is to provide information and potential stories to the media in the form of news releases and other means. Businesses like to see stories in the media about themselves, particularly positive stories about new products or new initiatives, because they create a positive image about the company.

The friction arises between the media and business when companies use advertising and public relations as pressure to receive favors or positive stories from the media outlets that regularly write about these companies. There are many examples of companies "reminding" media outlets of their large advertising budget, and companies have shut out some newspapers, magazines, or other media from talking to their employees or executives if they think the media outlet hasn't been favorable, or even fair, in previous coverage. A survey of writers for

BUSINESS JOURNALISM TIMELINE

1917 – BERTIE FORBES BEGINS PUBLISHING HIS BUSINESS MAGAZINE CALLED FORBES. THE UNITED STATES ENTERS WORLD WAR I.

1919 – THE WALL STREET JOURNAL STARTS BARRON'S, A WEEKLY BUSINESS NEWSPAPER NAMED AFTER ITS CURRENT EDITOR.

1920 – JOHN J. LEARY JR. OF THE NEW YORK WORLD WINS A PULITZER PRIZE FOR HIS COVERAGE OF THE COAL STRIKE A YEAR EARLIER.

1920 – ALEXANDER NOYES JOINS THE NEW YORK TIMES AS FINANCIAL EDITOR. THROUGHOUT THE DECADE, HE WILL BE THE MAIN BUSINESS JOURNALIST WARNING ABOUT A STOCK MARKET CORRECTION.

publications focused on the business of farming showed that about two-thirds of them say that advertisers have threatened their publications or withdrawn advertising in the past, or have attempted to bribe journalists with gifts and free meals.[6]

Advertising and public relations have probably had the biggest impact – positively and negatively – among the many outside forces acting on the development of business journalism in the past 200 years. The growth of advertising has led to the success of new publications such as *BusinessWeek*, *Forbes*, and *Fortune* that cover business. And public relations practitioners can be credited with helping thousands of business reporters tell better and more thorough stories about every possible topic related to business journalism.

However, because many media outlets in the 19th century did not see a conflict of interest in providing favorable mention of many major advertisers in their news and editorial content, the field of business journalism has had to overcome the belief that its coverage can be influenced or outright purchased. And today, some trade publications, particularly business-to-business publications, won't cover companies that don't advertise. The "hostage holding" can work both ways.

The issue swings in the opposite direction as well. There have been accusations of business media killing or softening the tone of stories to appease advertisers – even without the direct request to do so from the business. These orders may have come from the publisher or owner of the publication who fears the loss of a multi-million dollar advertising contract. In its Feb. 5, 1996, issue, *Fortune* magazine claimed that rival *Forbes* did not allow its writers to criticize its biggest advertisers and had watered down other stories.[7] *Forbes* denied the allegations at the time, but a biography of Malcolm Forbes noted several instances of how the former magazine owner killed certain stories that were critical of companies.[8] In 1939, press critic George Seldes noted example after example of newspapers suppressing news when it involved one of their major advertisers. "The press runs a three-column photograph of a new shoe counter at Lord and Taylor's, which it passes off on New Yorkers as straight news, but it ignores the Federal Trade Commission's order to Lord and Taylor 'to cease and desist from representing as silk any fabric not wholly comprised of silk.'"[9]

In the same week that Wal-Mart began its public relations campaign and angered the small-town newspaper publishers, the chairman of TCF Bank in Minnesota, Bill Cooper, wrote a letter vowing that his bank would no longer advertise in the *Minneapolis Star-Tribune* because of a column that suggested that the bank might be bankrolling a conservative Web blog and that customers of the bank who disagreed with the blog's political stance should withdraw their money from the bank.[10] Other businesses have withdrawn advertising from media when they felt they were attacked unnecessarily by the media – either by business journalists or others.

This chapter explores the relationship between advertising and public relations and the field of business journalism, and attempts to explain how these forms of mass communication have influenced each other. Throughout the years, business journalism and the media evolved in certain ways in part because of their perceptions – true and false – about advertising and PR. In addition, an understanding of the history of the relationship between the media and public relations and advertising helps expose some of the inherent issues and conflicts that many business journalists face when trying to perform their job.

"The antagonism many journalists feel toward public relations is firmly embedded in

shows growth & the impact

journalistic culture, and that antagonism influences the mass communication process," University of Houston professor Michael Ryan and Florida International University professor David Martinson concluded from a quantitative study, as well as from anecdotal evidence.[11] In the same study, the public relations practitioners felt that journalists were antagonistic because of past experiences with ineffective or unethical PR people. The hostility between PR and editors and writers hurts the public because it limits the amount of information disseminated, noted professors Lillian Kopenhaver, David Martinson, and Michael Ryan.[12]

A separate study by Ryan found that public relations officials restrained by their bosses or corporate culture when dealing with the media were limited in their effectiveness.[13] Management views PR as simply the mouthpiece to advocate their policies. Professors Lynne Sallott, Thomas Steinfatt, and Michael Salwen found that journalists and public relations officials agree that PR influences the news.[14] What they disagree on is the magnitude of that influence and how it is accomplished.

From a financial standpoint, good relations with businesses that advertise are vital to the success of a media operation. University of Toronto professor Harold Innis noted that in the 19th century, "competition for circulation and advertising compelled a policy of vigorous advertising of the paper which was reflected in the displacement of advertising by news on the front page and finally in the elaboration of the head lines."[15] Developments such as the telegraph increased the efficiency of newspapers as an "advertising medium" during that time. A comparison of newspapers in St. Louis in 1875 and 1925 showed that the space in the paper devoted to advertising increased from 28.9 to 60.5 percent.[16] Since then, most newspapers have followed a rule of offering 40 percent news and 60 percent advertising, according to studies, with some variance.

Whereas most media relied on subscribers in the early 19th century for the bulk of their revenue, by the end of the century they relied more heavily on advertising to pay the bills. And as media began to write more about business, the economy, and investing, a conflict arose between advertisers and business journalists. In many cases, the company relied on its public relations practitioners to correct the problem, which led to even more conflict.

BUSINESS JOURNALISM TIMELINE

1923 – W.M. KIPLINGER PUBLISHES THE FIRST ISSUE OF KIPLINGER'S WASHINGTON LETTER.

1920S – REPORTERS FOR THE WALL STREET JOURNAL ACCEPT BRIBES FROM INVESTORS TO WRITE FAVORABLY ABOUT CERTAIN STOCKS. THE BRIBES ARE DISCLOSED AT A 1932 CONGRESSIONAL HEARING ON THE STOCK MARKET CRASH.

1928 – CLARENCE BARRON DIES. A YEAR LATER, THE WALL STREET JOURNAL STARTS A WEST COAST EDITION.

SEPTEMBER 1929 – THE BUSINESS WEEK BEGINS PUBLISHING SHORTLY BEFORE THE STOCK MARKET CRASH. "THE" WOULD LATER BE DROPPED FROM THE NAME, AND THE TITLE WOULD EVENTUALLY BECOME ONE WORD.

Public relations in business

The creation of public relations, or publicity, can be traced to the desire by businesses to receive media coverage of their operations or events. Professors Fred Fedler and Denise Delorme note that P. T. Barnum used publicity to increase attendance at his circus events, and businesses copied his techniques.[17] Barnum's early strategies at garnering free publicity in the media drew the scorn of *New York Herald* editor James Gordon Bennett, setting the stage for future tension between PR and the media.[18] Barnum, a former newspaper editor, sent to newspapers stories that he knew would draw interest. He planted lies and then denied them and filed frivolous lawsuits just to attract coverage. He also concocted stunts, such as giving rides on the back of an elephant to the children of local editors. By the 1880s, publicists were being used by hotels, railroads, and steamboat lines.

The field of public relations began to grow dramatically in the latter part of the 19th century as companies grew larger, said professors Scott Cutlip, Allen Center, and Glen Broom.[19] Many of them did not want to be written about in the newspapers and magazines of the era, and the hiring of public relations practitioners was done to thwart articles. Eric Goldman noted that, "Big business was committed to the doctrine that the less the public knew of its operations, the more efficient and profitable – even the more socially useful – the operations would be."[20]

The first company to hire a full-time public relations person was Westinghouse, which needed to combat Edison General Electric Co.'s campaign of promoting direct current electricity versus its alternating current. In 1889, Westinghouse hired a Pittsburgh journalist to handle publicity for the company – a common practice because journalists were so underpaid – but did not create an actual in-house public relations department.[21] Eight years later, General Electric created its public relations department, becoming the first company to have PR practitioners work inside the company.

When the muckraking journalists of the early 20th century began attacking businesses and their tactics, many companies withdrew advertising rather than attempting to answer the concerns raised in the articles. At least one corporate president, John Dryden of the Prudential Insurance Co., was able to exert pressure on *Cosmopolitan* magazine through the company's advertising department to kill a critical article. The magazine pulled the story, which mentioned that Prudential's revenues had helped finance the Public Service Corporation, of which Dryden was an owner. Dryden, who was running for re-election to the U.S. Senate at the time, bought $5,000 in additional advertising in the October 1906 issue. The magazine's business manager then pulled the article, and the additional ads praised Dryden and were made to look like editorial copy.[22]

The journalists noticed what was happening. The magazine *World's Work*, in its June 1906 issue, concluded that information about companies would become more accessible in the future because many of the PR people being hired by businesses were former journalists.[23] Later, *American* magazine surmised that publicity would lead to the disclosure of facts that companies had previously withheld, although the article's writer, Sherman Morse, did caution that PR could be used "merely in obtaining for the corporations greater publicity for such facts as are directly favorable to them."[24]

By this time, the first public relations agency had already been founded. The Publicity

Bureau was established in 1900 in Boston by three former journalists, and its clients included Harvard University and the American Telephone and Telegraph Company. In 1906, it was hired by the railroad industry to lobby against legislation.[25] Two years later, another public relations firm opened in Washington and sought business from companies being affected by bills in Congress. One of the founders of this firm, William Wolff Smith, also worked for several newspapers while working in public relations.[26]

By this time, the media began to be wary about the increasing use of public relations by companies and industries. In 1908, the American Newspaper Publishers Association started a campaign against "free publicity," fearing it would decrease advertising. But the business journalists of the time generally saw PR people as being helpful to their work. The railroad editor of the Cincinnati *Enquirer* noted that publicity agents could improve the coverage of their clients if they knew what reporter or editor cared most about the topic.[27]

Two early public relations practitioners, Ivy Lee and Edward Bernays, helped shape PR's relationship with the business media. Both would have a profound influence on how business journalism viewed their clients, and both men would shape the media's perception of public relations. Both began their careers as journalists. Bernays edited two medical magazines, the *Medical Review of Reviews* and *Dietetic and Hygienic Gazette*,[28] while Lee worked for New York newspapers.

Bernays's first job in public relations occurred in 1915, when he took on the task of publicizing a Russian ballet's tour of American cities. Because of his success, the ballet's shows sold out before the tour began. Bernays later led successful public relations campaigns for the American Tobacco Company, including persuading women's rights groups to hold up Lucky Strike cigarettes as their symbol of freedom. His work for Procter & Gamble led to free publicity for its Ivory soap due to a contest he began for the best soap sculptures. He also created a widely covered event on the 50th anniversary of the light bulb in 1929 that was secretly sponsored by the General Electric Co.[29]

Bernays clearly understood the principle followed by celebrity publicists today of creating "buzz" about a company or product. His strategies of creating events and convincing groups not affiliated with his clients to support their products or services were firsts in public relations, and unknowing journalists were influenced to write about the products and companies. Bernays was credited with creating the term *public relations counsel,* and he wrote widely on the theory of changing people's opinions without them being aware.[30] To his credit, in the 1960s, Bernays reversed course on his promotion of cigarettes, leading an antismoking campaign after the health effects became widely known.

Lee had actually spent his journalism career covering business for the *New York World,* but left the paper in 1903 to work on the campaign for a New York mayoral candidate. In 1904, he worked for the Democratic National Committee. Two years later, he created a publicity firm and set forth a declaration of principles, which read in part:

> In brief, our plan is, frankly and openly, on behalf of business concerns and public institutions, to supply to the press and public of the United States prompt and accurate information concerning subjects which it is of value and interest to the public to know about.[31]

Implicit in this statement, however, is that Lee's firm would be the publicity agent and the businesses would decide the subjects of value and interest for the public to know. Lee's declaration also included a statement that accuracy was "our matter," yet some of his later work included deliberate lies and misstatements of fact that buttressed his clients' agendas.[32]

The anthracite coal mine owners hired Lee during a strike in Pennsylvania in 1906. Stung by criticism the operators received in newspapers during a strike four years earlier when they had kept silent while the unions cultivated a relationship with reporters, the owners hired Lee to present their side of the negotiations. Lee began providing a handout on the owners' positions as well as their perceptions of how the talks were proceeding. These handouts were the forerunners of the press releases that now inundate most media outlets by mail, fax machine, and e-mail. Lee's work was so successful in giving the mine owners better coverage in the press that his firm was hired to perform PR work for the Pennsylvania Railroad.

MOTHER JONES

In 1914, the Rockefeller family hired Lee to help present its views on the killing of striking miners, their wives, and children in Colorado at their Colorado Fuel and Iron Co. Known as the Ludlow Massacre – a term that the union organizers supported – the incident caused widespread criticism of the Rockefellers, who had resisted the public backlash after Tarbell's exposé of Standard Oil without commenting publicly but wanted to counteract media coverage about the Ludlow killings. John D. Rockefeller had actually hired a publicist, Joseph I. C. Clarke, to work for him after Tarbell's articles appeared, but Clarke resigned in 1913, frustrated by a lack of support for his work.

Lee worked to change the opinion of Colorado newspaper reporters and editors by regularly sending them bulletins titled "The struggle in Colorado for industrial freedom."[33] The first bulletin, dated June 22, 1914, included a letter signed by coal mine managers to President Woodrow Wilson and noted the "mass of misinformation and misrepresentation contained in recent issues of the public press."[34] The July 30, 1914, bulletin addressed the wages of the striking miners and noted that the salaries of miners had been examined by certified public accountants and newspaper editors.[35] The Aug. 3, 1914, bulletin noted that union "leaders have condoned, if not instigated, unnumbered acts designed to plunder property and to maim and kill loyal employe[e]s." [36]

Lee also used newspaper accounts to benefit his client, the Rockefellers' Colorado Fuel and Iron. In the Aug. 7, 1914, bulletin, he noted that editors of 25 newspapers in Colorado sided with the mines and their owners in the strike. The bulletin included a statement signed by representatives of the *Rocky Mountain News, Trinidad Advertiser, Boulder Camera,* and *Pueblo Chieftain.*[37] What was excluded from the bulletin was that these newspapers were owned or controlled by the coal companies.[38] And in perhaps his most infamous bulletin on the Ludlow Massacre, Lee's Aug. 17, 1914, missive noted the activity of an 82-year-old woman named Mother Jones, a well-known labor organizer involved in the strike who had been profiled in the July 1914 issue of *Metropolitan Magazine.* Lee's bulletin spent four pages criticizing Jones and her actions.[39]

Colorado State University professor Kirk Hallahan's research into Lee's bulletins and media relations work on behalf of the Colorado Fuel and Iron Co. finds no support for the premise that Lee was intentionally deceptive in his work, but Lee's testimony in 1915 before a congressional committee investigating the strikes showed that his bulletins only included information he obtained from the company or from those sympathetic to the owners.[40] And Hallahan added, " Perhaps a more dubious practice was the fact that his entire bulletin strategy was predicated on making it appear that the bulletins were published on behalf of the operators, not the Rockefellers."[41]

Although Lee's work for the Rockefellers was supported in *Financial World* magazine, his performance for Colorado Fuel & Iron and the work of other public relations practitioners such as Bernays began to set the tone for relationships between business and the business media. In the past, journalists writing about industry had been able to talk directly to company leaders by calling them on the telephone or visiting their officers. But with the inception of public relations staffs, many companies were placing a barrier to such direct communication with business reporters.

One of the most aggressive companies in using public relations was the American Telephone and Telegraph Company, known better as AT&T. Company executives believed that to accomplish their goal of creating a monopoly in the telephone system, the public's distrust of big business had to change. In 1903, the company hired one of the first public relations agencies. In 1907, a new CEO, Theodore Vail, placed an increased emphasis on PR and created an Information Department within the company. Vail was the first corporate leader to see public relations as a key component of a business's strategy. AT&T's plan was to position the company's phone system as a public service. The strategy worked, and for years the company's portrayal in the business media – as well as with consumers – conveyed this belief that the telephone system was a service.

WHAT LEE, BERNAYS, AND OTHERS DID IN THE EARLY DAYS of public relations was create a sense of mistrust among business reporters – and reporters in general – when covering companies. If the businesses had nothing to hide and wanted to provide information that was in the public interest, as Lee's principles had espoused, then why did presidents and chief executives often hide behind publicity and bulletins to get their messages delivered instead of delivering them themselves? The argument can be made that these executives were busy with the day-to-day running of their businesses. But with matters of such importance as the death of striking miners and general public opinion turning against the company as a result, Rockefeller and the Colorado Fuel & Iron Co. may have been better served, in the long run, with talking directly to the media instead of having Lee handle this task. Lee did convince Rockfeller's son, John D. Rockefeller Jr., to appear at the mines and talk to the press, increasing the family's visibility.

What Lee's work did for Rockefeller was give society the first glimpse at how public relations was being used to influence opinion about industry. Some rebelled against his tactics. Henry Luce's *Time* called Lee a "peripatetic representative extraordinary of U.S. Business."[42] And it showed other businesses how to use public relations to their advantage. The rise of public relations in the early part of the 20th century came at a time when the media overall were becoming less critical of big business and industry, and journalists overall were becoming more lazy, although there were some exceptions. The correlation between the two seems obvious in that public relations led to a softened attitude about business by many journalists. The positive slant toward business in *The Wall Street Journal, Forbes,* and other business-related publications in the 1910s and 1920s supported this theory, as does the fact that many journalists became public relations practitioners in the early years.

With the increasing emphasis on public relations by large corporations into the second half of the 20th century, many business reporters were unable to withstand the onslaught of friendly PR people offering story suggestions, friendly advice on stories, and their news releases. As authors Jeff Blyskal and Marie Blyskal wrote, "Contrary to what the press usually tells you, the poorly regarded business of public relations actually works. Business and government and other interest groups have realized what Hollywood studios and astute politicians have known for years: PR gets results." [43]

Even in *The Wall Street Journal,* it's estimated that as much as 50 percent of the daily content comes from press releases.[44] Journalists using information from releases isn't necessarily a bad thing. What causes problems for the business reporters is when they don't check out the information and simply trust the details in the release, or don't bother to call a person or company on the opposite side of an issue discussed in a release. Too often, as we'll later see, this happened with business journalism.

How ads helped business publications flourish

Another shift in mass communication in the late 19th and early 20th centuries also had an effect on how business and industry were portrayed in the media. The rise of advertising began to influence what was written about companies in a dramatic fashion. In addition, advertising influenced public relations in that many media outlets considered PR a free form of advertising, giving both advertising and PR a negative connotation.

The history of advertising in newspapers dates back to the 17th century, when a British periodical called *Mercurius Britannicus* carried an ad about an "excellent discourse concerning the match between our most Gracious and Mightie Prince Charles, Prince of Wales, and the Lady Henrietta Maria, daughter of Henry the Fourth, late King of France."[45] The first daily newspaper in the United States, the *Boston News Letter,* also contained advertisements for the return of merchandise stolen from an apparel shop and wharf. Julie Williams believed that advertising in colonial America was "perhaps the simplest form of the mass media, a direct offer from an individual to anyone." Williams later added that early Americans did not consider advertising to be the persuasive force that it is today.[46]

Like the growth of newspapers in the 19th century, the rise of the advertising industry was spurred by the Industrial Revolution. As businesses grew and shops opened in fast-growing towns and cities, advertising also increased. Businesses began giving their products "brand" names for consumers to better recognize them – and to create awareness for them in the minds of consumers. Products such as Levi's jeans, Maxwell House coffee, Budweiser beer, Ivory soap, and Coca-Cola also developed in the latter half of the 19th century. By the end of the 19th century, the first advertising agencies had opened, and department stores were among the heaviest advertisers in newspapers. Advertising became much more aggressive in enticing readers.

These advertisements generally contained no illustrations or pictures, and some newspapers, most notably the *New York Herald,* required that the ad copy be changed every day.[47]

Few newspapers turned down any advertisement, especially after the growth of magazines in the late 19th century. Because the newspapers did not have national circulation, they were not as effective in advertising as the national magazines that developed. *Harper's Bazaar* began publishing in 1867, and *Vanity Fair* started a year later. *Ladies' Home Journal* began operation in 1883, and *Cosmopolitan* started three years after that. These magazines would give businesses that wanted to advertise a bigger reach to potential consumers.

Verne Edwards points out that even today, advertising influences content in the media. A glut of retailer advertising around Christmas, for example, increases the size of a newspaper, allowing it to run more articles.[48] Such an influence by advertising has played a major role in business journalism. For example, in the 1990s, many business news departments at metropolitan newspapers developed separate sections on technology, spurred by interest in the Internet and gadgets. Many of these sections were supported by advertising from technology-related companies and retailers. But after the Internet bubble burst in the 21st century, many of these sections died when the advertising decreased. In addition, many city newspapers have business reporting staffs produce copy for special sections that list the largest companies in the area. These sections are full of advertising and typically a large moneymaker for the paper.

For most of the 19th century, the media ignored patent medicine advertising and were willing to accept the money for these ads.

One of the biggest advertisers in newspapers and magazines in the latter part of the 19th century were patent medicines. Many publications accepted advertising without concern for the actual value or efficacy of the product being advertised. By 1900, patent medicine sales had reached $75 million, although the ads that spurred these sales held curious claims. An ad for a medicine called "Bull's Sarsaparilla" claimed that it would keep the blood pure.[49] Bonnore's Electro Magnetic Bathing Fluid was advertised as a cure for everything from measles and rheumatism to paralysis and epilepsy. Other patent medicines claimed in ads to cure everything from venereal disease to cancer.

In 1892, *Ladies' Home Journal* announced that it would no longer accept patent medicine advertisements. The conflict between the patent medicine companies and business journalism erupted in November 1905, when *Collier's Magazine* ran a scathing article by Samuel Hopkins Adams showing how patent medicine companies had influenced what was being written about the industry in Massachusetts newspapers.[50]

Patent medicines had played a pioneering role in marketing, and advertisements for them appeared in the media as far back as the 18th century.[51] In the 19th century, when a reader complained to James Gordon Bennett of the *New York Herald* that patent medicine advertising in the paper hurt its credibility, Bennett responded by writing, "Business is business – money is money – and Dr. Brandeth is no more to us than Mr. 'Money Broker.'"[52] A few weeks later, another reader wrote to Bennett, noting that "you are crowding your first page full of quack doctors' advertisements, which are getting to be so indecent that the ladies do not pretend to look on that side of the paper."[53]

Patent medicines preyed on consumers who believed in miracle cures for certain fatal illnesses. Many of these "medicines" contained addictive drugs such as opium and alcohol. For most of the 19th century, the media ignored patent medicine advertising and were willing to accept the money for these ads.

Collier's changed the perception of patent medicine advertising. It printed a copy of a letter sent by a patent medicine company to every newspaper in Massachusetts that had a contract for patent medicine advertising. The letter noted that if certain legislation regulating these medicines passed in Massachusetts, the advertising would cease. *Collier's* showed that virtually no newspaper covered the patent medicine debate. The magazine also showed how newspapers wrote editorials against the legislation to save their patent medicine advertising revenue.[54]

The contract that the patent medicine companies had with newspapers across the country contained a provision that it would become void if legislation regulating the patent medicines passed in the newspaper's home state. By forcing the newspapers to sign such contracts to receive the advertising, the industry was forcing the paper to represent its positions, not the position of the public. Such contracts were rare between newspapers and advertisers, and were seen as a desperate attempt by the patent medicine industry to maintain sales.

Even without such contracts, there was pressure on the newspapers. When newspapers such as the *Cleveland Press* wrote articles criticizing the drug industry, six manufacturers canceled advertising contracts with the paper worth thousands of dollars. When the owner of the newspaper returned from a trip to Egypt, he promptly wrote a letter stating that similar articles about the drug industry would not appear in the future.[55]

Such disclosures hurt business journalists trying to fairly and accurately cover industry and commerce in a growing country. Not only were the editors and owners of newspapers and other media being pressured by some of their largest advertisers to limit the negative articles in their publications, their reporters interested in telling the public information about industry and the economy were being influenced in what they wrote.

As business and industry grew bigger, companies began spending billions of dollars on advertising. In 2003, for example, Coca-Cola Co., known for advertising its various soft drinks on virtually every medium, spent more than $1.9 billion in advertising. Automakers such as Ford Motor Co. and General Motors spent more. In comparison, total advertising spending in 1900 in newspapers and magazines was $450 million. By spending that amount of money, these large corporations wielded clout in the media.

The corruption of business journalists

Is it any surprise, then, that content in media about business, investments, the economy, labor and unions, and other commerce-related matters during the first half of the 20th century and on into the 1950s and 1960s was influenced by business forces? Although some publications such as *Consumer Reports* tried to provide an unbiased and analytical view of products, businesses and industries were committed to conveying their message in any way possible.

Newspapers responded aggressively between the years of 1917 and 1920 to the growing influence of advertising and public relations, primarily because of a shortage of newsprint – not because of ethical concerns about the separation of the editorial side of the business and the business side of the business, said communications expert Susan Lucarelli. "In the past, the boundaries between advertising and news had been more fluid, with many advertisers getting 'free or bonus reading matter' along with their paid ad," stated Lucarelli.[56] But *Editor and Publisher* and *The Fourth Estate*, both journalism trade journals, discouraged this practice, and the publications began to make a distinction between ads and stories.

Still, the public relations efforts of companies, as well as their advertising, influenced what was written about business. Media critic George Seldes noted that the media in the 1930s were notorious for suppressing news about their business operations, and argued "there is the general suppression of all commodity news favoring the consumer – the great American public whose servant the press proclaims itself to be."[57] As an example, he noted that Standard Brands spent millions of dollars in advertising its products, but when the Federal Trade Commission issued a cease-and-desist order against advertising a product designed to clean skin, it was mentioned in few newspapers. "Time after time, the government stopped this company from making false claims in the newspapers, but the press printed its advertising and kept quiet," said Seldes.[58]

According to Verne Edwards, many media owners tend to be conservatives, and they have sometimes favored their advertisers, although not as widely as some may believe. He cited as examples the "Truth-in-Packaging" bill debated in Congress in the 1960s. It was virtually ignored by magazines, he believed, because they feared a backlash from advertisers. And although problems with automobile safety were known as far back as the 1930s, many media outlets ignored the issue until Ralph Nader's "Unsafe at any Speed" attack on the Chevrolet Corvair led to hearings. "Editorial commentary too often steers clear of touchy subjects like Sunday-closing laws for fear of offending either Sunday-closed downtown merchants or retailers with suburban outlets," said Edwards. "Evidence of 'blackmail' advertising policies still crops up occasionally – both in the form of media persecuting non-advertisers and in the form of advertisers canceling contracts," Edwards writes.[59] Media critic Kent MacDougall notes that pharmaceutical companies withdrew $500,000 in advertising after *The New York Times* ran stories on adverse medical reactions, and the Pacific Gas & Electric Co. attempted to discredit a television reporter by accusing him of tampering with an interview.[60]

Ralph Nader on Time

Advertising has had a negative effect on consumers, with complaints including that it promotes unwise spending, and that companies could cut advertising and pass along the savings by cutting prices.[61] Public relations expert Michael Goodman, however, notes that companies place ads in business periodicals such as *The Wall Street Journal, BusinessWeek*, and *Barron's* to accomplish goals other than selling a product or service.[62] They may welcome a new corporate officer to the company or present a company viewpoint, such as the Wal-Mart ad mentioned earlier in the chapter. But MacDougall adds that television and radio are two media that often allow journalists to read promotional material for advertisers immediately after a news story. And many newspaper real estate, travel, and auto sections contain articles written by industry representatives.[63]

Public relations equally influences the work of business journalists, making many reporters and editors unwilling participants in promotional campaigns for companies and their products. Business reporters regularly write stories about new products being introduced, or new advertising campaigns for companies that heavily market to sell their products. In addition, business reporters cover dubious events such as news conferences that have been scheduled simply to produce stories. Goodman also notes that it is the job of PR people to "place articles explaining a corporation's position on a merger, acquisition, restructuring or downsizing."[64] The implication is that the public relations practitioner can convince the business journalist to write such an article from the angle that the company prefers. Another implication is that the public relations person knows what is considered newsworthy, which can also influence reporters.

For example, the public relations firm Burson-Marsteller created a PR campaign for drug company G.D. Searle's Dramamine, a motion sickness medicine, that included riding on roller coasters to determine if the drug was effective in preventing nausea. The campaign included Hollywood stuntmen and a roller coaster expert as spokesmen, and the group traveled across the country visiting theme parks to rate and ride their coasters – and to attract media attention. The story was picked up across the country and the world.[65] Many of these articles appeared in the business sections of newspapers and magazines.

A business editor for a metropolitan newspaper in the East claimed more column inches and stories devoted to industry and business activity than similar papers. "The only trouble," he confessed, "is that nobody reads it."[66] Business school professor S. Prakash Sethi notes that while the national media and the metropolitan newspapers do a decent job in covering business aggressively and fairly, "the vast majority of newspapers with primarily local orientation...are only too happy to accept press releases from the public relations department of various companies and print them as news stories."[67] In 1985, a *Fortune* writer noted that as business news coverage increased, the demand for information made "public relations-generated news materials all the more attractive and valuable to budget-conscious editors."[68]

Some relationships between business publications and public relations professionals have gotten the journalists into trouble. In 1984, a Washington, D.C., judge ruled that *Stock Market Magazine* violated federal investment laws for failing to register as an investment adviser. Some of the publication's content had been written by public relations employees of the companies profiled in the magazine.[69]

The examples mentioned here are extreme. They do suggest, however, that most journalists – not just business reporters – have faced the problem of how to cover a story based on influence from a public relations practitioner or the subject's advertising relationship with the journalist's outlet. And it would be safe to say that many business sections in the media, but not all, try to prevent or limit such influence. It also does not suggest that all public relations and advertising people try to be unethical.

But there has been a precedent of advertising and public relations influencing content about business and the economy. When these events have been exposed, business journalism has been hurt. Public relations practitioners and advertisers may feel that if they can influence one business journalist, they can influence many. In addition, readers notice. After *ComputerWorld* ran an advertisement for a book called "Does IT Matter" next to an excerpt from the book and an interview with the author, it was criticized by some of its subscribers. One reader stated, "Advertising should be kept at a distance from anything that represents the opinions of the media publishers. Otherwise it presents the appearance of impropriety."[70]

The most critical issue for business journalists is how to best get past these issues and work with a company or an industry with a fair relationship, moving beyond the distrust that has developed through decades of misuse of public relations and advertising. According to a study in the 1990s, more than a third of journalists and managing editors surveyed admit they treat business unfairly, while more than two-thirds of businesspeople say they are not always candid and truthful with journalists.[71] Those feelings have not likely dissipated a decade later, and on the journalist side, some of the unfairness may be in retaliation to what is perceived to be unfair treatment by corporate public relations practitioners in the past.

But PR must also take some of the blame. Public relations practitioners have taken advantage of the fact that in the 1980s and 1990s many business journalists didn't understand what they were writing about. Because of the growth in business journalism, many young reporters, with neither background nor experience, were placed in jobs writing and editing about the field. This was an opportunity for public relations. "Many business journalists have had to depend on PR people as security blankets to reassure them that what they're writing is correct, as the PR person pulls the strings," said Blyskal and Blyskal.[72]

To realize the goal of being watchdogs of business and industry, as well as Wall Street, business journalists must rise above the influence of advertising and public relations.

Footnotes

1 From "NNA president says community newspapers insulted by Wal-Mart PR strategy," available at http://www.nna.org/articles/walmartinsults.htm.

2 From "NNA president says community newspapers insulted by Wal-Mart PR strategy."

3 From "Wal-Mart CEO to counteract 'urban legend,'" by L. Grant, Jan. 12, 2005, USA Today, p. 5B.

4 See, "Wal-Mart and Eli Lilly turn to full-page ads to address their critics," by N. Ives, Jan. 14, 2005, New York Times, p. C1; "Battered Wal-Mart stands up to critics, launches ad blitz to improve image," by B. Yerak, Jan. 14, 2005, Chicago Tribune, p. C1; "Wal-Mart seeks to rebut critics; The giant retailer launched a national advertising campaign and started a Web site," Jan. 14, 2005, Philadelphia Inquirer, p. C2; "Wal-Mart lashes back at retail chain's critics," by D. Wethe, Jan. 14, 2005, Fort Worth Star Telegram, p. C2; and "Wal-Mart takes to airwaves, print to polish image; retailer discounts critics' claims that it isn't fair to workers, harms communities," by C. Leonard, Jan. 14, 2005, Arkansas Democrat-Gazette, p. A1.

5 See "Wal-Mart mounting huge media blitz intended to repair image," Jan. 14, 2005, CNN Daybreak; "Wal-Mart company fights back against bad press," Jan. 13, 2005, Good Morning America; and "Wal-Mart PR campaign draws fire," by W. Spain, Jan. 13, 2005, CBSMarketwatch.com.

6 From "Farm journalists and advertiser influence: Pressures on ethical standards," by R. G. Hays and A. E. Reisner, Spring 1990, Journalism Quarterly, pp. 172–178.

7 See Fortune, Feb. 5, 1996.

8 From Malcolm Forbes: The man who had everything, by C. Winans, New York: St. Martin's Press, 1990, p. xx.

9 From "News is suppressed," by G. Seldes, Aug. 2, 1939, The New Republic, pp. 351–354.

10 From "They can dish it out, but…" by M. Mosedale, Jan. 12, 2005, City Pages, available at http://www.citypages.com/databank/26/1258/print12851.asp.

11 From "Journalists and public relations practitioners: Why the antagonism?" by M. Ryan and D. L. Martinson, Spring 1988, Journalism Quarterly, pp. 131–140.

12 From "How public relations practitioners and editors in Florida view each other," by L. L. Kopenhaver, D. L. Martinson, and M. Ryan, Winter 1984, Journalism Quarterly, pp. 860–865.

13 From "Organizational constraints on corporate public relations practitioners," by M. Ryan, Summer 1987, Journalism Quarterly, pp. 473–482.

14 From "Journalists' and public relations practitioners' news values: Perceptions and cross-perceptions," by L. M. Sallot, T. M. Steinfatt and M. B. Salwen, Summer 1998, Journalism and Mass Communication Quarterly, pp. 366–377.

15 From "The newspaper in economic development," by H. A. Innis, December 1942, Journal of Economic History, p. 9.

16 From Newspapers and the news, by S. M. Kingsbury, H. Hart and associates, New York: G. P. Putnam's Sons, 1937, p. 195.

17 From "Journalists' hostility toward public relations: A historical analysis," by F. Fedler and D. DeLorme, a paper submitted to the Association for Education in Journalism and Mass Communication 2002 Convention, Public Relations division–research category.

18 From The shocking history of advertising, by E. S. Turner, London: Michael Joseph Ltd., 1952, p. 126.

19 From Effective public relations, eighth edition, by S. M. Cutlip, A. H. Center, and G. M. Broom, New York: Prentice Hall, 2000, p. 109.

20 See Rendezvous with destiny: A history of modern American reform, by E. F. Goldman, New York: Alfred Knopf, 1963, pp. 216–219.

21 From Effective public relations, p. 110.

22 From "The 1906 campaign to sway muckraking periodicals," by R. D. Reynolds Jr., Fall 1979, Journalism Quarterly, pp. 513–520.

23 See World's Work, June 1906.

24 From Public relations and business: 1900–1929, by A. R. Raucher, Baltimore: Johns Hopkins Press, 1968, p. 140.

25 From Effective public relations, p. 113.

26 From Effective public relations, p. 115.

27 From Public relations and business: 1900–1929, p. 142.

28 From PR! A social history of spin, by S. Ewen, 1996, New York: Harper Collins, p. 159.

29 From PR! A social history of spin, p. 216.

30 See Propaganda, by E. L. Bernays, 1928, New York: H. Liveright, and Crystallizing public opinion, by E. L. Bernays, 1934, New York: Boni and Liveright.

31 From Effective public relations, p. 117.

32 From PR! A social history of spin, p. 78.

33 From "The struggle in Colorado for industrial freedom," Bulletin No. 1, June 22, 1914, available at the Rockefeller Archive Center, North Tarrytown, N.Y.

34 From "The struggle in Colorado for industrial freedom," Bulletin No. 1, June 22, 1914, available at the Rockefeller Archive Center, North Tarrytown, N.Y.

35 From "The struggle in Colorado for industrial freedom," Bulletin No. 9, July 30, 1914, available at the Rockefeller Archive Center, North Tarrytown, N.Y.

36 From "The struggle in Colorado for industrial freedom," Bulletin No. 10, Aug. 3, 1914, available at the Rockefeller Archive Center, North Tarrytown, N.Y.

37 From "The struggle in Colorado for industrial freedom," Bulletin No. 11, Aug. 7, 1914, available at the Rockefeller Archive Center, North Tarrytown, N.Y.

38 From "Ivy Lee and the Rockefeller's response to the 1913–14 Colorado coal strike," by K. Hallahan, Winter 2002, Journal of Public Relations Research, p. 290.

39 From "The struggle in Colorado for industrial freedom," Bulletin No. 13, Aug. 17, 1914, available at the Rockefeller Archive Center, North Tarrytown, N.Y.

40 From PR! A social history of spin, pp. 79–80.

41 From "Ivy Lee and the Rockefeller's response to the 1913–14 Colorado coal strike," pp. 265–315.

42 From Luce and his empire, by W. A. Swanberg, New York: Charles Scribner's Sons, 1970, p. 90.

43 From How the public relations industry writes the news, by J. Blyskal and M. Blyskal, New York: William Morrow and Co., 1985, p. 27.

44 From How the public relations industry writes the news, p. 47.

45 From The shocking history of advertising, p. 15.

46 From The significance of the printed word in early America: Colonists thoughts on the role of the press, by J. H. Williams, Westport, Conn.: Greenwood Press, 1999, p. 220.

47 From The shocking history of advertising, p. 128.

48 From Journalism in a free society, by V. E. Edwards Jr., New York: William C. Brown Co., 1970, p. 185.

49 From Advertising and integrated brand promotion, third edition, by T. C. O'Guinn, C. T. Allen, and R. J. Semenik, Mason, Ohio: South-Western, 2003, p. 80.

50 See "The patent medicine conspiracy against the freedom of the press," Nov. 4 1905, Collier's magazine, p. 11.

51 From "Patent medicines: An early example of competitive marketing," by J. H. Young, December 1960, The Journal of Economic History, pp. 648–656.

52 From Main currents in the history of American journalism, by W. G. Bleyer, 1973, New York: De Capo Press, p. 202.

53 From New York Herald, July 20, 1836.

54 See "The patent medicine conspiracy against the freedom of the press," p. 11.

55 See "The patent medicine conspiracy against the freedom of the press," p. 12.

56 From "The newspaper industry's campaign against spacegrabbers, 1917–1921," by S. Lucarelli, Winter 1993, Journalism Quarterly, p. 888.

57 From "News is suppressed," p. 353.

58 From "News is suppressed," p. 353.

59 From Journalism in a free society, p. 177.

60 From Ninety seconds to tell it all: Big business and the news media, by A. K. MacDougall, Homewood, Ill.: Dow Jones-Irwin, 1981, p. 2.

61 From Journalism in a free society, p. 178.

62 From "Corporate communication and meeting the press," by M. Goodman, in Corporate communica-

tion: Theory and practice, edited by M. Goodman, Albany, N.Y.: State University of New York Press, 1994, p. 261.

63 From Ninety seconds to tell it all: Big business and the news media, pp. 99–111.

64 From "Corporate communication and meeting the press," p. 261.

65 From How the public relations industry writes the news, pp. 69–71.

66 From Journalism in a free society, p. 188.

67 From "The schism between business and American news media," by S. P. Sethi, Summer 1977, Journalism Quarterly, p. 247.

68 From "How much should companies talk?" by W. Guzzardi Jr., March 5, 1985, Fortune, pp. 64–68.

69 From How the public relations industry writes the news, p. 57.

70 From "Defending boundaries: Computerworld readers offer their views on the blurring boundaries between editorial content and advertising," by M. Johnson, June 7, 2004, ComputerWorld, p. 26.

71 From The headline vs. the bottom line: Mutual distrust between business and the news media, by M. Haggerty and W. Rasmussen, 1994, Nashville, TN: The Freedom Forum First Amendment Center.

72 From How the public relations industry writes the news, p. 55.

Chapter 6

The business magazine changes everything

In the first half of the 20th century, a new medium began to play a more prominent role in covering business and the economy, despite the increasing influence of public relations and advertising on the field. The rise of the business magazine in the early 20th century led to new structures of business coverage and opened new formats.

Forbes magazine was the first independent magazine solely devoted to business coverage. Bertie Charles Forbes was born in Scotland in 1880 as the sixth of ten children. His father was a tailor but also ran a general store. Bertie Forbes originally worked for the *Dundee Courier* in Scotland. Forbes moved to South Africa in 1902 and got a job at the *Natal Mercury*, but soon went to work for the *Rand Daily Mail.* It was in South Africa where Forbes became interested in business news.[1]

In 1904, Forbes came to New York. His first job was with the *Journal of Commerce*, where he became well known for reporting the importers' prices of raw silk – the deal they made with the buyers, not their asking price. The tactic caused consternation with the silk importers, but the reporting caused the market for silk to become more competitive as prices fell.[2] According to author Christopher Winans, "He brought enterprise reporting to business journalism, uncovering and reporting market-moving information, using a variety of investment-banker types as confidential sources, thus establishing himself as an influential source in business."[3]

Forbes added a column called "Fact and Comment" (a later staple in *Forbes*) to the *Journal* and also began writing the newspaper's weekly money market recap.[4] His work drew the attention of William Randolph Hearst, who hired Forbes in 1911 for the *New York American* as his main syndicated business and financial columnist.[5] The column ran in nearly 100 newspapers, and Forbes used his influence to become friendly with rich Wall Street investors and bankers.[6] He later used these contacts to find investors for a new venture.

Forbes started his magazine "devoted to doers and doings" in 1917. Originally, he wanted to call the publication *Doers and Doings*, but Walter Drey, the general manager of the *Magazine of Wall Street*, convinced his new business partner to use his last name because it was the writer's "brand" in the investment community.[7]

Others also saw the potential for magazines devoted solely to business. The U.S. Chamber of Commerce started *Nation's Business* in 1907, but its boosterish coverage was intended mainly for its members. *Financial World* started in 1902, but its focus at the time was strictly what its title implied – finance. In 1929, shortly before the Depression, *BusinessWeek* magazine entered the field, published by McGraw-Hill shortly after its stock had begun trading. And in February 1930, *Time* magazine founder Henry Luce started *Fortune* magazine. Each publication would make a major contribution to business journalism and change the way journalists wrote and reported about companies, the economy, investing, and other areas. In England, the *Economist* started as a newspaper in the 1840s but didn't evolve into a magazine format until the 20th century.

Later, the business magazine genre would add a new facet as well – the personal finance magazine devoted specifically to how readers should spend and invest their money. Although business magazines often wrote about investing, these new publications took the level of personal finance to a new high, discussing topics as far ranging as stocks and bonds to life insurance and cemetery plots.

What the magazine format did for business journalism was allow in-depth coverage of companies, industries, labor, Wall Street, and any other business-related issue. The articles were often three to four times longer than what appeared in newspapers, and the reporters sometimes spent months working on stories, interviewing everyone from company executives to customers, competitors to investors, and even disgruntled former employees. The magazine article on a company, particularly those that appeared in *Forbes*, *Fortune*, and *BusinessWeek*, often went beyond the basics of how well or how poorly the business was performing and assessed its future prospects. To compete with the daily newspapers, which also began to pay more attention to companies, though not always critically, the business magazine writer and editor had to think of an angle that hadn't been covered before, giving the reader an analysis that wasn't available in the daily press.

In addition, business magazines gave journalism new forms and styles for how the subject was covered, such as the profile of the corporate executive and the company profile, as well as the company strategy article. And they did all of this at a time when the main media of the past, the daily newspapers, struggled to understand the importance of business and industry coverage to their readers. In the 1920s, as the economy grew, readers wanted to know why the economy was expanding. Although much of the coverage at the time was positive, examples of more sophisticated coverage existed. And in the 1930s and 1940s, when the country's economy underwent massive changes, the business magazine assessed what the transformation meant for everyone from the factory worker up to the CEO.

Other general news magazines played an important role in business journalism. *Newsweek*, *Time*, and *U.S. News and World Report* all covered business and industry, occasionally putting such stories on the cover. Automakers and labor seemed a favorite subject for the mainstream magazines. Henry Ford II graced the cover of *Time* on Feb. 4, 1946.[8] Two decades later, General Motors President Jim Roche appeared on the cover on May 20, 1966.[9] *Life* magazine also paid attention to business issues. Its Aug. 9, 1943, issue focused on women working in factories because of the labor shortage during World War II.[10] On May 19, 1959, the photo-oriented magazine put Teamsters President Jimmy Hoffa on the cover, and on Aug. 26, 1966, the cover story was labor strikes.[11]

They also paid attention to Wall Street. *Time* (June 1, 1962), *Newsweek* (Aug. 21, 1961), and *Life* (June 5, 1970) each put a bull or bear on its cover at least once to signify a booming or shrinking stock market.[12]

But the breadth and depth of business coverage provided in the magazines that specialized in the topic overwhelmed the general interest magazines and became required reading for the serious businessperson, or for anyone interested in business.

Forbes

As with *Collier's*, *McClure's*, and other magazines in the early 20th century, new publisher B. C. Forbes named his publication after himself. The first issue of *Forbes* sold for 15 cents, and it included an explanation of an interview with John D. Rockefeller with the teaser on the cover noting, "How Forbes gets big men to talk."[13] The reverence of Rockefeller was in stark contrast to what Ida Tarbell had written about the businessman. "The man who built up the most wonderful business the world has ever known, not only tells, in the next issue of *Forbes* magazine, how he got on, but gives pointed advice to the young men – and the older men, also – of America, on how to succeed and how to live," wrote Forbes.[14] He noted that such interviews require careful preparation. The issue also contained articles on New York banking laws, utilities, and big bankers forecasting money rates. In a surprising addition, the first issue also included a piece called "Woman in Business" written by Marian Glenn.[15] At the time, few women wrote about business or anything else, and few women were in business.

In its first decade, *Forbes* magazine was filled with inspirational stories about business and rarely, if ever, practiced the reporting about business and the economy that the muckrakers had practiced. One exception appeared in the first issue, when Forbes criticized financier George Jay Gould, calling him the "Nicholas Romanoff of American Finance" and noting his "distrust of both sub-

Business Journalism Timeline

October 1929 – Stock market crash sends country into a Depression. Many business publications downplayed the severity of the market's drop.

February 1930 – Henry Luce begins publishing Fortune.

1933 – Federal government creates the Securities and Exchange Commission to regulate public companies and the stock market.

ordinates and rivals."[16]

An issue in 1918 was typical of the first years of the publication. It had a painting of a Marine on the cover. The inside story explained why the Marines were so efficient and what business could learn from the military force.[17] (Although the country had entered World War I five months before the start of the magazine, *Forbes* focused on the war only in respect to how it was being funded.) Author John Quirt notes that Forbes didn't always side with the executive. He also "scolded" companies when they fired workers during bad times.[18]

More than any other publication had done in the past, *Forbes* took on the persona of its founder and main writer, and his interest in the personalities within business led to a large number of profiles. "In the early decades of the twentieth century, prior to my grandfather's efforts, business reporting consisted of not much more than dry statistics," wrote Timothy Forbes in 1996. "There was little attention paid by the press to the people behind the figures. In a very real way, B. C. Forbes pioneered a new genre of journalism."[19] The June 1, 1930, issue was a prime example of this type of business journalism. In it, Forbes interviewed Walter Teagle, the president of Standard Oil Co. of New Jersey. The article concluded, "My prediction is that Walter Clark Teagle has not, despite his notable achievements, reached the zenith of his career."[20]

Forbes, unlike *Fortune* later, provided investment advice and catered to the investment community. With the stock market crash in 1929 and ensuing Depression, the magazine suffered as the founder continued to run articles trumpeting investing despite the economic crash. Forbes's column on the stock market in the June 1, 1930, issue predicted that, "1930 will not pass without quite an impressive bullish demonstration on Wall Street."[21] The rise in stock prices did not occur, and the misplaced advice hurt the magazine. In 1929, the magazine had more than 67,000 subscribers, but by 1936, it was third, behind *BusinessWeek* and *Fortune.* A decade later, things weren't much better. In 1946, *Forbes* had a circulation of 93,890, while *BusinessWeek* had 157,530 subscribers and *Fortune* had 234,987.[22]

Forbes kept the magazine afloat during the Depression with income from his syndicated column, which he wrote until 1943. He died in 1954. His son Malcolm became a well-known figure while running the magazine, and although its circulation rose in the 1950s and 1960s after languishing for most of the post-Depression period, *Forbes* magazine stayed behind its two greatest competitors. Malcolm Forbes, with the help of editor James Michaels, pushed the magazine to become more critical and to analyze the business world, not merely laud it. The strategy worked. By 1976, *Forbes* passed *Fortune* again in circulation.[23]

Forbes represents an important point in business journalism's history. Its founder was one of the first well-known business journalists in the country – not just to businesspeople but to all readers. And its brand of business journalism – focusing on the people and investing – would widen the focus of business reporting.

Forbes today remains a smart magazine typically ahead of the curve on business issues. In 1984, for example, it was the first business publication to explain Michael Milken's junk bond issues and how they were changing business. In its May 4, 1987 issue, it talked about spotting the top of the stock market. Five months later, the market plunged in its biggest one-day loss since 1929.

And from a business standpoint, *Forbes* remains the only major business publication that continues to be owned by the family that started it. Because of its independence, its coverage of companies has more credence than other corporate-owned business media. Still, its owners sometimes interfered in the magazine's coverage, as seen in Chapter 5, hurting its credibility.

BusinessWeek

A decade after *Forbes,* another magazine emerged to take advantage of the roaring business and economic world of the 1920s. And its brand of business journalism refined how journalists reported and wrote about business, the economy, and other matters for decades to come.

James H. McGraw and John Hill combined the book departments of their company in 1909. Their other operations, primarily publishing industry newspapers, were kept separate until 1917 when the McGraw-Hill Publishing Co. was formed. Hill was editor of *Locomotive Engineer,* while McGraw had purchased the *American Journal of Railway Appliances* in 1888.[24]

In 1929, seven weeks before the stock market crash, McGraw-Hill launched a new magazine called *The Business Week* with 14 staff members. While the fledgling company had no way of knowing that the next decade would be a time when dozens of trade business publications would falter and those that did succeed would struggle to maintain circulation, its creation of a weekly magazine devoted to general news about business and the economy gave the magazine format a new outlet for business journalism. Unlike *Forbes,* which at the time was the only major competitor in the business magazine field, *BusinessWeek* paid more attention to the economy of the country. One of the biggest indicators of its interest in the economy was a thermometer that appeared on the cover of the magazine for decades, from the 1930s to 1961, that gauged the temperature of the American economy.

The magazine was formed to provide interpretation to what was happening in the changing business world, said Malcolm Muir, president of McGraw-Hill at the time. He stated:

> *The Business Week* always has a point of view, and usually a strong opinion, both of which it does not hesitate to express. And all the way through, we hope you will discover it is possible to write sanely and intelligently of business without being pompous or ponderous.[25]

BUSINESS JOURNALISM TIMELINE

1933 – ARTHUR KALLET AND FREDERICK SCHLINK PUBLISH "100,000 GUINEA PIGS: DANGERS IN EVERYDAY FOODS, DRUGS, AND COSMETICS." IT IS "INTENDED NOT ONLY TO REPORT DANGEROUS AND LARGELY UNSUSPECTED CONDITIONS AFFECTING FOOD, DRUGS, AND COSMETICS, BUT ALSO, SO FAR AS POSSIBLE, TO GIVE THE CONSUMER SOME MEASURE OF DEFENSE AGAINST SUCH CONDITIONS."

1935 – CONGRESS PASSES THE WAGNER ACT, WHICH GAVE UNIONS THE RIGHT TO COLLECTIVELY BARGAIN WITH COMPANIES.

JULY 1935 — FORTUNE BEGINS A QUARTERLY FEATURE CALLED THE FORTUNE POLL, WHICH WAS DEVELOPED BY ELMO ROPER, RICHARDSON WOOD AND PAUL CHERINGTON.

1936 – SYLVIA PORTER BEGINS WRITING A PERSONAL FINANCE COLUMN IN THE NEW YORK POST. SHE INITIALLY USES INITIALS TO DISGUISE THE FACT THAT SHE'S A WOMAN.

The comment was an obvious slap at the existing competition. B. C. Forbes's magazine was considered self-important and haughty to many at the time. And one of the reasons that *Fortune* was later founded was that its creator considered *Forbes* to be "piddling and inexpressively dull."[26] *BusinessWeek* followed the format of *Time* magazine in many ways, creating distinct departments within the magazine that would become regular features.

In the first issue, for example, the Business Outlook section cautioned "stock prices are generally out of line with safe earnings expectations, and the market is now almost wholly 'psychological.'"[27] However, in the Nov. 2, 1929, issue, the magazine misinterpreted what the stock market crash meant, stating, "The Wall Street crash doesn't mean that there will be any general or serious business depression…For six years, American business has been diverting a substantial part of its attention, its energies and its resources on the speculative game. Now that irrelevant, alien and hazardous adventure is over. Business has come home again, back to its job, providentially unscathed, sound in wind and limb, financially stronger than ever before."[28] *BusinessWeek* was not the only business medium to miss forecasting the Depression.

Other sections of the magazine in those early years included production, marketing, labor, finance, management, transport, government and business abroad, as well as a Washington Outlook to accompany the Business Outlook. With such reporting, *BusinessWeek* became one of the first publications to routinely cover the regulatory and policy issues coming from the nation's capital that affected business and industry. In 1950, it published its first executive pay survey, which today remains a popular feature.

In addition, *BusinessWeek* had an advantage by publishing every week, giving it the ability to write about business events in a more timely fashion. *Forbes* was published every two weeks, and in the beginning *Fortune* came out monthly. In 1933, seeing the success of *Time* and *BusinessWeek*, *Newsweek* began publishing on the same weekly basis.

The magazine, like many other publications during the Depression, struggled, losing $1.5 million from its founding through 1935.[29] Where *BusinessWeek* succeeded and other business publications failed was in its ability to give a broad but comprehensive overview of issues and trends affecting industry and the economy. Every week, its content provided a cross-section of various industries and what the issues were in each of them, as well as analysis of the broader trends such as unemployment, the stock market, and trade. Its content changed with the economy. In the first decade, the magazine added sections called "Labor" and "Management," as well as "New Products" and "Business Abroad." It expanded its economics content in the 1940s, dropped an Agriculture section in the 1950s, and added a Personal Business column.[30] In 1969, it became the first magazine to devote a department to information technology, calling it Information Processing.

BusinessWeek wanted company managers reading its magazine, even if the articles were not about their company or companies in their industry. It believed that these managers and executives would want to know what was going on in other industries that affected their business, and that they might learn management tips or strategies from other industries.

The magazine's issues in the 1950s epitomized this strategy. The Aug. 14, 1954, issue was dominated by a package of stories on motivation – why people buy products and why people work.[31] That same year, on April 17, it put a woman – Brownie Wise of Tupperware fame – on the cover for the first time. On April 7, 1956, the cover story was on the growing economy in India, while the May 12, 1956, publication offered the advice of General Electric's Ralph Cordiner: "The work of organization is never done."[32] The Nov. 17, 1956, issue offered a guide to borrowing money in a tight economy.[33]

The June 22, 1957, cover story was on Ford and its new car, the Edsel, which was pictured under a protective wrap so that competitors wouldn't steal its design. Part of the story explained the strategy of the new vehicle and how the company had built its dealer network – issues that any manager at a national company would likely be interested in reading.[34] A week later, *BusinessWeek's* cover story was business in Europe and the idea of unifying countries in Europe in an economic community.

And unlike its competition, which staunchly maintained a pro-business outlook, *BusinessWeek* often looked beyond the boardroom for its stories and examined how business influenced society. In 1968, the magazine published a 33-page insert called "Business and the Urban Crisis," which examined the economic and social problems of American cities.[35] An analysis of its content in 1967 noted that about 10 percent of all its articles for the year were devoted to urban issues. It also focused on civil rights in the 1960s.[36]

June 1957
Business Week

For years, *BusinessWeek* also attracted readers in an unusual way. It was not sold on newsstands, but instead the magazine solicited subscriptions from corporate management. When applying for a subscription, the reader had to provide his or her title and employer, information that was used by ad salesmen to show that readers were executives.[37] The subscription strategy changed in the 1970s, when the magazine began soliciting readers outside the business world.

The magazine mastered the corporate strategy article. Its covers in the 1970s under editor Lewis Young frequently promoted two or three corporate strategies inside the magazine. The Feb. 6, 1978, issue, which examined how corporate jets were changing the way companies did business, included corporate strategy articles about Phoenix Resources, Standard Brands, and MacMillan Bloedel.[38] The Nov. 13, 1978, issue focused on the marketing at R. J. Reynolds and how Dow Jones, the parent of *The Wall Street Journal*, turned into a media conglomerate.[39] Another 1978 issue showed a can of Pepsi ready to take on a larger can of Coca-Cola, signaling the beginning of the Cola Wars.

In the 1970s, the magazine began adding bylines to its articles, giving its editors and reporters name recognition with readers. And in the 1980s and 1990s, *BusinessWeek* became an aggressive magazine under editor Steven Shepard, whose 20-year leadership of the publication included numerous National Magazine Awards. The magazine added an international edition, expanding its reach across the globe and tapping its foreign bureaus for more news and analysis. And it was ahead in defining many business trends. For example, in 1998, it helped define the notion of the New Economy. It also wrote about how the mafia had infiltrated Wall Street.

By 2005, under new editor Stephen Adler, the magazine added a column by CNBC commentator Maria Bartiromo and closed its European and Asian editions. It also began running a column by former General Electric CEO Jack Welch and his wife, and airing podcasts of the column on its Web site.

Fortune

Henry Luce started *Time* magazine on March 3, 1923.[40] The cover depicted Republican Speaker Joseph Gurney. But in the 1920s, Luce noticed the number of business stories the magazine had killed because there wasn't enough space.[41] With the fast-growing economy of the decade and the growth of investing, Luce thought a monthly business magazine could accomplish what his weekly news magazine had already achieved – provide a wide variety of readers across America with a better understanding of the news and issues that affected their lives.

Luce originally wanted to call his business publication *Power*, but was convinced to call it *Fortune* by his first wife who thought that name would be more subtle for readers.[42] In a prospectus for the magazine, Luce wrote, "Where is the publication that even attempts to portray Business in all its heroic present-day proportions, or that succeeds in conveying a sustained sense of the challenging personalities, significant trends, and high excitements of this vastly stirring Civilization of Business?"[43]

Two major events in 1929 could have affected the launch of the new business magazine. The first was the death of Briton Hadden, Luce's business partner who was not enthusiastic about the project. Luce had clearer sailing at launching the magazine without Hadden's opposition. The second was the October 1929 stock market crash, which would severely curtail interest in business information for the next decade as the country endured the Depression. The board of Luce's company tried to dissuade him from starting *Fortune*. And even after the market crashed, Luce placed the magazine's odds of success at just 50 percent.[44]

His idea was to produce a magazine unlike any other. The covers would contain striking art from some of the country's leading artists. The first cover was sketched on a tablecloth in a speakeasy in lower Manhattan by Thomas Maitland Cleland, at the time one of the country's leading experts on typefaces and design.[45] The photography inside would be the best in the world. Margaret Bourke-White, who later became a famous photographer, was the first staff photographer for *Fortune*.[46] Graphics and charts would help explain technical points of stories. And the writing would also be the best – Luce hired writers such as Archibald MacLeish and John Kenneth Galbraith to pen its stories. When approached by Luce to write for the magazine, MacLeish replied that he knew nothing about business.[47] Indeed, many writers had no experience in writing about business. But they were writers who could take arcane business subjects and explain them to anyone.

The first issue appeared in February 1930 and carried a cost of $1, with an annual subscription worth $10, a large sum for readers in a shrinking economy. But the magazine was visually appealing. It contained stories on the meatpacking and glass industries, the Biltmore Hotel, and Arthur Curtis James, then one of the richest men in the world. Other article subjects were a study of entertainment giant RCA and how to live in Manhattan on $25,000 a year.[48] At 184 pages, more than half of the magazine contained advertisements – a stunning contrast to other magazines during that time.

Luce declared that the magazine would contain no advice on how to run a business or on how to invest. And many of the initial issues contained articles more descriptive than taking a stance for or against business or an economic issue, which was surprising because each issue of *Time* espoused many of Luce's conservative Republican viewpoints. Luce withstood criticism after the second issue, which contained a "respectful" article about Texaco that some suggested had been paid for by the company.[49] Luce's article about Pittsburgh contrasted starkly to that written by Lincoln Steffens in *McClure's* just 30 years earlier. He wrote that "brass-knuckled steel barons" had been replaced by kindly businessmen such as the Mellons.[50] His depiction upset some of the magazine's writers. But as author David Halberstam noted, "He started *Fortune* magazine because as an emancipated young capitalist in the late twenties he thought most American businessmen were narrow sleeping Babbits unworthy of their rules and their duties and he wanted to seek out the handful of worthy businessmen and hold them up as examples."[51]

Luce's philosophy didn't last, and the Great Depression forced him to alter the magazine's content. As the country's economic condition worsened, *Fortune* became more adversarial toward business. Many writers were liberals or Socialists, and they constantly pushed for a more critical look at capitalism. They used examples from early issues to support their arguments. One of the most embarrassing early stories in the magazine was a profile of Swedish match king Ivar Krueger, who was called "brilliant" and "noble."[52] Krueger committed suicide in March 1932 just before his business failed because it had taken out loans that it was unable to repay.

The magazine began to reflect the problems of the economy. In September 1932, *Fortune* contrasted how a carpenter and a white-collar worker dealt with the Depression. Luce also had his magazine challenge businesses that didn't want to be the topics of articles, much as Ida Tarbell had done with the Standard Oil Co. "The public has the right to know how business works," said Luce. "You don't need much socialism if you have proper exposure to the capitalist process."[53] But in exposing business to the public, *Fortune* performed exactly the opposite of what Luce wanted, showing that capitalism could be corrupt and inefficient.

Among the companies that faced the wrath of *Fortune* were grocer A&P, U.S. Steel, and United Fruit Co. An exposé on European munitions companies in March 1934 led to a Senate investigation into similar companies in America.[54] When Allied Chemical President Orlando Webber refused to be interviewed by *Fortune* or to meet with Luce, the magazine sent a reporter to talk to Webber's parents in Milwaukee and obtained a picture of Webber – who as a kid was overweight. Luce sent an enlarged version of the picture to Webber with a note that explained that *Fortune* would run a story about his youth since he refused to talk. After receiving the note, Webber called Luce and granted the interview.[55] U.S. companies doing business in the Soviet Union were listed in the March 1932 issue with the suggestion that maybe they should pull out. Interestingly, such content did not cause the magazine to lose much advertising.[56]

MacLeish and Ralph Ingersoll, another *Fortune* writer, told the magazine's readers about societal issues such as starvation, homelessness, and begging that had been brought upon the country by business failures. A series of articles focused on how housing for the working class had fallen far behind that of Europe and explained how payments for bond issues to build town and city halls limited how local governments could help the poor. A 1937 article on unemployment pictured William Davis of Natchez, Miss., a sharecropper whose cupboard contained only a hunk of salt pork.[57]

Although Luce initially supported President Franklin D. Roosevelt's programs to rebuild the economy, *Fortune* grew sour on the president's plans when business conditions worsened in 1937. That year, the magazine reported a profit of nearly $500,000, but although *Fortune* was successful, Luce began changing the tone of the magazine's content to mirror his own business and political beliefs.[58] The publication became more pro-business in the late 1930s and in the 1940s. For example, the magazine rejected the work it had commissioned of writer James Agee and photographer Walker Evans, who had spent two months with Alabama sharecroppers. Their work was published in 1941 as the now famous book, *Let Us Now Praise Famous Men.* In the 1950s, the magazine also moved away from the striking and popular art on its covers and began using photographs and tying the cover to the main article.

The magazine extensively covered political issues and how they affected business, becoming one of the first publications to recognize the relationship. When Great Britain declared war on Germany in 1940, the magazine noted how the promise of increased business boosted steel stocks and the aircraft industry. But the war would also hurt the quality of journalism in *Fortune.* The February 1942 issue contained an article about a plant in western New York building tanks. But the location and other important details in the story were deleted and replaced with the word *CENSORED.* Editors argued that the plant's location was well known, and they published the article under protest.[59]

Although the publication later took on much of his political and business beliefs, Luce had at first created a publication that made it clear that business journalism could be interesting, informative, and entertaining without espousing certain viewpoints. He went out of his way to find the best journalists and moved away from the traditional strategy of having reporters and writers who knew something about business. By doing so, he attracted more interest to business journalism and opened the field to a more literary style.

In addition, *Fortune* should be credited with being the first publication to use the corporate profile as an article. The magazine's long, winding stories about companies served as the template for other business journalists to copy when writing about businesses, and it's used today in virtually every media form when a story is done about a company and its strategy. Galbraith noted that the early *Fortune,* "more than any other journal anywhere in the industrial world, saw the large modern corporation as a primary economic and social force."[60]

Fortune also took business journalism into new areas. In September 1936, it published an entire issue on Japan and reflected the belief that the Far East would become a vital part of U.S. business in the near future.[61] During World War II, it dispatched a writer to assess the British economy and how it might recover once the war was over. Never before had business journalism devoted itself with issues that were more political and societal in nature. And it examined unique businesses, such as syndicated cartoon strips and juvenile novels, traditionally outside the realm of business journalism.

In the 1950s, *Fortune* gave the world of business journalism a new feature that became increasingly popular. The magazine compiled a list of the 500 largest companies in the country for an issue in 1955. With $9.8 billion in revenue, General Motors topped the first list. Dubbed the *Fortune* 500, the annual compilation became immediately successful and turned into a barometer of American business.[62] The magazine later added other lists, including the

Global 500, the *Fortune* 1,000, the 100 Best Companies to Work For, and the Most Admired Companies. This last-named list would prove embarrassing for the magazine in the early part of the 21st century with the bankruptcy filing of Enron Corp., which had been at the top of the list for six years.

Fortune remained a bastion of pro-business writing, offering advice and analysis for managers at the country's largest businesses. But in recent years it has returned to a more adversarial relationship with the corporate world. Bethany McLean's criticism of Enron in February 2001 was perhaps the first crack in the energy company's façade. The more aggressive stance was spurred by John Huey, who took over the magazine in 1995 as managing editor and invigorated its pages. The cover stories became edgier, with headlines such as "The scariest S.O.B. on Wall Street"[63] and "Women, sex and power."[64]

Money, Worth, Kiplinger's, and Smart Money

Forbes, BusinessWeek, and *Fortune* were not the only business magazines to succeed. In the 1980s and 1990s, business-related magazines started that focused on giving readers advice on how to handle personal finances.

These new publications addressed societal changes in the United States in the 1960s and 1970s as more consumers began to own stock and take more responsibility for their investments. In 1975, more than half of the average American's assets were in bank deposits, according to Federal Reserve data. But by 2004, that number had fallen to 27 percent, as stocks, bonds, and mutual funds accounted for nearly three-fourths of an American's assets.[65] The percentage of U.S. households owning stock increased from 32.5 percent in 1989 to 49.5 percent in 2002, according to a 2002 survey by the Investment Company Institute and the Security Industry Association.[66]

W. M. Kiplinger created the nation's first personal finance magazine back in 1947.[67] Called *Changing Times, The Kiplinger Magazine,* the publication contained no advertising and offered advice on a variety of topics. Its slogan was "To help you master everyday problems and see your way to a better future." The magazine was part *Consumer Reports* and part investment and financial adviser. The October 1959 issue was representative of the topics the publication covered. In that issue was an article assessing the pros and cons of going into business for yourself, an assessment of homeowners' insurance policies, advice for making charitable contributions count, and strategies for buying a freezer to fit your needs. The news-brief section of the magazine also noted one interesting trend:

> Business news on the radio is becoming routine. Both ABC and Mutual have regular business news programs. ABC's features John Cameron Swayze broadcasting directly from the floor of the New York Stock Exchange. Comments are made on business reports, the stock market, and the general economic scene. The trend may spread to local stations and to TV. It's a sign of broadening public interest in what's happening in business and to stocks.[68]

In between the articles were short tips such as cutting fuel bills and choosing and caring for silverware. A huge chart that encompassed three pages at the end of the magazine compared taxes paid on a state-by-state basis.

But in the 1970s, *Changing Times,* which later changed its name to *Kiplinger's Personal Finance Magazine,* began receiving competition. Time Inc. started *Money* magazine in 1972 as a complement to *Fortune,* focusing the publication's content on investing and spending money.[69] (In 1967, *Institutional Investor* magazine started, but it focused on how Wall Street was investing money.) The separation continued Luce's long-held belief of keeping investment advice out of *Fortune,* although the publication today contains such content. In 1992, *Wall Street Journal* parent Dow Jones and magazine publisher Hearst Corp. started a joint venture that began publishing personal finance magazine *Smart Money.*[70] Another magazine, *Worth,* started in 1992 by mutual fund giant Fidelity Investments, eliciting comments that the publication would play favorites to its parent company.[71] Fidelity investment guru Peter Lynch was prominently featured in its advertising.

Like *Forbes* and *BusinessWeek* in the 1920s, these magazines fed off the Wall Street mania that gripped the country, offering investment advice to readers on everything ranging from stocks and bonds to variable annuities. They wrote about how consumers weren't getting their money's worth for certain products and services. *Smart Money* wrote a scathing article in July 2000, for example, on how hospitals and insurance companies were taking bigger chunks of personal injury lawsuit settlements than the consumer involved.[72]

But when the market slumped in the early 21st century, so did these publications, leaving only the stronger magazines. In 2001, *Individual Investor, Your Money,* and *Family Money* folded. The next year, Time Warner closed *Mutual Funds* magazine.[73] *Money, Kiplinger's,* and *Smart Money* all saw a drop in advertising and subscriptions, but remained in business.

Worth, which focused on the lifestyle of the well-to-do businessperson and entrepreneur, wasn't so lucky. The magazine was sold in April 1999 by Fidelity to a group of investors. By 2002, after losing more than $50 million during the past decade, the publication began seeking new capital.[74] The magazine eventually filed for bankruptcy court protection, and its assets were purchased in 2003 by the owner of the *Robb Report,* a glossy magazine filled with pictures of expensive cars and homes.

Despite the missteps, magazines have created their niche within business journalism. Walk past any newsstand today, and there's typically an entire section of business magazines, from the names mentioned here to specialty industry publications.

The business magazine also forced other media to pay more attention to coverage of business and industry since these publications showed that writing and reporting about the business world could be done in a way that the average reader would find interesting. In addition, these publications showed profits and circulation growth that caught the attention of their brethren in other media, particularly in newspapers and television. The former would begin to re-emphasize business coverage beginning in the 1960s and 1970s, while the latter would begin covering business and economic stories regularly.

These magazines also continued to focus society on money – how it was made, how it should be invested, who had it and who didn't, and how it should be spent. As the country's economy grew and expanded, and companies became larger, the consumer's appetite for information about why and how this was happening increased as well.

Did these publications fuel the appetite for information on how CEOs were successful or ran their companies into the ground? Perhaps, but they also provided a broad overview of what was happening in the business world. Their advice was not always on target, but business magazines became one of the standard bearers of business journalism in the middle part of the 20th century.

Their influence continues today. Publicists for companies try to get their executives on the cover of these magazines, knowing that hundreds of thousands of influential readers and investors will likely see the magazine, and business magazines can partly be blamed for the image of the CEO as cultural icon that permeated all media in the 1980s and 1990s. These magazines have also been known to cripple companies with negative stories and break down dubious investments for their readers, providing a service to society in rooting out the bad in business.

Footnotes

1 From Malcolm Forbes: The man who had everything, by C. Winans, New York: St. Martin's Press, 1990, pp. 21–22.

2 From Malcolm Forbes: The man who had everything, p. 22.

3 From Malcolm Forbes: The man who had everything, p. 23.

4 From Malcolm Forbes: The man who had everything, p. 23.

5 From The press and the world of money: How the news media cover business and finance, panic and prosperity and the pursuit of the American dream, by J. Quirt, Byron, Calif.: Anton/California-Courier: 1993, p. 86.

6 From More than I dreamed, by M. Forbes, New York: Simon and Schuster, 1989, p. 38.

7 From Malcolm Forbes: The man who had everything, p. 25.

8 See "Young Henry takes a risk," Feb. 4, 1946, Time, pp. 75–80. Note that a Ford advertisement appears on p. 12 of the same issue.

9 See "The rattles in the engine," May 20, 1966, Time, pp. 100–106.

10 See Life magazine, Aug. 9, 1943.

11 See Life magazine, May 19, 1959 and Aug. 26, 1966.

12 See Time, June 1, 1962, Newsweek, Aug. 21, 1961, and Life magazine, June 5, 1970.

13 From More than I dreamed, p. 22.

14 From The press and the world of money: How the news media cover business and finance, panic and prosperity and the pursuit of the American dream, p. 86.

15 From The press and the world of money: How the news media cover business and finance, panic and prosperity and the pursuit of the American dream, p. 89.

16 From Malcolm Forbes: The man who had everything, p. 26.

17 See "Why are U.S. Marines so efficient," by G. Bennett, Sept. 21, 1918, Forbes, p. 410.

18 From The press and the world of money: How the news media cover business and finance, panic and prosperity and the pursuit of the American dream, p. 87.

19 From Forbes greatest business stories of all time, edited by D. Gross, New York: John Wiley & Sons Inc., 1996, p. 2.

20 From "What the oil industry must do," by B. C. Forbes, June 1, 1930, Forbes, pp. 16–18.

21 From "Slow but steady improvement, stocks may boom," by B. C. Forbes, June 1, 1930, Forbes, p. 39.

22 From "How Forbes magazine got the way it is – and by whom," Sept. 15, 1977, Forbes, p. 121.

23 From "How Forbes magazine got the way it is – and by whom," p. 121.

24 See a corporate history of McGraw-Hill, available at http://www.mcgrawhill.com/about/history.html.

25 From "A time to celebrate," by S. B. Shepard, Oct. 11, 2004, BusinessWeek, p. 24.

26 From The press and the world of money: How the news media cover business and finance, panic and prosperity and the pursuit of the American dream, p. 60.

27 From "A time to celebrate."

28 From "The treacherous nature of bear market rallies," by M. Faber, Dec. 22, 2001, available at http://www.gloomboomdoom.com/marketcoms/011222.htm.

29 From "The last 60 years – and a look ahead," by S. Shepard, Sept. 25, 1989, BusinessWeek, p. 10.

30 From "The last 60 years – and a look ahead," p. 10.

31 See "People: What's behind their choices – in buying, in working," Aug. 14, 1954, BusinessWeek, pp. 50–61.

32 See "India walks tightrope into the industrial age," April 7, 1956, BusinessWeek, pp. 199–134, and "Big business explains itself on the lecture platform," May 12, 1956, BusinessWeek, pp. 68–74.

33 See "The money market, how to grab the scanty dollar," Nov. 17, 1956, BusinessWeek, pp. 64–106.

34 See "Ford gets full line at last," June 22, 1957, BusinessWeek, pp. 45–51, and "How to build a dealer empire: Strategy of the Edsel campaign," June 22, 1957, BusinessWeek, pp. 52–64.

35 From Magazines in the United States, third edition, by J. P. Wood, New York: The Ronald Press Co., 1971, p. 386.

36 From Magazines in the United States, third edition, p. 386.

37 From Magazines in the United States, third edition, p. 386.

38 See BusinessWeek, Feb. 6, 1978.

39 See BusinessWeek, Nov. 13, 1978.

40 From Luce, his life, time and fortune, by J. Kobler, New York: Doubleday & Co., 1968, p. 53.

41 From Luce, his life, time and fortune, p. 80.

42 From Luce and his empire, p. 82.

43 From An economy of abundant beauty: Fortune magazine and Depression America, by M. Augspurger, Ithaca, N.Y.: Cornell University Press, 2004, p. 6.

44 From "We're 70!," by J. Huey, March 6, 2000, Fortune, p. 5.

45 From "The art of covering business," by D. Okrent and T. Spencer, March 6, 2000, Fortune, p. F-90.

46 From Luce and his empire, p. 83.

47 From Luce and his empire, p. 83.

48 From "Finance finds a spokesperson: Fortune magazine, 1930–1937," by W. J. Chilman, Fall 2000, Financial History, pp. 20–23.

49 From Luce, his life, time and fortune, p. 82.

50 From Luce and his empire, pp. 83–84.

51 From The powers that be, by D. Halberstam, New York: Dell Publishing, 1979, p. 70.

52 "Finance finds a spokesperson: Fortune magazine, 1930–1937," p. 21.

53 From Luce, his life, time and fortune, p. 83.

54 From Luce, his life, time and fortune, p. 83.

55 From Luce, his life, time and fortune, p. 84.

56 From Luce and his empire, p. 91.

57 "Finance finds a spokesperson: Fortune magazine, 1930–1937," p. 22.

58 From Luce, his life, time and fortune, p. 85.

59 From "A tour through Fortune's past," March 26, 1990, Fortune, p. 188.

60 From "My debt to Harry Luce and Fortune," by J. K. Galbraith, in Writing for Fortune: Nineteen authors remember life on the staff of a remarkable magazine, New York: Time Inc., 1980, p. 119.

61 See Fortune, September 1936.

62 See Fortune, July 1955.

63 See Fortune, Dec. 9, 1996.

64 See Fortune, Aug. 5, 1996.

65 See "Individual ownership in equities grew steadily as households shifted asset ownership mix,"a report by the Investment Company Institute and the Security Industry Association, available at http://www.sia.com/research/html/key_industry_trends_.html#individualownership.

66 See "Individual ownership of equities continues to grow."

67 See Kiplinger's Web site at http://www.kiplinger.com/about.html.

68 From October 1959, Changing Times, The Kiplinger Magazine, p. 5.

69 From "Smart money vs. money; battle pits Hearst-Dow Jones against Time Warner," by S. Donaton and J. Mandese, March 16, 1992, Advertising Age, p. 21.

70 From "Dow Jones and Hearst to jointly test new personal finance magazine," by R. Gladstone, Aug. 14, 1991, Associated Press.

71 From "A magazine worth its price?" by P. Starobin, May 7, 1994, The National Journal, p. 1066.

72 See "Adding insult to injury," by M. Andrews, July 2000, Smart Money.

73 From "California publisher revives Worth magazine as guide for the rich," by K. Lynn, Nov. 27, 2003, Knight-Ridder Tribune Business News Wire.

74 From "Buyout of Worth magazine is planned by chief executive," by D. Carr, Feb. 11, 2002, New York Times, p. C2.

Chapter 7

The rise of The Wall Street Journal

Throughout 2002, reporters and editors at *The Wall Street Journal* scrambled to keep on top of the latest business scandal. They wrote about the problems at Enron, WorldCom, Tyco, Global Crossing, and Imclone in the United States. In Europe, the staff focused on the cash problems at Vivendi. And the reporting went deeper than just chronicling the latest events at each of these struggling companies; writers were searching for reasons why so many crises could occur at the same time. For its work in documenting the corporate scandals of the year, the *Journal* was awarded a Pulitzer Prize in explanatory journalism. Said managing editor Paul Steiger in his letter to the Pulitzer judges: "The Journal reporters responsible for these articles did more than just record a year of scandal, they also helped readers understand developments of vital importance to their lives and to sort out their larger meaning."[1]

In the last 75 years, no media outlet has done a more comprehensive, broader, or better job at documenting the ins and outs of the business world and the economy than the *Journal.* While such a statement may not seem surprising to those who read the newspaper and know that it is considered essential reading by most executives and important people on Wall Street, the newspaper's standing as the pre-eminent business journalism publication was not always the case.

In its early years, the *Journal* was nothing more than an industry newspaper that catered solely to the investment community. It was not initially eligible to win Pulitzer Prizes because it was considered to be an industry publication.[2] Not until after the Great Depression did the newspaper become one of the country's great publications, using its understanding of business, the economy, labor, and investing to explain their growing significance in society, the country, and the rest of the world.

Today, the *Journal* is the second largest newspaper in the country in terms of circulation, behind only *USA Today.* And it was the first newspaper to go national in the 1950s, being printed at plants across the country so that readers in San Francisco had the same news as readers in New York. Newspapers such as *The New York Times* and *The Washington Post* followed the *Journal*'s lead in catering to a national audience. In addition, the *Journal* was the first printed medium to understand the broad impact of business on everyone's life and to document those implications. Perhaps of most importance, the *Journal* developed business journalism into a segment of mass communication that demanded society pay attention to what was being written, showing other media outlets how the field should be documented and dissected.

Simply, the *Journal* became required reading for a large portion of the country, including other media outlets. In a 1982 letter to former editor Vermont Royster, CBS anchor Dan Rather wrote, "I read the *Journal* before anything else most days and have for years."[3] Politicians, chief executive officers, and people in other influential positions looked at the *Journal* to ascertain how issues and topics were being evaluated. In early 1970s, H. R. Haldeman, the special assistant to President Richard Nixon later implicated in the Watergate scandal, often wrote letters to Vermont Royster about items in the newspaper.[4] After his resignation, Nixon also wrote letters to Royster. In one letter, the former president noted, "I couldn't agree more with you that inflation will undoubtedly be the major political issue in the elections of 1978, and possibly in 1980 as well."[5] A 1974 study showed that the *Journal* had a higher readership than any other newspaper among "economic managers and owners, and much the same for labor union presidents." In addition, political party leaders read it more than any other newspaper.[6]

Such widespread influence was not the case when the newspaper was started by Charles Henry Dow, Edward David Jones, and Charles Milford Bergstresser in 1889, changing the name of its *Customers' Afternoon Newsletter* to its current moniker. For the first 50 years of the paper's existence, it was noted only for its overly positive coverage of the stock markets and its embarrassing ethical lapses in the 1920s.

But in the past 75 years, the newspaper and parent Dow Jones & Co. aggressively expanded into other territories and other media forms while becoming more objective, widespread, and incisive in business coverage. *The Wall Street Journal* now has editions in Asia and Europe, and its online site is the largest paid subscription news site on the Internet. It has been voted the most trusted publication in the country by the Pew Research Center Media Believability Studies since 1985.[7] Its other business jour-

BUSINESS JOURNALISM TIMELINE

MAY 1936 – CONSUMERS UNION REPORTS APPEARS, WITH ARTICLES ON GRADE A AND GRADE B MILK, BREAKFAST CEREALS, SOAP, AND STOCKINGS. A THREE-TIERED RATINGS SCHEME – BEST BUY, ALSO ACCEPTABLE, AND NOT ACCEPTABLE – IS ADOPTED TO PRESENT THE RESULTS OF SCIENTIFIC TESTS OF PRODUCTS.

1938 – NEW YORK FINANCIAL WRITERS ASSOCIATION IS FOUNDED.

1939 – SYLVIA PORTER PUBLISHES HER FIRST BOOK, "HOW TO MAKE MONEY IN GOVERNMENT BONDS," THAT OFFERED PRACTICAL ADVICE TO BOTH PROFESSIONAL INVESTORS AND THE GENERAL PUBLIC.

1941 – WESTBROOK PEGLER WINS A PULITZER PRIZE FOR THE NEW YORK WORLD TELEGRAM FOR HIS COVERAGE OF SCANDALS IN ORGANIZED LABOR THAT LED TO THE CONVICTION OF A UNION OFFICIAL.

nalism operations, such as *Barron's* and the Dow Jones Newswire, carry strong cachet in the business and journalism worlds. The writing and reporting by all the Dow Jones' subsidiaries are considered some of the best in the world – not just in the business journalism field but in all of journalism. The paper has won 29 Pulitzer Prizes, with most of those awards coming since 1970.

In addition, the company's name is now used in virtually every other medium, giving it further credence. The Dow Jones Industrial Average is considered one of the most important barometers of how the stock market is performing, and its use is widespread throughout business journalism. Dow Jones also has industry indices widely used in other media.

The *Journal* also created new forms of business journalism now considered standard in other media.

In 1988, the newspaper began a regular feature where investment professionals picked stocks and compared their performance to stocks picked by throwing darts.[8] The feature has been wildly successful and copied, and academics have studied its significance. The experts outperform the darts by a wide margin, but they outperform the broader market by a statistically insignificant spread, noted researchers Allen Atkins and James Sundali in *Applied Economics Letters*.[9] Another study of the picks by University of Massachusetts business professor Bing Liang showed that the picks by the professional investors have been "indistinguishable" from the dartboard picks 90 percent of the time.[10]

The *Journal* was among the first media outlets to survey economic experts about trends such as interest rates, inflation, consumer confidence, and bond yields, giving its readers a forward-looking analysis of future events. University of Alabama professors Robert Brooks and Brian Gray, writing in the *Journal of Portfolio Management*, found that the consensus forecast in the *Journal* for U.S. Treasury bond yields has been wrong nearly two-thirds of the time,[11] showing that there is some question about the usefulness and validity of this form of business journalism.

The *Journal* is considered the top echelon of business journalism throughout the world. It influences and shapes public opinion about industry and economics, and the newspaper's coverage is often followed by other media. No other media outlet writes about business and the economy – and everything that affects these subjects – with its breadth of knowledge.

Dow and Jones

The origins of what would become the most influential business newspaper in journalism began in the late 1870s, when its founders wrote about business for other publications. Charles Dow, for *The Providence Journal*, wrote about steamboats as well as the discovery of silver in Colorado. The silver story, in which Dow traveled with New York financiers across the country, allowed the young reporter to develop valuable sources among New York's bankers and market experts.[12] As a result, he moved to New York in 1880. Edward Jones also worked in Providence, and he met Dow at *The Providence Press*. He followed Dow to New York, and they both began working for the Kiernan News Agency.[13] Along with Charles Bergstresser, another Kiernan reporter, they left the news agency in 1882 and created a news service devoted to financial information.[14] Located in a basement at 15 Wall Street, they produced news bulletins written by hand and delivered them by messengers to subscribers. They were located next door to the New York Stock Exchange – and in the same building as their former employer, now their rival.

A year later, the fledgling news operation expanded by producing the *Customers' Afternoon Letter,* a compilation at the end of the day of information contained in the bulletins. Then, in 1889, Dow and Jones renamed the newspaper *The Wall Street Journal,* taking the name of another publication that had gone out of business.[15] The first issue was on Monday, July 8, and on the front page was a chart showing the average movement of prices in the market with this analysis: "There is some reason for believing that operators identified with the bear party sent early orders to London to depress Americans in that market as a preparation for the opening here."[16] Subscribers paid $5 a year for the paper, or 2 cents for each issue.

For decades, the paper's contents and format rarely differed, a trait that remains today. It included one important piece of information created by Dow and Jones that actually predated the newspaper. In 1884, Dow compiled a list of nine railroad and two industrial stocks (among the companies were Western Union, the Union Pacific, the New York Central, and the Louisville & Nashville railroads) and divided their prices by 11 to produce a stock market average. The average was first published on July 3, 1884.[17] Dow received complaints that the average was not representative of the overall market, so he refined his list, in 1885, 1886, and again in 1894.[18] In 1896, the *Journal* published the first industrial stock average of 12 stocks, including General Electric, American Tobacco, and American Sugar. The list would later be expanded to 20 stocks in 1916 and 30 stocks in 1928.[19] The Dow Jones Industrial Average remains the best known barometer of the market's performance, and today it also includes nonindustrial companies.

Another important contribution by Dow in the early days of the *Journal* was his simplistic explanation of how the market works. In 1899, Dow began writing a front-page column called "Review and Outlook" that assessed market performance. He advocated long-term holding of stocks, writing, "Nobody who plants corn digs up the kernels in a day or two to see if the corn has sprouted, but in stocks most people want to open an account at noon and get their profits before night."[20] The same year, Jones sold

BUSINESS JOURNALISM TIMELINE

1941-1945 – THE U.S. ENTERS WORLD WAR II WITH THE BOMBING OF PEARL HARBOR. THE AMMUNITION AND EQUIPMENT REQUIREMENTS OF THE GOVERNMENT TO FIGHT THE WAR PULL THE ECONOMY OUT OF THE DEPRESSION.

1942 — BUSINESSWEEK DEVELOPS A WEEKLY COLUMN CALLED THE "WAR BUSINESS CHECK-LIST" THAT IS A DIGEST OF NEW FEDERAL RULES AND REGULATIONS AFFECTING BUSINESS.

AUGUST 1942 — FORTUNE MAGAZINE PUTS AN ARTICLE TITLE ON THE COVER FOR THE FIRST TIME.

1945 – BARNEY KILGORE IS NAMED PRESIDENT OF DOW JONES & CO.

his interest in the company. Dow died three years later. The newspaper and the ticker operations were sold to the newspaper's Boston correspondent, Charles Barron, who had a wire service from his hometown.[21]

Barron had begun writing about financial news for the *Boston Evening Transcript,* but when he left the paper after a disagreement, he started a news service that delivered bulletins to businessmen on State Street, the Boston equivalent of Wall Street. Like Dow and Jones, he later expanded his news service to a financial newspaper called *The Boston News Bureau,* which Barron marketed as the "Financial Bible of New England."[22] In 1896, he added a business newspaper in Philadelphia called the *Financial Journal.*[23] When he purchased the *Journal* in 1902, Barron owned the three largest business newspapers in the country. Their operations were combined, and the newspaper's subscriptions grew, from 7,000 to 18,750 in 1920 and to as high as 52,000 in 1928 shortly before his death.[24] Barron also added in every major American city correspondents who regularly sent stories to New York for the newspaper, becoming the first business journalism since the Fugger newsletters in 16th century Europe to understand the importance of delivering information from a wide region to its readers.

At the time, the *Journal* printed morning and afternoon editions, primarily because the evening newspaper went to press before the final stock and bond prices were available. While the newspaper's subscriptions rose, the paper's content generally remained the same, providing readers with the latest from Wall Street and other financial centers. As one of the biggest advocates of the stock market boom of the 1920s, the *Journal* would suffer in the aftermath, losing thousands of subscribers and a large measure of its respect.

Barron died in 1928 before the market crashed. But before, he established *Barron's,* the weekly financial newspaper that provided a broader look at the markets. In an unsigned editorial in the May 9, 1921, issue, Barron wrote that the publication was "working from a new viewpoint, have secured an effective post of vantage, and will consistently supply a novel fulcrum on which the thoughtful investor may plan to get a purchase with this dollar level in a worth-while effort to budge the world of wealth."[25] In addition, the *Journal* started a West Coast edition shortly before the October 1929 market crash. These pieces of the Dow Jones operation would lose money for the next decade, and the company survived from the profits from its news service until new management would return the *Journal* to respectability with reliable coverage of business news.

Still, the formative years of the newspaper showed that news about business and the economy could sustain a daily publication. In addition, Dow Jones and the *Journal* became one of the first journalistic endeavors to quote people such as financier J. P. Morgan directly.[26] Using indices to gauge the performance of the market would become widespread after the Dow Jones index was introduced, with other media starting similar indices. However, none of them would be quite as successful, and today none is more widely quoted than the Dow Jones Industrial Average.

Barney Kilgore changes the paper

In the aftermath of the stock market crash, the *Journal* was left with two large black eyes. The first was from its pro-business and pro-Wall Street approach to news, which downplayed the significance of the October 1929 stock market crash. The second was from the actions of some of its reporters, who had accepted money from investors and others to promote specific stocks. The newspaper needed to rebuild its standing in the business community and in journalism.

Few people burned by the stock market in the 1920s wanted anything to do with the *Journal.* Dow Jones took to filling up the empty space on its ticker – which transmitted news events to subscribers by a machine – with jokes. The newspaper itself introduced a few new features, most notably the "What's News" column on the front page that gave a short synopsis of news from the previous day contained throughout the paper as well as items not in the paper.[27] The short rundown of news proved so successful that it survives today – and showed other newspapers how to attract readers to stories not on the front page.

The newspaper, if it were to survive the lean years after the crash, needed to change its focus. A young journalist named Barney Kilgore handled the task. Kilgore had been hired to work at the *Journal* directly out of DePauw University in 1929, and after a few months in New York was moved to the San Francisco office.[28] He immediately gained a reputation for the thoroughness of his reporting, primarily because he compared what banks reported for profits in press releases to what was reported in their audited statements and noticed some large discrepancies.[29] Kilgore returned to New York after writing the newspaper's first front-page feature story and was assigned to write the story about the newspaper's reporters taking bribes. In 1935, he went to run the Washington bureau, where he developed a popular feature called "The Washington Wire."[30] His fame grew when President Franklin Roosevelt, at a press conference, told other reporters to read Kilgore's stories if they wanted to understand part of his New Deal policies.[31] By 1941, Kilgore was back in New York and running the newspaper as managing editor. Barron's descendants, who had thought about shutting the paper to stem its losses, listened and agreed with Kilgore's radical plan to save the newspaper, whose name still reminded everyone of what had caused the Great Depression.[32]

Kilgore, along with editor Casey Hogate, wanted to make the newspaper the first delivered across the country. To make the newspaper appeal to readers across the United States, Kilgore radically changed the content of the

BUSINESS JOURNALISM TIMELINE

1946 – JOSEPH LIVINGSTON, THEN WITH THE PHILADELPHIA RECORD, BEGINS A SURVEY SUMMARIZING ECONOMIC FORECASTS FROM THE GOVERNMENT, ECONOMISTS, BANKS AND BUSINESSES.

1947 – W.M. KIPLINGER CREATES THE FIRST PERSONAL FINANCE MAGAZINE. IT'S CALLED CHANGING TIMES, THE KIPLINGER MAGAZINE.

1948 – THE WALL STREET JOURNAL STARTS A SOUTHWEST EDITION.

1950 — BUSINESSWEEK PUBLISHES ITS FIRST EXECUTIVE PAY SURVEY.

1951 – THE WALL STREET JOURNAL PURCHASES THE CHICAGO JOURNAL OF COMMERCE, TURNING IT INTO ITS MIDWEST EDITION.

1951 – CBS BEGINS ITS NEWS SHOW SEE IT NOW. IT HANDLES A NUMBER OF BUSINESS TOPICS.

newspaper. It would no longer be "The newspaper for the investor," as its slogan developed in 1903 noted. the *Journal* would be a mainstream newspaper that specialized in news about business and finance but also included news and information that anyone would want. A 1978 Dow Jones executive committee report noted that Kilgore's long-range plan to overhaul the newspaper was the first in the company's history and "was based on the belief that never again in the foreseeable future would the financial industry provide the type of market which would support a first-class daily newspaper."[33]

"Barney would talk of how the *Journal* ought to be – and could be – a national newspaper," said Vermont Royster, who worked with Kilgore in the Washington bureau and became editor in 1958. "Business, he said, and the political affairs that affected it, was the one topic of as vital interest to the reader in Omaha as the reader in New York. Why not give each the same important news each day? It was a fantasy, so most of his colleagues thought."[34] Royster was not all that impressed with the idea.

But Kilgore, who ran Dow Jones after Hogate died in the 1940s, was the first person at the *Journal*, or at any media outlet, to determine that useful news about business, the economy, and investing was important not just for the businessperson and the banker but also for the average person in society. He forced its journalists to focus on writing in a style that could explain arcane topics to nearly everyone in the country, not just those with business expertise. The jargon-heavy content in the newspaper was changed to a writing style that gave the readers more insight into the significance of events and how they would be affected. Said Royster, "In the beginning, we were so specialized that we were specialized only in what you might call a strictly financial, stock-market type of thing. And ironically, what we had to learn was to broaden our specialty and realize that business news actually embraces an enormous spectrum."[35]

the *Journal*'s front page on the day after the Pearl Harbor attack illustrated what Kilgore hoped to achieve with the newspaper. He realized that most readers would already know the details of the Japanese bombing, so the triple-deck headline on the front page focused on how manufacturers would speed up arms production and what effect the attack would have on the stock exchange and trading. One of the front-page stories began with this simple lead: "War with Japan means industrial revolution in the United States."[36] The actual attack was left for the "What's News" column, and took up just 12 paragraphs.

Kilgore understood that the *Journal* was not the only newspaper that most of its subscribers read. So it provided more analysis and delved deeper into a story to continue attracting readers. He broadened the traditional definition of business journalism to include political and sociological trends as well as issues in education and other stories that appealed to consumers. As a result, readers today come to expect widespread business coverage not only in the *Journal* but in other business journalism publications as well.

By the end of the Depression in 1939, the *Journal*'s subscription numbers had begun to rise. Kilgore's revamping of its content led subscriptions to soar. From the 41,000 copies it sold when he took over, the *Journal*'s total subscribers had risen to 1.1 million when Kilgore died in 1967.[37] At that time, the newspaper was printed at eight plants across the country, giving it the ability to reach a much broader audience than any other American newspaper.

Kilgore changed business journalism forever, altering how news about business was reported and written. In addition, when he realized that the newspaper's readership was filled with people with other interests, he added stories about national and world affairs, books, theater, and the arts as well. Peter Kann, publisher of the *Journal*, said that Kilgore "invented modern business journalism and the national newspaper."[38] TJFR Group, which published *The Journalist and Financial Reporter* newsletter, named Kilgore the Business Journalist of the Century in 2000.[39]

Kilgore had lots of help. Royster gave the newspaper a national presence with his editorial writing. In 1953, he won the paper's second Pulitzer Prize, and repeated the feat in 1984. *Time* magazine noted that Royster, following in the path of Kilgore's strategy of appealing to a broad audience, "makes high finance and big business friendly and folksy. He reduces economic intricacies to homilies anyone can understand. He takes the mystery out of Wall Street and makes it seem almost a neighborly kind of place."[40] In a 1963 speech at the University of Wisconsin, Royster summed up the *Journal*'s philosophy of reaching readers this way:

> The business man, for example, needs to know far more about economic trends, about political actions that affect business, about government actions, about things that happen in Europe than did his predecessor a generation ago.[41]

Royster, editor of the newspaper from 1958 to 1971, focused a lot of the *Journal*'s attention in the 1960s on politics and how the social unrest in the country was affecting the economy and business.[42] Along the way, the *Journal* expanded its reach. It started a Southwest edition in 1948 and added a Washington edition in 1955. In 1951, it purchased the Chicago *Journal of Commerce*, turning it into the paper's Midwest edition.[43] In 1962, the *Journal* started *The National Observer*, a weekly newspaper, although it folded in 1977 because of a lack of advertising.[44] In 1966, the newspaper passed the 1-million circulation mark. Kilgore created the national newspaper that he believed would cater to a wider audience. Said Royster, "He looked at the nation and saw it crossed by a single newspaper."[45]

The 800-pound gorilla of business journalism

Kilgore's changes to the *Journal* made the newspaper more respected because of its aggressiveness in business writing. The newspaper continued to be viewed as a conservative, probusiness publication, but it was a business newspaper that didn't hesitate to criticize business when criticism was warranted, or to aggressively seek exclusives without regard for what coverage corporations desired. In 1954, for example, after the *Journal* ran exclusive stories about new models from General Motors, the automaker became upset because its plans had been exposed and withdrew more than $250,000 in advertising.[46] A year earlier, the newspaper had reported the questionable background of the management of a company purchasing a company from Howard Hughes. After the stories ran, the management resigned.[47] As it continued to grow in the 1970s and 1980s, the *Journal*'s clout in journalism and the business world also increased. It began to regularly win Pulitzer Prizes, and its content began to be emulated by other journalists – those who covered business and the economy and many others who didn't.

The *Journal* still aimed to be the complete financial newspaper of record, documenting the ins and outs of Wall Street and the corporate world. But a practice begun by Kilgore and refined throughout the years brought the newspaper a respected place in journalism while giving its readers some of the best writing and reporting. The idea was to place the newspaper's best written story in the middle column of the front page each day, surrounding it with harder news. The story didn't necessarily have to be timely, or about business. But it was typically a unique focus, and it provided a unique look at society.

The story became known as the "A-hed" because of the shape of the headline. The first "A-hed" appeared on Dec. 17, 1941, and it discussed an unforeseen result of the country's entry into World War II – a shortage of American flags.[48] Kilgore created an editing staff for the front page of the *Journal* whose job it was to make everything that the reader saw first that day appealing. Bill Kerby, who had been put in charge of the front page by Kilgore, said his boss called it "our showcase." Kerby wanted sharp, clever writing that enticed the reader into the story. So stories began with lead sentences such as, "Do you like potato juice? You'll learn to love it in the days ahead." The story was about an impending ban on alcoholic beverages with grain due to a World War II shortage.[49]

The A-hed story was flanked by what the newspaper called "leaders." One appeared in the left-hand column of the front page, and the other appeared in the right-hand column. These stories were long, analytical articles about breaking news events of the day, and they included far more analysis and interpretation than what had been seen in other newspapers. A newsletter about business journalism said that these leader articles, if favorable, "can shift investor, Congressional and consumer opinion in your direction. A strongly negative story can literally lead to the collapse of your business and possibly the imprisonment of your top executives. Each has occurred, multiple times."[50]

One thing missing from the the *Journal*'s front page for decades was photographs and color, although many stories included pictures known as "dot-drawings" since 1979. Given that there were few visual appeals to the front page, how it was constructed each day became vitally important to its success.

The A-hed article provided a break between the two hard news stories, although it often dealt with serious issues. Once, the A-hed featured a story about efforts to save a sea otter smeared with oil in the wake of the 1989 *Exxon Valdez* oil spill off the Alaska coast. Another discussed the personal problems that faced Boston Red Sox first baseman Bill Buckner, whose error in the 1986 World Series was blamed for the team losing the sporting event.[51]

Within the newspaper, writing these stories became a prize many reporters cherished, and anyone was allowed to pitch story ideas. In the 1980s, a new reporter in the San Francisco bureau wrote a feature about how it was possible to travel across country for the same cost of one night's stay in an expensive New York hotel.[52] In the 1990s, a reporter in the Atlanta bureau wrote an A-hed about a historian and newsletter publisher who worked out of his basement in the suburbs and had details of virtually every Ferrari ever built. The story subject was often called to testify in court cases and for federal agencies such as the FBI on the value of the exotic cars.[53] The articles have become so famous that they have resulted in at least two anthologies. Ken Wells, a *Journal* writer, called them an icon of contemporary journalism:

> It is treasured by our readers, consistently ranking high in readership surveys...It is the funhouse of *The Wall Street Journal,* over the years attracting many gifted writers who might have otherwise fled the prospects of being turned into "business journalists" except that the paper offered as an incentive a chance to pen A-heds.[54]

The front page of the *Journal* is used for two reasons – to show its readers the best written and best reported stories in the paper and to give them an overview with small, one-sentence nuggets of information. For decades, the front page also included a special report about a specific sector of business. On Tuesday, it was news briefs about labor and workplace. On Wednesdays, tax news was detailed. On Fridays, the Washington Wire started by Kilgore ran.

Combined, these stories and features on the front page of the *Journal* made it what one critic called "the most influential page in American business news."[55] Competing against dozens of other publications on a daily basis, the *Journal* continually brought a perspective and an understanding to the business world and society. The front page of the newspaper has helped build its dominance in the field of business journalism, making the *Journal* the single media outlet that most others now look to when assessing business coverage.

Expansion and competition

As the success of the *Journal* grew in the 1970s and 1980s, however, it gained competition. *Investor's Business Daily* started publishing in 1984, and the *Financial Times,* a London-based business newspaper, began expanding in the United States, adding reporters to write about American business news. In addition, virtually every major metropolitan newspaper in the country expanded its business news staff and the space devoted to business coverage in the late 1970s and early 1980s. Newspapers such as the *Chicago Tribune* saw their subscriptions stagnate or fall when the *Journal* began selling papers in their circulation area, and they fought back with the same formula that made the *Journal* so successful – providing more in-depth business coverage that offered better analysis and understanding. Some of these newspapers succeeded, but many others failed.

Other newspapers such as *The New York Times* and *USA Today* began national editions in the 1980s, chipping away at the *Journal*'s dominance as the only newspaper offered across the country. Its circulation reached a high point of 2.1 million, but then fell to below 2 million by the time the newspaper celebrated its 100th anniversary in 1989.[56] The newspaper took its first major credibility hit since the 1929 stock market crash when one of its writers, R. Foster Winans, was convicted in 1985 of securities fraud for tipping stock traders to what he was writing in the newspaper. It had escaped criticism a decade earlier when star reporter Dan Dorfman, who had appeared on the cover of *Institutional Investor,* resigned from the paper in 1973 after receiving $500 in stock from a source.[57]

Throughout their history, Dow Jones and the *Journal* expanded their presence in business journalism. A one-section publication since its founding, the flagship newspaper expanded to two sections in 1980 and then added a third section in 1988.[58] The second section was called "Marketplace," and the third section was called "Money & Investing." *The Asian Wall Street Journal* started in 1976, and a European edition followed in 1983.[59] It stretched its operations overseas in other ways, joining forces in 1967 with the Associated Press to transmit business and economic news in dozens of countries.[60] The company also acquired a chain of small-town newspapers, a book publisher, and other business interests.[61] *Smart Money,* a personal finance magazine, was started in conjunction with Hearst Corp. And a syndicated television show has run nationally since 1982.[62]

The *Journal*'s business journalism remained strong, although critics note that it was behind competitors on several major stories – and missed several others altogether. Author Francis Dealy points out that the *Journal* missed the major stories that resulted in the savings and loan scandal of the late 1980s as well as the Michael Milken junk bond scandal during the same period.[63] Others criticized the paper for downplaying the excesses of the decade of the 1980s in the business world.[64] And like its reporting on the 1929 stock market crash, the *Journal*'s coverage of the October 1987 drop in the market – the largest single-day drop of the Dow Jones Industrial Average ever – was overshadowed by reporting in *The New York Times.*

Still, the newspaper won eight Pulitzer Prizes in the 1990s, including awards in the explanatory journalism category and the beat reporting category. Its reporting style became even more aggressive in the booming economy of the 1990s, as reporters urged sources to give them exclusive scoops on pending deals and announcements so that they could be prominently displayed in the *Journal* and not in competing media. In some cases, public relations practitioners encouraged their clients to leak breaking news to *Journal* reporters to gauge how investors or other interested parties would react, especially for stories to run in its Monday paper.

Like many other media outlets in the 1990s interested in business coverage, the *Journal* chronicled the rise of the Internet as a business tool and platform and marveled at the dramatic rise in the stock market. Its Web site was one of the first to sell subscriptions, and it has been one of the most successful pay sites on the Internet. Dow Jones expanded its business coverage online as well, in 2004 adding CBS MarketWatch Inc., a competing online business news service, to its business journalism offerings.[65] To further appeal to its business readers as well as mainstream consumers, the newspaper added a fourth section in 1998 called "Weekend Journal" that focused on leisure activities. And in 2002, it redesigned the entire newspaper, adding color and more graphics to the pages. The redesign included an overhaul of the front page for the first time in decades. The redesign has caused concern that the front page is now "too much like other daily publications and diluted the paper's franchise of investigative, behind-the-scenes business writing," wrote *New York Observer* reporter Sridhar Pappu.[66]

The newspaper also created a partnership with cable network CNBC, where its reporters and editors often appear. Some, such as former Moscow bureau chief Steve Liesman, a Pulitzer Prize winner, left the newspaper to become full-time CNBC commentators. And in 2005, the *Journal,* which dropped its Saturday edition in 1953 after the New York Stock Exchange stopped Saturday trading, added a weekend edition to the paper.[67]

These moves were designed to keep Dow Jones at the forefront of business journalism, pushing it into new media and new fields to provide the most comprehensive and fastest coverage of business-related issues, just as its founders had done back in the 1880s.

Despite the expansion into new media and new ventures, the heart of the *Journal* and Dow Jones remains reporting about business and the economy. Its editors, notably managing editor Norman Pearlstine and later managing editor Paul Steiger, broadened the definition of business journalism even further, assigning more investigative stories and encouraging the newspaper's longer stories to be more narrative. Even after the terrorist attacks on the World Trade Center on Sept. 11, 2001, which nearly destroyed the newspaper's main offices, the paper's coverage about the effects of the strikes on the business world won a Pulitzer. A year later, one of its reporters, Daniel Pearl, was kidnapped and murdered in Pakistan while trying to collect information about a terrorist. Pearl's death showed the steps many of the paper's journalists were willing to take to report a story that they thought their readers would want.

Interestingly, its editorial page maintains a strong conservative bent and defended businesses and the Republican Party while the reporters were finding corruption and illegal activities in corporations. One editorial page editor "is well aware that his corporate readers are interested in the things that are good for corporations, and he feels that such things more or less coincide with the national interest," said author Jerry Rosenberg.[68] What set the *Journal*'s editorial page apart from others newspapers was its pro-business stance on virtually every issue. Ben Bagdikian, a former assistant managing editor of the *Washington Post* and later a journalism professor at the University of California at Berkeley, noted that the newspaper's editorials focused on five themes – government regulation of business, spending for social benefits, taxes, any government budget other than defense, and programs that favor "special interest groups" about 80 percent of the time.[69] Sometimes the editorial page's opinions contradict what the journalists have written elsewhere in the paper, causing some conflict, wrote *Salon* senior writer Eric Boehlert.[70]

Those in business and those in journalism still closely watch the *Journal* to see what topics and issues it covers and how it uses its resources. In addition, the *Journal* is providing content for the Sunday business section of many regional newspapers. The newspaper remains at the top of the business journalism profession, and more than any other medium has come to illustrate the country's – and the world's – growing reliance on information about business and the economy. As it expands into new media forms and new coverage areas, the *Journal* is required reading for anyone interested in knowing what is going on in business anywhere in the world.

Footnotes

1 From "The corporate scandals of 2002: causes and effects," a collection of Pulitzer Prize winning articles by The Wall Street Journal staff, 2003, New York: Dow Jones & Co.

2 From Inside the Wall Street Journal: The power and the history of Dow Jones & Co. and America's most influential newspaper, by J. Rosenberg, New York: Macmillan Publishing Co., 1982, p. 201.

3 From Aug. 10, 1982 letter from Dan Rather to Vermont Royster, Southern Historical Collection, University of North Carolina at Chapel Hill.

4 See Vermont Royster papers, Southern Historical Collection, University of North Carolina at Chapel Hill.

5 From April 21, 1978 letter from Richard M. Nixon to Vermont Royster, Southern Historical Collection,

University of North Carolina at Chapel Hill.

6 From "What America's leaders read," by C. H. Weiss, Spring 1974, Public Opinion Quarterly, pp. 1–22.

7 See The Pew Research Center for the people & the press at http://people-press.org/.

8 From "The investment dartboard column," by J. R. Dorfman, Oct. 4, 1988, The Wall Street Journal.

9 From "Portfolio managers versus the darts: Evidence from the Wall Street Journal's dartboard column," by A. B. Atkins and J. A. Sundali, October 1997, Applied Economics Letters, pp. 635–637.

10 From "The dartboard column: The pros, the darts, and the market," by B. Liang, November 1996, http://ssrn.com/abstract=1068.

11 From "History of the forecasters," by R. Brooks and J. B. Gray, Fall 2004, Journal of Portfolio Management, p. 113.

12 From What's News, Dow Jones: Story of the Wall Street Journal, by W. Neilsen and F. Neilsen, Radnor, Pa.: Chilton Book Co., 1973, pp. 30–31.

13 From What's News, Dow Jones: Story of the Wall Street Journal, p. 33.

14 From The Wall Street Journal: The story of Dow Jones and the nation's business newspaper, by L. Wendt, Chicago: Rand McNally & Co., 1982, p. 25.

15 From Worldly power: The making of the Wall Street Journal, by E. E. Scharff, New York: Beaufort Books Publishers, 1986, p. 4.

16 From The Wall Street Journal, July 8, 1889, p. 1.

17 From The Dow Jones averages: 1885–1985, edited by P. S. Pierce, Homewood, Ill.: Dow Jones-Irwin, 1986, p. 1.

18 From The Dow Jones averages: 1885–1985, p. 3.

19 From The Dow Jones averages: 1885–1985, pp. 4–6.

20 From What's News, Dow Jones: Story of the Wall Street Journal, p. 37.

21 From The Power and the money: Inside the Wall Street Journal, by F. X. Dealy Jr., New York: Birch Lane Press, 1993, p. 22.

22 From Worldly power: The making of the Wall Street Journal, p. 14.

23 From Worldly power: The making of the Wall Street Journal, p. 14.

24 From Worldly power: The making of the Wall Street Journal, p. 15.

25 From "Foreward," Barron's, May 9, 1921.

26 From The Wall Street Journal: Purveyor of news to business America, by R. M. Feemster, New York: Newcomen Society in North America, 1954, p. 13.

27 From What's News, Dow Jones: Story of the Wall Street Journal, p. 49.

28 From Inside the Wall Street Journal: The power and the history of Dow Jones & Co. and America's most influential newspaper, by J. Rosenberg, New York: Macmillan Publishing Co., 1982, p. 73.

29 From The Power and the money: Inside the Wall Street Journal, p. 37.

30 From Inside the Wall Street Journal: The power and the history of Dow Jones & Co. and America's most influential newspaper, p. 74.

31 From Inside the Wall Street Journal: The power and the history of Dow Jones & Co. and America's

most influential newspaper, p. 74.

32 From The Power and the money: Inside the Wall Street Journal, p. 43.

33 From "Summary and Executive Committee Recommendation," by W. F. Kerby, Nov. 14, 1978, in the Vermont Royster Papers, Southern Historical Collection, University of North Carolina at Chapel Hill.

34 From remarks on Barney Kilgore, by V. C. Royster, Nov. 18, 1985, Princeton, N.J., in the Vermont Royster Papers, Southern Historical Collection, University of North Carolina at Chapel Hill.

35 From undated 1963 speech at the University of Wisconsin, in the Vermont Royster Papers, Southern Historical Collection, University of North Carolina at Chapel Hill.

36 From "All consumption curbs due to be stiffened; scarcity list will grow," by W. F. Kerby, Dec. 8, 1941, The Wall Street Journal, p. 1.

37 From The Wall Street Journal: The story of Dow Jones and the nation's business newspaper, p. 383.

38 From "Barney Kilgore," by P. R. Kann, Oct. 30, 1999, Editor & Publisher, p. 44.

39 From "Barney Kilgore selected as TJFR/Mastercard International Business Journalist of the Century," March 10, 2000, PR Newswire.

40 From Time, April 30, 1965, p. 73.

41 From undated 1963 speech at the University of Wisconsin, in the Vermont Royster Papers, Southern Historical Collection, University of North Carolina at Chapel Hill.

42 See Inside the Wall Street Journal: The power and the history of Dow Jones & Co. and America's most influential newspaper, pp. 77–78, 91–92.

43 From The Wall Street Journal: The story of Dow Jones and the nation's business newspaper, pp. 319–320, 329–330.

44 From The Power and the money: Inside the Wall Street Journal, pp. 83–84, 89.

45 From remarks on Barney Kilgore, by V. C. Royster, Nov. 18, 1985, Princeton, N.J., in the Vermont Royster Papers, Southern Historical Collection, University of North Carolina at Chapel Hill.

46 From The Wall Street Journal: The story of Dow Jones and the nation's business newspaper, pp. 346–348.

47 From A proud profession: Memoirs of a Wall Street Journal reporter, editor and publisher, by W. F. Kerby, Homewood, Ill.: Dow Jones-Irwin, 1981, p. 152.

48 From Floating off the page: The best stories from the Wall Street Journal's "middle column," edited by K. Wells, New York: Wall Street Journal Books, 2002, p. 1.

49 From A proud profession: Memoirs of a Wall Street Journal reporter, editor and publisher, p. 102.

50 From "The most influential page in American business news features a crew of inspired and talented story doctors," by D. Rotbart, July 1991, TJFR Business News Reporter, p. 1.

51 See "For Bill Buckner, it's life's small joys that offer reprieves," by J. H. Prager, July 24, 1998, The Wall Street Journal, p. 1A.

52 From Floating off the page: The best stories from the Wall Street Journal's "middle column," p. 4.

53 See "Don't ask Mr. Roush how much to pay for that old Ferrari," by E. DeLisser, June 9, 1997, The Wall Street Journal, p. 1A.

54 From "Tell me a story: The A-hed, a legendary editor's invention, is a gift for Journal writers and readers," by K. Wells, downloaded on Jan. 31, 2005 from http://www.wsjbooks.com/page-ahed.htm.

55 From "The most influential page in American business news features a crew of inspired and talented story doctors," p. 1.

56 From "Nation's business newspaper turns 100 at difficult time," by B. Ziegler, June 22, 1989, The Associated Press.

57 From "News hound: Tireless and excitable, Dan Dorfman chases stock-market scoops," by R. Smith, Jan. 18, 1988, The Wall Street Journal, p. A1.

58 From "The ups and downs of the Journal; on Wall Street an American institution celebrates its centennial," by E. Randolph, June 23, 1989, The Washington Post, p. F1.

59 From "The ups and downs of the Journal; on Wall Street an American institution celebrates its centennial," p. F1 and http://www.dowjones.com/TheCompany/History/History.htm.

60 From http://www.dowjones.com/TheCompany/History/History.htm.

61 From http://www.dowjones.com/TheCompany/History/History.htm.

62 From http://www.dowjones.com/TheCompany/History/History.htm.

63 From The Power and the money: Inside the Wall Street Journal, pp. 292–313.

64 From The Power and the money: Inside the Wall Street Journal, pp. 292–293.

65 See "Dow Jones & Company Closes $528 Million MarketWatch Acquisition," Jan. 24, 2005, PR Newswire.

66 From "At the Journal, identity crisis inside page one," by S. Pappu, Feb. 10, 2003, New York Observer, p. 1.

67 See "The Wall Street Journal to begin publishing weekend edition in September 2005," Sept. 15, 2004, PR Newswire.

68 See Inside the Wall Street Journal: The power and the history of Dow Jones & Co. and America's most influential newspaper, p. 202.

69 See Inside the Wall Street Journal: The power and the history of Dow Jones & Co. and America's most influential newspaper, p. 205.

70 For example, see "The Wall Street Journal's smear campaign,' by E. Boehlert, April 6, 2002, downloaded Feb. 1, 2005 from http://www.salon.com/news/feature/2002/04/06/pulitzers/print.html.

Chapter 8

Business journalism on radio and TV

The for-profit Career College Association didn't wait for a report on 60 Minutes before warning its members that the story might cause them problems. In a January 2005 memo to its members, association president Nicholas J. Glakas detailed a strategy to counteract the show that included full-page advertisements in *Roll Call*, a newspaper read by politicians and lobbyists in Washington, D.C., and sample letters to the editor that its members could send to local newspapers.[1]

The show accused for-profit colleges of using aggressive tactics in recruiting students and in being more concerned with profits than in educating students. It also discussed state and federal investigations into the industry and how some colleges were pushing students to apply for federal student aid to increase their revenue.

The power of electronic media – radio and television – to influence what the public thinks about business and industry is incredible, probably more so than any other medium because of its use of pictures, which visualize an issue for watchers. And throughout the latter part of the 20th century and into this century, television has been a major player in the field of business journalism, producing segments, shows, and even entire cable networks around news concerning industry, the economy, Wall Street, and other business issues. Even some local television stations have played a major role in business journalism. For example, a television station in Texas is credited with being the first media outlet to delve into the problem of Firestone tires coming apart on Ford vehicles.[2]

Despite the successes, some monumental failures in business coverage occurred on television. Jim Michaels, the editor of *Forbes* magazine from 1961 to 1998, criticized CNNfn and CNBC for their stock market coverage, calling it "frivolous and shallow." He added, "They're both doing the very antithesis of what the intelligent investor needs. They should be more challenging of business and not spew out the kind of crap they do."[3] *Washington Post* media critic Howard Kurtz criticized television's business coverage, primarily coverage of Wall Street and investing, in the late 1990s for being primarily positive and rarely warning the public watching that investing was risky and that many of the stocks being promoted on TV shows had no financial strength to back up their lofty stock price. "Some professionals voice concerns that cable financial news has contributed to a hyping of stock movements, at once feeding off and fanning a national frenzy of instant riches," added *Los Angeles Times'* writer Josh Getlin.[4] Yale economist Robert Shiller noted that television and Internet coverage of the markets ignored the realities of investing.[5]

A study by professors Bruce Plopper and Anne Conaway showed that some TV shows devoted to stock recommendations gave an overly positive representation of Wall Street at a time when the market underperformed.[6] However, a study of analyst recommendations on the show *Wall Street Week* showed that the stock suggestions of panelists on the show "do exhibit above-average performance beyond the first day following the program day."[7]

Television magazine shows, which have aggressively covered unscrupulous businesses in the past 30 years, turned out some embarrassing mistakes along the way. Sometimes these mistakes tarred the entire business journalism profession, and often gave business ammunition to fend off legitimate accusations. Among the large companies that have emerged from TV exposes with the upper hand against the reporting have been Philip Morris, General Motors, and Illinois Power.

Even on nightly network news, studies have shown that "bad news about business outweighed neutral and positive news. Stories about strikes, environmental threats, health hazards, product recalls, industrial accidents and illegal financial dealings accounted for almost 60% of the coverage devoted to business," suggesting that television business journalism exaggerates the flaws of business and industry while minimizing accomplishments.[8] The auto industry also receives more coverage than any other industry on network news shows.

In the early 21st century, as the market fell back, the number of viewers watching business-related news on television also fell, although ratings for cable television business networks and shows rose temporarily after the Enron scandal broke and became a major story in 2002.[9] Financial news, a lucrative segment of television because it brought in advertising from stockbroker firms, was cut on some networks, and entire shows were canceled. In 2004, the network CNNfn left the air.

The rise of business journalism on television in the 1980s and 1990s, however, forced other media to pay more attention to business and economic issues. In addition, television business news borrowed many of its best ideas and people from other media with a reputation of strong business coverage. Myron Kandel, who became a fixture on CNN covering business and the markets in the 1980s and 1990s, was a former newspaper financial editor with a well-deserved reputation for understanding industry-related issues. And many TV news magazine programs used segments on their shows to give viewers a profile of a company, similar to what the business magazines, particularly *Fortune*, had been doing since the 1930s.

On the negative side, television coverage of business has often been superficial. Journalism expert Kent MacDougall noted that the "twin tyrannies of time and pictures condemn many important but nonvisual business stories to TV oblivion." He also noted that television condenses complex business stories to where few understand their meaning, whereas other television coverage of business and the economy uses props to gain reader attention without actually helping the story.[10]

Coverage of business and industry on television also meant that companies and issues that may have previously slipped through the cracks and escaped the attention of business reporters in the print media were now being noticed. The additional coverage due to the rise of TV business journalism also meant that consumers had a variety of options from where to receive information about industry and the economy. Combined with the rise of Internet coverage of business, television's increased interest in business journalism meant that the field became more prominent overall in the media.

Radio has also had a similar influence on business journalism. As people turned to radios to receive information more immediately than newspapers and magazines, radio stations and networks provided coverage of business and economic issues. Many of the same networks, such as CBS, that provided television coverage also offered radio stations stories about business. By the 1980s and 1990s, radio shows such as National Public Radio's Midday Business Report and Public Radio International's Marketplace were heard around the country.[11]

Marketplace was the best known. It went on the air in January 1989, and it was the creation of executive producer Jim Russell, who had been approached in 1988 to listen to and critique American Public Radio's Business Update show. Russell developed an idea for a business radio show that brought public radio's sophisticated approach to news to business and targeted the show to a broad public radio audience, not business executives. The name was chosen over others that used the word *business* to try to attract listeners who weren't interested in a business news show. The strategy proved correct.

Bloomberg Financial Markets, which began offering a computer-based news service to Wall Street clients and media outlets in the late 1980s and early 1990s, added Bloomberg News Radio to its services.

Edward R. Murrow and business

In 1948, CBS became the first network to begin a nightly news show with its 15-minute *CBS TV News* airing five nights a week.[12] In the early years of broadcasts on television, many of the networks took to airing congressional hearings and other newsworthy events live. In 1951, CBS began the first magazine format news show with *See it Now.* Its primary host was Edward R. Murrow, already a well-respected journalist based on his coverage of World War II from London. A year later, NBC began its

BUSINESS JOURNALISM TIMELINE

OCTOBER 1953 — FORTUNE RUNS A 12-PAGE SPECIAL SECTION CALLED "THE COLORADO STORY" THAT IS THE FIRST TO COMBINE TEXT WITH ADVERTISING.

APRIL 17, 1954 — BROWNIE WISE, THE WOMAN WHO REVOLUTIONIZED THE TUPPERWARE PARTY, WAS THE FIRST WOMAN ON THE COVER OF BUSINESSWEEK.

1954 – BERTIE FORBES DIES. HIS SONS CONTINUE TO RUN THE MAGAZINE.

1954 – THE WALL STREET JOURNAL RUNS PHOTOS OF GENERAL MOTORS CARS THAT HAVE YET TO BE INTRODUCED TO THE PUBLIC. GM WITHDRAWS ITS ADVERTISING AND REFUSES TO SPEAK TO NEWSPAPER FOR A MONTH.

1955 – FORTUNE PUBLISHES ITS LIST OF THE TOP 500 INDUSTRIAL COMPANIES FOR THE FIRST TIME. GENERAL MOTORS TOPS THE FIRST LIST.

1957 – LOEB AWARDS CREATED TO HONOR BUSINESS JOURNALISM'S BEST.

Today morning news show.

Although Murrow is more famous for his coverage of World War II from London and his television shows in the early 1950s exposing the Communist baiting of Wisconsin Sen. Edward McCarthy, a review of his program content showed that Murrow, the first great television journalist, also spent a considerable amount of time concerned with business and economic issues.

Murrow was born in Greensboro, N.C., in 1908, but his parents moved across country to Washington, and Murrow graduated from Washington State University in 1930. After a few years working in other jobs, Murrow joined CBS in 1935 and was sent to Europe to report on foreign news. Most of his work for the next ten years focused on the impending war and then coverage of World War II. He began many of his radio reports with the trademark slogan, "This is London."[13]

While in England, however, Murrow also saw the importance of business. Upon returning to New York in September 1945 after the end of the war, Murrow remarked on the difference between the American economy and the European economy, noting, "The advertisements for new radios, cars, refrigerators, furniture, clothes, travel, frank – everything – speak a loud language of confidence."[14]

The 1950s were a time of economic expansion in the United States, and the media portrayed business as the driving force. Between 1950 and 1960, the gross national product of the country expanded 67 percent to $500 billion. The composition of the workforce also changed, with white-collar workers outnumbering blue-collar workers for the first time in 1956. It was in these economic conditions that the mainstream media began to once again pay attention to crucial business issues, and although Murrow spent a lot of time in the early part of the decade reporting for radio and television on the Korean War and McCarthyism, his reporting also set the tone in business.

Murrow reported the news. In September 1947, he told his radio audience that his network would "assist the listener in weighing and judging developments throughout the world, but refrains particularly with respect to all controversial political, social and economic questions from trying to make up the listener's mind."[15] In Murrow's mind, giving consumers news about the economy was on an equal plane with political and social issues. Two days later, he discussed providing economic aid to other countries, noting that "there are many who predict our economic collapse and not a few who hope for it."[16]

Murrow also frequently criticized the media on his broadcasts. After President Harry Truman's re-election in 1948, an event that surprised many in the media who had predicted a victory for Thomas Dewey, Murrow believed that the changing business climate was one of the reasons for miscalculating the election results. "Ours is a highly mechanized country," he said. "Our clothes are largely standardized; we tell pretty much the same stories, use the well-advertised goods of mass production. Much of our information is mass-produced, superimposed upon the country by syndicated columns written in New York or Washington, or by broadcasts originating in those two cities."[17]

On June 19, 1950, Murrow discussed the American economy on his radio show, quoting experts who believed that the rest of the year would see an expanding business world. Just before he went on the air, he penciled in "if nothing unexpected happens."[18] A week later, North Korea invaded South Korea. The war would take up much of Murrow's time in the next three years, but he still found business topics interesting. For example, his April 3, 1951, broadcast discussed attempts by the Federal Trade Commission to eliminate exaggeration from advertising by businesses such as the maker of Carter's Little Liver Pills.[19] On the last day of the same year, Murrow lamented the demise of the penny postcard, which he called "a victim of inflation" because the price was going up to 2 cents so that the U.S. Postal Service could raise $120 million.[20]

By April 1952, Murrow was flying over flooding in the Midwest and detailing the economic devastation. "There are trucks that were delivering fur coats and fancy dresses only last week," he reported. "They're now delivering sandbags. A delivery wagon with the name of a sewing machine firm painted on its side opens its doors and dispenses hot coffee."[21] He also followed the precedent set by Lincoln Steffens nearly a half-century earlier when discussing politics, noting in his Sept. 23, 1952, reporting on vice presidential candidate Richard Nixon that a group of California businessmen had created a fund for the politician to pay his expenses.[22] When he revisited Berlin in September 1953, he noted the difference in the city in business terms. "Now the shops are full of goods," he stated. "People are wearing better clothes and better shoes. One or two streets blaze with lights at night. The ballet and the opera are flourishing."[23]

Even the mundane business story sometimes drew Murrow's interest. In February 1954, he noted that the Senate Agriculture Committee had voted to regulate the coffee exchange.[24] In May 1954, when reporting on desegregation, Murrow speculated that one of the big issues for integration would be finance – the difference in spending per student depending on race. "It is this economic problem that accounts for much of the vociferousness of the southern outcry," said Murrow.[25] And when an October 1954 comment by Defense Secretary Charles Wilson – that fewer men being drafted would increase unemployment in the country – was criticized by union leaders, Murrow noted the significance of the issue. "He wasn't comparing auto workers to dogs," said Murrow. "But his phraseology, the smile notwithstanding, will bring no aid and comfort to Republican candidates where the labor vote is heavy."[26]

In 1954, Murrow showed his objectivity when it came

BUSINESS JOURNALISM TIMELINE

1960 – CBS AIRS HARVEST OF SHAME, A SHOW FROM EDWARD R. MURROW THAT DESCRIBED THE WORKING CONDITIONS OF MIGRANT LABORERS.

NOVEMBER 1960 – SYLVIA PORTER APPEARS ON THE COVER OF TIME MAGAZINE. SHE IS THE ONLY BUSINESS JOURNALIST EVER TO APPEAR ON THE COVER OF A MAJOR U.S. MAGAZINE.

1962 – RACHEL CARSON PUBLISHES SILENT SPRING, WHICH EXPOSES THE CHEMICAL INDUSTRY FOR PESTICIDES THAT HARM ANIMALS.

MAY 1963 — FORTUNE LAUNCHES JAPANESE EDITION CALLED PRESIDENT, AIMED AT AN ELITE AUDIENCE OF APPROXIMATELY 15,000 TOP EXECUTIVES.

1963 – JESSICA MITFORD PUBLISHES THE AMERICAN WAY OF DEATH, WHICH CRITICIZES THE FUNERAL INDUSTRY.

to reporting about his show's sponsors. ALCOA dropped its sponsorship after a program about a small newspaper's story of a land scandal in Texas where the company was expanding its operations.[27]

By 1957, Murrow returned to the issue of the Post Office, comparing its productivity to mail systems in Japan and Europe, and noting that the delivery of mail in the United States was much slower than elsewhere.[28] And in October 1957, after the Soviet Union launched a satellite that orbited the earth, Murrow noted the decline in engineering and scientific expertise coming from American companies.[29]

But Murrow's strongest reporting on business and industry came in 1960 with the report called "Harvest of Shame" that appeared on *CBS Reports*. The show, which aired nationally on Thanksgiving, showed the country the poor working conditions of migrant laborers and led to calls for legislation to improve how they were treated by employers.[30] The documentary would be Murrow's last. In 1961, he left journalism to work for President John F. Kennedy, and he died in 1965 from lung cancer.

But Murrow's lasting influence is felt in all of journalism, not just business journalism. He attacked stories with a vengeance and reported them with neutrality, letting the facts speak for themselves. He set the tone for radio and broadcast news coverage at its infancy. And his reporting showed how stories about politics, society, and business were all intertwined.

That understanding of the significance of business and economics would later spread to nightly television news in the 1970s.

Irving R. Levine and the economy

Like Murrow, another great business journalist in the field of television got his start in the field by covering stories overseas. Irving R. Levine's first job in journalism was for a Providence, R. I., newspaper, but by 1950, he was in Vienna reporting European stories for the International News Service. When the Korean War broke out, he volunteered to cover it, and while there began sending stories to NBC News. The network hired him full time in 1952 and sent him back to Europe. In 1955, he became the first network reporter accredited by the Soviet Union. Levine later worked as a foreign correspondent in Tokyo, Rome, and London, and by 1971, wanted to cover the State Department. But the executives at NBC News asked him to cover economics and business instead. Levine shuddered. "It was a barren time," he said. "Producers just weren't interested in those stories."[31]

Still, Levine was the first network correspondent to cover economics full time, and he reported on issues such as the recession, taxation, tariffs, and money that affected everyone. Although they were often dense topics, Levine explained them to his audience in a way that they could understand. Noted former television news producer and Syracuse University professor Robert Lissit, "He's often called to enlighten a television audience that has a limited background in such subjects. He's grabbed so much air time over the years that a CBS News president once said all NBC had for correspondents was a bunch of guys named Irving."[32]

Balding and wearing a bow tie, Levine made covering economics an essential part of broadcast TV. The 1970s was a period of inflation and stagnant business growth as well as rising unemployment. The stock market fell in the early part of the decade. Because of inflation, consumers began purchasing more products, which pushed up prices even further because of the demand. The first gas shortages arrived, leading to long lines at the pump. As a result, Levine was on the news virtually every night, explaining these issues and how they influenced the amount of money viewers had in their wallets or pocketbooks.

Levine first had trouble getting economic stories on NBC Nightly News. "I told him if he could make me understand them, the viewer would too," said Christie Basham, the show's Washington producer in 1971. "And he did. He taught me economics."[33]

Levine's break came when President Richard Nixon instituted price and wage controls on Aug. 15, 1971. When the oil embargo raised gasoline prices, Levine often began leading the evening news show. He followed five presidents to economic summit meetings around the globe and reported on their significance to American viewers, and he accompanied a delegation from the U.S. Treasury Department to China to cover trade talks.

Levine was in the right place at the right time. Before the early 1970s, stories about the economy were not often considered important enough to be included on television news shows. But what Levine did was take the issues and explain them in a way that even the uneducated viewer could understand. Levine became a workaholic in covering stories about the economy. When CNBC began airing, Levine contributed a weekly commentary piece. He also provided reports for the *Today* show and *News at Sunrise*.[34] As a result, other networks hired correspondents to cover the economy as well.

After Levine retired from NBC in 1995, he continued to maintain a presence in business journalism, delivering a commentary on *Nightly Business Report*, a show that aired in Miami, near where Levine had become dean of the College of International Communications at Lynn University.[35]

Louis Rukeyser and Wall Street Week

While Levine was making economics reporting a presence on the network news shows, another development in television business journalism was beginning.

Louis Rukeyser's journalism career began in the 1950s, and he spent more than a decade at the *Baltimore Sun* as a political and foreign correspondent. He left the newspaper for a job at ABC News, where he began covering business and economics stories in 1968, before Levine began his stint covering the same beat at NBC. Rukeyser had developed a number of economic specials for ABC, but found that network executives weren't as interested in his coverage as other correspondents. "The trouble with most television executives and producers is they think the economy is too dull and too complicated to do on TV," Rukeyser said after he left the network. "And that happens to be nonsense."[36] Two years later, he began a show on the Public Broadcasting System called *Wall Street Week*. By 1973, the show had become so popular that Rukeyser left ABC to devote his full-time attention to it. The show became a fixture on PBS channels around the country.

Every Friday night, *Wall Street Week* was taped at Maryland Public Television, with Rukeyser and a group of investment professionals talking about the market, individual stocks, the economy, and other business-related matters that concerned Wall Street. Rukeyser became known for his puns and his dry wit, and the show attracted millions of watchers. What was so interesting was how Rukeyser structured the show to cater to the average viewer. "The prevailing view is that the subject of economics is too dull and/or too complicated to hold an audience larger than the capacity of your average phone booth," he said. "I think that's nonsense. I think there is a hunger in the American public for clear, believable, understandable, usable pocketbook information."[37]

Initially, the show ran for 30 weeks, but expanded to 35 weeks in 1972 and became a year-round program in 1973.[38] Each week, Rukeyser and three investment experts discussed whatever had happened during the previous week. Rukeyser would provide the review, and then the panelists would offer some commentary. Viewer questions were answered. When responding to a question from a viewer about whether to invest in a hairpiece manufacturer, Rukeyser responded, "If all your money seems to be hair today and gone tomorrow, we'll try to make it grow by giving you the bald facts on how to get your investments toupee."[39]

The host prided himself on representing the views of his viewers, not those of his guests. In 1989, one of his panelists, Robert Nurock, who had been on the show for 19 years, quit because he claimed Rukeyser wouldn't let him freely speak about the market.[40] Rukeyser expanded the reach of the show, launching an investment newsletter based on the show and information provided by the host. The move upset Maryland Public Television, which felt that the host was unfairly exploiting the popularity of the show.[41] Some of Rukeyser's best known guests, including Peter Lynch of Fidelity Investments and John Templeton of Templeton Funds, endorsed the newsletter, but some money managers said the publication provided only basic information. There were other embarrassments to the show. One of its regular guests, money manager Alan Bond, was indicted in 1999 on taking kickbacks from brokers who received investments from his clients.[42] Enron was once a sponsor of the show as well. And in 2001, the *Columbia Journalism Review* criticized Rukeyser's practice of using analysts promoting specific stocks without disclosing that the analyst's firm had a banking relationship with the company.[43]

Still, Rukeyser dispensed valuable advice on his show. On the *Wall Street Week* after the October 1987 market crash, he brought a dose of reality to the situation by stating, "It's just your money, not your life. Everybody who really loved you a week ago still loves you tonight. And that's a heck of a lot more important than the numbers on a brokerage statement."[44] After the terrorist-hijacked planes struck the World Trade Center in September 2001, Rukeyser told his viewers that what had been attacked was "the very symbol of the economic revolution that has dramatically raised living standards on every continent."[45] His other famous sayings included, "Don't get mad, get rich" and "There's nothing like a bull market to bring out the crooks and a bear market to start catching them."[46] Rukeyser also wasn't afraid to criticize his panelists. In 1997, he said professional investors "excel and lead the world" in one area: "They're world champions at panicking and hysterical overreactions."[47]

Rukeyser's popularity extended beyond the television show and his newsletters. He held financial seminars on cruise ships and in Las Vegas. He spoke to groups across the country. In 2002, when Maryland Public Television dropped Rukeyser for a similar show with *Fortune* magazine, he quickly moved his show to CNBC, where he remained for two years before retiring. The *Fortune* show was canceled in 2005. Throughout the history of Rukeyser's show, it was the most watched business program on television.[48] The quality of his business journalism was recognized when he received a Loeb Award, becoming the first broadcaster ever to receive the honor.

Rukeyser brought a simple understanding of Wall Street and investing into millions of homes every week, giving viewers the confidence that they knew as much about buying and selling stocks as the professionals who received millions to do the same for clients. He made investing seem easy, and he deciphered complicated terms and strategies. More important, his 30-minute show spawned other shows about business and the economy on other networks, and it demonstrated the demand for business journalism on television that led to the creation of entire business news networks.

60 Minutes goes after business

At the same time that Rukeyser began reporting on the economy for ABC News, a new magazine show premiered on CBS. Today, *60 Minutes* is widely considered to be the top news program on television. And throughout much of the show's history, it has used stories involving companies, industry, the economy, labor, and other business-related topics to attract viewers.

60 Minutes had its origins in Murrow's old television show *See it Now.* Its producer, Don Hewitt, had also been the producer for the network's original 15-minute news segment every night, so the stories on the show were developed with definite news angles. The show, which aired for the first time in September 1968, covered numerous stories and issues, including many that delved deeply into businesses. In short time, companies and executives began to fear receiving a call from *60 Minutes.* Many began denying requests to be interviewed by the show.[49] Hewitt reacted by stating, "Business wants reported only what fits the carefully tailored profile that Madison Avenue and public relations people have put together."[50]

Not all the stories about business and businesspeople were critical. In the first year, the show profiled billionaire oilman H. L. Hunt in a laudatory, rags-to-riches profile.[51] More recently, Leslie Stahl reported a positive piece on GE CEO Jack Welch for the program. But many of the shows broke new ground in business journalism. In 1978, *60 Minutes* cooperated with the *Chicago Sun-Times* to set up a bar to catch government officials taking bribes.[52] The same year, the show ran a story on the Pinto that questioned the safety of the Ford Motor Co. vehicle.[53] The Pinto story ran despite Ford's being a sponsor of the show, and it continued the tradition of the business press aggressively covering the auto industry. Later that year, the show also ran an exposé on service stations making unneeded repairs. In 1979, the show ran a segment on a California chemical plant that was contaminating water in the area.[54]

One of the show's most famous pieces of business journalism occurred in 1979, when it ran a 16-minute segment on the construction of a nuclear power plant by Illinois Power. The Sunday night show accused the company of millions of dollars in excessive costs that would likely be passed on to consumers. Harry Reasoner began the show by explaining the situation like this:

> Take Illinois Power, for example, which wants its customers to help pay for a nuclear power plant whose costs have gone up three times since the original estimates. If the customers don't pony up, the company's financial

rating, their ability to sell bonds and meet their customers' energy needs, is in trouble.[55]

The next day, the company's stock fell in the busiest trading day of its history. Illinois Power replied quickly to the story, however, producing a 44-minute videotape that served as a rebuttal to the show. The company sent it to customers, shareholders and investors, corporate executives, and other journalists. It was a point-by-point reply to all the assertions made on the show. In January 1980, CBS admitted to inaccuracies in the story. One error was that the rate increase to consumers was attributed to the nuclear plant when the increase was only partly due to the plant's cost. And the other was that the Illinois Commerce Commission had denied the rate increase when it had actually been approved before the show aired. But *60 Minutes* stood by the rest of the story.[56]

And *60 Minutes* never stopped examining businesses, unscrupulous employees, and other problems in industry and exposing them to unsuspecting consumers. In 1980, a segment discussed the rising number of workers who were paid in cash never reported to the Internal Revenue Service, while another piece delved into the silver business and how Nelson Bunker Hunt was cornering the market.[57] The same year, it profiled the head of the Federal Trade Commission after businesses complained it was being heavy-handed with its regulations.[58] In 1989, the show ran an exposé on Freedom Financial Corp., a time-share resort company that offered outlandish gifts such as cars and money to get people to visit its locations.[59] The next year, it documented how used car dealers were rolling back the odometers on vehicles to increase their price.[60]

Even in recent years, the show has aggressively pursued the top business stories, interviewing former ImClone CEO Sam Waksal, for example, about Martha Stewart's alleged insider trading and problems at the company. *60 Minutes* also landed an interview with disgraced HealthSouth CEO Richard Scrushy. In the mid-1990s, the show was in the forefront of criticizing the tobacco industry and finding records that showed it knew that cigarettes were harmful.

60 Minutes contributed to business journalism by showing that investigative reporting about business and companies could be done in any medium. And it awoke many in the print media, which had primarily been silent in criticizing industry in the 1950s and 1960s, that there were important stories to be covered that were being ignored. In addition, the show spawned a number of similar shows on television that also began to aggressively pursue business stories as part of their regular segments. Among them were ABC's *20/20* and NBC's *Prime Time Live.* Many of these shows copied the *60 Minutes* format, and some of them may have gone too far when it came to reporting on business and industry. These transgressions would later taint business journalism on television.

Business news and ABC, CBS, and NBC

The news magazine shows on the networks were not the only coverage that companies and industry received on television. The nightly newscasts also devoted time to major business news stories, particularly after correspondents such as Levine and Rukeyser showed the value in reporting major business events. In a study published in 1989, however, a researcher showed that networks skewed their reporting on economics issues, giving more coverage to bad economic news in nonelection years and that comments by the president or a presidential candidate can influence the amount of coverage given to economic news in an election year.[61]

However, much of the business journalism on television that caught the attention of society occurred on other magazine shows. With the success of *60 Minutes*, many of these shows began attacking business. And many businesses reacted by attacking back.

In particular, television magazine show segments about companies as varied as supermarket chain Food Lion, cigarette maker Philip Morris, automaker General Motors, and others drew attention to the often questioned reporting tactics used by journalists to present companies in an unfair manner. While a majority of the business journalism coverage produced by the major networks was likely impartial, these episodes brought business reporting on TV into a bad light.

These companies were not the only ones that faced the glaring lights of television. Kaiser Aluminum was the focus of a *20/20* episode that alleged the company marketed unsafe house wiring. It responded by running newspaper ads in 1980 criticizing its "trial by television."[62] Exxon, Shell, and other companies complained about coverage they received, and a panel ruled that the coverage was "the product of unknowledgeable journalists who lack the qualifications to deal with the extraordinarily complex subject of energy."[63] Charter Medical, which ran a chain of mental hospitals, attempted to stop a *60 Minutes* segment about its operations by filing a lawsuit before it ran.[64]

The reaction by business against these shows led to increased tension between industry and the media. And while many complaints alleging unfair coverage were later determined to be unfounded, business journalism was perceived by many in the public as being biased against corporations.

...while many complaints alleging unfair coverage were later determined to be unfounded, business journalism was perceived by many in the public as being biased against corporations.

One of these highly publicized television stories about business occurred in November 1992, when NBC ran a segment called "Waiting to Explode" on its popular *Dateline* show about how certain General Motors' trucks were more likely to explode when struck from the side.[65] The show had taped staged accidents to support its claims, but the accidents did not result in fires that destroyed the trucks, as had happened in several actual accidents. The show went ahead and aired the footage, but a month later apologized to GM when threatened with a lawsuit. In addition, it was disclosed that the crash testers hired by the network to perform the accidents had placed incendiary devices under the trucks to promote a fire.[66]

At nearly the same time as the GM story, competitor ABC ran a story on its *Prime Time Live* show about North Carolina–based grocery chain Food Lion, accusing it of selling old and tainted meat to customers. The show used undercover reporters who were hired by Food Lion locations to work in the stores, and taped footage inside the stores without the company's permission. One of the producers wrote the following on her application: "I love meat wrapping. I have heard Food Lion is a great company. I would like to make a career with the company."[67]

The company launched a massive public relations campaign to counter the story, charging that the show selectively used footage that supported its preconceived angle and not footage that portrayed Food Lion positively. The company also sued ABC, but not for libel. It claimed fraud and business deception, noting that the producers had obtained jobs under false pretenses. Food Lion's stock price dropped 50 percent, and its sales fell after the segment aired. Although a judge initially awarded Food Lion $315,000 in damages, the award was later reduced to $2. However, the courts ruled that the reporters acted illegally.[68]

Two years after the GM debacle on *Dateline* and the Food Lion story on *Prime Time Live*, the ABC News program *Day One* ran an investigative story called "Smoke Screen" about how Philip Morris manipulated the nicotine in its cigarettes. The main reporter on the story was Walt Bogdanich, a former *Wall Street Journal* reporter who had won a Pulitzer Prize for investigating medical clinics. Two weeks later, Philip Morris sued ABC for libel, asking for $10 billion in damages.[69] In 1995, the network settled the case by apologizing on the air to the cigarette company. But a year later, ABC aggressively reported on the industry again, with Peter Jennings on the nightly news airing a segment called "Never Say Die – How the Cigarette Companies Keep on Winning."[70]

Although the *Day One* story was tarnished, few questioned the reporting. In fact, later stories and evidence proved the reporting correct. The end result, however, was a loss of credibility for this type of reporting, which included anonymous sources.

Overall, the television networks have done a good job of reporting about business, though their work has not been as measured as other types of media, notably newspapers and magazines. But what remains in the public's perception of how TV approaches business journalism is the cases where it was later determined that their tactics and approaches to a story were unfair. And by using such strategies, all investigative business journalism on TV during the time came under question. The success of the companies in fighting back made it harder for many journalists in any form of media to report and write investigative pieces about business and industry without being accused of being unfair and receiving threats of lawsuits. Many of the network magazine shows remain today, and they still often produce segments critical of businesses and executives. And even today, these stories can have a tremendous impact on consumers and society. In North Carolina, there remain people who refuse to shop at Food Lion, more than a decade after the story ran.

CNBC, CNNfn, and cable coverage

The business coverage by the networks on their nightly news shows and on special magazine shows demonstrated the rising interest in news and information about the subject. In the late 1970s and early 1980s, another part of the television industry – the cable networks – would take business journalism to new heights. What cable television did was create entire shows, and then later entire networks, devoted to business news. Unlike Rukeyser's *Wall Street Week*, these shows focused on the news events of the day, and later often broke news stories before their print counterparts.

The first cable business news show was *Nightly Business Report*, which began airing in 1979 on public television stations around the country. Produced at WPBT in Miami, *Nightly Business Report* covered business news as the networks covered politics, government agencies, sports, and other beats. Its broadcast typically started with the main business news developments of the day and then followed up later with features and interviews. Another segment recapped the market activity of the day in stocks, bonds, and commodities. Two years after it started, *NBR* was on 125 stations, and by 1999, it was carried on more than 272 stations in the United States and others across the world.[71]

The show was the idea of business executives on WPBT's board, which approached news director Linda O'Bryon about starting a business news show. Said O'Bryon: "Business news on television was not a subject that was thought of. It was not visual. It was not the type of subject that attracted a large audience – but we felt it was important."[72] They saw the success of Rukeyser's show and decided to expand the content to general business news. Initially, the program was 15 minutes long, but it later expanded to 30 minutes. What also set it apart was the lack of advertising.

Almost immediately, *Nightly Business Report* had competition. In 1980, Cable News Network began airing a show called *Moneyline* that featured host Lou Dobbs. And later in the 1980s, two networks – Financial News Network and NBC's Consumer News and Business Channel, later shortened to CNBC – debuted with a primary focus on reporting about business, the economy, and Wall Street.[73] In the 1990s, wire service Bloomberg added television programming to its media operations, obtaining time on the USA Network, and CNN launched CNNfn, putting Dobbs in charge of the operation.

As the first cable network devoted to news, CNN regularly gave space to business stories. But Dobbs also had his own show, and it regularly featured corporate executives, economists, and Wall Street investors. The show was later expanded into an hour-long broadcast, and Dobbs was the main voice covering major business news stories in the 1980s, such as the 1987 crash and the savings and loan crisis. Financial News Network, which had broadcast seven hours a day, was bought out by CNBC in 1991. For most of the 1990s, CNBC and CNN, which launched CNNfn in 1995, competed against each other daily to land scoops on business news and CEO interviews. Bloomberg News, a wire service, also added a cable television network in the 1990s to compete against these channels, offering a unique multiscreen format. *Washington Post* media writer Howard Kurtz, who wrote about the onslaught of television coverage of business news in the 1990s in *The Fortune Tellers*, likened the competition between the cable networks and the print media for business coverage as spotlighting "many of the same relentlessly optimistic traders and analysts who have been telling investors to buy, buy, buy stocks."[74]

The cable networks overwhelmed the local stations as well. In 1999, for example, few Chicago stations were bothering to report on the market and investing.[75] Indeed, the cable television business networks covered the booming stock market of the 1990s as if it were a sporting event, noting the meteoric rise of stock indexes with much fanfare. Celebrities were created, as Dobbs became one of the most recognized anchors on CNN, and CNBC's Maria Bartiromo, who often broadcast from the floor of the New York Stock Exchange in the 1990s, became known as the "Money Honey." Others on the show had nicknames as well, such as "The Brain" and "The Kahuna." CNBC's slogan was "Profit from it," the implication being that consumers could get rich by watching its programming.[76] And the mere mention of a CEO of a publicly traded company appearing on the network would send its stock upward – even before the executive appeared on the air.[77]

After Dobbs left CNN in 1999, CNBC expanded its competing show *Business Center* and signed Bartiromo to a five-year contract.[78] At the end of the 20th century, the future of business journalism on television couldn't have looked any brighter. The Dow Jones Industrial

Average had gone from 3,000 to above 11,000 in the decade, and every network had begun to be infatuated with business news, particularly news about how the stock market was making people rich.

Like the 1929 crash, which few media had predicted or correctly analyzed its impact, the drop in the market in the first few years of the 21st century hurt the credibility of business reporting. Particularly hurt were the cable networks, which came across as being boosters for higher stock prices. When stocks were mentioned in the show, a graphic showing how the stock had performed recently was typically added to the screen for viewers to assess. Even radio got into the act, as National Public Radio began a regular business show that included investment advice.

Viewership dropped for the business networks and shows in the wake of the stock market drop in 2000 and 2001, although it spiked when CNBC reporter David Faber broke the WorldCom fraud case in 2000. By the middle of 2002, CNBC's average audience was 25 percent lower than the previous year.[79] Many of the shows also toned down their pro-business approach, although Dobbs, who had rejoined CNN in 2001, criticized federal regulators for indicting accounting firm Arthur Andersen.[80] By 2004, when CNN shut down CNNfn, CNBC was left to compete with increasing business news on Fox News Network, the other networks, Bloomberg TV, and the *Nightly Business Report.*

What the cable networks learned in the 1990s was that they had sensationalized reporting and writing about investing and the markets. With stocks falling in the early part of the 21st century, viewers turned to other networks and other shows. Now, CNBC and other business journalism shows on television are attempting to recoup their audience by toning down their Wall Street coverage and providing a more balanced view of the business and economic world. Some of the shows, such as *Moneyline,* provided a more balanced view of industry, although Dobbs's credibility was questioned because of his comments about companies sending employees overseas and his defense of accounting firm Arthur Andersen. As *The Economist* assessed the situation in late 2004, it noted:

> A network devoted to business news is about business, in fact, during the 1990s when its popularity was peaking, business news was really about getting rich. Watching share prices crumble was less fun, and being misled by bulls was more costly than being misled by bears. Day traders have largely been wiped out. The reality of business – a tough, often tedious slog – and of investing may not be compelling enough for television.[81]

That is the challenge that business journalism on television faces as it enters an unknown stage of the business cycle and in investing. Can it recoup its lost viewers by offering more sedate programming? And is that really what its viewers want? Whatever the future holds for business journalism on television, the field has one major accomplishment: It has made CEOs look more comfortable while being interviewed in front of a camera.

Footnotes

1 From "For-profit colleges respond, in advance, to forthcoming '60 Minutes' report," by G. Blumenstyk, Jan. 27, 2005, The Chronicle of Higher Education, downloaded Jan. 28, 2005 at http://chronicle.com/temp/email.php?id=v49ssq3p610ltwz8324596gsmx250nbv.

2 From "The tire flap: behind the feeding frenzy," by S. Crock, with N. St. Pieree, Oct. 16, 2000, BusinessWeek, p. 126.

3 From "An old hand says TV's business journalism falls short," by D. Dorfman, Oct. 4, 2002, The New York Sun, p. 9.

4 From "Stocks: TV's newest sport," by J. Getlin, April 19, 2000, Los Angeles Times, p. A1.

5 See Irrational exuberance, second edition, by R. Shiller, Princeton, N.J.: Princeton University Press, 2005.

6 From "From Wall Street to Main Street: An analysis of stock market recommendations on TV business news programs," by B. L. Plopper and A. F. Conaway, 2001, a paper presented at the 2001 Association for Education in Journalism and Mass Communication national convention, Mass Communication and Society division.

7 From "Wall Street Week: Information or entertainment," by E. J. Ferreira and S. D. Smith, January/February 2003, Financial Analysts Journal, pp. 45–53.

8 From "Business coverage in network newscasts," by J. R. Dominick, Summer 1981, Journalism Quarterly, p. 185.

9 From "Enron scandal gives a boost to TV's business journalists," by G. Garvin, Feb. 15, 2002, The Miami Herald.

10 From Ninety seconds to tell it all: Big business and the news media, by A. K. MacDougall, Homewood, Ill.: Dow Jones-Irwin, 1981, pp. 47–48.

11 From "Radio finds news is strictly business," by E. A. Rathburn, July 21, 1997, Broadcasting and Cable, pp. 44–45.

12 From 60 Minutes: 25 years of television's finest hour, by F. Coffey, Los Angeles: General Publishing Group Inc., 1993, p. 19.

13 From In search of light: The broadcasts of Edward R. Murrow, 1938–1961, edited by E. Bliss Jr., New York: Alfred A. Knopf, 1967, p. 7.

14 From In search of light: The broadcasts of Edward R. Murrow, 1938–1961, p. 106.

15 From In search of light: The broadcasts of Edward R. Murrow, 1938–1961, p. 114.

16 From In search of light: The broadcasts of Edward R. Murrow, 1938–1961, p. 117.

17 From In search of light: The broadcasts of Edward R. Murrow, 1938–1961, pp. 138–139.

18 From In search of light: The broadcasts of Edward R. Murrow, 1938–1961, p. 161.

19 From In search of light: The broadcasts of Edward R. Murrow, 1938–1961, pp. 182–183.

20 From In search of light: The broadcasts of Edward R. Murrow, 1938–1961, pp. 205–205.

21 From In search of light: The broadcasts of Edward R. Murrow, 1938–1961, p. 211.

22 From In search of light: The broadcasts of Edward R. Murrow, 1938–1961, pp. 224–225.

23 From In search of light: The broadcasts of Edward R. Murrow, 1938–1961, p. 241.

24 From In search of light: The broadcasts of Edward R. Murrow, 1938–1961, p. 244.

25 From In search of light: The broadcasts of Edward R. Murrow, 1938–1961, p. 252.

26 From In search of light: The broadcasts of Edward R. Murrow, 1938–1961, pp. 274–275.

27 From Edward R. Murrow and the birth of broadcast journalism, by B. Edwards, Hoboken, N.J.: John Wiley & Sons, 2004, p. 126, and from Edward R. Murrow, an American original, by J. E. Persico, New York: McGraw-Hill Publishing Co., 1988, pp. 406–407.

28 From In search of light: The broadcasts of Edward R. Murrow, 1938–1961, pp. 305–306.

29 From In search of light: The broadcasts of Edward R. Murrow, 1938–1961, pp. 310–311.

30 From Edward R. Murrow and the birth of broadcast journalism, pp. 141–143, and from Edward R. Murrow, an American original, pp. 460–462.

31 From "As a beat, business is booming," by M. Landler, July 9, 1995, New York Times, p. 27.

32 From "Not just another pretty face," by R. Lissitt, July/August 1994, American Journalism Review, pp. 44–47.

33 From "Not just another pretty face," pp. 44–47.

34 From "Not just another pretty face," pp. 44–47.

35 From "The last of the scholar-journalists," by J. Martin, Nov. 1, 1995, Providence Journal-Bulletin, p. 1H.

36 From "TV talk: Louis Rukeyser and 'Wall Street Week,'" by T. Jory, May 8, 1978, Associated Press.

37 From "Wall Street's 'sex symbol' celebrates 20 years on PBS," by A. Dominguez, Nov. 11, 1990, Associated Press.

38 From "TV talk: Louis Rukeyser and 'Wall Street Week.'"

39 From "Wall Street's 'sex symbol' celebrates 20 years on PBS," by A. Dominguez, Nov. 11, 1990, Associated Press.

40 From "Rukeyser racks up TV ratings, detractors; Little guy's hero has stepped on big toes," by S. Antilla, Nov. 13, 1989, USA Today, p. 7B.

41 From "Rukeyser starts investment newsletter; left out of profit picture, Maryland Public Television reported angry," by B. D. Fromson, May 29, 1992, Washington Post, p. F1.

42 From "Money manager indicted," Dec. 17, 1999, Orlando Sentinel, p. B1.

43 From "Darts and laurels," March/April 2001, Columbia Journalism Review, p. 14.

44 From "Life and career of Louis Rukeyser," C. Mack, Dec. 31, 2004, Louis Rukeyser's Wall Street transcript.

45 From "Life and career of Louis Rukeyser."

46 From "Life and career of Louis Rukeyser."

47 From "Rukeyser finally gives his opinion," Nov. 23, 1997, Bloomberg News.

48 From "National Press Club luncheon with Louis Rukeyser," Oct. 20, 1995, a transcript from the Federal News Service.

49 From "Business strikes back against the press," by A. P. Sanoff, Oct. 26, 1981, U.S. News & World Report, p. 57.

50 From "Business strikes back against the press," p. 57.

51 From 60 Minutes: 25 years of television's finest hour, p. 43.

52 From 60 Minutes: 25 years of television's finest hour, p. 90.

53 From 60 Minutes: 25 years of television's finest hour, p. 91.

54 From 60 Minutes: 25 years of television's finest hour, p. 107.

55 From Punch, counterpunch: 60 Minutes vs. Illinois Power Company, Washington, DC: The Media Institute, 1981, p. 11.

56 From Punch, counterpunch: 60 Minutes vs. Illinois Power Company, pp. 28–29.

57 From 60 Minutes verbatim: Who said wait to whom, the complete text of 114 stories with Mike Wallace, Morley Safer, Dan Rather, Harry Reasoner and Andy Rooney, New York: Arno Press, 1980, p. 251 and pp. 445–450.

58 From 60 Minutes verbatim: Who said wait to whom, the complete text of 114 stories with Mike Wallace, Morley Safer, Dan Rather, Harry Reasoner and Andy Rooney, p. 308.

59 From 60 Minutes: 25 years of television's finest hour, p. 160.

60 From 60 Minutes: 25 years of television's finest hour, p. 166.

61 From "Economic news on television: The determinants of coverage," by D. E. Harrington, Spring 1989, Public Opinion Quarterly, pp. 17–40.

62 From "The business campaign against 'trial by TV,'" July 2, 1980, BusinessWeek, p. 77.

63 From "The business campaign against 'trial by TV,'" p. 77.

64 From "Charter asks court to stop CBS probe," by T. Steadman, April 21, 1999, Greensboro News & Record, p. A5.

65 From "Does TV News Go Too Far? A Look Behind the Scenes At NBC's Truck Crash Test," by B. Weiser, Feb. 28, 1993, Washington Post, p. A1.

66 From "G.M. resumes its advertising on NBC News," by B. Carter, Feb. 12, 1993, New York Times, p. A14.

67 From "The lion's share," by M. Gunther, March 1997, American Journalism Review, p. 18.

68 From "The lion's share," p. 18.

69 From "ABC, Philip Morris and the infamous apology," by S. Weinberg, November/December 1995, Columbia Journalism Review, pp. 29–37.

70 From "Peter Jennings explores tobacco tactics in 'Never say die,'" by F. Moore, June 26, 1996, Associated Press.

71 From "20 years and counting: Nightly Business Report, a pioneer program two decades ago, rights to retain viewers," by T. Stieghorst, Oct. 17, 1999, Fort Lauderdale Sun-Sentinel, p. 1G.

72 From "TV pioneer honored for distinguished achievement," by G. DeGeorge, April/Mary 2004, The Business Journalist, pp. 1–2.

73 From "20 years and counting: Nightly Business Report, a pioneer program two decades ago, rights to retain viewers," p. 1G, and from "Turner launches into business news and crowded field," by S. Hofmeister, Dec. 30, 1995, Los Angeles Times, p. D1.

74 From "On CNBC, boosters for the boom," by H. Kurtz, Nov. 12, 2002, The Washington Post, p. A1.

75 From "The local business broadcasting paradox: More investors, less reporting," by J. Kirk, June 13,

1999, Chicago Tribune, p. C2.

76 From "On CNBC, boosters for the boom," p. A1.

77 From "On CNBC, boosters for the boom," p. A1.

78 From "The business of covering business," by D. Bauder, June 22, 1999, Austin American-Statesman, p. C1.

79 From "CNBC struggles even as financial news abounds," by J. Rutenberg, July 29, 2002, The New York Times, p. C1.

80 From "Business typhoon Dobbs blows for middle class," by G. Sherman, Aug. 16, 2004, New York Observer, p. 11.

81 From "Bad business: business on television," Nov. 6, 2004, The Economist, p. 74.

Chapter 9

Business journalism begins to prosper

As the new medium of television began examining business and the economy, other media also began to focus more of their attention on companies and the economy and how they affected people. While magazines such as *Fortune, Forbes,* and *BusinessWeek* continued to cater to executives and managers at businesses, the daily newspaper filled a void and gave average consumers more news and information about Corporate America in the aftermath of World War II.

The 1950s was a time of prosperity for the U.S. economy, and much of the coverage reflected the good times. Few, if any, publications covered business with a critical eye or worked to uncover wrongdoing. Relationships between newspaper business desks and companies were often cozy.

Nevertheless, beginning in the 1950s, newspapers would allocate more space to business and economics stories, showing that they realized the growing importance of this information on their readers.

Many in the business journalism field today believe that the greatest boom time for coverage occurred in the 1980s and 1990s, as explosive growth in the stock market and in corporate profits led to many metropolitan newspapers creating separate business news sections for the first time and adding hundreds of reporters and editors in the field. However, business journalism also saw tremendous growth in the 1950s, 1960s, and 1970s as periods of greater prosperity followed by economic worries such as inflation and international imports made people more aware of business issues. Between 1955 and 1965, the gross national product nearly doubled to $670 billion, and the number of stockholders increased to more than 20 million, more than double the 8.6 million shareholders that existed a decade earlier.[1] On a percentage basis, the number of households owning stock grew from 4 percent in 1950 to 15 percent in 1970.

Strong growth occurred in business journalism throughout the period as well. Between 1952 and 1967, space allocated to business and financial information in a sampling of 17 newspapers increased by 76 percent, and the total number of pages increased 46 percent, according to an American Newspaper Publishers Association study.[2] The newspapers included the *Seattle Times, Charlotte Observer, The* (Raleigh) *News & Observer, Dallas News,* and *Des Moines Register.* The features added by these newspapers included an advice to investors' column and a local business column. Data, such as mutual fund asset values, were also added.[3]

During the same period, a survey of 162 daily newspaper business and financial editors noted that 81 percent estimated that readership demand for business news had "increased substantially" since 1960.[4] At newspapers with circulation between 15,000 and 100,000, a third of the editors felt that readership had more than doubled. The top three demands by readers were for more local business news, stock market news, and news about government economic policy decisions. The survey also showed that employees devoted to business news, as a percentage of total employees in the newsroom, was highest among papers with circulation below 15,000.[5]

Boosting business journalism's credibility at the time was the creation of the Loeb Awards in 1957 by Gerald Loeb, a highly successful financier and founding partner of E.F. Hutton who made it his mission to educate individuals about finance, investments, and economics. The awards recognized journalists who made significant contributions to the public understanding of business and financial issues. Since 1973, the awards have been administered by the UCLA Graduate School of Management and have become one of the most prestigious awards in journalism.

It was also at this time that business journalists formed their first national organization. The Society of American Business Editors and Writers was created in 1964. An earlier organization had existed for business journalists in New York.

ONE OF THE NEWSPAPERS MAKING MAJOR EFFORTS to improve business coverage in the 1960s was *The Washington Post,* which hired Hobart Rowen from *Newsweek* in 1966 to beef up its business reporting. Rowen started covering business at the *Journal of Commerce* in 1938 and moved in 1944 to *Newsweek,* where he wrote a page called "Business Trends" and later started a syndicated economics column. While deputy managing editor of finance from 1966 to 1975, he increased the *Post's* business desk from 4 to 30 members and boosted its coverage from 3 columns a day to more than 20 columns.[6]

Another newspaper pushing to improve business coverage in the 1960s was the *Los Angeles Times.* In 1968, it hired John Lawrence from *The Wall Street Journal* to be its financial editor. He separated the business section from the sports section, making the newspaper one of the first with a standalone business section, and Lawrence also pushed business stories for the newspaper's front page. One of Lawrence's early hires was Paul Steiger, who later became managing editor of *The Wall Street Journal.*[7]

Another paper that dramatically improved its business coverage in the 1960s was the *New York Herald Tribune.* Financial editor Myron Kandel believed that "the public interest was substantially affected by the activities of private commerce, which ought not to be exempt from the inquiring eyes of the press." Among the reporters he brought in was Dan Dorfman, whose investigative reporting would become well known in business journalism for the next 30 years. One of the major pushes that Kandel made in the paper's business coverage was to obtain an opposite side to the story from competitors, former employees, stock traders, analysts, and other sources.[8]

In 1976, another study of business and financial editors showed that more than two-thirds believed that popular business news had "increased substantially" and nearly 20 percent thought it had "more than doubled."[9] The editors also noted a sharp increase in investigative business reporting. More than 22 percent said they had increased their coverage of the stock market substantially, while more than half said they had increased local business coverage.

Still, the survey noted that managing editors at newspapers "fail to appreciate that business news can be as significant as that of politics and crime."[10] And business journalists suffered through ethical issues. One newspaper in Iowa, the survey found, was unwilling to report on the negative aspects of the city's largest employer because of the publisher's personal connections, while a newspaper business editor in Ohio felt as if "no business had been exposed here in my memory in the last 25 years" because of the publisher's influence.[11] Other editors reported that their business news staffs had been enlisted to write copy for the advertising department.

As space, reporters, and editors devoted to business journalism increased, so did criticism of the sometimes shallow coverage. In 1973, *Columbia Journalism Review* published a piece called "The bleak wasteland of financial journalism" by noted business journalist Chris Welles in which he noted that media have largely ignored the "pervasive influence of business" because of a "chronic blindness of journalism to the realities of business and finance – a collective self-deception that corporate power is either largely benign or not all that extensive anyway, that except for a few unfortunate miscreants businessmen have the public interest at heart."[12] How quickly, it seems, had the business journalism community forgotten about Rockefeller and the Ludlow mining massacre. Welles noted that *The Wall Street Journal* was the only "truly independent watchdog the business world has," while *BusinessWeek* "tends to be much blander and acquiescent," and *Fortune* "almost never presents a viewpoint that might unduly disturb the sleep of its readership."[13] Welles would later become a senior editor at *BusinessWeek* and helped train dozens of business journalists.

Other media also weighed in to criticize business coverage. *Time* excoriated economic news coverage in 1975, noting that the "business press is generally reluctant to question the basic assumptions under which government

BUSINESS JOURNALISM TIMELINE

SEPTEMBER 1963 — FORTUNE HAS ITS FIRST COVER TO FEATURE A PERSON — GM'S ALFRED P. SLOAN.

1964 – SOCIETY OF AMERICAN BUSINESS EDITORS AND WRITERS IS FOUNDED.

1965 – RALPH NADER PUBLISHES "UNSAFE AT ANY SPEED." THE BOOK CRITICIZES THE AUTO INDUSTRY FOR FAILING TO MAKE CARS SAFER TO DRIVE.

1965 – JOSEPH LIVINGSTON WINS PULITZER PRIZE FOR REPORTING ON EASTERN EUROPEAN ECONOMIES.

1966 – WASHINGTON POST HIRES HOBART ROWEN FROM NEWSWEEK TO IMPROVE ITS BUSINESS AND ECONOMICS COVERAGE.

1967 – DOW JONES LEADER BARNEY KILGORE DIES.

1967 — FORTUNE ESTABLISHES ITS FIRST OVERSEAS OFFICE IN BRUSSELS.

and private economists work."[14] A year later, the same magazine ran a story whose title – "The failings of business and journalism" – conveyed its belief that most journalists were unfamiliar with how corporations operated.[15] And in 1974, *Editor & Publisher* argued that "many business and financial writers don't understand what they are writing about and have the feeling readers and the business community don't care."[16] In 1975, *Columbia Journalism Review* questioned whether the media were making the country's economic malaise worse with their reporting. "Journalists tend to regard any upward or downward movement of these [economic] figures as good or bad news, but this can be misleading, particularly when the focus is on predicting the course of the economy," stated its article.[17]

The best known critique of the lack of improvement in coverage with the growth of business journalism in the 1960s and 1970s came in an opinion piece in *The New York Times* by Donald S. MacNaughton, chairman of the Prudential Insurance Co., who criticized business coverage – and how the corporate world responded. "Here we are, business and the news media, like two strange dogs, circling each other warily, suspicious of each other's intentions," he wrote.[18]

Although some in business criticized business journalism at the time because of its apparent anti-business sentiment, such feelings were not pervasive, according to studies. A 1984 study found that the general public was split about whether the news media were biased for or against business. The same study found that business editors had a positive opinion about capitalism – a more favorable opinion than the general public.[19] "Much of what businessmen perceive as bias involves nothing more than a conscientious reporter trying to deal with some large and sensitive issues," said a *Fortune* writer in a 1974 article titled, "Must business fight the press?"[20]

In addition, a 1980 study on the quality of business journalism found it had improved. It concluded that "daily newspapers are making a greater effort to interpret and explain business news and provide guidance and assistance for their readers. The larger newspapers, in particular, are devoting more space to interpretive and investigative stories."[21] The study also found that most newspaper business sections were ethical and did not accept anything of value from sources that might affect their reporting.

However, a 1978 study of business and economics coverage in Pennsylvania newspapers discovered that many editors were dissatisfied with their coverage, primarily because of the middling competence of their staffs and lack of interest. Half of the editors said that they were not covering business stories that should receive media attention.[22]

Despite the criticism, business journalism had taken a big step forward in the 1960s and 1970s and began to distance itself from the chummy relationships it had with many of the corporations it covered.

From the back sheet to the front page

By the late 1970s and early 1980s, some major changes in the field pushed business journalism forward even more. In 1978, under the direction of business editor John Lee, *The New York Times* started a standalone section called "Business Day" and beefed up its Sunday business section.[23] The move by one of the nation's most well-respected newspapers started a business journalism arms race in which virtually every major newspaper would add a business section. *The Wall Street Journal* devoted a front-page story to how the media were devoting more space and staff to covering business. Among the papers following the lead of the *Times* were *The Washington Post, The Los Angeles Times, Chicago Tribune, Philadelphia Inquirer,* and *Atlanta Constitution.* The *Tribune* expanded its staff from 8 to 22, while the *Fort Worth Star-Telegram* doubled its business reporting staff to 12.[24] At the *Miami Herald* in 1980, Larry Birger created the Business Monday section – a tabloid that offered coverage of local and regional companies and management trends – that became a staple of metropolitan newspapers in the next 20 years.[25]

Others followed with developments that shaped business journalism. *Fortune* changed from a monthly to a biweekly publication. *BusinessWeek* became the biggest seller of advertising for any magazine, allowing it to run more content. *Time* and *Newsweek* added space for business stories – and began putting business stories on the cover more regularly. When CEO Ross Johnson led a management buyout of RJR Nabisco, he graced the cover of *Time* as a symbol of corporate greed.[26] *The Financial Times* in London added a weekly publication in the United States, and *The Economist* began to boost its U.S. readership.[27] Many publications added business coverage because of an increase in advertising from corporations. But the economy of the 1970s was also forcing consumers to pay more attention to issues that affected their wallets and pocketbooks.

Other issues were also spurring better – and more – business coverage. In the 1970s, for example, Southern newspapers such as *The* (Raleigh) *News & Observer* and *Charlotte Observer* focused on how working conditions in textile mills made employees sick, bringing a health issue to their readers in terms of economic impact.[28] Growing debate about regulatory control of certain industries such as airlines in the 1970s also fueled coverage.

During the 1970s and early 1980s, another type of business newspaper began to emerge. Entrepreneurs started weekly business papers in major metropolitan areas. By the end of the 1980s, every major newspaper's business section was competing against a weekly that focused solely on business news. In the magazine field, business-related publications also proliferated. In 1988, more than 350 magazines were devoted to business and industry topics.

BUSINESS JOURNALISM TIMELINE

1968 – REUTERS EXPANDS ITS BUSINESS NEWS SERVICE INTO UNITED STATES.

1968 — CAROL LOOMIS BECOMES THE FIRST FEMALE WRITER TO BE ELECTED TO THE FORTUNE BOARD OF DIRECTORS.

SEPTEMBER 1968 – CBS BEGINS RUNNING 60 MINUTES. THE NEWS MAGAZINE SHOW WILL BE AN AGGRESSIVE REPORTER OF CORPORATE WRONGDOING.

1969 – BUSINESSWEEK ADDS A REGULAR SECTION TO THE MAGAZINE CALLED INFORMATION PROCESSING.

1970 – LOUIS RUKEYSER BEGINS A WEEKLY TELEVISION SHOW ON PBS CALLED WALL STREET WEEK.

1971 – IRVING R. LEVINE BEGINS TO COVER ECONOMICS AND BUSINESS FOR NBC NEWS.

By 2001, the number had nearly doubled to 682 – and 27 new business magazines were introduced in 1998 alone.[29] Reuters, Dow Jones, and the Associated Press, which had long dominated coverage of business and economic stories from a wire service perspective, received a new competitor in 1990 with the creation of Bloomberg News. This growing competition also spurred more coverage.

At newspapers, where more resources were poured into business stories in the 1980s and 1990s because of the different options consumers had in receiving news, a few trends emerged that further shaped business journalism. One was the push to provide what was called "consumer" stories that ran the gamut from discussing family budgets to investing in stocks and bonds. The economy was also written about with more regularity, and thankfully, somewhat more clarity. Reporters began to dig deeper into underlying trends affecting a business such as competition and the effectiveness of advertising and marketing. And business coverage also began to look more closely at how industry was affected by outside sources such as government regulation.

RACHEL CARSON

Despite these advances in business journalism and the field's past accomplishments in affecting society and informing people, business journalism could still improve and provide better coverage.

Following consumer spending

How wisely consumers spent their money became a topic that business journalists covered with increasing regularity in the 1960s and 1970s. This push toward more consumer-oriented reporting was in part spurred by the growing popularity of Sylvia Porter and *Consumer Reports*, but also by economic factors. With price controls, the Arab oil embargo, and inflation in the 1970s, the need for families to budget how their money was spent became an important issue for many households.

Another factor that spurred consumer reporting in the 1960s and 1970s was one man – Ralph Nader – who regularly attacked big business in the name of the average person. His organizations, such as Public Citizen and the Public Interest Research Groups, regularly issued reports lambasting companies.

There were a few muckraker-type exposés that made headlines in the early 1960s that boosted consumer-type reporting. Author and scientist Rachel Carson attacked the chemical industry in 1962 with the release of her book *Silent Spring*, which documented the effects of pesticides on birds and other wildlife. In it, she wrote:

> A strange blight crept over the area and everything began to change. Some evil spell had settled on the community: mysterious maladies swept the flocks of chickens; the cattle and sheep sickened and died. Everywhere was a shadow of death. The farmers spoke of much illness among their families. In the town, the doctors had become more and more puzzled by new kinds of sickness appearing among their patients. There had been several sudden and unexplained deaths, not only among adults but even among children, who would be stricken suddenly while at play and die within a few hours.[30]

Although she was attacked by the chemical companies, much as Upton Sinclair was attached by the meatpackers nearly 60 years earlier, her claims were supported by President Kennedy's Science Advisory Committee.[31] Carson's writing led to the creation of aggressive environmental reporting, which some media outlets have lumped into business reporting, and led consumers to question what chemicals were being used in the food they were eating. It also spurred the formation of the Environmental Protection Agency.

By the 1970s and 1980s, newspapers across the country were using stories about the environment to ask pointed questions of companies. The *Los Angeles Times, Charlotte Observer,* and *Louisville Courier-Journal* were among the papers paying close attention to how companies were polluting the environment and how it affected consumers. The reaction they received was to be expected. Companies "reacted defensively to even the most thoroughly researched and evenly balanced accounts, while holding the news media generally guilty of exaggerating environmental dangers," said journalism expert Kent MacDougall.[32]

Carson was followed a year later by another author, Jessica Mitford, who published *The American Way of Death,* a stinging critique of the funeral industry that became popular because the industry tried to stop people from reading it. The book became a *New York Times* bestseller by exposing the high costs of funerals and burials. Again, a muckraker forced regulatory changes as the Federal Trade Commission enacted standards for the funeral industry.[33] A revised edition of the book was published in 1998, two years after Mitford's death.

Unfortunately, much of the consumer reporting during this period lacked the punch and attention of earlier reporting. The issue with many of the early attempts at this type of reporting was the fact that it involved understanding statistics about economic factors, and many journalists became writers to avoid having to work with numbers. Offering stories and advice on how to better spend money became a dicey proposition for many business journalists since they had to rely many times on experts to crunch the numbers – or make sense of them. Sometimes, the conclusions seemed rudimentary. A 1974 report by the *Los Angeles Times* looked into changes of mid-

Business Journalism Timeline

1971 – Forbes begins publishing list of highest-paid executives.

1972 – Time Inc. starts Money magazine to complement Fortune.

1975 – Philadelphia Inquirer wins Pulitzer Prize for explaining how federal tax laws are applied unequally.

1975 — BusinessWeek devotes a cover story to the corporate woman. A year later, the magazine receives a National Magazine Award for Public Service for the story.

1976 – Asian Wall Street Journal begins publishing. A European edition follows in 1983.

1976 – Des Moines Register wins Pulitzer Prize for uncovering abuses in the grain export trade business.

1978 – New York Times begins standalone business section.

dle-class American budgets. They concluded that higher taxes caused families to cut back on spending, a conclusion that an eighth grader might be able to make. But they also reached the more profound conclusion that consumers had developed some expensive habits, such as relying on professionals more and more.[34] For example, the average cost of treating a sore throat had risen to $43.50 due to the cost of a doctor's visit and lab fees. Fifteen years earlier, a family would have simply given the sick person some aspirin and told him to stay in bed.

Other issues developed with consumer reporting. An insert into as many as 80 newspapers in the mid-1970s, *Common Cents,* promised to provide readers with stories that would help them with their everyday purchases while not upsetting advertisers.[35] It avoided naming product brands and did not test products in a laboratory. Instead, it published articles that gave basic advice. One article on purchasing U.S. savings bonds, for example, ignored the fact that these bonds offered lower interest rates than other investment opportunities and that the interest rate was less than the current rate of inflation. Indeed, the publication relied heavily on material provided by the government and by trade associations in its editorial content. The stories were also provided to a newspaper's advertising department in advance so that it could sell ads for the section. A *Columbia Journalism Review* critique of *Common Cents* noted that it was "blurring the line between editorial and advertorial even further."[36] The insert died out after several years.

At newspapers, consumer reporting turned to writing more about scams and ripoffs and providing more solid advice on topics such as taxes and investments. After she died, Sylvia Porter was replaced by Kathy Kristof, whose column ran in papers across the country via the Los Angeles Times Syndicate. Many newspapers hired consumer reporters to handle local stories.

For example, Gene Tharpe at the *Atlanta Journal-Constitution* wrote a regular feature called "Helpline." Readers were encouraged to write to Tharpe and receive help for their problems. A Jan. 21, 1991, column was typical. In it, Tharpe looked into issues ranging from a delayed tax refund to a watch ordered by mail that never arrived, and a magazine subscription cancellation.[37] Before agreeing to help readers, Tharpe asked that they send copies of documents related to their issue and give an address and daytime phone number. In 2000, the *Cleveland Plain Dealer* started a similar column when it hired consumer writer Sheryl Harris.[38]

This coverage, however, was also inadequate in some cases. *Washington Post* ombudsman Richard Harwood complained in 1989 that the "'new' consumer news involving ripoffs, commercial fraud, product safety and the like has tended to fall between the cracks. We haven't known how to handle it or where to put it in the newspaper. A radical idea would be to look at it as 'news.'"[39] Former *Post* reporter Morton Mintz agreed, noting two years later that "*Post* management has been content with weak or nonexistent coverage of automobile safety issues, while publishing every Saturday an evaluation of whichever new car the auto-industry reporter has test-driven."[40]

In addition, many newspapers added consumer reporting about personal finance issues such as saving for college, saving for retirement, balancing a checkbook, and investing in stocks and bonds. While this type of coverage provided a valuable service, some argued that it alienated traditional business section readers. "While going after the home economist and the do-it-yourself investor, newspapers, with few exceptions, appear to have ceded serious reporting on local and regional business to the scores of business weeklies that have cropped up," claimed *Editor & Publisher* in 1996.[41]

Still, by the 1990s, consumer reporting had become a mainstay of business journalism, helping publications such as newspapers that previously catered to executives and managers to cross over and provide stories about money that regular readers also wanted.

Increased attention to how consumers should spend their money – and how they should avoid being taken by unscrupulous businesses – occurred at the same time that economic coverage became more important.

The economy

Coverage of the economy and economic statistics has been a staple of business journalism for nearly 100 years. The New York Fed began holding weekly news conferences in 1915 on banking and financial data. In the 1960s, the event was dubbed "the oldest periodic press conference in the banking and financial world, and one of the most successful."[42] It was where business journalists who covered banking and the financial industries could get answers to their questions from central bankers on the record. The press conference ended in 2000, done in by the Internet and other technological advances.

During the 1950s and 1960s, most business news consumers were used to slow and steady economic growth. The coverage of economic trends and policies was also staid. Although many economists wrote columns for top newspapers and magazines, their stories about the economy had little meaning to the average reader. It wasn't until later, noted *The American Economic Review*, that reporters and economists "discovered that they not only enjoy each others' company but may even serve a public interest, a loose form of adult education."[43]

As inflation, price controls, oil shortages, and other economic-related issues took their toll in the 1970s, economics journalism grew in importance. What was happening in the economy, how the U.S. government was reacting, and what the average reader needed to do to prepare for the changing economic times became a major story.

Although television reporters such as Irving R. Levine and Louis Rukeyser helped explain economic data, the print media struggled in the early 1970s. For example,

BUSINESS JOURNALISM TIMELINE

1978 – INC. BEGINS PUBLISHING LIST OF 100 FASTEST-GROWING PUBLICLY TRADED COMPANIES.

1978 – FORTUNE CHANGES ITS PUBLISHING SCHEDULE TO BI-WEEKLY FROM MONTHLY.

1979 – NIGHTLY BUSINESS REPORT BEGINS AIRING ON PUBLIC TELEVISION STATIONS ACROSS THE COUNTRY.

1980 – WALL STREET JOURNAL EXPANDS TO TWO SECTIONS.

1980 – CNN BEGINS AIRING A SHOW CALLED MONEYLINE FEATURING LOU DOBBS.

1980 – LOU BIRGER AT THE MIAMI HERALD CREATES THE MONDAY TABLOID BUSINESS SECTION.

when the commerce department released data about the Gross National Product in 1978, it was covered in widely different ways by some of the country's most prestigious newspapers. *The New York Times* noted that corporate profits rose 26 percent, while the *Washington Post*'s headline claimed an increase of 44 percent. *The Wall Street Journal* used a figure of about 10 percent. In fact, none of them was correct. The number was 15.7 percent.[44] "The rest of the country's listeners were no better off," claimed the *Washington Journalism Review*. "They were exposed to the same confusion of reports as national TV and radio reporters and smaller papers picked up the stories carried on AP and UPI, and the wire services associated with three of the four influential papers."[45]

Even stories about bigger economic concerns, such as economy policy, were lacking in context and analysis, according to experts. "In this most important area of reporting, the media's performance is, I believe, seriously flawed," wrote Herbert Stein, former chairman of the President's Council of Economic Advisers, in *Columbia Journalism Review*.[46] Stein later said, "Not only do the media concentrate on the short-term aspects of the economy, they also dramatize them in ways that further exaggerate their performance."[47]

According to James Hamilton in *Nieman Reports*, readers want economic information from the media for three reasons: (1) to make personal economic decisions, such as with interest rates, (2) for entertainment in reading about the pay of a savings and loan executive or an out-of-work factory employee, and (3) to make decisions in their role as citizens and voters.[48] Said Hamilton: "What is missing from complaints about the quantity and quality of economic news is an economic analysis of the market for economic news."[49] What he found was that people are more interested in reading about economic issues that affect them directly than economic issues of a social or political nature. In addition, readers of newspapers understand economic news when it explains how it affects their lives, but they have little understanding of issues such as the federal deficit or the increase in the gross domestic product.

Explaining economics in human angles, however, does help the average reader understand. When business journalists began writing about economic information such as unemployment or the Consumer Price Index using examples of people and how they were personally affected by an increase or decrease in the number of jobs available in an area or the cost of a gallon of milk, they connected these concepts with readers. Putting economic trends and analysis into context for the average reader is one of the hardest tasks for business journalists to perform, but is it one that has occurred with increasing frequency in the last 15 years.

Pushing American business journalists to pay more attention to its economy has been the globalization of economies across the world. The U.S. economy now depends greatly on the economies of other countries, and vice versa. To understand what is happening in the local economy requires that American business journalists become more knowledgeable about what is happening in economies halfway around the world. In part, they have been forced to do so because of inroads made in the American media market by foreign publications such as *The Economist*, which in the 1980s and 1990s made a major push into the United States and which provided an analysis of the global economic situation that was lacking for many American readers.

The Economist, founded in England in 1843 to lobby against tariffs on imported grain, gave American readers a view of its economy without being parochial – and with a distinct opinion.[50] And it did a better job than most other publications in telling the readers how supposed noneconomic issues around the world such as wars and protests were actually tied to the economic situation in that particular region.

In addition to globalization forcing Americans to pay more attention to the economy, another change in the 1980s that gave economics reporting a boost was the appointment of Alan Greenspan as chairman of the Federal Reserve Board in 1987. Although other Fed chairmen had previously graced the covers of magazines, Greenspan's lengthy tenure and his ability to successfully ride the U.S. economy to one of its greatest eras of prosperity made him a media cult figure around the world. Suddenly, it became stylish to write – and read – about decisions the Fed made about the federal funds rate and what Greenspan was thinking.

When Greenspan succeeded Paul Volcker as chairman of the Fed, the move was analyzed and criticized. Hobart Rowen, writing in the *Post*, noted that Greenspan had a "dedication to reducing the budget deficit, vigorous support for free trade and a belief that a sharply declining dollar poses a major threat to the world's economy."[51] What his analysis didn't include was what that meant to the average reader.

Greenspan soon became synonymous with the country's economy, and the journalists writing about the Fed and economic policy hung on his every word, analyzing each phrase for what it meant. And the journalists got better at explaining how rising interest rates meant that consumers would pay more on their home mortgage or their car loan, but receive more interest on their certificate of deposit at the bank. They also better explained that lower interest rates would spur spending because products and services wouldn't cost as much. Still, some noted that economic coverage of Greenspan and the Federal Reserve occurs "the same way journalism covers sports – on the assumption that the people who really want to know the details will know where to find them. But informing the public about economic policy is more important than that."[52]

Sometimes, Greenspan was so vague that respected business journalists made different conclusions about what he said. On June 8, 1995, for example, *The New York Times* ran a headline stating, "Greenspan sees a chance of

Business Journalism Timeline

1982 – Forbes begins publishing list of the 400 richest people.

1984 – Investor's Business Daily begins publishing.

1984 – Reuters sells stock and becomes a public company.

1984 – Reporter J. Foster Winans uses the Heard on the Street column in The Wall Street Journal to promote stocks for friends. He is later convicted.

1984 – Mobil Corp. withdraws ads from The Wall Street Journal and refuses to talk to its reporters.

1988 – Wall Street Journal adds Money & Investing section.

1989 – CNBC is launched as a cable business news network by NBC.

recession,"[53] while the *Washington Post*'s headline stated "Recession is unlikely, Greenspan concludes."[54] Other major attempts at explaining the economy in the 1990s made similar nebulous conclusions or were criticized. In 1996, *The New York Times* ran a week-long series called "The Downsizing of America," later criticized for making the economy sound worse than it actually was.[55] Other economics stories such as trade negotiations failed to accurately portray the feelings of most Americans or businesses, noted former business editor Merrill Goozner.[56]

Still, economics coverage improved dramatically from a half-century earlier. Readers who once didn't know the significance of the Consumer Price Index or the Federal Reserve Board now understand how both can affect their everyday lives. They were helped by journalists such as *The Washington Post*'s John Berry, who "understands Greenspan like no one else" and whose "monopoly on interpreting the Fed is Microsoft-like."[57] In addition, changes in society and the world have made the economy more relevant to readers and viewers of the media. This is partly a reflection of the economy's performance.

More important, studies have shown that coverage of economics news influences people's opinions of the economy – either positively or negatively – showing the need for business journalists to more accurately reflect in their stories the true economic conditions in the country.[58]

What the increased coverage of the economy also showed business journalists was that they needed to pay more attention to government agencies that regulated business.

Government and business

Shortly after Rowen took over the business desk at the *Washington Post* in 1966, a young reporter by the name of Robert Samuelson was hired to work for him. At that time, a reporter on the paper's national staff covered the Federal Reserve. Two other reporters split the government agencies that regulated business. Samuelson took the Civil Aeronatics Board, the Interstate Commerce Commission, and the Federal Communications Commission. The other reporter was assigned the Securities and Exchange Commission, the Federal Trade Commission, and the Federal Power Commission. Before Rowen arrived, these agencies and their influence on business were hardly covered by the media.[59]

Because of the *Post*'s location near these government agencies, it has done the most complete job of documenting how the business world and regulation have interacted in the past 35 years. But other newspapers have performed just as well in writing about how state government and businesses sometimes clash.

Government reporting has been considered a prestigious beat at many newspapers and television stations. Covering city hall meant that you often interviewed the mayor and other important people. Writing about the state legislature meant stories about important new bills that had been promoted by powerful representatives and senators. The state beat might include the governor, whose job it partly was to make sure people from every corner had a job that paid them enough to support their families.

Increasingly, these government stories also became business stories. State public service commissions regulated the rates that electrical, water, and telephone companies could charge consumers. Insurance commissioners oversaw the premiums insurers charged for homes, cars, and lives. And as these stories became more complicated, the news desk turned to the business desk to help unravel what was actually the news.

Reporting on the intersection between government and business has never been more important than in the early 21st century, when new regulation after new regulation has been proposed and signed into law to prevent the business scandals that have so often occurred. A 2003 *Newspaper Research Journal* study found that newspapers rely heavily on government sources when reporting on business crises.[60]

However, many of these regulatory agencies still go largely uncovered, leaving many business stories untouched. One reason is the difficulty in mining information out of these agencies, which can be unwieldy and uncooperative.

As business journalists began to cover the government regulatory angle more, they also began developing specific beats centered on specific industries or businesses. Most metropolitan newspapers in the 1970s and 1980s, for example, had a banking reporter whose job it was to cover the major banks in the region. As banks began consolidating in the 1990s, that beat became important to cover the changing landscape, but the decline in the number of banks also decreased the importance of the beat to some newspapers where bank headquarters were lost.

Many business desks also had a full-time reporter to cover retailers, specifically when new malls or department stores were being built. This reporter often worked closely with a real estate reporter, who wrote about commercial and private developments. Newspapers located in areas with major airports often had a reporter writing about transportation.

The coverage expanded into previously uncovered areas as well. Mutual funds were typically written about in investment publications. But with the rise of 401(k) plans that included mutual fund options being offered by companies to their employees to help them save for retirement in the 1980s and 1990s, newspapers added mutual fund columnists and regular articles. In 1995, *The New York Times* changed its Sunday section to emphasize mutual funds.[61] In the same year, the *Boston Globe* added columns that covered marketing and advertising, business travel, and the workplace.[62] As technology and the Internet grew in usage in the 1990s, dozens of newspapers added special tech sections. In 1996, the *Los Angeles Times* introduced Cutting Edge, a new Monday section that replaced its regular business coverage.[63] Smaller papers such as the *Austin American-Statesman* also rolled out technology sections. The *Times* also introduced Wall Street, California, and Small Business as separate sections within the next year.[64] It should be noted that many of these special sections disappeared after the 2000 Internet bubble popped, and the coverage was rolled back into the traditional business section.

Business journalism experienced a heyday in the 1990s. With Greenspan steering the economy, the stock markets grew at dizzying rates for most of the decade, making many people millionaires overnight. Those who wanted in on the game looked to the business coverage in their local newspapers, on television, or wherever they could find it to learn what they too needed to do to make money.

Still some problems

Despite the many advances – more staff, more space devoted to the topic, better expertise, wider coverage – made by business journalism from the 1950s to the 1990s, there remained problems. Sometimes, business coverage was overly aggressive, and sometimes it wasn't aggressive enough. Sometimes, the reporting showed an appalling lack of understanding of the issues, and sometimes, the reporting went overboard in explaining everything.

There were some shining examples of business journalism during this period. In 1989, the *Atlanta Constitution* uncovered the practice of local banks refusing to lend money in poor neighborhoods in one of the first examples of computer-assisted reporting in business journalism.[65] In 1993, two reporters from *The Wall Street Journal* won a Pulitzer Prize for their coverage of the management turmoil at General Motors Corp.[66] In 1996, *The* (Raleigh) *News & Observer* received a Pulitzer Prize for its coverage of the hog farming business in North Carolina.[67] A year later, a Pulitzer Prize was awarded to the *Seattle Times* for its coverage of the aerospace industry and Boeing Corp., one of the area's largest employers.[68]

Others distinguished themselves in other ways. The *New Orleans Times-Picayune* took on one of the city's best known companies, Freeport-McMoRan, documenting environmental damage at its gold mine in Indonesia.[69] The *Omaha World-Herald* ran a five-part series in 1997 after an E. coli breakout at a local meatpacking plant.[70]

Yet one of the most embarrassing episodes in the field of journalism during this time occurred in 1998, when the *Cincinnati Enquirer* ran an 18-page special section that exposed a local company, Chiquita Brands International Inc., of bribing officials and other claims related to illegal environment and labor practices. Although the reporting was apparently accurate, less than two months later the newspaper apologized for its coverage, paid millions of dollars to Chiquita even though the company had not filed a lawsuit, and fired its reporter, who had broken into the company's voice mail system to obtain some of his information.[71] Although investigative business journalism had taken a back seat during the decade to more fawning coverage of the business world, the Chiquita story sent a chill through the field and signaled to many that business would aggressively defend its turf.

In the 1990s, some disturbing trends in business journalism emerged that would give the field its biggest black eye since the scandals after the 1929 stock market crash. Business journalism failed in one of its most important assignments – to serve as a watchdog. How business reporters and editors responded would get business journalism back on the right track.

Footnotes

1 From "The explosive demand for business news," by T. W. Hubbard, Winter 1966, Journalism Quarterly, p. 703.

2 From "News research for better newspapers: Volume four," by C. R. Bush, New York: American Newspaper Publishers Association Foundation, 1966, p. 24.

3 From "News research for better newspapers: Volume four," pp. 25–26.

4 From "The explosive demand for business news," p. 703.

5 From "The explosive demand for business news," p. 705.

6 From "Hobart Rowen: An expert 50 years in the making," by E. Whitney, Nov. 27, 1988, St. Petersburg Times, p. 1I.

7 From "John Lawrence, 70, pioneer in reporting on business," by J. Boyet, Jan. 5, 2005, New York Times, p. C14.

8 From The paper: The life and death of the New York Herald Tribune, by R. Kluger, New York: Alfred A. Knopf, 1986. pp. 687–688.

9 From "Business news in post-Watergate era," by J. T. W. Hubbard, Autumn 1976, Journalism Quarterly, p. 488.

10 From "Business news in post-Watergate era," p. 491.

11 From "Business news in post-Watergate era," p. 492.

12 From "The bleak wasteland of financial journalism," by C. Welles, July/August 1973, Columbia Journalism Review, pp. 40–49.

13 From "The bleak wasteland of financial journalism," p. 43.

14 From "Economic coverage: D as in dismal," Jan. 20, 1975, Time, pp. 62–63.

15 From "The failings of business and journalism," Feb. 9, 1976, Time, pp. 78–79.

16 From "Business page reporting examined by editors," by G. B. Healey, Feb. 23, 1974, Editor & Publisher, pp. 13, 36.

17 From "Are the media making things worse? Or are they just spooking themselves?" by F. Klein, March/April 1975, Columbia Journalism Review, p. 53.

18 From "Big, bad business in the hands of the devil press," by R. Otwell, April 1977, Quill, pp. 15–18.

19 From "Attitudes of newspaper business editors and general public toward capitalism," by R. A. Peterson, G. Albaum, G. Kozmetsky, and I. C. M. Cunningham, Spring 1984, Journalism Quarterly, pp. 56–65.

20 From "Must business fight the press?" by T. Griffith, June 1974, Fortune, p. 204.

21 From "Business coverage is getting better," by E. C. Hynds, Summer 1980, Journalism Quarterly, pp. 297–304.

22 From "Business and economic news in Pennsylvania daily newspapers," by J. N. Rippey, Spring 1978, Journalism Quarterly, pp. 130–134.

23 From "A bullish pulpit: The NYT's business desk," by R. Morris, May/June 1981, Columbia Journalism Review, p. 31.

24 From "Nation's press devotes more space, manpower to economic coverage," by D. McClintick, Dec. 8, 1978, The Wall Street Journal, p. 1.

25 From "Two S. Floridians who made journalism history," by B. Garcia, Dec. 28, 1999, The Miami Herald, p. 1C.

26 See Time, Dec. 5, 1988. The title is "A game of greed."

27 From "Nation's press devotes more space, manpower to economic coverage," p. 34.

28 From "The brown-lung controversy," by B. Hall, March/April 1978, Columbia Journalism Review, pp. 27–35.

29 From "Riding the wave," November/December 2001, Columbia Journalism Review, pp. 106–107.

30 From Silent Spring, by R. Carson, Boston: Houghton Mifflin, 1962, p. 1.

31 From Stories that changed America: Muckrakers of the 20th century, by C. Jensen, New York: Seven Stories Press, 2000, p. 117.

32 From Ninety seconds to tell it all: Big business and the news media, by K. MacDougall, Homewood, Ill.: Dow Jones-Irwin, 1981, p. 84.

33 From Stories that changed America: Muckrakers of the 20th century, p. 149.

34 From "Are the media making things worse? Or are they just spooking themselves?" p. 53.

35 From "The Common Cents approach to consumer reporting," by F. Pollock, September/October 1977, Columbia Journalism Review, pp. 37–38.

36 From "The Common Cents approach to consumer reporting," p. 38.

37 From "Tax fund arrives after long delay," by G. Tharpe, Jan. 21, 1991, Atlanta Constitution, p. C7.

38 From "Consumer woes? We'll try to help," April 16, 2000, Cleveland Plain Dealer, p. 3L.

39 From "No news for consumers," by R. Harwood, April 2, 1989, The Washington Post, p. C6.

40 From "The pro-corporate tilt," by M. Mintz, Fall 1991, Nieman Reports, p. 24.

41 From "Tuning out the business section," by T. Case, June 8, 1996, Editor & Publisher, p. 18.

42 From "Reporting on the reserve," by R. H. Hoenig, Winter 2001, Financial History, pp. 15–17.

43 From "Economists and reporters: A combination to promote/restrain trade," by B. D. Nossiter, The American Economic Review, 1972, pp. 381–383.

44 From "Corporate profits up? 44%, 26% or…" by C. Forsyth, June/July 1979, Washington Journalism Review, pp. 11–12.

45 From "Corporate profits up? 44%, 26% or…" p. 12.

46 From "Media distortions: A former official's view," by H. Stein, March/April 1975, Columbia Journalism Review, p. 37.

47 From "Media distortions: A former official's view," p. 39.

48 From "Lower pay for analysis," by J. T. Hamilton, Fall 1991, Nieman Reports, p. 19.

49 From "Lower pay for analysis," p. 19.

50 From "The Americanization of The Economist," by D. D. Guttenplan, May/June 1993, Columbia Journalism Review, p. 55.

51 From "Greenspan and the doubters," by H. Rowen, June 25, 1987, Washington Post, p. A17.

52 From "Demystifying Mr. Greenspan: How to fathom the Fed," by E. Shanahan, January/February 1995, Columbia Journalism Review, pp. 36–37.

53 From "Greenspan sees chance of recession," by K. Bradsher, June 8, 1995, New York Times, p. D1.

54 From "Recession is unlikely, Greenspan concludes; still, Fed watchers expect lower rates soon," by J. Berry, June 8, 1995, Washington Post, p. B10.

55 See critiques that include "Making too much of downsizing?" by K. Heyboer, May 1996, American Journalism Review, p. 10, and "Is the media making too much of downsizing?" a transcript of the CNN show Reliable Sources from March 24, 1996.

56 From "Blinded by the boom: What's missing in the coverage of the New Economy?" by M. Goozner, November/December 2000, Columbia Journalism Review, p. 23.

57 From "He stands alone," by J. Cramer, July/August 1998, Brill's Content, pp. 65–66.

58 From "The Economy and second-level agenda setting: A Time-Series Analysis of Economic News and Public Opinion about the Economy," by J. B. Hester and R. Gibson, Journalism Quarterly, Spring 2003, pp. 73–90.

59 From "Moving toward the mainstream," by R. J. Samuelson, Summer 2002, Nieman Reports, p. 22.

60 From "Government sources dominate business crisis reporting," by L. Powell and W. R. Self, Spring 2003, Newspaper Research Journal, p. 97.

61 From "NY Times upgrades business section," March 18, 1995, Editor & Publisher, p. 34.

62 From "Boston Globe expands, redesigns business section," Nov. 11, 1995, Editor & Publisher, p. 53.

63 From "New L.A. Times business section," March 30, 1996, Editor & Publisher, p. 27.

64 From "L.A. Times focuses business section," by D. Perucci, Sept. 27, 1997, Editor & Publisher, p. 27.

65 The series ran from May 1, 1988 through May 4, 1988 and included dozens of follow-up articles. The first of the series is "Atlanta blacks losing in home loans scramble: Banks favor white areas by 5-1 margin," by B. Dedmon, May 1, 1988, Atlanta Constitution, p. A1.

66 Among the articles that were entered in the Pulitzer competition were "Major restyling: At once-stodgy GM, management change is a generational one," by P. Ingrassia and J. B. White, Nov. 3, 1992, The Wall Street Journal, p. A1, and "Eminence grise: Behind revolt at GM, lawyer Ira Millstein helped call the shots," by J. B. White and P. Ingrassia, April 13, 1992, The Wall Street Journal, p. A1.

67 See "N&O hog series takes top Pulitzer Public service prize rewards stories on pork industry," by C. Whitlock, April 10, 1996, The (Raleigh) News & Observer, p. A1.

68 See "Can FAA adopt tougher attitude? 2 unsolved crashes have public uneasy," by B. Acohido, June 24, 1996, Seattle Times, p A1, and "NTSB delayed introducing 737 proposals Boeing fought," by B. Acohido, Oct. 2, 1996, Seattle Times, p. A1, among other articles.

69 From "A fire breather gets scorched: Two newspapers and a mining giant," by S. Dudley, March/April 1996, Columbia Journalism Review, p. 10.

70 From "A meat story, well done," by L. Kelliher, January/February 2004, Columbia Journalism Review, p. 14.

71 For details of the Cincinnati Enquirer-Chiquita scandal, see "How Cincinnati paper ended up backing off from Chiquita series," by A. M. Freedman and R. Balu, July 17, 1998, The Wall Street Journal, pp. A1, A8, and "After apology, issues raised in Chiquita article remain," by D. Frantz, July 17, 1998, New York Times, pp. A1, A14.

Chapter 10

The roaring '90s

No decade in business journalism's history has seen more dramatic change – good and bad – than the 1990s. Boosted by the decade-long rise in the stock market, the rapid development of the Internet as both a tool for businesses to sell products and services and for the media to distribute news and information almost instantaneously, and the resulting hoards of overnight millionaires, business reporting became caught up in the hysteria and went along for the ride.

The explosion in reporters and editors devoted to business journalism led to the field being the biggest growth area in journalism during the decade. In 1988, the number of business journalists was estimated at 4,200. By 2000, the number had surpassed 12,000.[1] Space for coverage also rose. The percent of the space in newspapers devoted to business coverage more than doubled in the 1990s, from 7 to 15 percent.[2] Other media followed the trend, as cable networks also gave more attention to business stories.

A number of these journalists, however, were unprepared to cover the top business stories of the time, such as the savings and loan scandal of the late 1980s and early 1990s, hostile takeovers, the rise in mergers and acquisitions, and the excesses of Wall Street. In addition, business journalists were "blindsided by globalization. How could a sneeze in Bangkok become pneumonia in Moscow and Sao Paulo – and galloping consumption in some American mutual funds?" asked *New York Times* business reporter Diana Henriques in 2000.[3]

As is the case with most dramatic changes in society, though, these shortcomings were not readily apparent to those practicing the craft or those reading business coverage. Society was obsessed with business in the 1990s; people began watching cable television network CNBC while they worked. People with respectable jobs quit to become day traders, thinking that was the path to riches. Stock tips and investment portfolios became common conversation among friends. Journalism merely followed along and recorded the breathtaking events.

Even the most cynical media observers were won over. *Columbia Journalism Review* called it "The Business Century" and noted how such coverage became hot news.[4] *American Journalism Review* called the explosion in business journalism "Follow the Money" and noted the insatiable demand for business information.[5]

The media industry complied in ways that were good – and bad – for business journalism. The good included the proliferation of media outlets devoted to business coverage. With more reporters focused on writing about the economy and the business world, previously uncovered issues now received some scrutiny. In addition, new strategies for covering business helped reader comprehension. The use of rankings in business journalism became a staple, although its practice has been criticized. And some media developed entirely new forms of business journalism. Bloomberg L.P. created a wire service in 1990 to compete against Dow Jones, Reuters and the Associated Press in a fashion that focused on the investment community. Its strategy was wildly successful, and it quickly became a dominant player in the field.

The bad trends in business journalism in the 1990s centered primarily on how stories were reported and then written. Business journalism overall became too trusting and too fawning in its coverage. Chief executive officers became magazine cover material as their company successes were attributed to their leadership and visionary management style in ways that were often oversimplified. New technology companies were treated in stories as the future of the business world even though few of them made money – and most of them would eventually go out of business or be sold. In the 1990s, business journalism too often accepted the company line about too many topics and neglected its role as corporate America watchdog.

There were many other parts of business journalism that were positive developments in the 1990s. Here is how business journalism got to its position in the 1990s, and how it rebounded in the early part of the 21st century to take on, once again, a more skeptical view of what it was covering.

The rise of rankings in business journalism

The first cracks in business journalism that led to the problems of the 1990s actually began decades earlier and were initially considered a major innovation in how the media tracked business. Today, many in business journalism still use rankings and lists. But over the years, this technique became overused, and it led to scorecard journalism that often missed the bigger story. Because of the rise of rankings, business journalism often became simply concerned with the biggest company, the fastest growing company, the largest increase in stock price in the past 12 months, the highest salary, the largest bonus, the richest people, and the best performing mutual fund, and not whether these companies, stocks, or executives reached the top through ignoble means.

At first, lists in business journalism were used to help identify potential stories. When reporters and editors at *Fortune* in the 1950s began to compile an annual list of the largest U.S. companies, it was not to share with its readers.[6] When the first *Fortune* 500 list was published in 1955, however, it became an instant hit. The term became part of business language, and each year readers rushed to see what companies had moved up – or down – in the rankings. All but two of the original 500 companies had revenue of more than $50 million, with the total revenue of the entire list at $136.9 billion and the profits at $8.3 billion.[7]

At first, the list, which ranked businesses in terms of revenue, included only industrial companies – General Motors Corp. ranked No. 1 for 31 of the first 40 years of the list.[8] (Exxon would top the list for several years through the 1970s and early 1980s.) *Fortune* later added a separate list of service companies and then combined the two lists. Wal-Mart Stores Inc. now has a stranglehold on the top spot with revenue that exceeds the total of the entire first list from 1955.

Although the ranking performed a valuable service to readers, providing context that allowed readers and executives to see how companies performed compared to their competitors, it later proliferated into a series of other rankings by *Fortune* and other business publications such as daily newspapers and weekly business papers. Such simplistic rankings likely clouded business journalists from understanding bigger trends and problems in industry and also likely led some executives to focus simply on the rankings and how they compared to others and not operating their companies to perform to the best of their ability. The other problem with some lists was their subjectivity. Many lists were subjective, such as the Most Innovative Companies or Most Admired Companies, where the rankings were based on opinion and not quantitative financial results.

Forbes countered in 1971 with another list that soon became popular in business journalism – the highest paid CEOs. The average company head had a salary and bonus of about $130,000, the survey found, though at the top of the list was IT&T CEO Harold Geneen, who had made $767,000 in 1970.[9] "Financial speaking, the CEO doesn't always have it made," noted the magazine in the first ranking. "He does not necessarily do as well as men of equal talent who rise to the top of other professions."[10] The magazine noted that doctors, lawyers, accountants, athletes, and entertainers at the time often made more than the average CEO.

By spotlighting this discrepancy, *Forbes* likely shed a light on executive compensation, forcing many corporate boards to consider paying their CEOs more. Today, executive pay has become a major story in the business world and is widely portrayed in the business press as often being out of touch with the rest of the job market. By 1991, the top CEO on the list was Time Warner's Steve Ross, who made $78 million.[11] *Forbes* is no longer alone in examining CEO pay. Lists of the top-paid executives are now annual stories at many magazines and newspapers.

By the late 1970s, lists became more popular. *Inc.* magazine, noting that the *Fortune* list slighted the smaller companies that were growing by leaps and bounds, began its annual ranking of the 100 fastest growing small public companies in 1978.[12] Some of the companies that would make its list in the first decade, such as Dell Computer, would later wind up on the *Fortune* list, whereas others, such as Tampa-based Silk Greenhouse, which was No. 31 in 1990, would file for bankruptcy court protection and go out of business. *Inc.* later added a list of the top 500 private companies.

BusinessWeek followed with its list of the Top 1,000 companies. *Forbes* countered with a list of the 500 largest foreign companies and its list of the top 500 companies ranked in four different ways – sales, profits, assets, and market value.[13] Not to be outdone, *Fortune* added other lists, including the most admired and least admired companies. By the 1980s, it also ran a list of the 50 biggest Mafia bosses and the 50 most fascinating businesspeople. "Filling space with lists rather than prose about the winners and losers may not be more enlightening, but it does offer the reader a means of joining the competition without being at risk," pointed out *The New York Times* in 1987.[14] The issues sold copies, and the magazines were in the business of making money, just like the companies on their lists.

Forbes found its niche in business journalism lists in 1982, when it launched the Forbes

400 richest people in America.[15] Although a daunting task, the list did nothing to promote strong business journalism except to encourage others to document the massive wealth that some business owners, executives, and their families had built throughout the years. But the pursuit of wealth – and the list of the wealthiest – was widely followed. Said *Forbes* in announcing the first list: "A periodic scorecard of who is really rich in this country – an intriguing enough inquiry anyway – but it will go beyond that: It will attempt to delve into the nature of wealth and wealthy, into how they got that way as well as who they are, and into how they conduct their lives."[16] First on the list was Daniel Keith Ludwig, a shipping magnate whose wealth was estimated at more than $2 billion.[17] Few profiles of Ludwig appeared at the time, though the people at the top of the list today, such as Bill Gates and Warren Buffett, routinely appear on magazine covers. Prior to his inclusion on the list, Ludwig's name had appeared in *Newsweek* in 1976 as one of the richest men in the world and in a *Forbes* article in 1979 about his South American business holdings. He was not quoted in either article.

The *Forbes'* list increased the public's fascination with the wealthy and how they had gotten that way. In turn, business journalism began focusing more on those who were in charge of accumulating the wealth – for themselves and for shareholders. A direct correlation between an increase in coverage of the net worth of individuals and the increase in coverage of CEOs can easily be made. No longer were readers of business coverage simply interested in the Rockefellers of Ida Tarbell's time from the perspective of the broader effect on society of their companies. Consumers of the business press now also wanted the details of their personal lives. Business journalism happily complied, although at first even *Forbes* was dubious. "'I thought it was pretty dicey at first," said editor James Michaels. "I thought how do you find out about somebody who owns six shopping centers and isn't on the society pages?"[18] By 1987, the magazine added lists of foreign billionaires and the highest paid entertainers. Three years later, it added a list of the top 40 highest paid athletes.[19]

Writing about the personal wealth and other private details of the richest families and executives is not neces-

BUSINESS JOURNALISM TIMELINE

1989 – ATLANTA JOURNAL-CONSTITUTION WINS PULITZER PRIZE FOR SERIES OF STORIES THAT UNCOVERS REDLINING BY BANKS USING COMPUTER DATABASES.

1989 – RAY SHAW PURCHASES AMERICAN CITY BUSINESS JOURNALS AND MAKES THE WEEKLY BUSINESS NEWSPAPER STANDARD READING IN MAJOR METROPOLITAN MARKETS.

1990 – MICHAEL BLOOMBERG STARTS BLOOMBERG BUSINESS NEWS. THE NAME LATER CHANGES TO BLOOMBERG NEWS.

1990 – WASHINGTON POST REPORTERS WIN PULITZER PRIZE FOR THEIR INVESTIGATION INTO SECURITIES AND EXCHANGE COMMISSION AND HOW IT REGULATES WALL STREET.

1991 – FINANCIAL NEWS NETWORK IS BOUGHT OUT BY CNBC.

sarily off limits for business journalism. Some of the best investigative business stories have uncovered wrongdoing in how the richest of the rich operated their businesses and squandered their inheritances. Less than half the people on the original wealthy list remained a decade later, a great story unto itself. But writing about wealth simply to ascertain the wealthiest led business journalism down a path of simplified coverage that caused many publications to ignore more substantive stories.

In the 1990s, this list form of business journalism exploded into the personal finance area as well, giving readers "Eight top investments that never lose money," according to the cover of *Money* in March 1994.[20] The same issue included a ranking of America's best jobs. *Smart Money* blasted its July 1999 cover with "10 stocks now."[21] Yet an analysis of such investment lists by *Brill's Content* found that they rarely beat the overall market.[22] One editor of *Smart Money*, who complained that *Brill's* needed to look at a longer term view of the stock portfolios, ignored the fact that many readers likely don't hold on to investments for five years.

And today, virtually every business publication or newspaper section runs some sort of annual ranking list. Newspapers in almost every state run a list of the top public companies in their geographic region. Regional weekly business newspapers run a list of the top businesses in a certain industry – ranging from the largest hospitals to the biggest contractors or accounting firms – almost every issue. Every year, they combine these lists and sell them in book form.

Such lists are a way for business journalism to keep a running scorecard of industry and executives. In that respect, they do serve a valuable purpose. Yet they have also turned a good chunk of financial reporting into simply looking at the rankings to determine stories. For years, Enron made the list of most admired companies compiled by *Fortune*. Such stories are based on reputation and not hard-nosed reporting.

Perhaps more important is that the rankings have turned into a public relations tool for the companies that these publications are supposed to be covering objectively. Many businesses that make these lists use their standing in their press releases and in other literature to promote themselves. Such usage makes it seem as if the business publications have given the companies a stamp of approval. That's a dangerous association.

CEO from celebrity to the crime log

As business journalists paid more attention to the performance and size of companies, and the compensation of executives, chief executive officers became a bigger focus for stories. It was the company CEO who typically had the final say on the important decisions, and it was the CEO whom increasingly people within the company and outside the company looked to for guidance about the future of the business.

Business journalists have long written about company leaders. But throughout the years, the tone of such articles has made subtle changes to where in the 1990s much of the coverage about corporate heads seemed to treat the CEO as a movie star whose every move was the result of brilliant strategy and skilled planning. In fact, that was often untrue, and many CEOs who received laudatory coverage in the 1990s would later be accused of crimes and fired because of some of their actions.

In the 1950s and 1960s, CEOs received coverage in the media based on how their strategies or operating styles were different and might be of help to other companies struggling to manage their business. The May 12, 1956, cover of *BusinessWeek*, for example, is of General Electric President Ralph J. Cordiner, but the story inside the magazine never mentions his background before he took over running the company or details of his personal life.[23] Instead, it's an explanation of Cordiner's opinions of how big companies can be managed effectively and what their problems will be in the future. The article has an academic tone, dispensing advice and analysis, yet is written using words common among businesspeople, not everyday citizens. It's obvious the article is intended solely for a business audience.

Other CEOs appeared on magazine covers during this period simply to provide art for an industry analysis. The Dec. 1, 1957, *Forbes* gives a detailed analysis of why oil companies were selling stock on Wall Street to raise cash. On the cover is Eugene Holman, chief executive officer of Standard Oil of New Jersey, the world's biggest oil company at the time. Yet the article rarely mentions Holman and never directly quotes him.[24]

When *Fortune* magazine put a portrait of General Motors' Alfred P. Sloan on its cover in September 1963, he became the first executive to grace its front. And yet the article that accompanied the cover was not about Sloan. Instead, it was written by Sloan and detailed the management of GM for the previous 50 years. Sloan had retired from the company seven years earlier, but was considered one of the greatest industrial leaders of the first half of the 20th century. The story, and the subsequent five-part series, were more a primer of Sloan's management philosophy of delegation than an homage to his business acumen.[25] He downplayed personal leadership for teamwork.

Through the years, however, the role of the CEO changed. And with it, so did the way CEOs were covered by business journalists. When many American companies failed to anticipate issues such as foreign competition in the 1970s, CEOs were replaced with a different breed of manager. A CEO had run a company in the past by direct order. Now, the new breed of CEO, who began seeing many of his moves analyzed and criticized by the growing business press, became a manager of people, a leader, and a coach.[26]

In addition, according to Rakesh Khurana in the *Harvard Business Review*, other important changes occurred

Business Journalism Timeline

1991 – The Wall Street Journal wins a Pulitzer Prize for examining the human impact of the leverage buyout of Safeway Stores Inc.

June 1991 – Sylvia Porter dies.

1992 – Wall Street Journal parent Dow Jones and magazine publisher Hearst Corp. entered the fray with a joint venture that begins publishing personal finance magazine Smart Money. Mutual fund company Fidelity Investments starts Worth magazine.

November 1992 – NBC's Dateline runs a segment showing how General Motors trucks explode when involved in accidents. The automaker sues the network, which later apologizes for staging the accidents to make them look worse than they appear.

1994 – Marketwatch.com starts posting business news online.

that led to a change in coverage:

> Investors were suddenly looking for CEOs who could shake things up and put an end to business as usual. This important change coincided with two other shifts. The first was the emergence of an almost religious conception of business, exemplified by the appearance of words such as "mission," "vision," and "values" in the corporate lexicon. The second shift was the rise of the so-called populist capitalism, whereby ordinary Americans made investing the country's most popular participatory sport.[27]

One of the ways CEOs found they could lead their companies to develop new strategies and consider new management or operating styles was by communicating with the media. No longer were CEOs likely to turn down interviews with journalists. By talking to the business reporter, the CEO was now presumably also able to communicate with his employees who read the story. And with this shift came the first celebrity CEOs – Chrysler's Lee Iacocca, Apple Computer's Steve Jobs, and General Electric's Jack Welch all rose to prominence in the early 1980s by being on the covers of business magazines and the front pages of business sections. Coverage of these executives differed from what was written about corporate leaders in the past. Now, the stories lauded their successes instead of examining their management style. Acerbic managers were praised as long as their companies produced results.

Surprisingly, these early CEO stars emerged at a time when some companies and executives were being convicted of wrongdoing. LTV chairman Paul Thayer was sentenced to four years in prison for lying about insider trading. E.F. Hutton engaged in a check-kiting scheme, and the First National Bank of Boston failed to report more than $1 billion in transactions that involved laundering drug money.[28] And yet, CEOs continued to be routinely lauded in the press for pushing companies to new heights. "Top executives and shrewd investors are good bets to emerge as media heroes, unless or until they appear to be headed for prison," said Norman Solomon in *Nieman Reports*.[29]

By the 1990s, the CEO was a full-fledged celebrity. *Time* magazine noted in 1996 that seven of the ten most powerful people in the country were CEOs, and only President Clinton was more powerful than Microsoft co-founder and long-time leader Bill Gates.[30] The software computer guru has himself been the cover photo of dozens of magazines, including *Time* and media watchdog *Brill's Content*, which in September 1998 analyzed the company's public relations effort to turn Gates into a savvy business executive by manipulating the media. The magazine noted how Gates devoted considerable time to maintain relationships with key journalists and invited a dozen to stay with him at his family's vacation home.[31]

In the 1990s, Gates's strategy was how many CEOs dealt with the business media, and it led to often fawning coverage of corporate leaders as visionaries and demigods when in fact many of them would later show tragic flaws. "The rise of such CEOs partly reflects a broader trend, the personalization of everything," concluded *The Wall Street Journal* in 1997. "People make sense of the world by attaching names and faces to impersonal forces."[32]

But business journalism missed a story in making superstars out of CEOs such as Gates, Intel's Andy Grove, Coca-Cola's Roberto Goizueta, and others. The success of their companies was the result of thousands of employees, and the leader was merely successful in convincing workers that the CEO's vision of the company would lead to higher profits and an increasing stock price. In the 1990s, as the market pushed upward nearly every month, it was easy for workers to believe in their CEO because, for the most part, profits did continue to rise, and stock prices continued to hit new highs.

In addition, CEOs began to speak out about other issues. Before the 1992 presidential election, Welch warned that a victory by Clinton would return "flat earth" thinking to Washington. The comment was duly picked up by the adoring media and published in newspapers across the country the next day.[33]

The business journalists were eager to accept the often breathless stories told to them as they profiled these executives. Tyco CEO Dennis Kozlowski was portrayed in *Barron's* and *Time* as having played high school basketball and football, yet his high school yearbook showed he played neither.[34] In a profile in *Forbes,* Kozlowski was noted to have had talent with numbers at a young age, yet he waited on tables.[35] A *Barron's* story even took the PR pitch that Kozlowski was the next Jack Welch.[36] Later, Kozlowski's PR handlers at Tyco changed the details of where he was born in New Jersey and gave him an MBA that he didn't earn.[37] These details were reported without questioning by journalists until Kozlowski was indicted for tax evasion and lost his job. Only then did the press uncover the problems with his past.[38]

Not all superstar CEOs remained unscathed in the 1990s. Sunbeam CEO Al Dunlap received criticism in 1996 and 1997 even while Wall Street analysts praised his management ability. Dunlap's problem? He changed his image from a CEO who cut expenses at companies to make them run more efficiently to a builder of businesses. The media would have none of it and criticized this about-face.[39]

But for most CEOs in the 1990s, dealing with the business press was easy. They were given nicknames like "Neutron Jack" Welch and "Chainsaw Al" Dunlap by the media, even if the nicknames were not flattering. As the overly positive coverage of CEOs continued, some began to get uneasy with the coverage. Noted journalism critic Ben Bagdikian warned in 1997 about the "unrelieved glo-

BUSINESS JOURNALISM TIMELINE

1994 – JOHN HANCOCK AWARDS FOR EXCELLENCE IN BUSINESS JOURNALISM ARE DISCONTINUED AFTER 27 YEARS.

1995 – CNNFN IS LAUNCHED.

OCTOBER 1995 — BUSINESSWEEK PUBLISHES A STORY CALLED "THE BANKERS TRUST TAPES" THAT DETAIL THE INNER WORKINGS OF HOW BANKERS TRUST SOLD COMPLEX FINANCIAL INSTRUMENTS KNOWN AS DERIVATIVES TO CORPORATE CLIENTS. A FEDERAL JUDGE PREVENTS THE MAGAZINE FROM PUBLISHING THE STORY FOR THREE WEEKS AFTER PROCTOR & GAMBLE SUES BANKERS TRUST FOR FRAUD. A FEDERAL APPEALS COURT DECLARES THE JUDGE'S ORDER UNCONSTITUTIONAL.

NOVEMBER 1996 – THESTREET.COM IS FOUNDED BY HEDGE FUND MANAGER JAMES CRAMER. IT GOES PUBLIC IN 1999.

rification of business people, not just in advertisements where corporations pay for self-praise, but in 'news' that is assumed to be dispassionate."[40] Coverage of Goizueta's death in 1997 was likened to a "beatification…He was an American saint to match Britain's Diana and India's Mother Teresa."[41] Still, little criticism of corporate wrongdoing appeared in the media in the 1990s, according to a 2000 report.[42]

In no other industry in the 1990s was the corporate CEO so lauded as in technology. Overnight, Internet companies were being taken public, and twenty-something CEOs became instant millionaires. Their success, and how they had made millionaires of workers who owned stock, were considered the Great American Story.

It all came crashing down, unfortunately, leaving business journalism with some well-deserved egg on its collective face. Internet stocks plummeted, causing thousands of companies to go out of business. Even once laudatory companies such as Tyco, Coca-Cola, GE, and Microsoft lost their luster in differing ways. Some were accused of monopolistic practices by the federal government, while others were unable to find another CEO to ride the company as successfully as past leaders. "There's a good side and a bad side to being a celebrity CEO," said *Newsweek*'s Allan Sloan in 2001. "When the world loves you, you can do no wrong, no matter how badly you're behaving. When you're out of favor, though, you can do no right."[43]

After the turn of the century, the CEO went from being a star to being part of the crime log. CEOs were indicted with regularity for breaking various laws, and their court hearings became daily coverage. The former leaders of Tyco, Enron, HealthSouth, WorldCom, Cendant, Adelphia Communications, ImClone Systems, and other firms became more familiar with the courtroom than the boardroom. As a result, their coverage in the media changed as well. A 2002 study suggested that scrutiny of a company's poor performance increased the likelihood the business would change its CEO.[44]

What is known today about the role of business journalism making CEOs celebrities in the 1980s and 1990s is that the executives believed their positive coverage, and in so doing crippled companies in many ways. One *Strategic Management Journal* study found that "the greater a CEO's celebrity, the more a CEO will commit to continuing the actions that are associated with the celebrity and the greater the strategic inertia of the firm."[45] In other words, a CEO became more concerned with continuing his celebrity status and less concerned with addressing company problems. The study also found "evidence that CEOs who gain greater praise in the press become overconfident about their ability to extract greater acquisition returns and to pay higher acquisition premiums."[46]

Despite the problems with overly positive coverage of corporate executives, two developments in business journalism in the 1980s and 1990s led to more coverage and dramatically changed how many business news readers obtained information.

The growth of specialty business publications

As business coverage became a regular staple, new forms of delivering news about companies and the economy developed as well. Two of the more interesting trends in this respect in the last 20 years have been the development of the weekly business newspaper in large and medium-sized cities around the country and the startup of a new business news wire service that challenged the hierarchy of coverage and forced its competitors to get better.

In the late 1970s, weekly business newspapers entered many metropolitan markets. They gave business managers and executives coverage of stories that affected their operations, but weren't being included in the daily newspaper's business section. Their stature in the business world – and in journalism – increased in the 1980s as they gave their niche readers straightforward coverage. Some of these early publications included *Business Atlanta, Capital District Business Review, Texas Business,* and the *Wisconsin Business Journal.*[47] They were successful financially as well because their average reader made more money than regular newspaper readers, meaning advertisers wanted to reach them. Often, they competed against monthly business magazines and bi-weekly publications.

The owners of weekly newspapers discovered an untapped area for business journalism – providing coverage of small, privately held businesses in a community. While traditional newspapers focused coverage on the large, publicly traded entities in the city, they virtually ignored smaller companies. The weekly business newspapers found that there were plenty of good stories to be told about these companies as well.

In the early 1980s, the weekly business newspapers were owned by one of several companies. Newspaper chain Scripps-Howard owned business tabloids in 13 markets, while American City Business Journals operated publications in 5 cities. The Business Journal Group ran six weekly newspapers, while Crain Communications and MCP each had three.[48]

By 1984, the fight for readers among these publications reached the country's biggest media market – New York. In that year, monthly *Manhattan inc.* and weekly *Crain's New York Business* both debuted, joining bi-weekly *New York CityBusiness.*[49] Crain had already successfully launched a weekly in Chicago. By 1985, the fight for business readers among these publications gained the attention of *Newsweek,* which assessed the coverage as "flattering (if somewhat boring) takeouts on executives and industries, plus spot news that sometimes scoops the metropolitan daily newspapers."[50] That same year, American City sold stock and began buying weekly business papers in other markets. By 1987, it owned 36 publications, pri-

Business Journalism Timeline

1997 – The Wall Street Journal wins a Pulitzer Prize for its examination of the business aspects of the war on AIDS.

April 1998 – The Industry Standard is launched. Fueled by Internet company advertising, it lasts until late 2001.

June 1998 – Financial World ceases publication.

1999 – The Oregonian wins a Pulitzer Prize for its coverage of how the Asian economic crisis is affecting a local company that exports frozen French fries.

February 2000 – Houston station KHOU TV reports on problems of Firestone tires on Ford Explorer vehicles.

August 2000 – Bloomberg News becomes victim of Internet hoax by writing story based on fake news release.

marily in smaller metropolitan markets such as Kansas City and Honolulu.[51]

By 1989, the company was strapped for cash and ended up being sold to Ray Shaw, a former journalist at *The Wall Street Journal* who had risen to become president of Dow Jones, the *Journal*'s parent. In 1989, Shaw bought the American City papers with a partner and continued to expand the operation, buying additional papers in Boston, Philadelphia, Minneapolis, Pittsburgh, and San Jose.[52]

In 1995, American City Business Journals was sold to Advance Publications, the parent company of Newhouse newspapers and *Vogue* and *Vanity Fair* magazines, but a decade later Shaw remained in charge of the operation, which had since expanded its reach even further and now includes 41 weekly business newspapers.[53] By comparison, Crain's had business publications in six markets, including two in Mexico.[54]

These publications broadened the scope of business journalism, pushing it down to a level that the small business owner wanted. In addition, because the publications came out weekly, the newspapers focused on trends and long-term events instead of the daily happenings at businesses. Today, American City Business Journals is one of the largest employers of business journalists in the country, and many larger media outlets such as *The Wall Street Journal* and daily newspapers look to its publications to hire reporters and editors.

Bloomberg takes on Reuters, Dow Jones, and AP

If the weekly business newspapers found a niche providing coverage for the small business owner, then Bloomberg LP found in the 1990s that there was a similar position at the top of the business journalism spectrum – providing news on an immediate basis for traders and Wall Street professionals.

Started in 1990 to complement financial data and analysis of stocks and bonds, the Bloomberg news service grew quickly and became a major competitor of the existing business wire services at Reuters, Dow Jones, and the Associated Press. With a new player in the market, the other wire services improved their coverage and the speed at which they reported major stories.

When Bloomberg started, Reuters had 1,300 journalists in 116 bureaus around the world, and globally was considered the pre-eminent provider of business information.[55] Founded in London in 1851 by Paul Julius Reuter, the news service used carrier pigeons to deliver information the 76 miles between Brussels and Aachen, a town on Germany's western border. The pigeons gave Reuter an advantage over other wire services because they delivered the news twice as fast as trains.[56] When telegraph lines were laid between the cities, Reuter moved his operation to London and began providing opening and closing stock prices in the London and Paris markets as well as news. His service was the first to report the assassination of President Lincoln in 1865 to European newspapers. Reuters, which expanded its financial data offerings in the 1970s, went public in 1984.[57]

While Reuters was well known throughout the world, the Associated Press and Dow Jones wires were formidable business news services in the United States. The Dow Jones wire was augmented by stories compiled by reporters at *The Wall Street Journal*, while the Associated Press operated a business news desk in New York and had reporters in bureaus throughout the country and world. In addition, the AP collected business stories from its newspaper clients and placed them on the wire.

By the mid-1990s, Bloomberg had placed one of its computer terminals – which carried its stories as well as vast amounts of data on companies – in virtually every major business newsroom for free. In return, all Bloomberg asked was that the publication give it credit when it ran one of its stories or used its data to create a chart or graphic.[58] (Bloomberg made its money by charging thousands of dollars each month to its Wall Street clients. In the late 1990s, it also began charging its newspaper clients.) Many newspapers began regularly running stories from the Bloomberg wire, preferring its coverage to its competitors at times because of the speed at which it was delivered and the focus on the market. In the 1990s, as the stock market went through a decade-long boom, information about the market became required coverage.

As Bloomberg grew in importance, its competitors became wary. "Bloomberg found niches that Dow Jones and Reuters news didn't fill," said founder Michael Bloomberg. "From the start, it was easier for us to add to our basic product what they provided, than for them to add what we built to theirs."[59] In 1998, Reuters was accused of stealing confidential data from Bloomberg in an attempt to copy some of its services.[60] Five years later, Reuters reported a loss, and it cut its reporting staff.[61] A competing business news service called Bridge Information Systems also started in the 1990s and was run by former Reuters managers, but it went out of business after the market fell in 2000. By 2001, Bloomberg had more than 1,100 reporters in 79 bureaus.[62]

Bloomberg was successful in giving the same information to Wall Street traders and its newspaper clients, and it provided the information in various formats, from its computer terminals to its television network. As consumers of business news received more detailed information, they became more knowledgeable about what was going on in the markets and the economy. In addition, Bloomberg pushed for more access to business information. It was one of the biggest proponents of Regulation Fair Disclosure, a Securities and Exchange Commission rule that went into effect in 2000 and required companies to disseminate information to everyone at the same time instead of doling it out to favored analysts and investors in private conversations or on restricted conference calls.

The word *Bloomberg* has become nearly synonymous with business news and data, just as Reuters and Dow Jones have been for the previous 100-plus years. And by providing an additional news service that focused on business and economics coverage, Bloomberg showed the growing importance of such news to readers everywhere.

Puff piece to aggressive coverage

As the stock markets fell back in 2000 and 2001 and corporate scandals that helped prop up companies – and their celebrity executives – increasingly were uncovered, the business press reacted in a natural way, turning in the opposite direction from its soft coverage to become more critical and aggressive.

Many business reporters and editors felt that they had been duped into believing that companies operated ethically and that their projections for future growth were accurate. As their eyes opened, the reporters and editors realized they needed to be more skeptical of what they were told. The market didn't always go up, and neither did corporate profits. Sometimes, companies reported higher results because of illegal maneuvers taken by executives.

Business journalism, with few exceptions, simply repeated the mistakes from the 1920s before the Great Depression. "The press has been a participant in the misinformation that often accompanies periods of high speculation," said Jeffrey Madrick, the editor of economics magazine *Challenge.* "There was never a golden age when that didn't happen. But there was a time when the financial press was on the whole considerably more skeptical."[63]

Madrick says the business press failed in the 1990s because it had became "market oriented and more profit oriented on average."[64] As a result, the business media became reluctant to cover bad news.

Some business journalists argued that they were duped into believing companies such as Enron and executives such as Dennis Kozlowski because they were pillars of society who were supposed to act in the proper way. Journalists did not have the tools and expertise to uncover the wrongdoing, they say. But that thesis can only go so far. The business press didn't do the serious work required of its job. It also was too quick to bill itself as an all-knowing expert and anoint companies and executives as successes without examining all the facts.

Business journalism is now rebuilding its credibility with society by tackling its coverage in a more aggressive manner. More questions are being asked. Harder news stories have begun returning to business sections and magazines, replacing softer stories. Business journalism is actually better than it ever has been, argue many in the field.[65]

But it can continue to improve and remember the mistakes of its past, focusing instead on the required reporting techniques of reading SEC filings and digging into lawsuits. "Only that kind of serious, sober, independent reporting can give the public the insights into American business it now knows it needs to learn," said Philip Longman, a senior fellow at the New America Foundation. "Let's hope the business press learns the hard way what happens when journalism never dares to be dull."[66]

Footnotes

1 From "Business reporting: Behind the curve," by D. Henriques, November/December 2000, Columbia Journalism Review, p. 18.

2 From "Follow the money," by L. M. Simons, November 1999, American Journalism Review, p. 56.

3 From "Business reporting: Behind the curve," p. 19.

4 See "The business century: How the economy became hot news in the last 100 years," by B. Saporito, March/April 1999, Columbia Journalism Review, pp. 47–52.

5 See "Follow the money," pp. 55–68.

6 From "Forty years of the 500," by C. Loomis, May 15, 1995, Fortune, p. 182.

7 From "Box score of business bigness," July 1955, Fortune, pp. 96–97.

8 From "Forty years of the 500," p. 182.

9 From "What is the chief executive worth?" May 15, 1971, Forbes, p. 164.

10 From "What is the chief executive worth?" p. 164.

11 From "What 800 companies pay their bosses," May 27, 1991, Forbes, p. 236.

12 From "The Inc. 100: The 12th annual ranking of America's fastest growing small public companies," by R. A. Mamis, May 1990, Inc., p. 32.

13 From "Those list-crazy business magazines," by P. Passell, Aug. 5, 1987, New York Times, p. A26.

14 From "Those list-crazy business magazines," p. A26.

15 From "The Forbes Four Hundred," by H. Seneker, Sept. 13, 1982, Forbes, p. 100.

16 From "The Forbes Four Hundred," p. 100.

17 From "The Forbes Four Hundred," p. 102.

18 From "Forbes hunts for richest four hundred," by N. R. Kleinfeld, Sept. 11, 1982, New York Times, p. 35.

19 From "Throw a tantrum, sign a contract," by P. Newcomb and C. Palmeria, Oct. 1, 1990, Forbes, p. 68.

20 See Money, March 1994.

21 See Smart Money, July 1999.

22 From "Magazine showdown," by M. R. Baker, October 1999, Brill's Content, pp. 110–112.

23 See BusinessWeek, May 12, 1956. The article appears on p. 68.

24 See Forbes, Dec. 1, 1957. The article appears on p. 13.

25 From "My years with General Motors – Part I," by A. P. Sloan Jr., September 1963, Fortune, pp. 135–142, 196–203.

26 From "Faces of the '90s: CEOs are stars now, but why? And would Alfred Sloan approve?" by G. P. Zachary, Sept. 3, 1997, The Wall Street Journal, p. A1.

27 From "The curse of the superstar CEO," by R. Khurana, September 2002, Harvard Business Review, September 2002, p. 60.

28 From "White-collar crime is big business," by M. Green and J. F. Berry, June 8, 1985, The Nation, p. 689.

29 From "Money makes headlines in today's news coverage," by N. Solomon, Summer 2002, Nieman Reports, p. 17.

30 From "You've read about who's influential, but who has the power," by R. Lacayo, June 17, 1996, Time, p. 80.

31 From "Making Bill," by E. L. Stevens, September 1998, Brill's Content, pp. 100–114.

32 From "Faces of the '90s: CEOs are stars now, but why? And would Alfred Sloan approve?" p. A1.

33 See, for example, "Election spices up CEO talks; some chiefs back Clinton on trade," by M. Fetterman, Oct. 12, 1992, USA Today, p. 2B.

34 From Testosterone Inc.: Tales of CEOs gone wild, by C. Byron, New York: John Wiley & Sons, 2004, pp. 32–33.

35 From Testosterone Inc.: Tales of CEOs gone wild, p. 33.

36 From Testosterone Inc.: Tales of CEOs gone wild, p. 311.

37 From Testosterone Inc.: Tales of CEOs gone wild, p. 80.

38 From "Nantucket still a welcome port to 'exiled' Kozlowski," by M. Brelis, Dec. 1, 2002, Boston Globe, p. G1.

39 From Testosterone Inc.: Tales of CEOs gone wild, pp. 266–267.

40 From Media monopoly, by B. Bagdikian, Boston: Beacon Press, 1997, fifth edition.

41 From "Lionizing Coke's King: Media, myth, capitalism, and the death of Roberto Goizueta," by P. J. Priest and N. Kohn, a paper presented at the Association for Education in Journalism and Mass Communication 1999 annual meeting.

42 From "The sound you hear is silence," by M. Mintz, Summer 2000, Nieman Reports, pp. 60–64.

43 From "Now playing!!! The celebrity CEO," by A. Sloan, Sept. 17, 2001, Newsweek, p. 55.

44 From "Monitoring the financial press and forced CEO turnover," by K. A. Farrell and D. A. Whidbee, 2002, Journal of Banking and Finance, pp. 2249–2276.

45 From "Believing one's own press: The causes and consequences of CEO celebrity," by M. L. A. Hayward, V. P. Rindova and T. G. Pollack, July 2004, Strategic Management Journal, pp. 645–646.

46 From "Believing one's own press: The causes and consequences of CEO celebrity," pp. 645–646.

47 From "Local business press: New phenomenon in the marketplace," by B. G. Vanden Bergh, A. D. Fletcher, and M. A. Adrian, Spring 1984, Journalism Quarterly, pp. 645–646.

48 From "Business paper shootout headed for New York," by R. Fannin, October 1984, Marketing & Media Decisions, p. 62.

49 From "Business paper shootout headed for New York," p. 62.

50 From "Boom in the business press," by J. Alter, Jan. 7, 1985, Newsweek, p. 66.

51 From "Demand-side journalism," by R. McGough, Feb. 23, 1987, Forbes, p. 68.

52 Much of the history used in this section came from "ACBJ: Serving up local business," a paper written by Colin Sutker, a student in "Business and the Media" during the Spring 2005 semester at the University of North Carolina at Chapel Hill.

53 From "ACBJ: Serving up local business."

54 A list of the Crain publications can be found at http://www.crain.com/po.html#citypubs.

55 From "Bloomberg is starting financial news service," by B. Feder, March 29, 1991, New York Times, p. D4.

56 From Breaking News: How the wheels came off at Reuters, by B. Mooney and B. Simpson, London: Capstone Publishing Ltd., 2003, pp. 5–6.

57 From Breaking News: How the wheels came off at Reuters, pp. 21–33.

58 From "How Bloomberg pressures editors: They can't pay for the machine, but they can get it for credit," by D. Kadlec, September/October 1997, Columbia Journalism Review, p. 38.

59 From "Bloomberg by Bloomberg," by M. Bloomberg, New York: John Wiley & Sons, 1997, p. 86.

60 From "Memos said to detail Reuters effort to obtain Bloomberg data," by K. Eichenwald, Feb. 2, 1998, New York Times, p. D1.

61 From "Can Reuters recover? The venerable agency needs a new strategy for success," by J. Matloff, July/August 2003, Columbia Journalism Review, p. 49.

62 From "The cult of Bloomberg," by A. Pogrebin, June 2001, Brill's Content, p. 96.

63 From "Financial reporting: Lessons of the Enron collapse," by J. Madrick, Winter 2003, Harvard International Journal of Press/Politics, p. 3.

64 From "Financial reporting: Lessons of the Enron collapse," p. 4.

65 From "Grading business journalism," by G. Harmon, www.businessjournalism.org, available at www.businessjournalism.org/content/5764.cfm.

66 From "Bad press: How business journalism helped inflate the bubble," by P. Longman, Washington Monthly, October 2002, p. 18.

Chapter 11

The business media and the auto industry

On April 6, 2005, *Los Angeles Times* automotive critic Dan Neil reviewed the new Pontiac G6. He was unimpressed with the vehicle and the recent performance of General Motors, Pontiac's maker. Neil concluded his column by stating, "When ballclubs have losing records, players and coaches and managers get their walking papers. At GM, it's time to sweep the dugout."[1] The implication was that General Motors CEO Rick Wagoner should be fired.

The Detroit-based automaker reacted immediately. The next day, it pulled its advertising from the newspaper "for the foreseeable future." A company spokeswoman stated it heard "strongly voiced objections from our dealers in California and from within GM regarding factual errors and misrepresentations."[2] The annual advertising spending by GM in the newspaper was estimated at $10 million.[3]

The dispute between one of the world's largest companies and one of the most respected newspapers in the United States wasn't unique, however. Throughout business journalism history, the auto industry and the media have constantly clashed over what auto companies feel is unfair and improper coverage.

The incidents include a May 1954 boycott of *The Wall Street Journal* by General Motors, which was upset that the newspaper printed details and sketches of some of its 1955 models before the company wanted them released to the public. The company stopped purchasing ads in the newspaper and also severed relationships with the editorial staff.[4] The boycott ended a month later when the company was criticized by other media.

In the 1960s, General Motors spied on consumer advocate Ralph Nader after the publication of his book "Unsafe at Any Speed," which criticized the Corvair. In a statement, the company acknowledged its investigation was "promoted by Mr. Nader's extreme criticism of the Corvair in his writings, press conferences, TV and other public appearances."[5]

In 1983, Chrysler pulled its ads from industry publication *Car and Driver* after the magazine published a story about the damage a Dodge suffered when it was being test driven in Mexico and struck a steer.[6]

In 1992, General Motors pulled its advertising from *Automobile* magazine for three months after its editor, David E. Davis Jr., criticized the company's management during a speech at the Washington Automotive Press Association's black-tie gala.[7]

The same year, GM sued the "Dateline NBC" television show for its report on the manufacturer's pickup trucks. The report showed one truck exploding after a collision because the crash was rigged by the producers of the show. After the automaker filed a defamation lawsuit, NBC apologized in a three-and-a-half-minute statement for making the accident look worse. After the apology was read, GM resumed advertising.[8]

In 1994, auto dealers pressured the *San Jose Mercury News* to apologize for a May 22 article on buying cars that quoted the author of a book on negotiating stating, "One reason God gave you feet was so you could use them to walk away from car salesmen." Three days after the article appeared, three dozen dealers met with the paper's publisher, and 40 pulled their advertising, costing the paper $1 million in revenue.[9]

The relationship between the media and the auto industry ... is contentious because of the billions of dollars carmakers and dealers spend each year on advertising.

Similar boycotts have occurred at papers throughout the country. In addition, dealers have influenced newspaper coverage in other ways. In 2005, *The Virginian-Pilot* in Norfolk dropped the syndicated auto column of Tom and Ray Magliozzi after complaints from local dealers.[10]

In 1997, before he went to the *Los Angeles Times,* Dan Neil wrote a road test of the 1997 Ford Explorer for *The* (Raleigh) *News & Observer.* In the review, he wrote that the vehicle was a good place to have sex. After complaints from dealers, he was put on probation and then later fired. His firing was covered in *Media & The Law* with the following lead: "Covering cars just got more boring in North Carolina."[11] Neil later won a Pulitzer Prize for criticism in 2004 for his auto reviews in the *Times.*

The conflicts haven't been confined to carmakers. The oil and gas industry, reliant on the auto industry to provide customers for its products, has also had a contentious relationship with the media. In 1984, Mobil Corp. canceled its advertising in *The Wall Street Journal* and refused to provide information to its reporters after what it termed "five years of problems."[12]

These conflicts are more than a pattern. They show the media's intense interest in the auto industry, perhaps the one business that has the biggest impact on the U.S. economy. In fact, it could be argued that no industry has garnered as much attention and examination from the media as the auto industry. Partly because of the American fascination with cars and other types of vehicles – from monster trucks to motorcycles – the press has covered automakers consistently, thoroughly, and sometimes overwhelmingly in the past 100-plus years. But sometimes, the media has also shied away from aggressive coverage for business reasons.

At newspapers such as the *Detroit Free Press* and the *Detroit News,* teams of reporters and editors are devoted to covering the auto manufacturers. The national magazines and newspapers such as *BusinessWeek* and *The Wall Street Journal* also have full-time reporters and editors on the auto beat. And then there are the trade publications that write solely about cars and their makers.

The relationship between the media and the auto industry, however, is contentious because of the billions of dollars carmakers and dealers spend each year on advertising.

Unwilling to upset some of their largest advertisers, publications, TV stations, and other media outlets shy away from aggressively covering the business. And when they report a story mildly critical of the car business, the reporters and editors routinely receive complaining phone calls from someone in the industry.

In some ways, the relationship between the media and the auto industry helps define business journalism. The rise – and stumbles – of the auto industry have gone hand in hand with the developments of business and the economic reporting. The rise to dominance of GM and Ford Motor Co. as huge companies controlling a sizeable chunk of the economy demanded that the media cover them in great detail. Their leaders graced magazine covers well before executives in other industries. Their new products were dissected well before other products received the same scrutiny. Their financial performance was a reason for curiosity well before other company earnings. Their struggles became front-page news as well. A car purchase was a huge investment for readers, who wanted to know what was going on at these companies.

Because of the intense coverage, the auto industry has tried, sometimes successfully, to push back against the media. The relationship between auto companies and business journalists is one that is closely watched because of the intense competition among the media outlets to scoop one another.

It's also been the industry where business journalism has, in some respects, had its greatest accomplishments and setbacks in the past 40 years.

Ralph Nader and *Unsafe at Any Speed*

The media's interest in automobiles began with the inception of the motorized vehicle. Beginning in 1898, newspaper coverage in Peoria and Chicago was prolific as Charles and Frank Duryea kept the press informed about their orders and the number of Duryeas shipped. Coverage intensified when Henry Ford began offering his Model T in 1908 for $850. The first affordable vehicle for most Americans transformed society by making travel easier and faster. Six years later, Ford had a bigger impact on society when he announced, with voluminous press coverage, that he would pay factory workers $5 per day – about twice the going rate. When word reached the South, people moved North to find work.

The media documented other dramatic auto developments throughout the years. In 1917, Ford was sued by the Dodge brothers, and the settlement in the case allowed John and Horace Dodge to start their own company. Newspaper owner E. W. Scripps kept a steady correspondence with automakers such as Ransom E. Olds, David Dunbar Buick, and George Studebaker, and encouraged coverage in his papers. Ford unveiled the Model A in 1927, while General Motors passed Ford in sales in 1931. In 1937, a strike in Flint, Michigan, led to widespread coverage and criticism in the media about General Motors' handling of worker issues.

In the early 1950s, smaller automakers garnered widespread coverage when they merged to form American Motors to compete against the bigger companies. In 1953, Chevrolet introduced the Corvette to combat European sports cars, and in 1964, the Ford Mustang and Pontiac GTO ushered in muscle cars.

Some in the media were also examining car safety and other related auto issues. In 1952, *Consumer Reports* published its first frequency-of-repair charts for autos based on reader responses. A decade later, the magazine published a guide to auto insurance, calling for reforms after it discovered that rates varied by hundreds of dollars across the country for similar drivers.[13]

But in 1965, a book criticizing the Detroit automakers would receive widespread attention for its accusations after General Motors, the largest company in the country, was found to have investigated its author.

Ralph Nader was unknown in the United States in the early 1960s. A lawyer, Nader wrote an article in *The Nation* in October 1963 noting that some cars seemed to be more accident prone than others and that the safety of a car was a function of how the car was built as well as how it was driven. "Slaughter on the highways has been a perennial phenomenon for nearly half a century, and still an industry is permitted to produce, unhindered, vehicles full of accidents and tragedies waiting to happen," wrote Nader.[14]

The article was virtually ignored, and the auto industry successfully thwarted attempts to force it to build safer vehicles for nearly a decade. In the spring of 1965, a Senate subcommittee led by Connecticut Sen. Abraham Ribicoff began investigating highway safety. Nader, a subcommittee advisor, testified about a Cornell University study showing a relationship between a car's design and fatal accidents.[15]

On Nov. 30, 1965, Nader's book *Unsafe at Any Speed* was published. It criticized the safety of several cars, particularly GM's Corvair. On the same day, *The New York Times* ran an article on p. 68 in which Nader blasted the auto industry, the tire producers, the National Safety Council, and the American Automobile Association for ignoring safety problems. The second paragraph of the article read, "Ralph Nader, a Washington lawyer, says that auto safety takes a back seat to styling, comfort, speed, power and the desire of automakers to cut costs." The story later stated, "Mr. Nader charges that the President's Committee for Traffic Safety is little more than a private-interest group running a public agency that speaks with the authority of the President."[16]

The industry reacted swiftly. The next day, the *Times* ran an article on p. 37 in which the automobile industry denied Nader's charges.[17] Articles on Nov. 30 and Dec. 1 also mentioned his book. In the Nov. 30 article, the book was mentioned in the sixth paragraph, but in the Dec. 1 article, where the car companies denied ignoring safety, it was mentioned in the third paragraph.

Interest in Nader's accusations and his book would have likely died if not for General Motors' actions. The company hired private investigators to pry into Nader's life. When the investigation into Nader became public, Ribicoff and others were outraged. On March 9, 1966, the *Times* reported that two senators – Ribicoff and Gaylord Nelson from Wisconsin – called for a Justice Department investigation into the harassment. "No citizen of this country should be forced to endure the kind of clumsy harassment to which Mr. Nader has apparently been subjected since the publication of his book," said Ribicoff. "Anonymous phone calls in the middle of the night have no place in a free society."[18]

A day later, General Motors admitted it had investigated Nader. By this time, the *Times* moved the story to the front page of the paper.[19] With GM backtracking, the media covered the story aggressively. On March 23, the apology to Nader from GM was prominently written about on page one of the *Times*, along with Nader's picture, as Ribicoff had held a hearing the day before on GM's spying.[20] On April 21, 1966, the *Times* noted that the CBS network would air in May an hour-long special on automobile safety, and its story mentioned

Nader in the fifth paragraph.[21] On May 21, 1966, the *Times* ran an article in which GM President James Roche said publicity of the safety issue surrounding the Corvair had hurt sales. The article, based on the company's annual meeting, noted that Nader had been nominated as a director of the company, but received just 217 votes out of more than 232 million cast.[22]

On Oct. 24, 1966, the *Times* noted the passage of the Traffic Safety Act, which would set federal safety guidelines for cars and tires, due to "the insistent efforts of Ralph Nader."[23] The article said the turning point in getting the legislation approved was when Nader revealed he had been spied upon.

The media covered Nader and the auto safety issue closely during this period because of the public relations gaffes that plagued General Motors. The company at first denied it had investigated Nader, and then, when caught in the lie, confessed. Once that happened, the media sensed that automobile safety was an issue that the industry didn't want to address. Because of Nader and the media coverage, the carmakers were forced to handle the issue sooner rather than later.

On May 13, 1969, the *Times* carried one more front-page article that mentioned Nader, General Motors, and the Corvair. The company announced it was discontinuing the car. The story noted that the Corvair had helped Nader build "his attack on the automobile industry" and was the car that "indirectly led to Government regulation of the auto industry."[24] By the time the car was pulled, its sales had fallen 93 percent.

Without Nader's fight for car safety and the consistent reporting of the topic, society might still have safer automobiles than 40 years ago. But without the coverage, the safety features installed in virtually every make and model would not have happened as soon. "In the klieg lights of national television, a folk hero was born – and the modern consumer movement got underway," said *Columbia Journalism Review* in 1990.[25] By the end of 1969, Nader appeared on *Time*'s cover with the headline, "The consumer revolt."[26]

The energy crisis and Japanese invasion

The industry's dealings with Nader showed the media that the auto companies were unprepared to deal with harsh criticism. Although these companies had been successful for decades and had become the country's largest corporations, they were not immune to mistakes. One of their biggest blunders – failing to anticipate the move to more fuel-efficient cars – occurred in the early 1970s, and journalists, having seen the public's interest in the auto industry's travails with Nader and car safety, jumped on the story.

Japanese automakers had been in the United States since 1957, when Toyota entered the market. But initially sales were slow, and the business media ignored the overseas competition. One of the first articles that noted the potential for Japanese companies to take sales away from the U.S. carmakers was on Nov. 10, 1968, when a *Times'* story noted how Toyota and Nissan planned to boost sales in the United States. The response of the U.S. companies in the article was to lobby for tariffs against the imports or convince the Japanese government to lower tariffs so they could compete in that market.[27]

Three years later, the coverage was on the impact of Japanese auto sales in the wake of a tariff increase. The *Times* wrote in August 1971 about how Toyota customers who had ordered, but not yet received, their cars were calling dealerships to see if they would have to pay the increased tax.[28] *Forbes*, meanwhile, began to raise concerns about the impact of Japanese imports on the American automakers one month later. It reported that Japanese cars were outselling American models in Southern California. "Detroit's problem was compounded by the fact that it somehow failed to recognize how determined the Japanese can be," said the magazine.[29]

By 1973, the Japanese car invasion into the United States exploded in the aftermath of the Arab oil embargo, which led to gasoline shortages across the country. Because the Japanese cars got better gas mileage, they became more economical for many U.S. consumers. A Nov. 10, 1973, article in the *Times* on the impact of the energy crisis, however, ignored the Japanese companies except for a brief mention that the gas shortage was increasing "interest in small cars."[30] Most of the story focused on plans by the American companies to roll out compact cars in coming years. A similar focus was taken by the *Times* in a Dec. 14, 1973, story detailing steps being taken by the American car builders to come up with more fuel-efficient cars. The article noted "decisions that are being made now as a result of the fuel crisis will not, however, become part of products rolling off the assembly line until at least 1976."[31]

The Japanese auto companies, however, had already flooded the market with cheap, fuel-efficient cars and took sales away from Ford, General Motors, Chrysler, and American Motors, the four big American car companies at the time. *Forbes*, in its Jan. 1, 1974, issue, was the first to question the U.S. manufacturers' strategy with a story that used the headline, "The writing was on the wall, but Detroit didn't bother to decipher it." The story noted that the American companies were "making more big cars than [they] could sell" and that "the Big Three all misjudged the strength of the trend toward smallness."[32] Only American Motors, which at the time made the compact cars Gremlin and Hornet, had been unscathed.

The *Times* finally caught on in April 1974, noting sales at the American car companies had fallen dramatically, but its coverage added that some Japanese automakers were also struggling due to inflation in their home country.[33] One that was not struggling was Datsun, but it faced the issue of getting its cars from Japan to America because of a shortage of ships. The Subaru importer chided the American companies, stating, "They were brought up with the big-car point of view. How do you change your value systems?"[34]

In 1975, *U.S. News & World Report* weighed in on the failure of the American car companies to compete effectively in the small car market. On June 16, it commented that Detroit had thrown in the towel and would now try to compete in the small car market against its Japanese competitors.[35] A month later, its July 28 issue questioned whether the 1976 models from the American car companies would sell because they had yet to incorporate design features to improve fuel efficiency.[36]

Another problem for the companies was credibility, the magazine pointed out. Detroit auto executives had claimed that they couldn't achieve federal standards for safety and pollution, but then met them. "It may also be one reason why some buyers have turned to imported makes," said *U.S. News*.[37]

By 1977, the domestic car companies rebounded against the Japanese imports, and the tone of the coverage was more upbeat for the industry. The *Times* reported on Oct. 23, 1977, that Ford was about to introduce its Fairmont model, "a 2,700-pound gas-sipper of unmistakably foreign heritage."[38]

In its Jan. 16, 1978, issue, *Fortune* heralded "How G.M. turned itself around" from its standing at the end of 1973 of having the worst average gas mileage among U.S. automakers. In 1977, GM's gas mileage was better than either Ford or Chrysler. But the magazine also criticized the company's past strategy with the analysis that "G.M. was slow to realize what besides efficiency made the imports so attractive: agility and a certain sporty functionalism were increasingly appealing to a broader public than what G.M. understood."[39]

At the end of the month, the *Times* took the same tone with a story titled, "Meeting the imports head-on." In it, the newspaper's main auto writer at the time traveled to domestic car dealerships and found that their new compact cars were selling.[40]

By the end of the decade, stories about the Japanese car invasion and its effects on the American auto industry had died out. In the early 1980s, the story became how the U.S. companies responded to the threat, although the Japanese companies maintained a large market share. Since the 1980s, the Japanese automakers have become increasing part of auto industry coverage as they build plants in the United States.

In the 1980s, however, the story in the auto industry also shifted in a way that mirrored a growing problem in business journalism.

Lee Iacocca woos the business press

Many articles written about the Japanese invasion into the American auto market in the 1970s quoted Ford executive Lee Iacocca. But in July 1978, Henry Ford II fired Iacocca, then Ford's president. Within months, Iacocca moved to Chrysler, where he became president and chief operating officer. By the end of 1979, he convinced Congress to back $1.5 billion in loans to the company so it could avoid filing for bankruptcy court protection.

With his marketing background, Iacocca was one of the few auto industry executives who believed in using the media to promote his agenda. In 1964, he appeared on the covers of both *Time* and *Newsweek* as the creator of the Ford Mustang.[41] After joining his new company, Iacocca wasted no time in courting business reporters and editors by telling them his strategy for turning around the ailing Chrysler. In November 1978, barely one week into the job, Iacocca was interviewed in the *Times* explaining that Chrysler's marketing and service needed to be overhauled.[42] The next year, he sent telegrams to publishers of the country's largest newspapers, inviting them to a meeting at Chrysler headquarters for a "private but on-the-record preview" of the company's models for the next five years.[43] For Iacocca, now Chrysler's chairman and CEO, the meeting had an obvious purpose – turn media coverage of his struggling company around.

By 1982, as Chrysler's financial performance improved, the media obliged. Iacocca became one of the first celebrity CEOs created by press coverage. On Aug. 29, 1982, he was pictured on the front page of the *Times'* business section with a story titled, "Iacocca rides high in Detroit."[44] Quoted throughout the article were Wall Street analysts lauding the executive's performance. One analyst even noted Iacocca had become the industry spokesman, a spot normally reserved for the leader at General Motors. *Time* magazine also noticed, examining how the company used Iacocca in its commercials to sell cars. The general-interest magazine gushed, "Chrysler's recovery is largely Iacocca's doing, a triumph of brains, bluster and bravado."[45]

Columnist Russell Baker of the *Times* became smitten with Iacocca, writing on March 27, 1983, that, "I like Lee Iacocca, though we've never met. I like the cut of his jib and the jut of his jaw as he walks and talks. He strikes me as one corporation leader who is interested in making something."[46] Later, Baker imagined Iacocca on the floor of a Chrysler factory, talking to workers on how to construct a dashboard or build a radiator. Baker's entire impression, however, was based on watching Chrysler's commercials featuring the CEO.

By this time, Iacocca's ascendancy to media darling was complete. There was speculation about him running for president. In 1984, Chrysler made as much money as it had in its previous 58 years combined. That year, when Iacocca led a pep rally at a Michigan assembly plant, *Time* described the reaction as a "roar worthy of the crowds in Latin American soccer stadiums when their national teams take the field."[47] The next year, the same magazine called him "a spunky tycoon turned superstar" and "America's hottest new folk hero" for turning around Chrysler.[48] The CEO added to the media coverage by writing a book and making public appearances. "Not since William Randolph Hearst has there been a tycoon who has occupied the national imagination as vividly as Iacocca," wrote *Time*.[49] In 1985, Iacocca was named the country's most influential person outside government.

Compared to other auto executives reluctant to talk to the business media, Iacocca seemed liked a breath of fresh air.

The business press's coverage of Chrysler and its charming CEO turned him into the first of what would become a series of executives viewed as celebrities and heroes. Explained John Huey, then a *Wall Street Journal* reporter:

> When Chrysler Corp. was down for the count, Mr. Iacocca took a page from the lives of Joe Namath and Muhammad Ali (both bona fide heroes), and went before Congress to stage the corporate equivalent of personally guaranteeing he would beat the Colts, while simultaneously taunting Sonny Liston. When Chrysler got up and staggered back to its corner to continue the fight, the modern chief executive hero was born. Forget that the turnaround at Ford Motor Co. is in many ways a more impressive business achievement; how many Americans can identify Donald Petersen?[50]

Indeed, compared to other auto executives reluctant to talk to the business media, Iacocca seemed liked a breath of fresh air. And as such, he received more leeway from reporters and editors. His appearances in more than 80 Chrysler television commercials made him a public figure to the average consumer, many of whom were likely recognizing their first CEO when they saw Iacocca's picture in the paper. Iacocca would reappear in the company's commercials in 2005, long after he had stepped down as its leader.

According to one analysis of how Iacocca was portrayed in the press, "Media attention to Chrysler's problems suggested that assurances from the person in control would be most effective."[51] Many of his actions, such as cutting his salary, were designed to elicit favorable coverage. Another assessment of Iacocca's communication skills noted, "Part of his popularity is that he doesn't impose on the press for a non-event," and "I'm convinced one of the reasons media people attend Iacocca's press conferences in such large numbers is his well-known gift for turning a phrase, for giving them a quotable quote."[52] A third evaluation of the Iacocca-as-celebrity-CEO phenomenon concluded that the positive media coverage was the reason for his success and popularity.[53]

Coverage of Iacocca and Chrysler during his tenure, which lasted from 1979 to 1992, showed how the media could turn a CEO into a cult-like figure with boosterish coverage. In many respects, stories about Iacocca were the first in the media to portray an executive as some sort of all-knowing and all-powerful person and started the trend of reporting about CEOs of other companies in a similar fashion.

But auto industry reporters, who have a reputation of often being too close to the companies they cover, didn't always roll over and cater to their sources. In the 1990s and on into the 21st century, business journalism aggressively uncovered other embarrassing problems at the U.S. car companies.

The SUV and *The New York Times*

Outside of Detroit, no daily newspaper has written more unconventional stories about the auto industry than *The New York Times.* For decades, the paper has put some of its top reporters in its Detroit bureau and told them to stand out from the pack of other journalists writing about the car business. Other national papers also devoted resources to Detroit. *USA Today* has had two full-time reporters on the beat, while *The Wall Street Journal* has had five reporters covering the industry.

Despite the overly positive coverage of Chrysler and Iacocca, the auto industry continued to struggle for much of the 1980s and 1990s, and many reporters documented its issues. Alex Taylor III, *Fortune's* primary auto industry writer, wrote an exhaustive look at the industry in 1992, noting that the Detroit companies had a chance to take back the lead in car sales from their Japanese competitors but failed when given the same opportunity a decade earlier.[54]

Among the major auto stories in the 1980s was Chrysler's acquisition of American Motors in 1987. The deal included the Jeep brand, and the company and other domestic auto manufacturers pushed so-called sports utility vehicles – automobiles that were similar to Jeeps but with back seats and more luggage area – to consumers as a way to counteract Japanese car sales. Because SUVs were designated as light trucks by regulations, they were exempt from many rules regarding gas mileage and emissions. The vehicles were attractive to many consumers because they conveyed an active, outdoor lifestyle. By 1996, SUVs accounted for 44 percent of vehicle sales.

Entering the auto beat the same year was Keith Bradsher, a *Times* reporter who moved to Detroit to become bureau chief. Bradsher had spent time on other business beats, but he was not an auto expert or a car enthusiast. His first stories on the beat were typical of stories from most reporters. A May 1996 article noted that the increased competition in the SUV market could reduce profits for Detroit companies.[55] But in July of that year, Bradsher wrote his first story that raised the question of SUV pollution and poor gas mileage. The title: "What not to drive to the recycling center?" Bradsher wrote, "The first signs of backlash against sport vehicles are emerging. While the vehicles continue to fly off the dealers' lots, some people are objecting that they burn too much gasoline and spew out too much pollution."[56]

Bradsher continued to dig deeper into the SUV's impact on society and switched his coverage from pollution and gas mileage to another consequence. On March 19, 1997, his first bombshell appeared on the front page of the *Times.* In the story, Bradsher documented how people driving smaller cars struck by SUVs in accidents were much more likely to die than the person driving the SUV.[57] Accompanying the story was a chart that compared the weight of light trucks to sedans, and the height of the bumpers.

Four days later, Bradsher followed with an article looking into the psychology of why people buy SUVs. One of the main reasons was to feel safer and to improve their view of the road. In addition, "Sport utility vehicles appeal to an aging population desperately seeking security at a time of widespread worries about corporate downsizing, family breakups and crime," wrote Bradsher.[58] On June 11, 1997, Bradsher wrote another article titled, "Sport utility vehicles pose growing danger to car occupants" that reported on a Department of Transportation study of accidents between SUVs and cars.[59]

By September, Bradsher was back on the front page, writing about the same issue. This time, he carried his reporting further, noting that despite the increase in accidents between SUVs and cars, regulators in Washington and the car companies in Detroit were ignoring the issue. The story also noted that the Detroit companies made virtually all of their profits on light trucks and barely broke even selling cars.[60] He continued his aggressive reporting in October with a front-page story that disclosed that insurance companies planned to increase premiums on SUVs[61] and followed that up with a front-page article in November that detailed how light trucks emitted more pollution than cars.[62]

In December, two more front-page articles by Bradsher noted additional safety problems in SUVs when they rolled over[63] and detailed how light trucks were able to avoid rules on pollutions.[64] In January 1998, Bradsher followed the pollution story with one that noted how Ford and GM planned to cut emissions in sport vehicles.[65] A month later, Bradsher disclosed that insurance companies were urging the car companies to revamp designs of sport utilities.[66]

Interestingly, few other business journalists followed Bradsher's lead. Although he eventually won a George Polk Award for his coverage, his stories were criticized by other auto reporters in addition to the company executives.[67] Industry publication *AutoWeek* issued a press release when it ran a cover story on Bradsher's reporting. The press release stated, "It was the *Times* which chose to pick up the sword against trucks and SUVs – and it is *AutoWeek's* duty to not only support car and truck passion, but also to bring fairness to the discussion."[68]

But like the stories by muckrakers nearly 100 years earlier, Bradsher's reporting forced the government to act. After his stories began appearing, regulatory agencies paid more attention to SUVs. The National Highway Traffic Safety Administration conducted its first test of light truck crashes in 1998 and put pressure on the Detroit companies to improve safety features. The Environmental Protection Agency increased its examination of light truck emission standards.[69]

In 2002, Bradsher wrote a book called *High and Mighty: SUVs – The world's most dangerous vehicles and how they got that way,* going into further detail about the rise and dangers of the SUV. But the book never had the widespread impact of Sinclair's *The Jungle* or Tarbell's

History of the Standard Oil Company. People continued to purchase such vehicles, although the car companies did improve their safety.

Ford and Firestone's debacle

While Bradsher was still covering the auto industry, an even bigger story about SUV safety and accidents surfaced that would give one of the car companies its biggest embarrassment. Reporting on the problems with Firestone tires on Ford Explorers would later place stories by a Houston television station in a compilation of the top muckraking pieces of journalism of all time.

The relationship between Ford and tire company Firestone dated back to 1895, when Henry Ford asked Harvey Firestone to supply him with tires for his new cars. Later, members of the two families would marry each other.[70] In 2000, the relationship became tense because of an increasing number of accidents due to problems with Firestone tires on Ford's most popular SUV.

Anna Werner, a reporter for KHOU-TV in Houston, was a member of the station's investigative unit called "The Defenders." In November 1999, she called an attorney to talk about story ideas. The attorney alerted her to a case in which the tread had come off a Firestone tire and caused an accident.[71] In February 2000, the station ran its story, using examples of accidents and people's deaths to explain the problem. The story disclosed similar accidents elsewhere in the country, and it also quoted a former National Highway Traffic Safety Administration head stating that the tires needed to be recalled. Firestone immediately sent a letter to KHOU, accusing it of "falsehoods and misrepresentations."[72]

No other media picked up the story until the summer, when journalists were spurred by other issues related to the Firestone–Ford problems. Regulators began an investigation in early May, shortly after a *Chicago Sun-Times* series on other tire problems.[73] Two judges ordered that depositions in two Firestone lawsuits be opened to the public in May and July, and in late July, KHOU learned that Ford was replacing Firestone tires on its Explorers in three South American countries.[74]

On Aug. 2, 2000, however, two business reporters for *USA Today* wrote a story that added pressure on the companies and the federal government to act. The story disclosed that Firestone and Ford had known about the problem dating back to 1992, and that the National Highway Traffic Safety Administration was also aware of the problem.[75]

Within a week, Firestone announced a recall of 6.5 million tires after negotiations with Ford and the federal agency. Ford CEO Jacques Nasser lauded KHOU's coverage during the news conference, saying, "They deserved a medal, actually."[76]

Once again, the auto industry had failed to anticipate the negative reaction it would receive from coverage related to the safety of its vehicles, and it took the media to force action. The Ford Explorer–Firestone tire story became front-page news for months around the world as business journalists focused on how the recall and the publicity would affect the financial performance of the two companies and how they were likely to recover from the embarrassment.

On Aug. 26, the *London Times* examined Ford's handling of the situation.[77] In early September, *The New York Times* gave credit to KHOU reporter Werner for breaking the story.[78] In September, *Newsweek* wrote about the increasing litigation facing both Ford and Firestone and the effects of the deaths on their images.[79] For Ford, the accidents were a more serious matter, as the Explorer provided a quarter of the company's profits.

By October, the story shifted to more of a financial angle than the consumer issue of defective tires. *Fortune* wrote about why chairman Bill Ford Jr. had kept quiet about the issue with the Explorer and its tires.[80] By May 2001, when Firestone announced that it would stop supplying tires to Ford, the story became the bickering between the two companies over which was at fault for nearly 100 deaths.

BusinessWeek explored the battle between the two companies in its June 11, 2001, issue, and neither company came out looking good.[81] Firestone argued that the Explorer was more accident prone than the Ford Ranger, while Ford rolled out data showing the Firestone tires were more likely to fail than Goodyear tires used on the same vehicles. In the end, executives lost jobs, and consumers became less confident in their products. Throughout coverage of the Ford–Firestone story, executives for the tire maker went to great pains to make it clear it was not admitting any guilt for the accidents. In the end, the desire to avoid taking blame in the beginning of the crisis is what may have hurt them the most. In May 2002, *Forbes* lauded Firestone's return by admitting its mistakes.[82] Both Firestone and Ford used their chief executives in commercials in an attempt to address consumer concerns.

Coverage of wrongdoing by large corporations has become increasingly rare in the 21st century because of economic pressures on business reporters and editors, argues journalism professor Joe Saltzman. "To be printed, it would have to go through a rigorous gauntlet of checks and double-checks because a story like this could mean a loss of significant advertising dollars, to say nothing of lawsuits," he wrote in November 2000, three months after the product recall.[83]

Yet the Ford–Firestone coverage shows that not only are such investigative journalism pieces good reporting, they are necessary to keep companies from harming consumers. Without the media, the companies and government regulators would not have acted as quickly as they did. And because virtually every family in America owns an automobile, strong coverage of the industry is needed in the future to keep it in check.

Such aggressive coverage of the auto industry continues. In June 2005, CNN investigated the number of fires that resulted from a faulty switch installed in millions of Ford vehicles between 1992 and 2003.[84] Ford recalled more than 1 million cars at the time the story ran, but more had yet to be recalled. And earlier in the year, the National Highway Traffic Safety Administration began investigating the switches.

What is learned from examining the relationship between business journalism and the auto industry is that an aggressive, adversarial relationship can exist for decades and result in positive changes for society. One of the newest industries, the Internet, had a much different relationship with the media.

Footnotes

1 From "An American idle; The Pontiac G6 is a sales flop. At General Motors, let the impeachment proceedings begin," by D. Neil, April 6, 2005, Los Angeles Times, p. G1.

2 From "GM pulls ads from Los Angeles Times," by J. P. Miller and J. Mateja, April 8, 2005, Chicago Tribune, p. C3.

3 From "GM has little to gain in paper fight," by B. Steinberg and J. T. Hallinan, April 11, 2005, The Wall Street Journal, p. B5.

4 From "Effect of Mobil news boycott," by A. S. Jones, Dec. 5, 1984, New York Times, p. D4.

5 From "G.M. acknowledges investigating critic," by W. Rugaber, March 10, 1966, New York Times, p. 1.

6 From "G.M.'s snub of the Los Angeles Times is just the latest battle between marketers and media outlets," by S. Elliott, April 11, 2005, New York Times, p. C6.

7 From "When car makers retaliate against critical magazines," by D. P. Levin, June 26, 1992, New York Times, p. D9.

8 From "Did TV news go too far? A look behind the scenes at NBC's truck crash test," by B. Weiser, Feb. 28, 1993, The Washington Post, p. A1.

9 From "Those sensitive auto dealers strike again, and another newspaper caves," by A. C. Shepard, September 1994, American Journalism Review, p. 14.

10 From "Click and Clack dropped from paper after advertisers complain," by D. Astor, May 26, 2005, Editor & Publisher, downloaded May 26, 2005 from http://www.editorandpublisher.com/eandp/news/article_display.jsp?vnu_content_id=1000937090.

11 From "An auto section reluctantly pulls punches," Oct. 17, 1997, Media & the Law.

12 From "Mobil boycotts the Journal," by J. Alter, Dec. 17, 1984, Newsweek, p. 101.

13 From http://www.consumerreports.org/main/content/aboutus.jsp?FOLDER%3C%3Efolder_id=457439&bmUID=1119013190863.

14 From "Penny whistle or public's advocate?" by R. L. Bishop and J. Kilburn, Winter 1972, Public Relations Quarterly, p. 7.

15 From "Penny whistle or public's advocate?" p. 8.

16 From "Lawyer charges auto safety lag," Nov. 30, 1965, New York Times, p. 68.

17 From "Car makers deny a lag in safety," Dec. 1, 1965, New York Times, p. 37.

18 From "Investigation asked," March 9, 1966, New York Times, p. 38.

19 From "G.M. acknowledges investigating critic," p. 1

20 From "Penny whistle or public's advocate?" p. 8.

21 From "C.B.S. to examine car-safety issue," by V. Adams, April 21, 1966, New York Times, p. 79.

22 From "G.M. sales hurt by safety issue," by W. D. Smith, May 21, 1966, New York Times, p. 38.

23 From "89th Congress enacted laws that benefited the consumer," by N. Robertson, Oct. 24, 1966, New York Times, p. 34.

24 From "G.M. drops Corvair, a failure at age 10," by J. M. Flint, May 13, 1969, New York Times, p. 1.

25 From "Ralph Nader: News creator," by D. Bollier, May/June 1990, Columbia Journalism Review, p. 51.

26 See "The U.S.'s toughest customer," Dec. 12, 1969, Time, p. 89.

27 From "The Japanese are coming: U.S. auto makers worry," by J. M. Flint, Nov. 10, 1968, New York Times, p. F1.

28 From "Customers waiting for Toyotas flood office with price queries," by I. Barmash, Aug. 17, 1971, New York Times, p. 18.

29 From "How the Japanese blitzed the California auto market," Sept. 15, 1971, Forbes, p. 28.

30 From "Auto industry in two-way squeeze," Nov. 10, 1973, New York Times, p. 39.

31 From "Auto industry facing lasting changes," by A. Salpukas, Dec. 14, 1973, New York Times, p. 1.

32 From "Automotive: The writing was on the wall, but Detroit didn't bother to decipher it," Jan. 1, 1974, Forbes, pp. 141–142.

33 From "The energy crisis spurs demand for small cars," by J. M. Flint, April 7, 1974, New York Times, p. 1.

34 From "The energy crisis spurs demand for small cars," p. 1.

35 From "Detroit concedes: Little cars are here to stay," June 16, 1975, U.S. News & World Report, p. 26.

36 From "Can Detroit sell the '76 cars?" July 28, 1975, U.S. News & World Report, p. 45.

37 From "Can Detroit sell the '76 cars?" p. 45.

38 From "It had to be a better idea," by W. K. Stevens, Oct. 23, 1977, New York Times, p. F1.

39 From "How G.M. turned itself around," by C. G. Burck, Jan. 16, 1978, Fortune, p. 88.

40 From "Meeting the imports head-on," by W. K. Stevens, Jan. 29, 1978, New York Times, p. Auto 1.

41 See "The Mustang, the newest breed out of Detroit," April 20, 1964, Newsweek, and "Ford's Lee Iacocca," April 17, 1964, Time.

42 From "Iacocca's plan for Chrysler: Focus on service and marketing," by R. Stuart, Nov. 7, 1978, New York Times, p. 70.

43 From "Chrysler team seeks support for aid; Chrysler's new team pitching," by W. H. Jones, Oct. 14, 1979, The Washington Post, p. G1.

44 From "Iacocca rides high in Detroit," by J. Holusha, Aug. 29, 1982, New York Times, p. F1.

45 From "Iacocca's tightrope act; With brains, bluster and bravado, the boss struggles to salvage Chrysler," by A. L. Taylor III, March 21, 1983, Time, p. 50.

46 From "Peripatetic pitchman," by R. Baker, March 27, 1983, New York Times Sunday Magazine, p. 26.

47 From "A spunky tycoon turned superstar; straight-talking Lee Iacocca becomes America's hottest new folk hero," by K. Andersen, April 1, 1985, Time, p. 31.

48 From "A spunky tycoon turned superstar; straight-talking Lee Iacocca becomes America's hottest new folk hero," p. 30.

49 From "A spunky tycoon turned superstar; straight-talking Lee Iacocca becomes America's hottest new folk hero," p. 30.

50 From "That's no hero, that's a CEO: No matter how hard they seem to try, business execs don't get any respect," by J. Huey, March 20, 1987, The Wall Street Journal, p. 1.

51 From "C.E.O. performances: Lee Iacocca and the case of Chrysler," by M. W. Seeger, Fall 1986, The Southern Speech Communication Journal, pp. 52–68.

52 From "Iacocca still charms the media," by J. L. Tolley, September 1987, IABC Communication World, pp. 21–23.

53 From "A case study in print media and heroic myth: Lee Iacocca 1978–1985," by G. N. Dionisopoulus, Spring 1988, The Southern Speech Communication Journal, pp. 227–243.

54 From "U.S. cars come back," by A. Taylor III, Nov. 16, 1992, Fortune, p. 52.

55 From "Competition may thin profits in sports utilities," by K. Bradsher, May 9, 1996, New York Times, p. D1.

56 From "What not to drive to the recycling center," by K. Bradsher, July 28, 1996, New York Times, p. E2.

57 From "Collision odds turn lopsided as sales of big vehicles boom," by K. Bradsher, March 19, 1997, New York Times, p. A1.

58 From "Domination, submission and the Chevy Suburban," by K. Bradsher, March 23, 1997, New York Times, p. E2.

59 See "Sports utility vehicles pose growing danger to car occupants," by K. Bradsher, June 11, 1997, New York Times, p. A20.

60 From "A deadly highway mismatch ignored," by K. Bradsher, Sept. 24, 1997, New York Times, p. A1.

61 See "Big insurers plan to increase rates on large vehicles; collision costs blamed," by K. Bradsher, Oct. 17, 1997, New York Times, p. A1.

62 See "Light trucks increase profits but foul air more than cars," by K. Bradsher, Nov. 30, 1997, New York Times, p. A1.

63 See "Further problems of safety found for light trucks; danger of rolling over," by K. Bradsher, Dec. 12, 1997, New York Times, p. A1.

64 See "Loophole for trucks; plan allows big vehicles to skirt rules on pollutants," by K. Bradsher, Dec.19, 1997, New York Times, p. A1.

65 From "Auto makers plan cuts in emissions of sport vehicles; criticism is addressed," by K. Bradsher, Jan. 6, 1998, New York Times, p. A1.

66 From "Insurers saying utility vehicles need redesign; auto insurers urge makeover of sport utilities," by K. Bradsher, Feb. 10, 1998, New York Times, p. A1.

67 From "Awards and anguish for a driven reporter," by C. Butler, September/October 1998, Columbia Journalism Review, p. 57.

68 From "Awards and anguish for a driven reporter," p. 57.

69 From "Awards and anguish for a driven reporter," p. 57.

70 From "Ford treads a fine line with U.S. public over Firestone recall," by A. Jones, Aug. 26, 2000, The (London) Times, Business.

71 From "Local TV uncovered national scandal," by J. Rutenberg, Sept. 11, 2000, New York Times, p. C17.

72 From "Local heroes," by A. Shepard, December 2000, American Journalism Review, p. 42.

73 From "News media get in line to take credit for bringing about Firestone tire recall," by A. Zimmerman, Sept. 12, 2000, The Wall Street Journal, p. A4.

74 From "Local heroes," p. 44.

75 From "Officials have known SUV tire suspicion for a decade," by J. R. Healey and S. Nathan, Aug. 2, 2000, USA Today, p 3B.

76 From "Local heroes," p. 43.

77 From "Ford treads a fine line with U.S. public over Firestone recall," Business.

78 From "Local TV uncovered national scandal," p. C17.

79 From "Ford vs. Firestone," by K. Naughton, Sept. 18, 2000, Newsweek, p. 26.

80 From "Why Ford's chairman has kept mostly mum," by A. Taylor III, Oct. 2, 2000, Fortune, p. 43.

81 From "Ford vs. Firestone: A corporate whodunit," by J. Muller and N. St. Pierre, June 11, 2001, BusinessWeek, p. 46.

82 From "Flats fixed: Thought Firestone was as good as dead? Look who's rolling," by J. Fahey, May 27, 2002, Forbes, p. 40.

83 From "Media silence is not golden," by J. Saltzman, November 2000, Society for the Advancement of Education, p. 29.

84 From "Ford document: Millions of vehicles have fire risk part," by D. Griffin, June 16, 2005, CNN Primetime.

Chapter 12

Business news on the Internet

In April 1998, Todd Woody walked into the San Francisco offices of a new publication called *The Industry Standard* to apply for a job. Hired as a senior writer, he helped build the magazine into a weekly publication that documented the ins and outs of the growing Internet industry. There were beer parties on the roof of the building on Fridays attended by venture capitalists and CEOs. By late November 1999, the publication was putting out issues with more than 200 pages. The next year, its issues topped 300 pages and were filled with stories documenting the latest development in how the Internet would change business. Its founder claimed that the company would become a $1 billion operation. Covering the Internet was a major business story, and providing business news on the Web was the wave of the future.

By September 2001, however, the magazine was out of business, and Woody was looking for another job. By 2005, he became the business editor of the *San Jose Mercury News,* which had also heavily covered the Internet boom and bust, after joining the paper in 2003 as assistant business editor for technology. Although his paper provides business news on the Internet and through a blog called "Silicon Beat" in addition to the regularly printed newspaper, the *Mercury News,* as well as other publications, is now more skeptical of Internet companies.

In the 1990s, the Internet changed how businesses operated. It gave businesses the opportunity to sell their goods and services by computer, without customers leaving their home. It also allowed people to communicate with each other across the globe without using telephones.

The Internet also caused a major transformation in the media world, as newspapers, magazines, television stations, and other forms of media began providing information to readers and viewers by computer. No longer did someone have to wait until the paper arrived on his driveway in the morning or for the 6 o'clock news to find out what had happened that day. News was now instantaneous, and nowhere was the process of immediately gathering and disseminating news more important than in business journalism because of stock price fluctuations based on breaking news.

For decades, business wire services competed against each other based on whose story ran across the wire first. The ability to have information about important business events mere seconds before someone else often meant millions to Wall Street traders. With that information, they traded stocks involved in the news ahead of others who also wanted to buy or sell the stock based on the news. Even newspapers with scoops that appeared in their business sections caused investors to frantically place calls to brokers.

The Internet, however, sped up the flow of information even more and quickly became the primary source of information for many interested in business news. With the creation of Web sites devoted solely to business news, investors more and more turned to their computers to obtain the latest important news about stocks, bonds, and other investments. The Internet became quick and easy, but it also threatened the tenets on which business journalism's credibility had been carefully built in the previous 50 years.

As a result, the business journalism landscape changed forever in the 1990s. How business journalism was delivered to a core reader was overhauled, and how most business reporters and editors performed their daily journalism tasks was dramatically altered. In addition, online business information services demanded experienced reporters and editors to deliver news as quickly as possible. Because many of them were flush with cash, they offered exorbitant salaries and other perks to entice business journalists to the Internet. Newspapers, magazines, and other traditional forms of media had to rethink how they delivered business news to remain competitive. Many developed an online site offering business coverage in addition to the stories that appeared in their print offerings.

One of the most successful business journalism Web sites was WSJ.com, the online site of *The Wall Street Journal.* Launched in 1996, the online *Journal* became one of the first successful Web sites that charged subscribers to access its stories and information. Ten years later, the site had more than 700,000 paying subscribers, paving the way for other business news Web sites.

Even after the Internet bubble popped in 2000, many of the changes remained that occurred in business jour-

BUSINESS JOURNALISM TIMELINE

MARCH 2001 – FORTUNE PUBLISHES CRITICAL ARTICLE ABOUT ENRON BY BETHANY MCLEAN.

APRIL 2001 – INTERNET STOCK BUBBLE BURSTS, ENDING DECADE-LONG PERIOD OF OFTEN LAUDATORY BUSINESS COVERAGE.

OCTOBER 2001 – AFTER CEO JEFF SKILLING RESIGNS, ENRON'S STOCK FALLS DRAMATICALLY AFTER INTENSIVE COVERAGE LED BY THE WALL STREET JOURNAL. COMPANY EVENTUALLY FILES FOR BANKRUPTCY COURT PROTECTION.

2002 – MARYLAND PUBLIC TELEVISION DROPS LOUIS RUKEYSER, WHO TAKES HIS SHOW TO CNBC.

2002 – GRETCHEN MORGENSEN OF THE NEW YORK TIMES WINS PULITZER PRIZE FOR COVERAGE OF WALL STREET SCANDALS.

nalism as a result of this new technology. Although only a few pioneers in Internet business journalism remain, the Web is seen is a valuable tool for the media to communicate to their audience, particularly in the fast-paced world of Corporate America. Media outlets today post breaking news on their online site – for those wanting the information immediately. The media then expand the story in their print versions delivered on doorsteps and in mailboxes – for those willing to wait so that they can get a better perspective from an article with more analysis than the online version.

Although the Internet is seen as a real threat to traditional forms of media, it now has also evolved into a tool used by newspapers, magazines, television stations, and others to augment printed publications by presenting data online such as stock prices and bond values, or the latest data from the government on inflation. In addition, business journalism stories adjusted to the Internet. Newspapers, wire services, and magazines will now write stories about companies or business topics, and at the end of the story direct the reader to an online site where he can look at charts and other information about the company or the issue. Some papers, such as Woody's *San Jose Mercury News*, provide URLs in the printed business section to documents posted online, such as company lawsuits or patent applications.

The Internet also improved business reporting in many ways. The technology gave government agencies such as the Securities and Exchange Commission the ability to make regulatory documents for thousands of companies available online. Journalists started putting their e-mail addresses underneath their bylines or at the end of their stories, encouraging readers and sources to get in touch with them if they had a question or comment. Some readers would provide tips or ideas for future stories.

But the Internet also caused some pain for business journalism. As more sites provided business news and information, they hired reporters and editors away from existing publications, which in turn hired news reporters and editors to replace those who had left. Eventually, the hiring increase led to journalists entering the field of business coverage without much experience. Others had never covered business except during the growth economy of the 1990s and didn't know how to cover a business or an industry in difficult economic times or what it meant when the stock market dropped precipitously.

For consumers, going to the Internet to look for news and information also became a problem. Few knew what sites contained reliable stories and data and who was operating them.

The new wave of business reporting

The bull market for Internet stocks for much of the 1990s resulted in a bull market for business journalists as well. Nowhere was this more prevalent than in the Silicon Valley area of California and in New York, where many Internet news sites had set up shop.

In a 12-month period in the late 1990s, the *San Jose Mercury News* lost 11 business technology reporters and editors who took jobs at various Internet companies.[1] The *San Francisco Chronicle* lost a similar number, and even *The Wall Street Journal* was raided for talent.[2] Dave Kansas, a reporter at the *Journal*, left the prestigious business newspaper to become editor of TheStreet.com, a Web site devoted to news and commentary about investing.[3] Herb Greenberg, a nationally known columnist from the *Chronicle*, left the newspaper and also joined TheStreet.com.[4]

Kansas and Greenberg were just two of hundreds of business journalists who left the traditional print media for online jobs. Most of them had been offered jobs with higher salaries, and some were given stock options in their new companies. The idea, popular at most Internet companies at the time, was that these online news ventures would soon go public and those holding stock would become instant millionaires. And for some journalists, that did happen – for a fleeting moment. Kansas held stock in TheStreet.com that was worth more than $9 million at one point.[5]

Business journalists have long left the field to work for the industries they covered as reporters. Most of the public relations staffers at the large Detroit automobile manufacturers were once journalists. The difference this time, according to journalists, was the ability to leave their traditional media job and get paid much more than they had in the past. Such moves called into question their motives when they were covering the companies at which they later became employed. When *Fortune* reporter Jodi Mardesich left the magazine to join www.drspock.com, she had written about the company just one month before. And her farewell column on the magazine's Web site abandoned any pretense of journalistic objectivity and gushed about the opportunity she saw in her new job.[6] Other journalists who received offers from Internet ventures they wrote about refused to turn in stories on the companies.[7]

In addition to leaving for jobs at Internet companies, journalists left positions for work at publications focusing on the Internet industry, such as *The Industry Standard, Red Herring,* and *Fast Company.* These magazines grew exponentially during the Internet craze. By 2000, for example, *Fast Company* was printing more than 500,000 copies and publishing issues with more than 400 pages, due to the volume of advertising from Internet companies.[8]

The Industry Standard would come to illustrate the dramatic rise and precipitous fall of many Internet companies. Launched in April 1998, the weekly magazine chronicled what was happening on the Web at a breathtaking speed, and within a year was publishing 200-plus page issues. Internet companies clamored for attention – and coverage – from its reporters. "For the magazine's veteran

BUSINESS JOURNALISM TIMELINE

2003 – DONALD W. REYNOLDS NATIONAL CENTER FOR BUSINESS JOURNALISM AT THE AMERICAN PRESS INSTITUTE IS FOUNDED. IN FEBRUARY 2004, IT UNVEILS WWW.BUSINESSJOURNALISM.ORG.

2004 – CBS MARKETWATCH.COM COMMENTATOR THOM CALANDRA RESIGNS FROM THE ONLINE FINANCIAL JOURNALISM SITE AFTER IT WAS DISCLOSED THAT THE SEC WAS INVESTIGATING HIS TRADING.

2004 – CNNFN GOES OFF THE AIR.

2004 – DOW JONES PURCHASES MARKETWATCH FOR MORE THAN $460 MILLION.

2005 – FOX NEWS DEVELOPS PLANS TO LAUNCH NEW CABLE BUSINESS NEWS NETWORK.

journalists, accustomed to banging on the doors of people who expressly did not want their story told, the unrelenting flack attacks and rock-star treatment constituted a disconcerting role reversal," wrote Woody, who was a senior editor.[9]

Even after the NASDAQ market, where virtually all public Internet stocks traded, crashed in April 2000, the magazine and its staff kept covering the industry as if everything were still all right. The magazines remained thick with ads until the end of the year, but by January 2001, the magazine starting laying off workers. By August of that year, the magazine had ceased publication.[10]

There were other magazines that suffered a similar fate. *Business 2.0* was sold to AOL Time Warner, but its subscribers simply shifted to *eCompany* and the magazine shuttered.[11] *Red Herring*, another Internet publication, closed its doors after publishing its March 2003 edition.[12] *Upside*, yet another magazine, also failed. *Fast Company* remained in existence in 2005, but it had been sold twice – the second time for about one-tenth of what it fetched in 2000.[13]

Business journalism was swept along for the ride. Some prominent business reporters and editors wrote about the Internet, and many of them hoped to become rich by joining one of the startup publications or Web sites and then hoping that it would surpass the traditional media in consumer usage.

Astonishingly, what many business reporters and editors failed to grasp in the late 1990s was that many of these companies were losing money and unlikely to start producing cash anytime soon. When the economy changed, many Web sites and publications didn't know how to adapt.

Influencing mainstream media

The increase of business journalism on the Internet and in Web-oriented publications forced newspaper business sections, business magazines, and other traditional business media to change how they covered all industry, not just technology.

Many newspapers rolled out special once-a-week technology sections to cover the Internet and related industries, whereas others took a hard look at their coverage of companies in the industrial, financial, and other industries. Newspapers also became serious about their Web sites and introduced a number of new features on the Internet. Some newspapers, for example, began offering updated stock information online as a way to combat competing Web sites. Other newspapers began posting breaking news first online, providing a bare-bones story of major news events.

Newspapers changed the strategy of how they covered business in the daily paper. Knowing that the savvy business reader would have likely logged on to get the headlines and breaking news, newspapers began writing news with more analysis and more explanation of what deals and other developments meant to the readers. Knowing that the Internet reader likely skimmed a Web site for information, the newspaper's goal became to give that reader insight that they wouldn't receive elsewhere.

Magazines also adjusted. *Fortune* and *BusinessWeek* saw the potential impact of the Internet early on, and both added online Web sites and beefed up their technology coverage overall. *Forbes* lagged behind and didn't begin to improve its tech reporting until the late 1990s, just as the bubble was about to burst. *BusinessWeek* added an Information Processing section to the magazine in 1969, nearly two decades before *Forbes* added a computer section. *Forbes* didn't open an office in Silicon Valley near the technology companies until 1998.[14]

Newspapers developed trends in coverage that weren't followed on the Internet. A study of business journalism news online for three weeks beginning Feb. 12, 2001, showed that three prominent Web sites – CNNfn, CNBC, and CBSMarketwatch – paid more attention to stock market news and individual company news than the business coverage found in the three largest newspapers – *The Wall Street Journal, USA Today,* and *The New York Times.* The newspapers reported more coverage of the economy, international business news, legal issues, and executive news than the Web sites.[15]

But the Internet has not taken over business journalism – yet. That's despite a 1998 survey of company executives by Yankelovich Partners that predicted that the Internet would be the primary distributor of daily business news by 2005. More than 90 percent of the executives believed the Internet would be where they would receive news. Nearly three-fourths thought that e-mail would be a key source for business news.[16] The predictions haven't come true. Although the Internet crash might have had something to do with changing the euphoric attitude among executives, some likely downplayed the staying power of other media forms.

There remains smart and savvy business journalism performed on online sites. TheStreet.com and Marketwatch.com are two early Internet business journalism sites that remain today and win awards for their coverage. In 2003, for example, Marketwatch.com was named the best Internet business service by Editor & Publisher.[17] In addition, major media outlets have an Internet presence as well that provides certain facets of coverage that their print or broadcast formats ignore.

But the Internet has not replaced printed newspapers and magazines, or television and radio, for delivering business news and information to society. In many respects, it has augmented business journalism, providing a new outlet for information, reaching an audience that previously may not have looked to the mainstream media for business stories.

Some experts predict the demise of the printed publication. But with its ability to provide a depth and breadth of coverage, especially in terms of business journalism, print business reporting is not likely to be replaced by online media anytime soon.

However, some Internet news sites have made their presence known in the field of business journalism.

The Street.com's rise and impact

As online business news Web sites began to proliferate in the mid-1990s, the traditional business journalism outlets noticed and watched. In 1995, *BusinessWeek* reviewed Web sites that provided information for traders.[18]

By the next year, the Internet's influence on stock prices became an increasing issue. A Minnesota computer supply company saw its stock rise and fall in early May 1996 after an investor wrote on an America Online Motley Fool bulletin board about his purchases and sales of the stock, according to the *Minneapolis Star-Tribune.*[19]

Other Web sites also promoted stocks to savvy investors and curious readers without much investment expertise. One of the most popular in the late '90s was www.ragingbull.com, a financial message board Web site founded in 1997.[20] It joined Motley Fool and Silicon Investor as the largest sites where people could post messages – pro and con – about stocks. Raging Bull used freelance writers who also posted articles about the market each day.[21]

Many Internet sites that talked about stocks and Wall Street often played up comments from professional analysts and investors. And in the latter half of the decade, no analyst was more prominent than Henry Blodget when it came to promoting stocks, particularly those of Internet companies. In December 1998, it was Blodget who made the prediction that Amazon.com's stock, which had been trading at near $240, would top $400. (The stock was trading in early 2006 at about half the value that it was at its 2000 peak.) The next day, Blodget's prediction was covered in virtually every business section in the country – and on financial Web sites across the Internet.[22]

One of those sites was TheStreet.com, which was founded in November 1996 as an online financial information service. Within a year of its founding, the site had 3,500 members paying $12.95 per month to access its articles, and it was expanding coverage to include company earnings and mutual funds.[23] TheStreet.com was founded by hedge fund manager Jim Cramer, and he became the face of the fledgling business news site, but many didn't consider him a business journalist even though he wrote a column on the site. Cramer's in-your-face style was also seen on CNBC, and he had previously been a columnist for *Smart Money*, the investing magazine started by Dow Jones in 1992.[24]

By the time the Web site went public in 1999, it had a staff of more than 50 reporters and editors and another two-dozen outside contributors, with more than 40 stories being posted every day.[25] Reporters were motivated to break news with $2,000 bonuses.[26] The subscriber base had grown to more than 37,000 by February 1999, and the site hoped to capitalize on the growth of online brokerage accounts, which were expected to grow from 3.5 million at the end of 1997 to 24 million by the end of 2002.[27] In other words, TheStreet.com hoped to attract subscribers from people who believed they could get rich playing the market. "The whole premise of Cramer's financial writing was that he would bring the average Joe inside Wall Street and explain the intricacies of the game as he risked his own cash," noted *Washington Post* media critic Howard Kurtz. "That meant he had to be candid about his setbacks as well as his triumphs."[28] When TheStreet.com's stock began trading in May 1999, it went from $19 to $71 in the first day, receiving a huge run-up similar to other Internet stocks that had gone public.[29]

Cramer touted the immediacy the Web site could offer to readers compared to magazines and newspapers that also included pages and pages of investment advice. "It's impossible for magazines like *Worth, Money, Smart Money* to deliver a serious financial product at a time when other people can deliver information instantaneously," he said.[30] Although he might have been exaggerating, Cramer did have a point. Most financial magazines were printed days before subscribers received them. During that period, a major news event such as a merger, acquisition, or executive shakeup could affect a stock or an entire industry featured in the print publication.

Some thought Cramer used the Web site to boost the performance of his hedge fund by writing positively about stocks in which he was invested and trashing stocks that he had sold. The criticism hurt TheStreet.com's credibility, and all Internet news sites struggled to build trust with readers.

The Web site, however, did present some strong business journalism. Columnist Peter Eavis was one of the first to criticize Enron's financial accounting, and he also was ahead of other business journalists in examining the problems at life insurer Conseco, which eventually went bankrupt. On Oct. 6, 1999, TheStreet.com's Adam Lashinsky wrote a column about the pending Webvan Group Inc. initial public offering, breaking details about the company's business plan that had not been in its government filings. The day the column was published, the company postponed its IPO until it could update its public documents.[31] In addition, Lashinsky's efforts, as well as those by other business journalists, pushed the Securities and Exchange Commission to require companies to disclose information to all investors at the same time.

Despite its problems, TheStreet.com showed business journalism had the ability to offer an editorial product online for a price and have people pay for the information. By the end of 1999, the site had 94,000 subscribers.[32] Although the site struggled financially for many years, it remains in existence today as a player in business journalism.

One of the competing Web sites that TheStreet.com mentioned in its prospectus with the SEC was Marketwatch.com, which had started two years before it in 1994. The Marketwatch site received a boost in 1997 when it sold a stake in the operations to CBS in exchange for use of the television network's name and promotions on its radio, TV, and billboard operations.[33] Later dubbed CBS Marketwatch.com, the site focused on hard business news, whereas TheStreet.com's forte was market commentary. Marketwatch also went public in 1999 and saw its stock increase more than eightfold before falling. Along with the Motley Fool site and others, Marketwatch competed with TheStreet.com for readers looking to obtain business news online. Another smaller site called Jagnotes.com also carried Wall Street gossip and stock news.

These business news sites brought investing information to the masses. As Internet locations for business reporting started, so did sites that offered access to company conference calls, Wall Street analyst reports, and other data. The once secretive world of Wall Street became available to anyone with the click of a few buttons on his keyboard. "The biggest force behind technological change in investing is the Internet," claimed *The Wall Street Journal* in 2000. "It has redefined two important steps in the investing process: the way people learn about investments, and the way they place their trades."[34] Online business journalism was vitally involved in the former, and more people turned to the Internet to find information about stocks. Many times, they used news sites.

Along the way, many online sites adjusted their strategies to make themselves more credible to readers. TheStreet.com generated additional revenue by offering subscriptions to other information services. Real Money, another one of its sites, offered analysis of the stock market, while Real Money Pro targeted professional investors and included trading diaries from hedge fund managers.[35]

The Journal's parent, Dow Jones, realized these online sites served a business news niche for consumers who weren't being served by the online version of its flagship newspaper. So in late 2004, it agreed to buy Marketwatch.com for $463 million.[36] That deal validated the role that online business news sites play in the field. After years of struggling, the Internet news sites that remain will likely play an important role in business journalism.

Reporting rumors and gossip

For all the advancements that business journalism made using the Internet to tap into an expanded audience, there were still major problems with delivering news and information about the corporate world and the economy on the Web. Because of the technology's youth and lack of regulations as to who could run a site proclaiming to provide business information, the credible news sites were hurt by others – and by scams that frequently occurred using the Internet to promote stocks.

Said Kansas, the former editor of TheStreet.com, in 2001, "The Internet has become a trusted medium for the delivery of news. Not that all news sources on the Internet are to be trusted, of course. As with print and broadcast media, some are more reputable than others."[37] Business journalists soon discovered that there were some less than reputable operators using the Internet for their own financial gain. This problem exposed issues with how business news was reported on the Web, since many readers were fooled by Web sites that actually weren't valid news organizations.

In many cases, information posted on Web sites about stocks and companies is simply unsubstantiated chatter.

The rumors and gossip that infiltrated many online business news sites disguised as objective journalism were no different from the banter on the television programming on cable networks such as CNBC and CNNfn or the speculation about companies and stocks that appeared in virtually every major business publication, from Gene Marcial's column in *BusinessWeek* to the Heard on the Street column in *The Wall Street Journal.* A 1989 *Washington Journalism Review* article traced the rise of competition in Wall Street reporting in the early 1980s to an increase of business journalism, including rumors and gossip.[38]

What made the Internet-based rumors and gossip so different was their effect on society. They fueled rampant speculation by novice traders with no expertise in how the market operated. With access to information on the Internet, these Web surfers changed the dynamics of Wall Street and business journalism. "Using the Internet, an investor can have almost as much information at his fingertips as a professional in a well-stocked Wall Street office," claimed *Forbes* in 1994.[39] The Internet and business journalism's portrayal of its power in society made average people want to buy Internet stocks even though they knew little about the companies and even less about the stock market.

Rumors that started on the Internet and eventually found their way into other media forms were called "geyser journalism" by one former ombudsman in 1998.[40] In some cases, the rumors got out of hand because the speed of the Internet affected companies and their stock prices in ways that could not be easily corrected. Business journalists have had to learn how to assess the comments they find on the Internet and quickly determine their veracity.

For example, in 1999 consumer product giant Procter & Gamble refuted allegations begun on the Internet that household cleaner Febreze would poison household pets.[41] It took the company about four months before calls to the company about the false allegations began to die down. Although P&G's stock price was not affected, in other cases, companies have seen their shares take huge hits from Internet rumors.

In 1999, PairGain Technologies Inc. saw its stock price rise dramatically after an employee posted a news article about the company that looked as if it were from the Bloomberg News Web site.[42] In March 2000, a fake Lucent Technologies Inc. news release was posted on an Internet message board, warning that the company's profits would fall short of estimates.[43]

In August 2000, the California-based technology company Emulex Corp. was the victim of one of these rumors. A phony press release was sent out on the Internet stating that the company was adjusting its earnings downward, its chief executive officer had resigned, and that the Securities and Exchange Commission was investigating it. The release was immediately picked up by the Bloomberg and Dow Jones wire services, and its contents were also broadcast on cable network CNBC.[44] The stock began falling, and it was off 60 percent before the NASDAQ market halted trading in the shares at the request of the company.

It was not until two hours later that the company issued a press release rebutting the false release. Bloomberg and Dow Jones apologized to the company, but the damage had been done. The stock rebounded when trading began later in the day, but it still closed more than 6 percent down.[45] A week later, Bloomberg and the public relations distribution service that issued the press release were sued by a Florida investor.[46] Eventually, a 23-year-old college student was arrested and charged with sending out the fake press release and receiving nearly $250,000 in profits from trading in Emulex stock.[47]

Two years later, a similar incident caused the stock of drug company Cel-Sci Corp. to rise before the release was discovered to be a fake.[48] Concluded *Forbes* of such shenanigans: "You can accuse us – being a print product – of sour grapes, but from where we sit most of what passes for business news on the Net is nothing of the kind. It's mostly stock market chatter, seemingly aimed at stimulating people's trading juices."[49]

The Emulex and Cel-Sci examples are the extremes of what can be found on the Internet. In many cases, information posted on Web sites about stocks and companies is simply unsubstantiated chatter, and many people who spend time reading these chat rooms take it as such. Business journalists scan these chat rooms for information about the companies they cover, and sometimes they run across tidbits that seem viable enough to pursue as legitimate stories.

Still, what these incidents of rumors and gossip posted on Internet message boards or Web sites have done is to give the public the perception that the business news and data available online are not to be trusted, when a lot of it actually comes from reliable sources. In addition, these incidents fueled the belief that business journalism has lowered itself to simply trying to move stock prices by reporting on rumors and speculation.

Business journalism on the Internet has even been blamed for fueling the Internet bubble that caused technology stocks to rise dramatically in the late 1990s and then burst in April 2000, causing thousands of investors to lose billions of dollars. But, business journalism was not smart enough to push the market rally all by itself, and it wasn't savvy enough to explain why the market was rising to new highs until after the fact.

Causing the Internet bubble?

In many respects, business journalism on the Internet – and in print publications such as newspapers and magazines – helped fuel the growing hysteria about the stock market in the

1990s, and in particular, Internet stocks. In virtually every publication, there were stories about how the Internet was going to revolutionize the business world and how this new technology would overthrow traditional media. "The press bears some responsibility for the economic euphoria of the late 1990s," stated columnist Robert Samuelson. "We not only reflect the nation's mood swings, we help cause them."[50]

There is some merit to Samuelson's statement. A June 2005 study by Wall Street investment firm Bear Stearns traced the history of investment bubbles dating back to the tulip bubble in 17th century Europe. It found that history repeated itself in certain categories, giving investors the ability to predict when another bubble might occur. One of those categories involved the media and their portrayal of the economy. "Again, publications claimed that America was entering a new era of prosperity," as they had done so before past economic bubbles, read the report about the Internet stock bubble.[51] The study also noted, "Scores of periodicals emerged, focusing on different aspects of the industry."[52] For the railroad stock bubble of the 19th century, for example, a number of publications were created, including *The Railway Express, The Railway Examiner, The Railway Globe, The Railway Standard,* and *The Railway Mail.* Similarly, a number of Internet publications emerged in the 1990s.

More traditional publications pushed the Internet mania as well. *BusinessWeek,* in its June 22, 1998, issue, wrote that the Internet had revolutionized the way people did business, calling it the "Click-Here" economy. "In just three years, the Net has gone from a playground for nerds into a vast communication and trading center where some 90 million people swap information or do deals around the world," proclaimed the magazine, which had become available on the Internet in 1994.[53] The next year, the magazine published its "e.biz 25" – a list of innovators in Internet technology. It should be noted that *BusinessWeek's* economics editor, Michael Mandel, published a book called "The Coming Internet Depression" in 2000.

Even those who covered the Internet economy of the 1990s now know they were too optimistic in their coverage. "Our own businesses were too far inside the beat we were covering," wrote James Ledbetter, a former staff member at *The Industry Standard.*[54] His publication, he added, was built around a premise that didn't lend itself to editorial freedom. The magazine:

> ... had the same start-up mentality as many of the companies it covered. Inevitably, some of their worldview rubbed off on us. At exotic conferences in Aspen and Barcelona, our management mingled with the leaders of high-flying tech firms, some of whom were simultaneously advertising in the magazine, sponsoring a section of our Web site, speaking at magazine-sponsored conferences they had helped pay for, selling us software and giving colorful quotes to our reporters. This was not a formula for sustained independence.[55]

Philip Longman, a senior fellow at the New America Foundation, concurred with Ledbetter, writing, "Large parts of the media came to have a huge stake in promoting and flattering the boom's most flamboyant figures, as well as the products and ideas they were selling."[56] Business journalism grew thanks to the advertising dollars of many Internet companies.

Yes, publications such as *The Industry Standard* and *BusinessWeek* also aggressively reported about shady and unethical companies, even in the Internet industry, during the time. *The Standard,* for example, wrote critically about American Online and Priceline.com.[57] All it would have taken for most of the business journalism field, however, to prevent a repeat of its coverage from another boom time in U.S. history would have been to look back at how businesses and the economy were covered in the years leading up to the 1929 stock market crash and ensuing Great Depression.

History does repeat itself, particularly in business journalism. Only the industries and those writing about them change.

Footnotes

1 From "Crossing over," by C. Winston, May 2000, Brill's Content, p. 125.

2 From "Bull market for business journalists prompts defections at Journal," by D. Fost, May 18, 2000, San Francisco Chronicle, p. B1.

3 From "Reporter's market: Online services offer new avenues for job seekers," by D. Kopecki, August 1997, The Business Journalist, pp. 1, 9.

4 From "So Long, San Francisco, It Has Been a Truly Wonderful Run," by H. Greenberg, Feb. 20, 1998, San Francisco Chronicle, p. D1.

5 From "A nice piece of change for a simple guy," by A. Kuczynski, May 17, 1999, The New York Times, p. C11.

6 From "Journalists seduced by the dark side to jump ship to the Internet," by D. Fost, April 20, 2000, San Francisco Chronicle, p. B1.

7 From "Crossing over," p. 126.

8 From "A magazine giant weighs in on Internet business," by A. Kuczysnki, June 5, 2000, The New York Times, p. C1.

9 From "When boom went bust at the 'country club,'" by T. Woody, January/February 2002, Columbia Journalism Review, p. 58.

10 From "New economy; a writer chronicling the Internet revolution recalls living the experience he covered," by E. J. Savitz, Nov. 5, 2001, The New York Times, p. C5.

11 From "Party ends for Net magazines," by S. Goody, Aug. 23, 2001, London Daily Telegraph, p. 2.

12 From "Red Herring sinks; business magazine unable to secure enough ads," by P. Sarkar, March 1, 2003, San Francisco Chronicle, p. B1.

13 From "Biz business mags going Fast," by B. Arends, June 8, 2005, Boston Herald, p. 33.

14 From "Forbes bytes back," by E. L. Stevens, February 1999, Brill's Content, p. 55.

15 From "Business news web sites differ from newspapers in business content," by J. Jung, Spring 2003, Newspaper Research Journal, pp. 114–119.

16 From "Internet use changing U.S. industry," April 4, 1998, Editor & Publisher, p. 23.

17 From "CBS Marketwatch receives Eppy Award for 'Best Internet Business Service,' the latest in a suc-

cession of honors," May 12, 2003, Business Wire.

18 From "An online feast of business news," by S. Wildstrom, April 17, 1995, BusinessWeek, p. 16.

19 From "Online mention by Motley Fool takes Zytec stock on wild ride," by S. Alexander, May 9, 1996, Minneapolis Star Tribune, p. 1D.

20 From "Herd on the net," by M. Heimer, May 1999, Brill's Content, p. 53.

21 From "Herd on the net," p. 54.

22 From "Bullish on Blodget," by R. Rosenwein, June 1999, Brill's Content, p. 55.

23 From "The trader who won't shut up," by M. Warner, May 12, 1997, Fortune, p. 19.

24 From "The trader who won't shut up," p. 19.

25 From Form S-1 filed Feb. 23, 1999 with U.S. Securities and Exchange Commission. Document No. 0000889812-99-000614., p. 2.

26 From "Story bonuses for online reporters," by D. Noack, April 11, 1998, Editor & Publisher, p. 22.

27 From Form S-1 filed Feb.23, 1999 with U.S. Securities and Exchange Commission, p. 2.

28 From "Risky business: James Cramer made big money on the high-tech boom and took his expertise public through TheStreet.com, CNBC and other media," by H. Kurtz, Aug. 27, 2000, Washington Post Magazine, p. W08.

29 From "TheStreet.com makes big splash, yet analysts fear undertow," by S. Lacey, May 17, 1999, IPO Reporter.

30 From "Shouting financial advice in crowded field," by R. Pogrebin, April 13, 1998, The New York Times, p. D1.

31 From "Selective disclosure," by R. Schmidt, December 1999/January 2000, Brill's Content, p. 118.

32 From "The rise and fall of TheStreet.com," by R. Walker, December 2000, Money, p. 168.

33 From "The top financial Website is nobody's 'fool,'" by M. Gunther, Feb. 21, 2000, Fortune, p. 54.

34 From "How technology has changed the way we invest in stocks," by G. F. Ceron, Nov. 13, 2000, The Wall Street Journal, p. R32.

35 From "TheStreet.com strategic content," by P. S. Cohan, May 2002, Econtent, pp. 48–49.

36 From "Big payday for MarketWatch; Dow Jones agrees to buy S.F. financial Web site for $519 million," by D. Fost, Nov. 16, 2004, San Francisco Chronicle, p. E1.

37 From "New economy: A dot-com editor sheds his five-year 'cocoon' and looks at how journalism has changed in the age of the Internet," by D. Kansas, July 16, 2001, The New York Times, p. C5.

38 See "Chasing hot stocks," by T. J. Mullaney, December 1989, Washington Journalism Review, pp. 39–43.

39 From "Time to get hooked," by S. Kichen, Sept. 26, 1994, Forbes, p. 158.

40 From "First or right?" by B. Kirtz, March 1998, Quill, p. 25.

41 From "When those nasty rumors start breeding on the Web, you've got to move fast," by A. P. Crawford, Winter 1999, Public Relations Quarterly, p. 43.

42 From "Man gets probation, home detention in PairGain Internet stock hoax," by Michael White, Aug. 30, 1999, Associated Press.

43 From "Investors beware: Swindlers abound as net lures fools," by K. Kristof, July 2, 2000, Chicago Tribune, p. C3.

44 From "Bogus report sends Emulex on wild ride," by T. Ewing, P. Waldman and M. Rose, Aug. 28, 2000, The Wall Street Journal, p. C1.

45 From "Bogus report sends Emulex on wild ride," p. C1.

46 From "Bloomberg, Internet wire sued over Emulex," by N. Volpe, Sept. 1, 2000, Reuters.

47 From "Bloomberg, Internet wire sued over Emulex."

48 From "A hoaxer strikes online news service with bogus release," by M. Rapoport, June 12, 2002, The Wall Street Journal, p. C4.

49 From "Market buzz," by J. Smith, May 22, 2000, Forbes, p. 76.

50 From "Moving toward the mainstream," by R. Samuelson, Summer 2002, Nieman Reports, p. 24.

51 From "Asset bubbles: A look at past and future manias," by F. Trahan, K. D. Walters, and C. S. Portny, Bear Stearns Equity Research, June 2005, p. 6.

52 From "Asset bubbles: A look at past and future manias," p. 10.

53 From "The 'Click-here' economy," by R. Hof, G. McWilliams, and G. Saveri, June 22, 1998, BusinessWeek, p. 122.

54 From "The boys in the bubble," by J. Ledbetter, Jan. 2, 2003, The New York Times, p. A17.

55 From "The boys in the bubble," p. A17.

56 From "Bad press: How business journalism helped inflate the bubble," by P. Longman, October 2002, Washington Monthly, p. 18.

57 From "The boys in the bubble," p. A17.

Chapter 13

The scandals that were missed

June 2005 was a good month for journalists to cover business – and a bad month to be a corporate executive accused of wrongdoing. On June 18, former Tyco International Ltd. Chief Executive Officer Dennis Kozlowski, together with former Tyco CFO Mark Swartz, was convicted of stealing $170 million from the company through unauthorized loans and bonuses.[1] Two days later, Adelphia Communications Corp. founder John Rigas and his son Timothy, the company's former chief financial officer, were both sentenced to prison terms for bank fraud, securities fraud, and conspiracy. The elderly Rigas was blamed by the judge for "one of the largest frauds in corporate history."[2]

On June 9, HealthSouth Corp. agreed to pay $100 million to settle civil fraud charges brought against the company by the Securities and Exchange Commission. Jurors also spent most of the month deliberating the fate of former HealthSouth CEO Richard Scrushy, accused of inflating the company's financial performance and money laundering.[3] He was later found not guilty.

At the beginning of the month, the insurance industry reeled from New York Attorney General Eliot Spitzer's civil fraud charges against former American International Group Inc. CEO Maurice "Hank" Greenberg, once considered the leading executive in the business.[4]

In perhaps the biggest business story of the year, former Enron CEO Kenneth Lay was spending his time preparing for his trial, scheduled to begin in 2006, related to the collapse of the energy company in one of the largest bankruptcies ever. Before his trial began, *New York Times* business reporter Kurt Eichenwald spent the summer promoting his book "Conspiracy of Fools," which lays out the case against the Enron executives.[5] And playing in movie theaters across the country was "Enron: The Smartest Guys in the Room," based on the book by the same name written by two *Fortune* writers, Bethany McLean and Peter Elkind.[6] Business journalism had come a long way; the movie was the first big screen depiction of anything written by a business journalist for a business magazine.

Those were just the highlights. Other big business stories in June 2005 were the bankruptcy of grocer Winn-Dixie Stores Inc., causing the chain to close stores across the Southeast,[7] and the appointment of a new head of the SEC, Christopher Cox, likely to take a more laissez-faire approach to finding corporate criminals than former head William Donaldson.[8] In 2006, Cox was faced with upset business journalists who had been subpoenaed by the SEC as part of an investigation, and he quickly attempted to diffuse the situation by implementing guidelines on when reporters would be subpoenaed by the government agency.

All these stories were front-page news in business sections across the country. It seemed as if everything written about business during this period was about a corporate scandal or a company that had done something wrong and ended up losing millions for investors.

But that wasn't always the case. Comparing business coverage in June 2005 to coverage exactly six years earlier shows a stark contrast – and perhaps where business journalism went wrong in covering corporations.

In June 1999, *The Boston Globe* called Tyco the "quiet giant" and described Kozlowski's role at the company as "the chief executive who has built Tyco into a giant conglomerate with unglamorous business interests across the globe and even in the ocean's depths."[9] At the beginning of the month, the *International Herald Tribune* gushed, "Investors can't seem to get enough of Tyco International Ltd."[10]

For the elder Rigas and Adelphia Communications, the news was how his company was plastering its name all over the sporting world to increase recognition. At the end of June, the company agreed to spend $30 million to puts its name on the football stadium for the NFL Tennessee Titans.[11] And at the beginning of the month, Rigas received favorable press for purchasing the NHL's Buffalo Sabres and saving the team from moving to another city. "People love me," Rigas said, amused by the attention. "Everybody wants to pat me on the back."[12]

Analysts and investors, meanwhile, hailed Scrushy in business coverage for his decision to split HealthSouth into two companies. HealthSouth's stock rose 10 percent on the day the news was unveiled.[13]

The front page of the business section of *The New York Times* on June 27, 1999, carried a glowing story on how Enron encouraged entrepreneurs within the company to develop new businesses. Writer Agis Salpukis called the company "a model for the new American workplace – every bit as much as the Silicon Valley start-ups that usually come to mind when the subject is entrepreneurship or innovation."[14] Earlier in the month, *The Houston Chronicle* carried coverage of the initial public offering of Azurix, Enron's water utility, noting the stock sale was the second biggest in Houston in the decade.[15]

A review of the media coverage during this period – right at the end of the decade-long stock market boom and near the beginning of when these companies began to falter and crack – shows that rarely were stories critical of the CEOs or their strategies. Many business reporters lauded the executives for their moves and how they were transforming the business world.

One of business journalism's failures in the 1990s was that the coverage missed out on breaking huge corporate scandals. Instead of acting as a watchdog, many business reporters and editors went along with what they were being told by the business world. And once those in the business world who had acted unethically were uncovered, the business press moved right along. "The sober business press got drunk on a potent mixture of ad revenue and newsstand sales," said Douglas McCollam, a business reporter who wrote about his own failings during the 1990s. "We moved from the numerology of success (seven best mutual funds) to the numerology of failure (seven sins of corporate America) without much pause for introspection in between."[16]

The business press became too enamored with the celebrity CEO and with "list" journalism during the 1990s, and had its credibility hurt by the growing pains of the new Internet medium for business coverage. But journalism about the corporate world and the economy in the 1990s had deeper problems that for years went ignored until they were exposed when the scandals involving Enron, WorldCom, Adelphia, HealthSouth, and other companies exploded. These scandals led the business journalism field to begin to ask how so many could have been duped for so long.

The answer was that few business journalists bothered to examine a company's accounting of its performance or read its public filings with regulatory agencies. In other words, they weren't doing the basics.

Missing out on the accounting

Shortly after the stock bubble burst in April 2000, business journalism began to take a closer look at the financial statements, balance sheets, and cash-flow statements in the wake of its sometimes numbers-light reporting on the Internet industry. But when the Enron scandal related to inflating its earnings erupted in the fall of 2001, many business reporters and editors claimed that they couldn't have uncovered the company's problems even if they had known what to look for.

That argument doesn't hold when looking at how Enron was covered. Some business journalists had gotten close to the company's accounting before the scandal broke. And once the company began to disclose its problems, reporters, notably at *The Wall Street Journal*, found more accounting irregularities before regulators or the company could get an accurate handle on the situation.

Fortune reporter Bethany McLean is credited by most observers as being the first to question Enron's accounting. A review of her March 5, 2001, article shows that her reporting did raise some serious questions about the company, but she ultimately failed to find what was wrong. Even McLean admitted the shortcomings of her reporting in the article. "The inability to get behind the numbers combined with even higher expectations for the company may increase the chance for a nasty surprise," she wrote at one point. "The numbers that Enron does present are often extremely complicated."[17]

McLean's reporting raised enough concerns that other business journalists should have been more aggressive in examining Enron. She noted how Enron's debt had increased substantially and that its cash flow had slowed. She also pointed out that no analyst covering the company knew what was included in a division called Assets and Investments.[18] McLean dug into the company's financial statements and found where some potential accounting moves were being made to make Enron look better. Although she had training in investment banking, her analysis was simple enough that it could have been accomplished by anyone with a basic understanding of how to read a balance sheet and a financial statement – training an increasing number of business journalists are receiving.

Another reporter brought a skeptical accounting look to Enron before its problems emerged. Adam Levy, Atlanta bureau chief of Bloomberg News, wrote a story about the company in the May 2001 *Bloomberg Markets*, a magazine that goes to the company's terminal customers. He documented how the value of many of Enron's operations had been overstated and that the company's estimates for future profit growth were aggressive.[19] Other reporters, such as one at *The Wall Street Journal*'s Texas edition, also questioned the company's accounting.

Wall Street Journal reporters Rebecca Smith and John Emshwiller dug deeper into Enron's accounting and found where problems were buried. In a series of articles for the paper in the fall of 2001, the two reporters disclosed accounting tactics used by the company to make its financial performance look better than it was. Their first story to examine Enron's accounting looked at limited partnerships run by Chief Financial Officer Andrew Fastow and how the executive received millions from the deals.[20] Days later, they pointed out that Enron would have to issue more stock to satisfy some of its financial obligations from the partnerships.[21]

By the next month, Smith and Emshwiller explained the complicated financial structure that had been used at Enron that helped boost its earnings – and was now causing its problems.[22] And by the end of the month, Smith documented how the company was near filing for bankruptcy court protection because of its inability to untangle its finances.[23]

These stories were written by business journalists at three of the most prestigious business publications, and they likely had help from financial experts and other journalists with an accounting understanding. But these stories could have been written anywhere. Smith and Emshwiller had no particular insights into Enron. Neither had covered the company in any detail, and neither was based in Houston, the location of Enron's headquarters. McLean had spent just a handful of years in journalism and had no real interest in energy companies. Her interest in the Enron story was spurred by a comment made by a source. Levy's beat was more the Southeast economy.

The Enron story showed business journalism that it needed to know accounting. Business reporters and editors needed to have an understanding of how to read financial numbers and explain them to readers. Too many journalists don't have that training. And even some of the journalists who did help break the story were not as critical as they should have been early on. Smith, in writing about Enron in 2000, wrote stories that were "entirely devoid of skeptical voices," noted *Columbia Journalism Review.*[24] McLean's *Fortune* listed Enron as one of the country's "most innovative" companies in its annual list of "Most Admired Companies" for six years in a row.[25] Some business journalists previously called into question how companies were manipulating their performances with accounting. They just hadn't specifically focused on the Enron scandal or any others that had surfaced. Sarah Bartlett, writing an Oct. 5, 1998, cover story in *BusinessWeek* with the headline "Who can you trust?" wrote:

> It's the gnawing sense that companies that should know better are regularly pushing the limit, accountants are AWOL, and analysts are too enmeshed with their investment-banking brethren to provide objective advice. Even investors bear some responsibility: They've been so eager to cash in on the bull market that they've frequently ignored or optimistically interpreted restructuring charges, acquisition write-downs, and other accounting ploys that camouflage what's really going on.[26]

Few media outlets followed her lead. *American Journalism Review* criticized the lack of reporting focusing on company accounting by stating that stories like Bartlett's "were lost in a cacophony of naïve reportage that assured us the system was sound, analysts and auditors were basically trustworthy, and the market boom might go on forever."[27] Said Glenn Lewin, a business journalist advocating the need for accounting training: "Accounting is the process of recording, measuring, interpreting and communicating financial information to a variety of users, so it's important to understand its concepts and terminology."[28]

While regulators have attempted to close some of the accounting loopholes, new ways of getting around the accounting standards will always be found. Making accounting more important for today's business journalist is that the large accounting firms audit the bulk of the large companies in any industry, from petroleum to airlines, and sometimes these firms practice "aggressive" accounting methods that may obscure the facts.

Accounting is likely to continue to play a big role in business journalism's future. A 2004 study of business editor attitudes found that they were more likely to pay a job candidate more money if he had training in accounting, and nearly 90 percent of business editors either "strongly agreed" or "somewhat agreed" that an accounting class should be required of journalism majors.[29]

Some news organizations have begun hiring accountants. Bloomberg News, for example, had a forensic accountant on its staff in 2005. He answers questions for reporters, looks at company financial statements, and provides accounting training for the wire service's news staff.[30] Jeffrey Madick, editor of *Challenge Magazine,* suggested more media outlets do the same. "I think the financial media should find help," he said in 2002. "They should hire an accounting expert when things get too rough or an investment banking expert when things get too rough, and stop relying on the alleged sophistication and authority of their reporters."[31]

Following the footnotes

In addition to the accounting clues that business journalists could have seen to unravel the impending failures of Enron and other companies, an additional step in their reporting could have resulted in a bigger step toward uncovering the story. Buried in Enron's filings with the Securities and Exchange Commission – and in the public documents of other companies – were disclosures about shady deals these companies conducted with related companies. Called "off-balance sheet transactions," they should have been questioned by at least a few journalists. Instead, they were ignored.

Some nonjournalists had already uncovered the transactions. Hedge fund managers and other investors read about them in a report in May 2001 by Off Wall Street, a private research firm.[32] Another hedge fund manager used the Internet to find former Enron employees, calling them at home to question them about the transactions.[33] These were reporting tools a business journalist could – and should – have used as well.

Reading a company's financial statements requires more than examining the numbers. They should be read along with the company's explanation in its SEC filings. *Columbia Journalism Review* noted that footnotes to financial statements are "too often ignored," but "often contain crucial information that is not included in the main body of the statement."[34]

Today, more journalists are examining footnotes, but it's likely that not all footnotes are being explored for potential stories.

Paul Steiger, the managing editor of *The Wall Street Journal*, noted that Smith and Emshwiller based their reporting on the accounting that "showed that Enron's profits were heavily based on aggressive accounting, the liberal use of off-balance-sheet partnerships and misleading statements to regulators and the public."[35] One of the reasons others in the media did not follow their reporting is that writing about accounting is often seen as boring and hard for a reader to understand. But Smith and Emswhiller's stories, as well as their book, *24 Days*, about the fall of Enron, should be required reading for business journalists who want to know how to look at the accounting and financial statements of a company. What Peter Behr, who wrote about Enron for the *Washington Post*, argued is that "Enron took great pains to conceal what it was doing and create illusions of success in the quarterly and annual securities reports it issued."[36] But he also admitted that there were clues about Enron's actions.

The 2004 study of business editor attitudes found that 97 percent of them felt it was important for reporters to be trained to examine a company's financial reports. "Business editors and newspaper publishers know their readers demand this kind of reporting, and the news of the day dictates it," concluded the study by Missouri State University journalism professor Mary Jane Pardue, former business editor of the *Memphis Commercial Appeal*. "If reporters were skilled in digging out questions about creative financial reporting, stories like Enron, Adelphia and Tyco would have been faster and more comprehensively reported. Better training would have led to more immediate identification of slippery accounting."[37]

Lessons learned

Will business journalists, along with the investing public, be duped by another major corporate scandal sometime in the future? The answer is yes because new ways of conning the world are being created every day. But if business journalists learned any lessons from what it did, and more importantly didn't do, in covering the corporate scandals at the beginning of the 21st century, those scandals will not be about off-balance sheet transactions or executives inflating earnings or using the corporate till for their own purposes.

If there is anything positive that has come out of the corporate scandals, it is that they have served as a Watergate for business journalism. In the mid-1970s, political reporting, and journalism in general, received a boost in stature by the reporting of Bob Woodward and Carl Bernstein of the *Washington Post* about the break-in at the Democrat Party headquarters at the Watergate hotel. Their stories eventually led to the resignation of President Nixon. Young writers growing up at that time entered journalism in droves as a result.

Although business journalism had no "Deep Throat" to lead it to where the problems exist in the business world, the reporting of corporate scandals led many to view writing about business in a more positive light. Business journalism is now seen as a way for a reporter or editor to make a name in the field, and many of the newest lessons on what to look for in writing about companies and executives have come out of stories about Enron, WorldCom, Adelphia, and HealthSouth.

The scandals have also fundamentally changed business journalism's reporting. There is skepticism about many of the sources that business journalists used with common regularity in the past. Investment bankers, analysts, consultants, accountants, and lawyers were all tainted in one way or another by their roles in the recent scandals. Many business journalists considered these people to be, for the most part, objective sources who could be quoted in stories about companies. The scandals taught reporters that many people and companies have their hand out, receiving money from these companies to keep quiet about what is really going on.

The journalists were equally guilty. A number of reporters and opinion writers had been paid money by Enron, for example, for consulting work and for speeches.[38] Among them was *Wall Street Journal* columnist Peggy Noonan and *New York Times* columnist Paul Krugman.[39] Few business journalists accepted money from the company, but their credibility was still questioned because nonbusiness journalists had taken money from a company that had cost thousands of people money out of their retirement plans.

In addition, business journalists are now more aware of the places to find information about companies. Public documents filed with the Securities and Exchange Commission, once just the domain of the hard-core business reporter, became common knowledge to journalists as a result of Enron and others. More journalists are using public documents filed with state regulatory agencies to report stories about companies. These documents could be used with even more regularity. "Most of the press, not all of it, bought the story and didn't bother taking a close look at the numbers," said Madick, editor of *Challenge Magazine*.[40]

The blowups by companies were a rude awakening for reporters who wrote glowing stories about these businesses.

What also happened in business journalism was a change in mindset. Business journalism had grown used to the stock market continuing to rise and corporate profits going higher and higher. Many writing these stories were in college or high school the last time a recession occurred or a major corporate scandal created uncertainty about the business world. Among the media outlets that looked bad was the *Houston Chronicle*, whose coverage of Enron was way behind the national media and laudatory of the company up until right before it filed for bankruptcy court protection.[41] Afterward, the newspaper changed many business editors and reporters, as well as the top editor.

The blowups by companies were a rude awakening for reporters who wrote glowing stories about these businesses. Because many felt they had been lied to, business coverage in general has taken an increased watchdog role. While business reporting in the 1990s might have been too positive about the corporate world, in the 21st century it has become more probing and more inquisitive. The coverage is not overly hostile, but it does ask more questions about how companies are being managed and whether strategies are the right moves.

That skepticism needs to remain, particularly during times when the stock market is overly priced. Studies show that corporate malfeasance rises during periods when the stock market is at historical highs. And as business journalism becomes more focused on the markets because more than half of the country now has an investment in stocks, it needs to warn readers and viewers of the dangers inherent in investing.

Pessimism in business journalism

The skepticism in business journalism today brings the field into a new era where critical analysis of companies, industries, executives, and deals can match the analysis and depth found more regularly in reporting fields such as politics, government, crime, and education. After the 1950s and 1960s, when business journalism rarely questioned business, and the 1970s and 1980s, when the quality of reporting improved but the field became more complicated, and the 1990s, when reporters and editors got caught up in the euphoria, the next few decades will determine the direction the field takes.

There are some promising signs that the quality of business journalism is on the upswing. Business magazines have become more caustic in their coverage and are less likely to put the face of a CEO on their covers. Almost immediately after the corporate scandals broke, *Fortune* ran a cover story for its March 18, 2002, issue about white-collar criminals.[42] *Business 2.0*, one of the magazines that hailed the Internet industry, used its April 2002 cover to chronicle the "101 Dumbest Moments in Business."[43] Commented *Washington Post* reporter Peter Carlson: "Business magazines have turned into pit bulls, printing stories excoriating these once-deified entrepreneurs as crooked, mendacious, rapacious robber barons. To tell you the truth, I much prefer these new stories."[44] Another critique of scandal coverage by the business magazines stated, "Some of the best magazine pieces used a combination of strong commentary that put ethical problems directly before readers and significant reporting that fleshed out the rhetorical claims."[45]

The cable business networks and business television shows toned down bullish outlooks as well. Although credited with creating interest in Wall Street by presenting business news in a fashion that most people could understand, cable business networks were then criticized for promoting the stock market bubble. Afterward, "in a stock market that has soured and in a world where military maneuvers could easily surpass investing as a national obsession, CNBC is trying to evolve with the times," noted one critic.[46]

Newspapers changed their role in reporting about business. On the day that Rigas, two of his sons, and two other Adelphia executives were arrested on fraud charges, the *Buffalo News* ran five stories about how their management of the cable company had backfired.[47] *The* (Jackson) *Clarion-Ledger*, the newspaper in Mississippi where WorldCom's headquarters was located, treated CEO Bernard Ebbers and the downfall of his company as front-page news for years. Stories with headlines such as "Auditor who blew whistle praised" and "Scandal fallout could include criminal charges" showed that the newspaper's coverage would be firm despite the fact that Ebbers had brought more jobs to the local community in the previous decade than any other employer.[48] One analysis of how newspapers covered corporate scandals pointed out that, "Newspaper discourse was notable for its use of commentaries by both news organization staffers and outside contributors with business expertise to bluntly put the scandals in a context that extended beyond the individual companies."[49]

Overall, business journalism waited to see if trends would last before jumping on the bandwagon. In August 2002, a CBS Marketwatch editor noted that the Standard & Poor's 500 index, a barometer of the overall stock market, had risen 20 percent from its low – the definition of a bull market. But editors suggested that it shouldn't be called a bull market for fear of its coverage appearing overly positive.[50]

In the wake of the corporate scandals, business journalism has examined government regulation of industry more closely. Previously, regulatory stories were shot down by editors or killed outright because they weren't interesting. Now, regulatory stories are front-page news because regulators are trying to fix the problems in the business world. But, added Lewin, "The SEC is understaffed," which means that the media also must act in a quasi-regulatory function toward businesses by looking for wrongdoing.[51]

Overly hyped corporate public relations, sometimes called spin, is also becoming more recognizable to business journalists, say observers. "Corrupt corporations collude, monopolize," said *Harper's* Bill Wasik. "They mislead and strong-arm consumers. They pollute the air, water and land, and falsify data to obscure it. They break union drives through illegal firings. They pad contracts with falsehoods. Overseas they retain the services of thugs, traffickers, dictators."[52] But Wasik also points out that business journalism has succeeded in the past partly "because of meticulous PR by free-market partisans."[53]

Business journalism is indeed at a crossroads. After building itself up to a critical mass, the field now needs to take the next step and become the watchdog that other areas of journalism reached decades earlier. It has taken the first few steps along that path, but needs to continue walking forward.

Impact on corporate America

How corporate America reacted to this new treatment by the media shows that business journalism is headed in the right direction. The heavy coverage of corporate scandals, even though the critical stories came after executives looted the companies, forced the U.S. government to enact a set of laws designed to make companies more accountable for their actions and make relationships with accounting firms more independent. In addition, companies have been pushed to add more outside independent directors to their boards to keep a closer eye on what's going on.

For the most part, companies have sat back and worked to abide by the new rules instead of blaming the media for their problems.

Interestingly, the regulations came despite no change in the American public's opinion about more business regulation in the wake of the corporate scandals. In a survey by the Pew Research Center for the People & the Press released in February 2002, 50 percent of those surveyed felt that regulation was needed to protect the public interest, while 41 percent believed that government regulation did more harm than good. The results were similar to those in 1999 when the question had also been asked.[54]

The same survey found that attitudes about businesses had changed based on what consumers had read in the media. More than 40 percent said that corporations put the interest of executives first, while in 1995 46 percent said that companies put the interest of shareholders first. And the number of people who believed that businesses strike a balance between profits and the public interest had fallen to 40 percent in 2002 from 45 percent in September 1999.[55] Clearly, consumer opinion supported the media taking a more aggressive role.

Business reporters and editors complied. The WorldCom scandal broke in June 2002. Within a week, *The New York Times* had a front-page story titled "The latest corporate scandal is sudden, vast and simple."[56] The article explained the accounting mistakes that had caused the company's downfall. *The Economist*, one of the more skeptical business-oriented publications in the 1990s, weighed in with an article called "When something is rotten" that noted that wrongdoing occurred in companies with weak cultures.[57] It then cited businesses where culture was weak – Global Crossing, Enron, and WorldCom.

Fortune explained in its Nov. 25, 2002, issue how a rise of corporate ethics officers had occurred in the aftermath of the scandals.[58] A column in the May 12, 2003, *Fortune* noted that the corporate scandals all occurred because of greed. "The founders and many others at these companies believed deeply that they deserved everything they got," wrote Geoffrey Colvin, "regardless of how they got it, because they had created their success."[59]

The business media pushed for more regulation – and this time was ahead of a corporate scandal. *The Economist* asked for an overhaul of the regulations of mortgage lenders Freddie Mac and Fannie Mae in June 28, 2003.[60] Other media followed suit, long before Fannie Mae's own accounting scandal was uncovered in 2004.

Even the mainstream media took a more aggressive stance toward business. After Enron's CEO Kenneth Lay was indicted in 2004, *Time* magazine wrote a story detailing how prosecutors would prove his guilt and explained the creation of a Justice Department team called the Enron Task Force.[61] Even the *Houston Chronicle* changed its view and took a skeptical look. Its columnist, Loren Steffy, began one column after Lay's indictment with the following sentence: "Let's take a trip inside the fantasy world that Ken Lay has created in his defense."[62]

Under pressure from increasing coverage, the business world made other changes in questionable tactics. Analysts were no longer tied to investment banking fees, and in some cases were even encouraged to write critical reports on companies. Investment bankers, having seen some of their brethren indicted for giving stock in initial public offerings to favored clients, stopped that practice. Stock options, seen as a way to align the interest of shareholders with executives, were downplayed as it become obvious that executives were pumping up company performance just to win more options. Board members now spend more time understanding merger and acquisition proposals – instead of the cursory meetings like the two-hour review the WorldCom board managed before offering a $6 billion bid for Intermedia Communications.[63]

Business journalism played a role in those changes, although how big a role could be debated. But as business journalism moves further into the 21st century, its reporters and editors have a firmer grasp on the business world and are less likely to be overwhelmed by a smooth-talking executive and his brilliant strategy.

The business journalism field has also become more knowledgeable about how to handle its sources in the investment community.

Footnotes

1 From "Ex-Tyco chief, top lieutenant found guilty; face 25-year terms for grand larceny," by L. Lazaroff, June 18, 2005, Chicago Tribune, p. C1.

2 From "Adelphia founder John Rigas sentenced to 15 years in prison," by E. McClam, June 20, 2005, Associated Press.

3 From "HealthSouth paying $100 million to settle SEC civil fraud charges," June 9, 2005, Associated Press.

4 From "Spitzer may get his day in court," by P. Coy, June 13, 2005, BusinessWeek, p. 40.

5 See "Enron chronicle trips over itself," by M. Lillich, June 11, 2005, Indianapolis Star, p. 13A.

6 See "Enron documentary unravels the issues; Film has funny, scary moments," by D. M. Kimmell, June 3, 2005, Worcester Telegram & Gazette, p. C3.

7 See "Winn-Dixie closing to hurt neighborhood," by R. Roger and M. Kempner, June 22, 2005, Atlanta Journal-Constitution, p. C1, and "Winn-Dixie plans retreat from Atlanta; Thousands to lose jobs when grocer closes 326 stores," by R. DeGross, June 22, 2005, Atlanta Journal-Constitution, p. A1.

8 See "Bush's choice for SEC chairman likely to be questioned on past work for company," by M. Gordon, June 10, 2005, Associated Press, and "Investors still have to beware," by J. Brown, June 10, 2005, St. Paul Pioneer Press, p. 2C.

9 From "The quiet giant: Tyco takes unglamorous road to riches," by S. Syre and C. Stein, June 30, 1999, The Boston Globe, p. F1.

10 From "For Tyco investors, more (and more) is better," by A. Sullivan, June 5, 1999, International Herald Tribune, p. 18.

11 From "Titans stadium to be named 'Adelphia Coliseum,'" June 28, 1999, Associated Press.

12 From "Rigas feeling crunch despite Sabres' success," by R. Cook, June 7, 1999, Pittsburgh Post-Gazette, p. C1.

13 From "HealthSouth stock jumps 10% on news company will divide," by J. Underwood, June 16, 1999, Birmingham News, p. 7D.

14 From "Firing up an idea machine; Enron is encouraging the entrepreneurs within," by A. Salpukis, June 27, 1999, The New York Times, p. C1.

15 From "Azurix's initial stock offering expected to raise $ 695 million," by J. Walsh, June 10, 1999, The Houston Chronicle, p. 2.

16 From "In review: Sliding on the bubble," by D. McCollam, September/October 2002, Columbia Journalism Review, p. 6.

17 From "Is Enron overpriced?" by B. McLean, March 5, 2001, Fortune, p. 122.

18 From "Is Enron overpriced?" pp. 123–124.

19 From "Enron's CEO Skilling takes company in new directions," by A. Levy, May 1, 2001, Bloomberg News.

20 From "Enron CFO's partnerships had millions in profits," by R. Smith, Oct. 19, 2001, The Wall Street Journal, p. C1.

21 From "Enron may issue more stock to cover obligations," by R. Smith and J. R. Emswhiller, Oct. 24, 2001, The Wall Street Journal, p. A2.

22 From "Fancy finances were keys to Enron's success, and now its distress," by R. Smith, Nov. 8, 2001, The Wall Street Journal, p. A1.

23 From "Enron's swoon leaves a grand experiment in state of disarray," by R. Smith, Nov. 30, 2001, The Wall Street Journal, p. A1.

24 From "Enron: Uncovering the uncovered story," by S. Sherman, March/April 2002, Columbia Journalism Review, p. 22.

25 From "Enron: Uncovering the uncovered story," p. 23.

26 From "Who can you trust?" by S. Bartlett, Oct. 5, 1998, BusinessWeek, p. 132.

27 From "Ignoring the alarm," by C. Layton, March 2003, American Journalism Review, p. 22.

28 From "The watchdog role business reporters need to play," by G. Lewin, Summer 2002, Nieman Reports, p. 19.

29 From "Most business editors find news reporters unprepared," by M. J. Pardue, Summer 2004, Newspaper Research Journal, p. 73.

30 One of the accountants at Bloomberg News is Tom Contiliano, who previously had worked for an accounting firm and taught accounting. Contiliano is also involved with training at universities that offer business journalism programs.

31 From "Financial reporting: Lessons of the Enron collapse," by J. Madick, Winter 2003, Harvard International Journal of Press/Politics, p. 7.

32 From "Looking for answers in the Enron story," by P. Behr, Summer 2002, Nieman Reports, p. 8.

33 From "Looking for answers in the Enron story," p. 8.

34 From "Avoiding future Enrons," by A. Schiffrin, March/April 2002, Columbia Journalism Review, p. 29.

35 From "Not every journalist 'missed' the Enron story," by P. Steiger, Summer 2002, Nieman Reports, p. 10.

36 From "Looking for answers in the Enron story," p. 8.

37 From "Most business editors find news reporters unprepared," p. 74.

38 From "Enron's helpers," by J. Lipton, March/April 2002, Columbia Journalism Review, p. 13.

39 From "Enron's helpers," p. 13.

40 From "A good story isn't always the right one to tell," by J. Madick, Summer 2002, Nieman Reports, p. 6.

41 From "Under their noses, smelling like a rose," by H. Kurtz, Feb. 11, 2002, Washington Post, p. C1.

42 See "White-collar criminals: They lie, they cheat, they steal and they've been getting away with it for too long," by C. Leaf, March 18, 2002, Fortune, p. 60.

43 See "The 101 dumbest moments in business," by T. Carvell, A. Horowitz, and T. Mucha, April 2002, Business 2.0, pp. 64–74.

44 From "Post-Enron, a reversal of fortune," by P. Carlson, March 26, 2002, Washington Post, p. C4.

45 From "Bad apples or rotten culture? Media discourse on the corporate scandals of 2001 and 2002," by D. A. Craig and K. A. Turner, July 30, 2003, paper presented at the Association for Education in Journalism and Mass Communication annual meeting.

46 From "Dull business news? CNBC transforms it into a breezy romp," by M. Hill, Oct. 22, 2001, Philadelphia Inquirer, p. C2.

47 See "Business journalists honor the News for Adelphia stories," April 10, 2003, Buffalo News, p. E1.

48 See "Auditor who blew whistle praised," by C. Harden, July 2, 2002, The (Jackson) Clarion-Ledger, p. 1C, and "Scandal fallout could include criminal charges," by J. Mitchell and R. Schoenberger, June 27, 2002, The (Jackson) Clarion-Ledger, p. 1A.

49 From "Bad apples or rotten culture? Media discourse on the corporate scandals of 2001 and 2002."

50 From "How the U.S. business media is failing its audience," by C. Pummer, Aug. 29, 2002, CBSMarketWatch.

51 From "The watchdog role business reporters need to play," by G. Lewin, Summer 2002, Nieman Reports, p. 21.

52 From "Dismal beat: The march of personal-finance journalism," by B. Waski, March 1, 2003, Harper's Magazine, p. 81.

53 From "Dismal beat: The march of personal-finance journalism," p. 81.

54 From "Views of business and regulation unchanged by Enron," a survey from the Pew Research Center for the People & The Press, Feb. 21, 2002, available at http://people-press.org/reports.

55 From "Views of business and regulation unchanged by Enron."

56 See "The latest corporate scandal is sudden, vast and simple," by K. Eichenwald, June 27, 2002, The New York Times, p. A1.

57 From "When something is rotten," July 27, 2002, The Economist, p. 53.

58 From "Keeping an eye on Corporate America," by A. Wheat, Nov. 25, 2002, Fortune, p. 44.

59 From "History repeats itself at HealthSouth," by G. Colvin, May 12, 2003, Fortune, p. 40.

60 From "Crony capitalism: Time to overhaul the regulation of America's giant mortgage companies," by R. Baker, June 28, 2003, The Economist, p. 70.

61 From "The case against Ken Lay," by J. Rawe, July 19, 2004, Time, p. 62.

62 From "Lay's world: All fantasy, all the time," by L. Steffy, July 11, 2004, Houston Chronicle, p. B1.

63 From "The corporate scandals and American capitalism," by I. M. Stelzer, Winter 2004, The Public Interest, pp. 19–31.

Chapter 14

Media and Wall Street

In the late 1990s, Salomon Smith Barney analyst Jack Grubman was a telecommunications reporter's best friend. He was always willing to take phone calls to discuss companies in the industry, particularly businesses such as Global Crossing and WorldCom, two of his favorites. What few journalists ever reported, in addition to Grubman's bullish prospects for these businesses, was that he was heavily connected to these companies, helping them recruit executives and advising them on acquisitions. In addition, Grubman's company Salomon Smith Barney acted as an adviser to telecom companies involved in the transactions.

When the telecom industry imploded in the early part of the 21st century, sending companies into bankruptcy court and executives such as WorldCom's Bernard Ebbers to prison, Grubman was portrayed as the huckster who fed business journalists and readers false information while he reaped millions. The reporters were criticized for not questioning Grubman's motives.

Perhaps nowhere more in journalism has the relationship between reporters and editors and their primary sources been criticized and analyzed than in business writing. This is primarily because of how professionals such as analysts, investors, hedge fund managers, investment bankers, and others who work on Wall Street have used reporters and their publications for their gain and the enormous amounts of money at stake with how businesses are covered in the media.

Analysts try to get investors to buy stocks so their firms receive commissions from these trades, so they like to talk about these stocks in the press. Favorable comments, they believe, will attract attention to the stock and could cause readers or viewers who hear or see the comments to call the analyst's company, typically a stock brokerage, and purchase shares of the stock.

On the other side, reporters view Wall Streeters as experts in the inner workings of the stock market, mergers and acquisitions, corporate finance, and other issues. These Wall Street pros can be valuable sources, providing exclusive information about deals. They are often the first people to know whether a company is going to be sold, or whether its stock is going to rise or fall. And because they have this information, many journalists fight to gain access.

These relationships have existed for more than 100 years. And yet only the naïve business reporter today is unaware of the inherent conflicts of interest that surround Wall Street sources. The journalists failed in the past by not disclosing those conflicts to readers or viewers. More and more, however, those conflicts are being disclosed, even though concerns about the relationship between business journalists and investors have existed since the early 20th century. In 1951, University of Minnesota sociology professor Arnold Rose noted that rumors in the stock market were so established "that some newspapers have made an attempt to organize it into the 'gossip columns' of the financial pages."[1] These rumors and gossip often appeared in trade journals and newspapers, and they are sometimes given to business reporters from investors who wished to influence the price of their holdings.

Only the naïve business reporter today is unaware of the inherent conflicts of interest that surround Wall Street sources.

Coverage of Wall Street is not just these conflicts and these analysts, or investors and money managers attempting to use the media for financial gain. Wall Street and investing is one of business journalism's hallmark beats because of its importance in society. It is where publicly traded companies – and lots of private companies – are evaluated on a daily basis. It's also where fortunes are made and lost. Although it can be argued that the media haven't been Wall Street's watchdogs in many cases, in many other incidents the media have focused their coverage on illegal investment schemes, shysters, and bad companies.

The good role that business journalism has played in evaluating, criticizing, and lauding Wall Street definitely outweighs the bad that has come from its relationship with the world's biggest market. And the people overwhelmingly turn to the media when needing information about Wall Street. A November 1997 study by the Pew Research Center for the People & the Press found that most consumers turned to news media sources for information about the Oct. 27, 1997, market crash instead of talking with others, such as their stockbroker. The most used medium was cable news, followed by the major networks.[2]

Some major news events that have affected people around the world have been stories coming out of Wall Street. The Great Depression that enveloped this country for most of the 1930s was triggered by the stock market crash in October 1929. Market crashes, or corrections, in 1987 and 2000 were also major news that signaled a changing economy in the country, at least temporarily. And while the media have always been there to report about it, in some cases, the analysis has been lacking. The Associated Press, however, succinctly captured what was happening in its Oct. 23, 1929, lead when it wrote, "Wall Street was thrown into the nearest approximation of a stock market panic experienced in years during the last hour of trading on the Stock Exchange today. A new and wholly unexpected method of selling swept over the market carrying scores of stocks down, and wiping more than $3,000,000,000 in paper values in the brief interval of about an hour, an average of about $50,000,000 a minute."[4]

The story later explains that the stock prices have fallen to "disasterously low levels" and described the scenes of "wild disorder on the trading floor." Anyone who read the account realized that a news event of major importance had occurred. The AP followed with a story the next day that began, "Four hours and eight minutes after the close of the New York Stock Exchange today the ticker recorded the final sale of the most frantic day of stock trading in history. This last quotation on the tape, appearing at 7:08 o'clock, was a final clarification of the confusion that hung over the wild course of prices as the record total of 12,894,650 shares was traded. Closing prices presented a picture of havoc among quoted values, hundreds of shares selling at or near low levels for the year, and from $20 to more than $100 below the record prices reached in recent months."[5]

The media have been fixated on money matters since the beginning of the country. How quickly the media were able to report major investment and financial news has often affected who made money and who lost money. For example, in January 1790, Alexander Hamilton, the secretary of the fledgling U.S. Treasury, delivered a report on the country's debt to Congress. The report detailed his plan to reorganize the debt and refund the existing debt at face value. Ships that set sail from New York – then the capital of the country – that month for the Southern states carried with them that information. Investors on those ships were able to go into Georgia, South Carolina, and North Carolina and purchase the country's debt at 10 to 20 percent of face value because the news that the debt would be repaid had yet to reach newspapers in those areas. They reaped the value of having that information first.[6]

NEW YORK STOCK EXCHANGE

As the financial world changed, so did how the media covered it. The United States began issuing paper money in $5, $10, and $20 denominations in the 1860s as the invention of the telegraph helped end some of the advantageous use of financial information. The laying of the transcontinental telegraph in 1861 and then the cable that was laid across the Atlantic Ocean in 1868 meant that overseas investors had information about stock prices on a daily basis.

In 1870, Thomas Edison brought out an improved stock ticker that also sped up Wall Street information. The stock ticker had been originally invented by Edward Calahan in 1867, but Edison made changes to it. He had arrived in New York in 1869, and fixed the Gold Indicator Co.'s telegraph that relayed gold prices to customers. He became superintendent of that company at $300 per month, and then later formed the first electrical engineering company. The Gold and Stock Telegraph Co. paid Edison $40,000 for his stock ticker.[7]

The resulting huge amount of immediate financial information flowing to investors around the world brought about dramatic changes in the media. Dozens of newspapers began following Wall Street. The most famous was *The Wall Street Journal*, founded in 1889. And they covered news that wasn't purely financial. In September 1920, a horse-drawn cart filled with dynamite and fragmented steel exploded outside the offices of J.P. Morgan & Co., near the busiest part of the financial district, killing dozens. The *Washington Post* called the explosion an "act of war," but it was a reaction of anarchists to the growing capitalistic-focused society.

The mainstream papers of the 19th century also paid attention to Wall Street, typically providing readers a chart of recent stock prices. When major news occurred, they also covered the Street with as much vigilance as a house fire or a murder. In an analysis of the five largest daily New York newspapers in 1889, Central Washington University journalism professor Cynthia Mitchell discovered that all of them criticized the New York Stock Exchange's attempt to cut off ticker service from its floor in an attempt to cut off information to a rival exchange. Mitchell points out that the press acted as a watchdog on the exchange at a time when it was not regulated by the government.

Investment schemes have also been uncovered. A so-called Ponzi scheme occurs when someone collects money from new investors to pay off old investors. The scheme typically collapses when the flow of new investors stops. The term came from a man named Charles Ponzi, who convinced thousands to invest in postage stamps, promising huge returns. His company unraveled when his claims of solvency were disputed by accounts in the Boston newspapers. Without their reporting, Ponzi's scheme may have ensnared more people than it did.[8]

Fifty years ago, the *Journal* covered financial news on Wall Street, but it had also expanded itself. A 1954 story detailed research showing women with charge cards spent more at department stores than those who paid cash. Another story noted that a factory in South Carolina that would employ only blacks had begun production. And a front-page article harked the beginning of a new eating sensation called fish sticks. All these stories, however, still affected Wall Street, for it was the companies whose stock and debt were traded every day that were being affected by these societal trends.[9]

Today, how the media covers Wall Street and financial news is changing, but the coverage is just as important as it has been in the past. With the invention of the Internet, media outlets rush to place their stories online as fast as possible. Wire services such as the AP, Bloomberg, and Reuters compete daily to beat each other with stories. In their newsrooms, they measure by seconds how much quicker their story reaches the wire in advance of the competition about a stock rising or falling.

With more than 50 percent of U.S. households owning stock in some form or another, coverage of Wall Street has grown increasingly important to many readers and viewers. "The job of writing daily about the Dow Jones industrial average and other esoterica of Wall Street changes dramatically from the abstract to the concrete at times of market stress," notes Bill Barnhart, the financial markets columnist of the *Chicago Tribune*. "Suddenly, you are a lifeline to your readers and an outlet for their anxieties and frustrations."[10] Still, Barnhart notes that some of the daily reporting about Wall Street fails to help society because there is a tendency to call "dial-a-quote Wall Street commentators who have built careers on providing sound-bite quotes to the news media on the dullest day in the market."[11]

Quid pro quo

To be sure, excellent reporting about Wall Street occurs daily. Stories break dramatic ground in explaining to the readers and viewers what is going on and how their investments are being affected. In 2002, Gretchen Morgenson of *The New York Times* won a Pulitzer Prize in the beat reporting category for her coverage of Wall Street.

On November 18, 2001, she wrote a damning article about Salomon Smith Barney analyst Grubman that detailed how the stocks of telecommunications companies that he had been recommending to investors had lost billions of dollars. "It is impossible to tell how many investors profited from Mr. Grubman's advice on the way up," she wrote. "But those who stuck with him until the end, heeding his advice and holding on to the stocks, have fared dismally. In one telecom arena that Mr. Grubman dominated, among the so-called competitive local exchange carriers, some $140 billion in stock market value has vanished — 95 percent of the cash raised."[12]

In a May 27, 2001 piece titled "Buy, they say, but what do they do?" Morgenson excoriated Wall Street analysts who were selling stocks they were telling clients to purchase. "Now the effect of research analysts' rosy reports on the stocks of untried companies is also coming under the microscope," wrote Morgenson. "At the height of the I.P.O. craze, some analysts became the Wall Street equivalent of rock stars. They could push stock prices to unheard-of levels with positive research reports and appearances on financial news shows and in the press — investors lapped it up."[13]

And in a March 18, 2001, article titled "How do they value stocks? Count the absurd ways," Morgenson wrote with a forceful conviction of attempting to right an obvious wrong – how Wall Street had overvalued stocks. "Perhaps the biggest mistake investors made during the bull market was to believe corporate propaganda about which numbers supposedly provided the best window on the state of their operations," she wrote.[14] The assertion came just one week after the Internet bubble that had caused stock prices to run up had been burst, and the market was headed downward for most of the rest of the year. Morgenson's writing showed she was looking out for her readers and ready to let them know what went wrong without holding back. Her writing likely upset many on Wall Street, but it was accurate and on the mark.

There were others. In 1990, two reporters from the *Washington Post* won a Pulitzer in explanatory reporting for their investigation of the Securities and Exchange Commission and its regulation of Wall Street. Also at the *Times*, Floyd Norris and Diana Henriques constantly found stories to write about that brought to light an unflattering look at Wall Street. In an evaluation of Henriques, the *TJFR Business News Reporter* in 1991 noted that her stories about Wall Street are like "mini-lectures – imbued with a strong moral sense of right and wrong, they educate and enliven, and often criticize."[15] Henriques, much like Ida Tarbell a century earlier, gives off the appearance of a mother ready to scold her children for any transgression. But her writing brought attention, and for good reason. "Part of the business of the Fourth Estate is to represent that public trust in the financial market," she said. Norris and Henriques held the feet of Wall Street sources to the fire for the benefit of their readers.

Perhaps the writer who critiqued Wall Street the most during the last 30 years of the 20th century was Alan Abelson of *Barron's*, the sister publication of *The Wall Street Journal.* While the stock market rose to new heights for most of the 1990s, Abelson criticized the run-up on almost a weekly basis. Unfortunately, many investors ignored his rants. For example, he wrote this about IBM investors in December 1992: "By our crude reckoning, these hapless souls have lost something over $28 billion this year, and of course, neither the year nor possibly the damage is over. Contrast that to the $16 billion estimated cost of Hurricane Andrew, and the case for an official designation of IBM as a disaster area seems unanswerably compelling."[16] A critical word from Abelson, who had trained Henriques, punctured more than one financial bubble, or caused stocks to rise with a kind word. His reputation of discovering scams and finding the truth on Wall Street is legendary. After his "Up and Down Wall Street" column lauded SEEC, which developed software to maintain computer systems, the stock rose 52 percent in one day in November 1998. And after he criticized PMT Services

Inc., in consecutive issues of *Barron's* in 1996, the company put out a press release to dispute his assertions in an attempt to keep the stock from falling. It didn't work.

Even as far back as the 1970s, Abelson drew the ire of hedge funds before their operations and tactics became commonly known on Wall Street and to the investing public. Many hedge funds short stocks, meaning they believe they will fall in price, not rise. A lawsuit brought by a Technicare Corp. shareholder accused Abelson of providing tips to these short sellers in advance of negative articles about companies. Abelson denied the charges, which were never proved. "Back in the 1960s, people used to threaten to punch me in the nose when I said something negative about a company," responded Abelson. "Now we live in different times. The suit is obviously an attempt to keep me quiet."[17]

ALAN ABELSON

Keeping Abelson – and other critical watchers of Wall Street – quiet has been hard for anybody to accomplish. Their reporting on the financial markets has brought to light illegal dealings, dozens of shady stock propositions and countless scam artists. Their work is respected by the scrupulous operators on Wall Street for acting as a semi-regulatory body. With their writing, they sometimes alert federal regulators at the Securities and Exchange Commission to potential transgressions. They sell newspapers and attract viewers to their media outlets. This reporting is what the quid pro quo should be for readers, viewers, and listeners who often are investors. Unfortunately, that's not always the case.

Heard on the Street

For all the good work that the media perform in acting as the watchdogs of Wall Street, some reporters and editors have been caught trying to profit financially with the information they obtain through their reporting. Such an act is the highest violation of business journalism ethics, and when caught, the offenders have often been sent to jail and have never been able to work in the media again.

The early days of the media's relationship with Wall Street didn't include such ethical rules for reporters and editors as banning trading in stocks based on information received in the course of reporting and editing. And there were dozens and dozens of reporters in the early 20th century who successfully used such information to personally profit. But as business journalism developed more fully in the latter part of the century, such actions were first frowned upon and then outlawed altogether. The SEC, which came into being in 1933, developed laws that made it illegal to trade stocks based on information not available to the general public. While these rules have most commonly been used to keep corporate executives from profiting, they have also been applied to journalists. And such actions, when exposed, have caused consumers of business journalism to question the motives of the reporters and editors – not just the ones who performed the illegal acts, but all of them.

In June 1969, financial columnist Alex Campbell published an item in the *Los Angeles Herald Examiner* about Amer Systems Inc. Unknown to readers, Campbell had purchased 5,000 shares of the company shortly before the article ran in the newspaper. The article, which praised the company, caused the stock to rise. Campbell then sold his stock in the company at a profit. A judge who ruled in Campbell's case called his actions "reprehensible."

The most famous illegal act involving using the media to profit financially occurred at *The Wall Street Journal,* the publication with the best reputation among the financial community. In the 1980s, *Journal* reporter R. Foster Winans was writing the "Heard on the Street" column in the newspaper. He met some stockbrokers and agreed to provide them information about what was going to appear in the column before it was published. The brokers then used that information and made nearly $700,000. They also paid Winans some of their profits. In one case, Winans promoted the stock of American Surgery Centers in the column while Abelson criticized the company.

Winans and the two brokers were convicted of mail and wire fraud charges and for violating securities laws by using confidential information for personal use. In addition, Winans violated the newspaper's conflict of interest code. He argued that he broke no laws during his trial, but still served time in prison. Merrill Brown, the financial correspondent for the *Washington Post* at the time, wrote, "If there is a seemingly sure thing in the stock market it is that the *Journal's* 'Heard on the Street' moves company stocks and bonds quicker and probably more decisively than any information source in the nation."[18] Despite the transgressions of Winans, the "Heard on the Street" column and the *Journal* remain well respected today among financial journalists and readers.

Such transgressions of journalists using information in articles before they were published to trade in stocks happened elsewhere as well. In 1989, Seymour Ruderman, an editor at *BusinessWeek,* was sentenced to six months in prison for trading on information in the magazine before it was published. He had earned $39,000 in profits with the information. The SEC also brought charges against the editor. The information came from the "Inside Wall Street" column written by Gene Marcial, whose reporting of tips in the piece has been criticized in the past because they often come from Wall Street analysts and investors who could potentially profit from what he writes.

Noted Norris from the *Times:* "To avoid sources with conflicts of interest is to avoid sources who know what is going on. But to rely on them is to invite criticism that reporters are being used by people trying to make a buck."[19] More importantly, perhaps, is how those relationships are viewed by media users and whether they cause consumers to distrust what they're reading about Wall Street and the financial world. Norris said that he sometimes passes on exclusive information provided by such sources. "There is no easy way to know if a money manager is using a publication to find buyers for his mistakes," said Norris. "But I routinely warn managers that if I think they are doing that, I will never quote them again."[20]

In many cases, society has had every right to question relationships between business journalists and their high-powered sources.

Dan Dorfman's faux pas

Promoting stocks for personal gain has been a problem in the media for a long time. In 1995, money manager Jim Cramer was criticized for writing in *SmartMoney* magazine about stocks that his investment firm owned. "The episode underscores the power and pitfalls of personal finance journalism in an age when thousands of investors are willing to bet real money on a columnist's hot tip," said Howard Kurtz, the media reporter for *The Washington Post.* "In what can only be described as a bull market, newspapers, magazines, television and radio stations are rushing to inundate consumers with all manner of investment advice."[21] Kurtz questioned whether this journalism was providing a service to its readers and viewers, or whether it was hype. He noted that in such reporting "unsubstantiated rumors are routinely reported, justified by the notion that even false information can move stock and bond prices."

Some reporters use these rumors and talk to make a name for themselves on Wall Street and in the media. But their ethics have still been questioned, causing the relationship between the media and the financial word to undergo another assessment of their respective roles.

Dan Dorfman was perhaps the biggest proponent of such reporting about Wall Street in the 1980s and 1990s. A former *Wall Street Journal* reporter, Dorfman had written the "Heard on the Street" column, as had Abelson. By the late 1980s, he was writing two columns a week for *USA Today* and providing commentary about the markets on Cable News Network. "My goal is to be an equalizer, to let the little guy know what the big guy knows," said Dorfman.[22] But he had his critics. After reporting on CNBC in 1995 that Coca-Cola would make a bid for Quaker Oats, the Atlanta-based soft drink company put out a statement that simply read, "Dan Dorfman does not have a clue."[23]

Some reporters use these rumors and talk to make a name for themselves on Wall Street and in the media.

He was right on other occasions. He reported on CNN Moneyline that Time Inc. and Warner Communications were merging before it was announced. In 1989, he broke the story of Paramount Communications' hostile offer for Time. And his reporting moved stock prices, showing that people paid attention to what he wrote or said. "The reason Dorfman rose so rapidly in recent years to become the highest paid and most influential business reporter in the United States isn't because he's a market genius," wrote *Newsweek* business columnist Allan Sloan in 1995. "It's the hunger for the simple way to make money, the quick hit, seven stocks to buy now, 10 mutual funds for the '90s, the 12-step computer program that guarantees you won't have to live on cat food when you retire."[24]

Another business publication, *BusinessWeek*, called to question Dorfman's reporting tactics and noted his relationship with a public relations executive used as a source for several stories. The magazine broke the story in 1995 that the U.S. attorney was investigating Dorfman and the PR person, Donald Kessler, for possible illegal insider trading. Dorfman was placed on a leave of absence by *Money* magazine, which had lured him from *USA Today.* The magazine then fired Dorfman after he refused to reveal his sources. Though Dorfman was never found to have profited by mentioning stocks in his writing, he was deemed guilty by his association with Kessler, who later pled guilty to two counts of securities fraud. Dorfman later made a comeback on the Internet.

Others have also been tarnished. Money manager Cramer, who helped found online financial news source TheStreet.com, where he wrote regularly, and appeared on CNBC, was accused of trying to influence the prices of stocks in which he invested. In December 1998, CNBC required its reporters to disclose their investments. In 1999, the *San Jose Mercury News* reassigned its high-tech columnist after it discovered she had made $9,000 profiting in an

IPO by being able to purchase stock at an insider's price. CNBC came under criticism in 2003 for allowing reporter Maria Bartiromo to interview Citigroup Chairman Sandy Weill. Bartiromo disclosed her investment of 1,000 shares in the company on the air.

And in early 2004, CBS Marketwatch.com commentator Thom Calandra resigned from the online financial journalism site after it was disclosed that the SEC was investigating his trading. Calandra had written in a stock-picking newsletter about an energy company in which he owned shares. He had also traveled to Asia on a trip paid for by the company. As a result, CBS Marketwatch.com thereafter required its journalists to register stock trades with the company, which also began conducting random audits of its financial reporters.

In many cases, the media outlets acted quickly to quell fears from readers and viewers that their Wall Street reporting was improper or unethical. And the journalists who were caught provided a symbol for the thousands of other reporters and editors involved in reporting about financial news that the credibility of their jobs lies with themselves and their actions. Without that credibility, they would have no integrity when it came to informing consumers about investing and Wall Street.

Analysts and the media

In recent years, the major issue the business media have faced in dealing with Wall Street is their reliance on the use of analysts as sources. These analysts typically work for large brokerage houses that buy and sell stocks for their clients. It's the job of the analysts to conduct research on these companies and determine when the firm's clients should buy and sell the stock. In theory, that's how it should work. And for decades, that was the practice, because the analysts were truly independent and could give objective viewpoints.

But in practice, something else happened for most of the 1980s and 1990s. Many analysts gave favorable ratings to companies in which their firms had a banking relationship. In other words, the analyst was there to curry favor with the company he or she was tracking so that the analyst's firm would get more business from it.

Many journalists ignored this practice and continued to interview and quote analysts when writing about a company. These analysts would often give glowing accounts of the company to the reporter because their firm wanted business from it. The business journalists would use those comments in their stories. At first glance, the usage of these analysts seemed an effective reporting tool. These analysts knew more about the company than most other sources used by journalists. The analysts had access to more information from the company than the journalists.

But as Morgenson's reporting, and that of many other journalists, later disclosed, these analysts were not an objective source. To maintain credibility with society, the business media have now shied away from using the analysts as much as they had in the past, and the analysts in turn have also stopped talking to the media in some cases. "It became a custom, a staple and a bad habit of business journalism, even at many of the best news organizations, to rely on analysts for interpreting news," said Joshua Mills, director of the master's program in business journalism at Baruch College in New York and a former business journalist at the *Times*.[25]

Others played the game as well. In the 1980s, investors would purchase a large stake in a company and imply that they planned to take over the business, sending the stock price higher. The stake would be reported in the media, and then the investor would sell his stake in the company – at a profit. In many cases, the media were serving the interest of the investor, not of society. This practice lost its luster after the journalists discovered the true intentions of their sources – although it still occurs in some cases and is still reported. In many cases, the journalists continued to use the investor as a source, but began disclosing the investor's potential motives.

Today, business journalists are also using other sources on Wall Street with more credibility to maintain their respect among readers and viewers. Other analysts, such as those who work for mutual fund companies or institutional investors, have little financial incentive to promote the buying and selling of stock. They do not need publicity. These analysts are being increasingly used in reporting on Wall Street.

The usage of analysts who lacked objectivity, however, tainted business journalism in the eyes of society, since many were looking for a scapegoat to blame for their investment losses. The smart journalists curtailed their use of these sources many years earlier. "The fact that most analysts are shills may be news to you, but it's not news to us," said Allan Sloan in a 2001 column in the *Post.* "Some of us did the right thing by warning you or by not spreading analyst opinions that we considered nonsense, but many of us spread the bubble gospel nationally and internationally. Now that things have gone bad, journalists who used to shill for whatever was hot now blame the likes of Morgan Stanley's Mary Meeker or Merrill Lynch's Henry Blodget instead of themselves."[26]

But who is to blame – the journalist for using the analysts and portraying them to the public as an objective source or the analysts for trumpeting stocks even when they didn't believe what they were saying? Many argue that many in society should be smart enough to realize that sources quoted by journalists always have a hidden agenda and that they should take those comments with a grain of salt. Others contend that it is the media's job to protect society from those on Wall Street looking to take advantage of them.

In many cases, such as Marcial's "Inside Wall Street" column that runs in *BusinessWeek* and often quotes analysts and investors with positions in the stocks they are talking about, studies have shown that the reporting does not help investors in the long run.[27] In other cases, financial analysts who recommended stocks on television without disclosing that their firm has a financial tie to the company was commonplace in the 1990s on CNBC and other networks.[28]

In one area of business journalism and its relationship with Wall Street, however, the media may have overstepped its bounds in trying to do for society what many in society didn't trust Wall Street to do.

Investment pornography

As business journalism became more sophisticated in its coverage of Wall Street and financial news, many in the field began writing stories that offered advice to consumers on how to invest their money, or how to spend their money wisely. This type of service journalism grew in popularity for much of the 20th century, and when done right, it provided readers and viewers with valuable information to help them lead better lives. One of the pioneers of this type of business journalism was Sylvia F. Porter, whose column began appearing in the *New York Post* in the 1930s.

In 1939, Porter published her first book, *How to Make Money in Government Bonds,* which offered practical advice to both professional investors and the general public. In the 1970s, a book titled *Sylvia Porter's Money Book: How to Earn It, Spend It, Save It, Invest It, Borrow It and Use it to Better your Life* sold more than 1 million copies, and the proliferation of personal finance journalism took off. At the time of her death in 1991, Porter's column reached 40 million readers in 450 newspapers around the world.

Others followed Porter. Jane Bryant Quinn gained a wide following with her personal finance column in *Newsweek, Good Housekeeping,* and *The Washington Post.* She also wrote a book offering financial advice called "Making the Most of Your Money," but began to worry about how much of the financial advice being offered through the media was being accepted by society. "These readers aren't greedy or dumb – which is how they'll be pictured when the music stops," said Quinn in 1998, two years before the market bubble burst. "They believe the stuff we're telling them. It's almost shocking to see how much they trust the press. That should frighten us more – especially those of us in the personal finance press."[29]

Quinn was referring to the glut of articles in the media and on business TV shows that offered advice on where to put money. Magazines touted their top 10 stock picks or the 20 best mutual funds. Newspaper writers pointed out undervalued stocks that savvy investors could profit from. TV shows were handing out stock tips. Personal finance columnist Humberto Cruz called such writing "financial pornography" and added "much of the financial pornography today is propagated by a financial press sinking to new depths of shallow formula reporting and sensationalism."[30] The most dangerous form, said Cruz, was the magazine cover headline that screams what stocks and mutual funds should be bought NOW. He used as an example the June 1999 issue of *Money* magazine, which touted "The 100 Best Mutual Funds. The Only List You Need." Two months later, in the August issue, the same magazine had a new cover headline: "Your Best Moves Now!" In that issue, however, some of the mutual funds recommended were not on the list of 100 best funds just two months earlier.

What are the readers to believe? Do they understand that the best mutual funds may have changed in two months, or is that even a correct assumption to make for a reader going back and evaluating the difference between the two issues? In many ways, the media are confusing society with the oversaturation of such financial advice, turning many away from service journalism that provides the readers with news and information they can use to make decisions about their lives.

And there is also the bigger, unstated problem of where the personal finance journalist is receiving the information used to provide investment advice to readers and viewers. "In many ways, the personal finance press covers a world of predators and prey," said Quinn. "We're supposed to stick up for the prey. Who will defend them, if not us? Yet we tend to dine with the predators, innocently, without even thinking about it."[31]

Yet, if the readers are not given this information from the media, then where would they get it? They could go to financial advisers, but many of them won't provide the array of options that the media might explore. While the media may have become too aggressive in taking on the role of investment adviser for society in the 1990s, many have toned down such advice-oriented reporting in the past few years as the markets have fluctuated up and down. Criticism from Quinn and Cruz also caused many in the media to evaluate their brand of personal finance journalism.

It can also be argued that the media are still providing a service, even if some of that service can be described as pornography. And as consumers see more of this reporting, they become smarter and can pick out what is sound advice and what should be ignored.

A critical relationship

The media have come off as being too cozy with its sources on Wall Street and in the investment community. *The Fortune Tellers: Inside Wall Street's Game of Money, Media and Manipulation* by Howard Kurtz shows time and time again that journalists have been manipulated by investors, analysts, bankers, and others in the financial world for the gain of their clients or themselves.

The media have come off as being too cozy with its sources on Wall Street and in the investment community.

Yet, a critical relationship between the media and Wall Street is vitally important to how society works. Readers of the Internet, newspapers, and magazines; watchers of CNBC and other business programs; and listeners to stock market reports on the radio rely on the media to counterbalance the message that they're receiving from the financial world. Without the media to question the financial world and call it on the carpet for wrongdoing, many more people would be duped. Do consumers increasingly turn to the media for investment advice? Yes, and that's probably not the wisest choice to be made, but the business media have done a good job of portraying themselves as sifting through the morass of Wall Street and providing clear and concise analysis of what's right and what's wrong. Transgressions made by business journalists in covering Wall Street and personal finance make society more attuned to the realization that they shouldn't be relying on the media for investment advice.

The media have made their fair share of mistakes in covering Wall Street.

After the stock market bubble burst in 2000, former *Forbes* editor Jim Michaels said, "The whole thing was a Ponzi scheme, yet during much of it, business journalists were cheerleaders for it. We in the media let our public down and helped the tremendous swindle of the public."[32] He suggested that journalists rely more on SEC documents to report about Wall Street than analysts. That's a move in reporting that is occurring.

Philip Longman, a senior fellow at the New America Foundation, was more critical of business journalism's failures leading up to the 2000 market fall. "Just as Americans put far too much faith in the integrity and intellectual prowess of stock analysts and other supposedly disinterested financial watchdogs during the boom," he wrote, "they also put far too much stock in business journalism and have a right to be disappointed and angry."[33]

While it's doubtful that most Americans are disappointed and angry at business journalists, they do feel somewhat deceived. However, journalists such as Morgenson and newspapers such as *The Wall Street Journal* still remain credible resources used on a daily basis by society to remain informed about stocks, bonds, and other investments as well as the inner workings of the financial world. And consumers have been well served by reporting that has exposed wrongdoing.

Many business media outlets are restoring that credibility though old-fashioned reporting – reading documents and talking to sources such as employees who know more about what's going on at a company than an analyst or investor. What many journalists who write about Wall Street have learned is that their role in covering the largest financial market in the world depends more and more on their knowledge of the games being played by everyone involved.

Footnotes

1 From "Rumor in the stock market," by A. M. Rose, Autumn 1951, Public Opinion Quarterly, pp. 465–466.

2 From "Stock market down, new media up," by the Pew Research Center for the People & The Press. Nov. 9, 1997. http://people-press.org/reports/print.php3?ReportID=101.

3 From "Business news coverage," by H. J. Caswell, October 1938, Public Opinion Quarterly, p. 615.

4 From "The Crash Begins," by the Associated Press, Oct. 23, 1929. http://www.epals.com/20thcentury/29marketcrash.tpl.

5 From "The Crash Begins."

6 From "The market, the media & the means," by J. Zweig, Summer 2000, Financial History, pp. 21, 36.

7 From "The market, the media & the means."

8 From Muckraking! The journalism that changed America, edited by J. Serrin and W. Serrin, New York: The New Press, 2002.

9 From "The pages of The Wall Street Journal, 50 years ago," by C. Crossen, May 2004, The Wall Street Journal classroom edition. http://www/wsjclassroomedition.com/archive/04may/deja_journal.htm.

10 From "Assignment: Watching the markets," by B. Barnhart, October-November 1998, The Business Journalist, p. 14.

11 From "Assignment: Watching the markets," p. 14.

12 From "Telecom's Pied Piper: Whose side was he on?" by G. Morgenson, Nov. 18, 2001, The New York Times, p. C1.

13 From "Buy, they say, but what do they do?" by G. Morgenson, May 27, 2001, The New York Times, p. C1.

14 From "How did they value stocks? Count the absurd ways," by G. Morgenson, March 18, 2001, The New York Times, p. C1.

15 From "This reporter does ample homework, but watch out if she thinks your company is abusing the public's trust," by T. K. Grose, October 1991, TJFR Business News Reporter, pp. 1, 7–9.

16 From "Changes at Barron's, acerbic column stays, for now," by J. Cox, Dec. 23, 1992, USA Today, p. 2B.

17 From "The hedge fund enigma: Hidden treasure," by J. Egan, May 8, 1977, The Washington Post, p. G1.

18 From "Leaks are inevitable, even at the Journal," by M. Brown, April 5, 1984, The Washington Post, p. B1.

19 From "In the dance between business journalists and their sources, who is leading whom?" by F. Norris, Jan. 8, 1996, The New York Times, p. 41.

20 From "In the dance between business journalists and their sources, who is leading whom?" p. 41.

21 From "The power of personal finance journalism; Some columnists offering investment advice also bend the rules," by H. Kurtz, Feb. 18, 1995, The Washington Post, p. A1.

22 From "Dan Dorfman is not afraid to stand up against big boys," by E. Whitney, June 5, 1989, St. Petersburg Times, p. 9.

23 From "Coke splashes cold water on Dorfman's TV rumors," by G. Collins, Jan. 14, 1995, The New York Times, p. 39.

24 From "Beyond the Dan Dorfman affair, business journalism's deeper ill," by A. Sloan, Oct. 31, 1995, The Washington Post, p. D3.

25 From "A primer on Wall Street analysts," by J. Mills, February 2004, Donald W. Reynolds National Center for Business Journalism, available at http://www.businessjournalism.org/content/3223.cfm.

26 From "Why to put little stock in the words of Wall Street analysts," by A. Sloan, June 12, 2001, The Washington Post, p. E3.

27 From "How inside is 'Inside Wall Street?'" by R. Rosenwein, November 1998, Brill's Content, p. 75.

28 From "Analyze this," by J. Oxfeld, April 2000, Brill's Content, p. 105.

29 From "When business writing becomes soft porn," by J. B. Quinn, March/April 1998, Columbia Journalism Review, pp. 48–49.

30 From "Financial pornography is a temptation best avoided," by H. Cruz, Aug. 23, 1999, Orange County Register, p. C7.

31 From "When business writing becomes soft porn," p. 49.

32 From "Investment bubble enticed journalists, Forbes official says," by K. Gallagher, Oct. 31, 2001, Milwaukee Journal Sentinel, p. 2D.

33 From "Bad press: How business journalism helped inflate the bubble," by P. Longman, October 2002, Washington Monthly, p. 18.

References

C. Mitchell. (2004). Checking financial power: Newspaper coverage of the New York Stock Exchange's bid to control the ticker, June 1889. A paper presented at the University of Tennessee at Chattanooga's Twelfth Annual Symposium on the 19th Century Press, the Civil War, and Free Expression.

Chapter 15

Business media and society

On Nov. 28, 2005, the Monday after Thanksgiving, media outlets across the country provided the online retail industry with some positive coverage about how the day was called Cyber Monday because of the large number of shoppers who purchased items on the Internet. The coverage included features on NBC's Today show and on MSNBC, as well as a story on the Reuters wire and in the *Chicago Sun-Times*. All these stories had been spurred by a press release from the National Retail Federation giving the day its new nickname. Online retailers saw the coverage as positive for it raised awareness of how consumers could shop by using their computer.

The Nov. 29, 2005, the Tuesday after Thanksgiving, online retailers and their industry association had likely changed their minds about the treatment they were receiving from the business media. *BusinessWeek* reporter Robert Hof called Cyber Monday a "marketing myth" and criticized the spin put on the date by the retail association, noting that it was only the 12th biggest shopping day of the year for online retailers. Other media outlets followed, and there soon appeared a backlash against the industry.

For the most part, businesses and the media that cover them have had a love–hate relationship. Business executives want the media to help them. They distrust the media because they feel as if the newspapers, magazines, television and radio stations, and Web sites are out to get them, to make them look bad and to expose even the smallest wrongdoing at their companies. And when they have been forthright with reporters and editors, their comments have been taken and used against them in some cases. Said journalism critic and former *Wall Street Journal* reporter Kent MacDougall more than two decades ago:

> Many a business executive can go on at length about how journalists are giving profits a dirty name, exaggerating environmental hazards, sensationalizing marketplace ripoffs, and sowing public distrust of business at a time when the capitalist system is under increasing strain and needs the media's understanding and support more than ever.[1]

The business media, on the other hand, distrust the corporate world. Maybe it's because those who work for big business have lied to them in the past, and that makes journalists wary of being lied to again. Maybe there are some reporters and editors wronged by a company in their personal life and taking it out on other businesses in their reporting. But quite often, business journalists have been unfairly blamed for problems in the corporate world. MacDougall noted that business journalists "don't agree that going beyond corporate news releases constituted giving business the business. And they were sick of businessmen reacting defensively to even the most thoroughly researched and evenly balanced accounts."[2]

In addition, dozens and dozens of corporate communications executives and managers of companies believe the media do a good job in reporting about industry. Many go out of their way to help reporters who call with questions and who simply want to understand their business and how it operates, spending hours and hours on the telephone or in meetings with journalists. They believe that the best way to deal with the business media is to be as accessible and honest as possible. Yes, the PR people may be presenting their specific viewpoint about topics such as workers' compensation costs or trade tariffs on their products that don't accurately represent opposing views, but the savvy reporter will always try to present both sides of the story by talking to others.

In addition, many reporters and editors have developed trusting relationships with CEOs and other executives at some of the largest companies in the world. Some of their largest scoops have been given to them by these executives, or their PR people.

What is society to make of this love–hate relationship between the media and corporate America? The watchful eye of the journalist helped expose some of the largest problems in the business world in the last 100-plus years and will likely continue to do so for years to come. Without hard-hitting business stories from newspapers, magazines, and other media, consumers today may not have the protections afforded them from regulations requiring safe consumer products and healthy foods, for example. Investors could be taken by con men. Yet, many in society appear uncaring or unconvinced about this benefit. Journalists typically rank among the least trusted by society in recent surveys.

Has the view of the business world been changed by what has been reported about it in the media? In many cases, the skeptical stories dating back to the muckrakers and continuing today on Enron and WorldCom are a byproduct of what society thinks about industry. Without the skepticism of society, and therefore reporters in society, that all companies are organized simply for the good of the employees and to provide consumers with the best product or service possible, there would be no uncovering of how businesses have circumvented the law for their own financial benefit or have inflated their performance so that executives can personally profit by selling stock. This distrust of business grew primarily from the scandals that the media wrote about.

Have journalists gone after companies and industry for the wrong reasons? In some cases, the answer is likely to be yes. And in some cases, the media have had to retract stories that they have aired or published criticizing the practices of businesses that made it seem as if they didn't care about the safety of the consumer. The *Orlando Sentinel*, for example, ran a correction about a series of articles related to OxyContin, a pain medication drug made by Purdue Pharmaceutical. The stories overstated the problems with the drug, and the bad publicity hurt Purdue's sales.

But the overriding result of more than a century of the media digging and uncovering the truth in the corporate world has been a better society for all of us to live in, whether or not we recognize this achievement. Where would we be without the government making sure the foods we eat are sanitary – a result of Upton Sinclair's *The Jungle*? Where would we be without the watchdog journalists uncovering every type of imaginable scam and financial trickery known to man?

The job of business journalists – even though they weren't known by that name 100 years ago – has been to document the human desire of greed and avarice. What business journalism basically boils down to is who has money and who doesn't and how that money was obtained or lost. In the past two decades, the sophistication of business journalism has arguably increased, improving its ability to serve as a watchdog over business – and protect society.

Corporate America's perceptions

Yet not everyone feels that way about business journalists, particularly those who regularly deal with such reporters. Put yourself in the shoes of a public relations professional or a company executive who has received a phone call from a reporter at the local paper. The reporter has uncovered an embarrassing fact about one of the company's products just days before a major advertising campaign has been scheduled to begin about the same product. The journalist wants to know whether the company is going to fix the problem and how it happened. And the reporter is pressing to find out how the mistake occurred and whether anyone was fired as a result.

Should the company be forthcoming with the journalist, who will then write a story that will appear in tomorrow morning's newspaper about the error? The PR person weighs the issue and realizes that the story is big enough that a wire service such as the Associated Press or Bloomberg News will likely pick it up from the newspaper, making it accessible to media outlets around the world, causing likely further embarrassment to the company. Does the company deny the fact? Or does it admit the mistake and lay out how it's going to correct the problem?

In many cases such as this, the company's corporate communications department is likely weighing the issue of whether the reporter and his or her media outlet will accurately tell the story and how the company will be portrayed – as a bumbling conglomerate that dropped the ball or as a proactive business handling the issue. While most PR people at companies understand that they're going to be criticized every once in a while in the media, their hardest job may be in explaining that negative story to their bosses, the executives who actually run the company. And it's the upper layer of management that truly distrusts the media and its motives.

Time and time again, surveys of executives show a low belief in the media's ability to tell a business story that is fair, accurate, and balanced. In 1989, the Gallup Organization conducted a survey for The Times Mirror Center for the People and the Press. It asked Fortune 500 executives whether they thought the media deal fairly with all sides or favor one side when dealing with political and social issues. Only 8 percent said the media were fair.[3]

A 1992 poll by Louis Harris and Associates for Boston-based life insurer John Hancock Financial Services Inc. found that only 54 percent of executives had a positive view of the quality of business journalism in America. In comparison, 79 percent of journalists polled had a positive view of business journalism. Only 27 percent of the executives polled believed that business journalism was fair, balanced, and accurate, whereas 84 percent of journalists agreed with that statement.[4]

In addition, the Harris poll found that just 41 percent of executives rated business journalism positively on producing stories that were well written and well researched. In comparison, 78 percent of journalists felt that business journalism was well written and well researched.[5]

Interestingly, these negative opinions about business journalism occurred at the beginning of one of the biggest boom times in America's economy, the stock market, and in business. As a result, a sizeable portion of business coverage in the early 1990s was favorable to business, as the media covered the technology boom related to the Internet and personal computer advances with a "gee-whiz" mentality – for the most part. "Many reporters, editors, and even a few media moguls were sincerely caught up in the same irrational exuberance that affected even Alan Greenspan in the end," said Philip Longman, a senior fellow at the New America Foundation. "And many business reporters simply didn't know what they didn't know about business."[6] If this was how executives thought about business journalism during a time when coverage leaned toward the positive in most media, think how they felt during other periods.

The boom in the market and in bubbly stories by business journalists also came at a time when the executives said they had become more accessible to journalists than they had been ten years earlier, according to the Harris poll. Journalists agreed on this point, one of the few points in which executives and journalists responded in the same manner. Even though executives were more accessible, corporate management and the journalists that covered them disagreed on the information that was being discussed. Eighty-one percent of executives said they were more honest than ten years earlier, but just 48 percent of journalists felt the same way.[7]

What were the problems? According to corporate executives, too much emphasis was being placed on "personality" reporting. They also felt that too many business journalists let their political views influence their reporting, and executives also felt that the media relied on stories that were "all style and no substance." Naturally, the business journalists disagreed, but in some cases, the executives may have been right. The fawning coverage of many CEOs in the 1990s through personality profiles resulted in the media making people such as General Electric Co.'s Jack Welch and Microsoft's Bill Gates seem larger than life and gave them credit for successful moves within their company that were actually the byproduct of the hard work of those below them.

Two years later, a similar study found that the opinions of business executives toward the media hadn't changed much. A national survey of executives and journalists by the Freedom Forum First Amendment Center found that 68 percent of executives felt the news media are biased against management, while 81 percent of journalists disagreed with the statement. About half the executives surveyed said they were usually not quoted accurately, while 84 percent of journalists believe they do quote management accurately. Nearly three-fourths of the executives believed that journalists portrayed business in a negative light, while nearly 40 percent of the journalists thought that business was presented in a positive light in the media.[8]

When it comes to the relationship between the media and executives, just more than 50 percent of the executives felt that the antagonism between the two was inevitable, while 81 percent of the journalists surveyed thought that was the case. Two-thirds of executives also thought that reporting does not enhance the status of business, while 42 percent of journalists felt it did. Clearly, the adversarial relationship that began decades earlier was still prevalent in a time of a strong economy. The Freedom Forum survey also found 56 percent of business journalists and 49 percent of editors disagreed that the relations between business executives and reporters had gotten worse in the past five years, but 45 percent of executives believed the relationship had worsened.[9]

Finally, Selzer & Co. conducted a business journalism survey of executives for the American Press Institute nearly a decade after the John Hancock survey. It found opinions about business reporting among corporate leaders had not changed much. Although the survey showed that CEOs expressed little concern about accuracy, they still gave local daily newspapers low marks for content and credibility. One in three was dissatisfied with the quality of business news in the local newspaper, and more than 60 percent gave reporters low marks for their ability to ask intelligent questions about their business.[10]

What exists is a corporate world that has not changed its opinion about the media in the past decade and is unlikely to change that viewpoint even if their suggestions such as better education take hold at newspapers, magazines, and in broadcast. This is a view likely ingrained in the culture of many corporations that deal regularly with the media and feel it has been burned at one point or another.

Should this change? A healthy distrust on both sides of the battle is likely good. What is perhaps more important is what the nonexecutive and the nonjournalist think about the relationship.

Is there a solution to the distrust? Should executives and company managers try to work more with the business journalism community? Many corporate heads would likely say no. They fear the treatment they'd receive. But the reporters might appreciate their openness. That might lead to even better coverage, helping everyone.

Public and consumer perceptions

Unfortunately, there is scant quantitative proof – except for perhaps the circulation figures of business publications – that the general consumer of business news and information appreciates the battle between industry and the media. Perhaps the more effective proof of the desire to see such a relationship is how society forces the government to enact legislation to prevent the abuses from occurring again.

Some polls and surveys have touched the issue of consumer perception of business coverage. In the 1992 John Hancock/Harris poll, deans and professors of graduate business schools were surveyed, and 72 percent rated the overall quality of business journalism in America as positive. Interestingly, their opinion was higher than that of deans and professors of journalism schools. Sixty-four percent of the journalism educators rated the overall quality of business journalism as positive. Sixty-four percent of the business school professors and deans also believed that business journalism was fair, balanced, and accurate.[11]

But business school professors can't be considered an accurate representation of the general public who read newspapers and magazines, watch television, and listen to the radio. They are more knowledgeable about business issues and have likely formed opinions about corporate malfeasance, executive compensation, and other topics discussed in the media.

Surveys about the quality of business journalism and the relationship with corporations have queried journalists and editors about the state of coverage. Nearly two-thirds of journalists and 63 percent of managing editors disagreed with the statement that most journalists covering business and economics introduce their selective perspective rather than report objectively. Twenty-one percent of the journalists and 19 percent of the managing editors agreed with the statement.[12]

In addition, 38 percent of business journalists and 36 percent of the managing editors felt that business journalists don't always treat their subjects fairly. Considering that this is one of the beliefs held by many corporate executives, it's somewhat surprising to see that many journalists believe the same thing.

When asked whether they agree with the statement "antagonism between the news media and business people is inevitable, because news often deals with change, unsolved problems and divisive issues," 81 percent of the business journalists and 74 percent of the managing editors agreed. Said Russell Rein of the *Santa Barbara News-Press:* "Most of the problems occur because business people are ignorant of the role of a free press in covering business. They want control just like they have in their business."[13]

ONE CAN PRESUME THAT THE PUBLIC APPRECIATES the role of the business media in making their lives better. But do they actually want critical stories of companies? It's likely that employees of a company would not be happy with a report that could cause them to lose their jobs, for example, if the business suffers as a result of the information being disclosed. Investors with a lot of money in a company may not like seeing negative stories that cause the stock price to fall.

Maybe the public isn't even paying any attention. While many readers and viewers will call a media outlet to complain about story content that they believe to be false or disagree with, they are likley the minority of those who have seen the story. Little is known about what the others think. The social responsibility role of the media presumes that the public benefits from stories that expose wrongdoing at companies and in industries, and that has happened countless times.

But has the public actually told the media that this is what they want? Many business journalists argued in the 1990s that their fawning coverage of Internet companies and investment ideas gave readers and viewers what they wanted although they provided no quantifiable proof.

But when the media stopped writing such stories, few in the public clamored for newspapers, magazines, Internet sites, and television stations to go back to that style of reporting. The same can be said of other types of business journalism coverage. That the media would discontinue examining business critically is highly unlikely, but as many outlets have looked inward to assess their business coverage in the wake of the Enron and Arthur Andersen scandals, as well as others, it's interesting that few have taken the time to assess the views of their readers. The lack of such a widespread study makes the media come off as being too arrogant to care about what its consumers think about the business news it's covering.

The future of business journalism

Business journalism is not what it was 10 years ago or 25 years ago or 100 years ago when Ida Tarbell and Upton Sinclair were bringing accusations to the public about unscrupulous operations. That also means that the business journalism of the future won't look as it does today or tomorrow.

We've seen a dramatic change in the reporting tactics of business journalists and how their information is disseminated to the public due to technology. More business reporters access public records of companies, for example, with a few clicks of their mouse. And their stories are often transmitted via e-mail and on Internet sites at a faster pace than a newspaper can be thrown on the driveway each morning.

These changes can be good and bad. Access to public records by computers can speed the process of reporting a story for a business journalist. But does it also make them lazy, making them more reliable on documents that they can read while sitting at their desk instead of getting out of the newsroom and talking to people at companies? Transmitting stories online makes the exposure of information immediate, but many Web sites report with more opinion in their content, decreasing their emphasis on objectivity, a precept that business executives believe is necessary for good coverage. There is an ongoing debate as to whether these changes have made journalism better or worse.

Still, business journalism overall is also much better than it was in the past. Gone are the days when business reporters at large newspapers accepted gifts from the companies they wrote about, or even handled freelance work on the side such as writing news releases. Gone are the days in the 19th century when much of the business journalism was based on rumors. The content has also gotten better, although it still could be improved. But many more journalists know now how to read a company's financial statement and can look through arcane regulatory filings and find news stories. They also have a better understanding of how businesses operate and are more knowledgeable about a company's operations. Yes, there will always be a learning curve for new reporters. But more and more, reporters have just as good an understanding about accounting, finance, management, and other issues as the people that they are interviewing.

The stories they're writing are becoming more sophisticated and tackle harder issues. Off-balance sheet financing was rarely written about before Enron, likely because few journalists knew its importance. Hedge funds were rarely, if ever, written about 20 and 30 years ago. Now, they're a common staple in business journalism coverage.

How business news is delivered is also changing. More and more, users of business news now receive stories on personal digital assistants and Blackberries. How business news stories will be delivered to readers, viewers, and listeners in the next century can only be imagined.

To be sure, reporters at *The Wall Street Journal, The New York Times, Fortune, Forbes, BusinessWeek*, and other major business publications have a better understanding of business topics and issues than most business journalists. But even at the smaller and mid-sized papers, Web sites, and TV stations, knowledge and understanding of the importance of reporting about business has increased exponentially. More, and better, business journalism is being practiced. And that can only mean there's more scrutiny of companies going on, more journalists are experiencing that adversarial relationship, and more stories are being critically written about how business is affecting society.

The question is whether the improvements in business journalism are permanent, or whether the field will regress, failing in its mission to serve society as it seems to have done in the aftermath of the muckrakers. "I'd like to believe that those of us who witnessed the tech bubble will be smart enough to prick the next bubble that comes along before too many investors get duped," writes James Ledbetter, business editor of *Time* Europe. "But in more skeptical moments, I fear that the rise of any boom sector in the American markets will bring with it an attending press that is at least compliant, if not out-and-out boosterish."[14] Many believe in the adage that those who don't know history are doomed to repeat it, and that could apply to business journalism as well.

Improving the quality

How has this improvement in business journalism taken place? A number of educational groups, industry organizations, and academic institutions have taken up the goal of improving the quality of business journalism going forward, not just in the United States but across the globe. Many of them believe that a better trained business reporter will lead to more respect from the corporate executive and more cooperation from companies and industries.

The impetus was shown in surveys. The Freedom Forum study, for example, found that 45 percent of business journalists and managing editors felt that reporters who cover business are not well enough educated.[15] More recently, a study in the Spring/Summer 2002 *Newspaper Research Journal* found that journalists believed that classes in business were needed to do their jobs more effectively. They also believed that the training should be for all journalists, not just those covering business and the economy.[16]

The Society of American Business Editors and Writers was founded in 1964, and one of its missions was to promote better coverage of business and economics issues. For decades, it has held conferences and seminars for business reporters and editors to learn more about their jobs and to write with a better understanding of the arcane topics they sometimes encounter. The organization was founded after two seminars for editors drew large crowds, and it has become the largest group for business journalists. It now has more than 3,000 members. In addition, groups such as the American Press Institute, Associated Press Managing Editors, and state and regional media associations have held seminars and workshops for business reporters and editors. The Southern Newspaper Publishers Association held two dozen workshops in 2002 and 2003 from Dallas to Roanoke, Virginia.

Most recently, the American Press Institute created the Donald W. Reynolds National Center for Business Journalism in late 2003. Funded with a $3 million grant from the Reynolds Foundation, the center has been holding 60 free workshops a year at locations throughout the country on topics such as reporting on the markets and the economy, investigative business reporting, and basic business reporting. The idea behind the workshops is that they will reach out to journalists desperately seeking training in the field.

Others have promoted quality in business journalism by giving awards for the best work. The John Hancock Awards for Excellence were given out for 27 years until 1994. The Gerald Loeb Awards for Distinguished Business and Financial Journalism and the Financial Writers and Editors Awards, sponsored by Northwestern and Strong Financial Corp., are two other prestigious awards that have sought out the best work in business journalism. SABEW also has well-known awards. In addition, the Pulitzer Prize committees have regularly selected business reporting among the winners. In 2004, a Pulitzer was awarded to reporters at the *Los Angeles Times* for their explanation of how Wal-Mart became the largest company in the world.

Some universities have seen the need for more training in business journalism and have begun offering majors in the field. Washington & Lee University in Lexington, Va., and Baruch College in New York City offer undergraduate degrees, while Columbia University and Northwestern University are offering master's degrees in the field. New business journalism programs at colleges such as Southern Methodist University and Florida Atlantic University were started in 2006. These majors require students to take classes at the business school in accounting, finance, economics, management, and other topics, giving them a better understanding of how businesses operate – one of the complaints that executives state about reporters covering their companies.

Still, these schools are in the minority. The American Press Institute study by Selzer & Co. found that not one journalism school administrator rated their journalism program as doing an excellent job training students in business journalism. Just more than a quarter said they believed they were doing a good job. Many of them expressed the belief that journalism students don't have the time to take courses in business or business journalism because accrediting standards force them to take required courses in liberal arts and other fields.[17] Some of the business journalism programs have struggled to maintain enrollment because many aspiring journalists avoid anything to do with numbers.

In addition, respected schools such as Duke University and the University of Pennsylvania have opened their doors for decades to professional business journalists to take a sabbatical from the newsroom and learn about business topics and issues for a week or several months. The Wharton program at Penn gives business journalists the chance to run their own company against other business journalists in the same industry. In the past, a similar program was run for years at the University of Missouri. The reporters and editors who have taken advantage of these programs have gone back to their newsrooms with an increased understanding of the corporate world.

All these programs and their participants – the Reynolds Center had more than 1,500 journalists attend its seminars in the first year – are a candid acknowledgment on the part of the business journalism community that the quality of the reporting and the writing can be better even though it has gotten better in the past two decades. Like a business that continuously seeks to improve its products and lower its expenses, reporters and editors who write about these businesses also want to make the situation better. It seems, perhaps, that the business executives and the reporters and editors who cover them have something in common.

What is lacking, however, is that there are still thousands of reporters and editors handling stories about business or industry who do not have a proper understanding of the issues or of how companies work, despite the efforts of educational institutions and industry organizations. Many of them think that they know enough to write about business until they encounter a story where they are clearly in over their heads. Others believe that they can write about sports or city hall without having to know the difference between net income and revenue.

One other problem is that many media outlets still continue to spend less on their business staff than they do in other areas, such as sports.

Business journalism has improved its quality and continued to have an impact on society because those in the field who are truly interested in the topic have a desire to become better at their craft. They realize that the business executive likely knows more about debt financing than they do but they want to be on a level playing field when it comes time to interview him or her about the topic. And to accomplish that, education is the only way. They may understand the history of the relationship between media and business, but until they have experienced it first-hand, their true understanding of what needs to be learned to do the job effectively won't be realized.

Whether that would change the relationship between corporate America and the journalism community remains to be seen. One simple tenet that many agree upon when arguing for more education in business journalism is that a better trained business journalist would be able to examine business more critically and would potentially be able to uncover more sophisticated problems. Some – in the minority – argue that business journalists are better off knowing just basic concepts of business and that a better understanding of business could make them more sympathetic and less objective.

Knowledge, however, is power. And for journalists, the more they know about business, the better they should be able to serve society. Ledbetter argued for improving the quality by keeping the skepticism alive.

Why media and business will always be adversarial

Business journalism is getting better every day. It is through the efforts of hard-working reporters and editors that the mistakes of the past won't be repeated in the future. Yes, new mistakes will be made. These will be mistakes that haven't even been considered yet, mistakes brought on by changes in reporting tactics or changes in how corporations operate or disclose financial information. Decades ago, and even in the 1990s, many reporters wrote stories about public companies and industries without checking the SEC filings of the businesses to look for investigations or accounting issues. Today, that would be considered a lapse in reporting – we hope!

But it's unlikely that corporate executives and their staffs will ever have a completely open relationship with the media. Many of them inherently distrust journalists for fear of telling them something that may hurt them once published. Others see how similar companies have been treated in the media and are fearful that their company may be next for the journalism chopping block, even though their operation has done nothing wrong. Perhaps exacerbating the issue is the fact that many companies hire former journalists to work for their companies. These former journalists help train executives and managers on what a reporter or editor is interested in learning about a company and how the company should respond to the questions.

But as we've seen time and time again, from Tarbell's treatment of John D. Rockefeller and the Standard Oil Co. to *The Wall Street Journal* and Bethany McLean's reporting of Enron, such an adversarial relationship is good for society. It brings about changes in corporate America and it exposes unethical, illegal, and immoral practices, acting as a self-policing mechanism that shows other companies what not to do. Reporting on wrongdoing in business has improved the quality of life of millions of consumers and saved lives. While it may have been embarrassing to the company, its survival – or failure – many times depended on how it responded to the crisis, particularly through the media.

Business journalism has clearly had a tremendous impact on all of our lives, whether or not the corporations and their executives want to admit it. Although people may not recognize this watchdog relationship by business journalists, for society to continue to improve, it needs to exist. Business journalism will affect millions of people in the future in ways that we can only imagine.

Footnotes

1 From Ninety seconds to tell it all: Big business and the news media, by A. K. MacDougall, 1981, Homewood, Ill.: Dow Jones-Irwin, p. 2.

2 From Ninety seconds to tell it all: Big business and the news media, p. 5.

3 From "The headline vs. the bottom line: Mutual distrust between business and the news media," by M. Haggerty and W. Rasmussen, 1994, Nashville, TN: The Freedom Forum First Amendment Center, p. 20.

4 From "The quality of business journalism in America," a Louis Harris Poll, 1992, Boston: John Hancock Financial Services, p. 3

5 From "The quality of business journalism in America," p. 5.

6 From "Bad press: How business journalism helped inflate the bubble," by P. Longman, October 2002, Washington Monthly, p. 18.

7 From "The quality of business journalism in America," p. 6.

8 From "The headline vs. the bottom line: Mutual distrust between business and the news media," p. 9.

9 From "The headline vs. the bottom line: Mutual distrust between business and the news media," p. 10.

10 From "Business journalism surveys," a Selzer & Co. poll, 2002, Reston, Va.: American Press Institute, p. 2.

11 From "The quality of business journalism in America," p. 4.

12 From "The headline vs. the bottom line: Mutual distrust between business and the news media," p. 11.

13 From "The headline vs. the bottom line: Mutual distrust between business and the news media," p. 12.

14 From "The boys in the bubble," by J. Ledbetter, Jan. 2, 2003, The New York Times, p. 17.

15 From "The headline vs. the bottom line: Mutual distrust between business and the news media," p. 16.

16 From "Business journalists need specialized finance training," by M. Ludwig, Spring/Summer 2002, Newspaper Research Journal, pp. 129–141.

17 From "Business journalism surveys," pp. 4–5.

Acknowledgements

The idea of documenting the evolution of business journalism and its effects on how people interact with Corporate America was developed more than four years ago, and it combined two of my personal interests for the past 20 years – history and reporting about the business world.

The first person I discussed it with was Jan Yopp, then the associate dean for undergraduate studies at the School of Journalism and Mass Communication at the University of North Carolina at Chapel Hill. Jan was also the head of a search committee looking for a new journalism professor, and I was a finalist for the position. I used the idea of this book in January 2002 as my creative presentation in front of the School's faculty, and Jan told me afterward that she thought it would be a best seller. Since that time, she has been one of my most trusted advisers – and not because of that comment.

Unfortunately, work on the book didn't begin until nearly three years later, but a number of people have played an important role in its development and in shaping my thinking for what it should accomplish.

Although the University of North Carolina Press did not publish this book, Senior Editor Chuck Grench was instrumental in its evolution. He read an initial proposal and some sample chapters and provided some excellent suggestions. Chuck and I met twice to discuss the book's development, and talked by e-mail a number of other times. Another book editor, Lawrence Erlbaum Associates' Linda Bathgate, also provided advice.

At UNC, I have been fortunate to have colleagues on the faculty who have also been a tremendous help. Donald Shaw, one of the foremost scholars of the past 30 years in journalism, read the first four chapters and provided some guidance. Dulcie Straughan and Lois Boynton, who are public relations professionals, helped shape the chapter on how business journalists and public relations practitioners have interacted through the years. Carol Pardun, a former UNC advertising professor who now runs the school at Middle Tennessee State University, also provided some feedback on the relationship between advertisers and business journalism. Telecommunications professor Charlie Tuggle reviewed the chapter on business journalism in television. Frank Fee, a journalism professor who is interested in the field's history, also read drafts of a few chapters and offered advice. Journalism professor Rhonda Gibson, an expert on grammar, read the entire book as a copy editor.

Professors at other universities have also been helpful. Business journalism professor Pamela Luecke at Washington & Lee University read a rough first draft. Gerald Baldasty, a professor at the University of Washington who has written journalism history books, also read some chapters and offered advice. Maurine Beasley, a journalism professor at the University of Maryland and noted historian, read the proposal and encouraged me to write this book, noting that business journalism had been virtually ignored in historical work performed in the field. Angel Arrese, a professor at the University of Navarre in Spain who also has an interest in business journalism history and has written on the topic, also read the manuscript.

One of Maurine's former students, Rick Sine, gave me the kick in the pants to write this book. He wrote a paper for her graduate level mass communications history class about the lack of understanding of business journalism's role in media that was forwarded to me and coalesced my thinking about the need for such a book, especially today when business journalism has become increasingly important to consumers for various reasons such as rising levels of stock ownership. After Rick re-entered the field of journalism, he critiqued more than half of the book and pushed for more analysis.

Other students also played in a role in the formation of this book. Students in my "Business and the Media" class in the Spring 2005 semester were required to read some of the early chapters and discuss their contents. Graduate assistant Chaise Nunnally researched some of the topics discussed in this book and helped find academic and newspaper articles for reference. Another graduate student, Eric David, spent six weeks reading all of the chapters and did research for chapters nine through 13, collecting articles and other pieces of information with the help of money I received from a Junior Faculty Development Award at UNC. Eric also tracked down a handful of rogue footnotes near the completion of this book. Another grad assistant, Anne Hillman, put together the index.

Lastly, Ed Avis at Marion Street Press expressed great interest in the idea for this book from when he first heard about it and saw its role in providing a better understanding of business journalism. He has been a proponent for it ever since and quickly moved to have it published.

Without the help of these people, and many others who I know I am forgetting, this book would not have been possible. I thank them all.

Chris Roush
Chapel Hill, NC

Photo credits

P. 15 Jacob Fugger: Courtesy of City of Augsburg, Germany

P. 17 Zenger's Trial: Courtesy of the New York State Unified Court System.

p. 25 Paul Julius Reuter: Courtesy of Reuters Group

p. 25 Frank Leslie's Illustrated Newspaper: Chris Roush personal collection

p. 29 The Economist: Chris Roush personal collection

p. 41 Charles Dow: Courtesy, Dow Jones & Company Archives

p. 43 Charles Bergstresser: Courtesy, Dow Jones & Company Archives

p. 45 Financial World: Chris Roush personal collection

p. 47 Lincoln Steffens: Library of Congress, Prints & Photographs Division, [reproduction number, e.g., [LC-B2-1234]

p. 49 Collier's: Chris Roush personal collection

p. 55 Lincoln Steffens: ???

p. 55 History of the Standard Oil Co.: Courtesy of Dover Publications

p. 71 Forbes magazine of World War I: Chris Roush personal collection

p. 73 The Business Week first issue: Courtesy, McGraw-Hill Co.

p. 76 Mother Jones: Credit Line: Library of Congress, Prints & Photographs Division, [reproduction number, e.g., [LC-F82-1234]

p. 81 Time magazine of Ralph Nader: Courtesy, Time Inc.

p. 88 Time magazine "Looking beyond the bear": Courtesy, Time Inc.

p. 89 Fortune magazine of small town: Chris Roush personal collection

p. 93 June 1957 BusinessWeek: Chris Roush personal collection

p. 94 Fortune magazine: Chris Roush personal collection

p. 105 Barney Kilgore: Courtesy, Dow Jones & Company Archives

p. 121 Jessica Mitford: Courtesy of The Mitford Institute

p. 139 Irving R. Levine: Credit: Lynn University

p. 140 Rachel Carson: Courtesy of the Lear/Carson Collection, Connecticut College.

p. 143 Lou Birger: Credit: The Miami Herald

p. 213 New York Stock Exchange: Credit Line: Library of Congress, Prints & Photographs Division, [reproduction number, e.g., LC-USZ62-90145]

p. 216 Alan Abelson: Courtesy, Dow Jones & Company

A

B

C

D

G

H

I

J

K

L

M

Q

R

S